The Almanac of Consumer Markets:

A Demographic Guide to Finding Today's Complex and Hard-to-Reach Customers

Margaret Ambry

American Demographics

PROBUS PUBLISHING COMPANY
Chicago, Illinois

© Copyright 1990 by American Demographics Press
A Division of American Demographics, Inc.
108 N. Cayuga Street
Ithaca, NY 14850

ALL RIGHTS RESERVED. No part of this publication may be reproduced, stored in a retrieval system, or transmitted by any means, electronic, mechanical, photocopying, recording, or otherwise, without the prior written permission of the publisher and the copyright holder.

This publication is designed to provide accurate and authoritative information in regard to the subject matter covered. It is sold with the understanding that the publisher is not engaged in rendering legal, accounting or other professional service. If legal advice or other expert assistance is required, the services of a competent professional person should be sought.

Library of Congress Cataloging in Publication Data Available

ISBN 1-55738-104-6

Printed in the United States of America

1 2 3 4 5 6 7 8 9 0

In memory of my Uncle Philly who taught me and my sisters something about the value of laughter, stories, Chiclets, and discretionary income.

TABLE OF CONTENTS

ACKNOWLEDGEMENTS x

INTRODUCTION xi

GLOSSARY xiv

CHAPTER 1
Children Under Age 5

Highlights 1

POPULATION
Share of total population 2
Sex, race, and ethnicity 3
State populations 4
State-by-state changes, 1990–2000 7

WORKING MOTHERS 8

HEALTH
Health status 9
Acute conditions 10
Chronic conditions 12
Activity restrictions 14
Cause of death 15

CHAPTER 2
Children Aged 5 to 17

Highlights 17

POPULATION
Share of total population 18
Sex, race, and ethnicity 19
State populations 20
State-by-state changes, 1990–2000 23
School enrollment 24

WORKING MOTHERS 25

LABOR FORCE
Labor force status 26
Extent of employment 27
Kinds of jobs 28
Labor force, participation rates, 1990–2000 30

HEALTH
Health status 31
Acute conditions 32
Chronic conditions 34
Activity restrictions 36
Cause of death 37

CHAPTER 3
Consumers Aged 18 to 24

Highlights 39

POPULATION
Share of total population 40
Sex, race, and ethnicity 41
State populations 42
State-by-state changes, 1990–2000 45

HOUSEHOLDS
Number of households 46
Types of households 47
Future household types 48

MARITAL STATUS AND FERTILITY
Marital status 49
Number of marriages and divorces 50
Childbearing patterns 51

EDUCATIONAL ATTAINMENT
Age and education 53
Enrollment in higher education 54
Sex, race, and ethnicity 55
Householders' education 56

LABOR FORCE
Labor force status 57

Almanac of Consumer Markets v

Extent of employment 58
Kinds of jobs 59
Labor force, participation rates, 1990–2000 61
INCOME
Household income 62
Individual income 63
Income and age 64
Income of married couples 65
Income of other family households 66
Income of nonfamily households 67
Income and race, families 68
Income and race, nonfamilies 69
Income of Hispanic households 70
Income of dual-earner married couples 71
Income and education 72
Future income 73
EXPENDITURES
Annual expenditures 74
Expenditures by income 76
Weekly shopping 78
Future expenditures 79
WEALTH
Owners and renters 81
HEALTH
Health status 82
Height 83
Weight 84
Acute conditions 85
Chronic conditions 87
Activity restrictions 89
Cause of death 90

CHAPTER 4
Consumers Aged 25 to 34

Highlights 91
POPULATION
Share of total population 92
Sex, race, and ethnicity 93
State populations 94
State-by-state changes, 1990–2000 97
HOUSEHOLDS
Number of households 98
Types of households 99
Future household types 100
MARITAL STATUS AND FERTILITY
Marital status 101
Number of marriages and divorces 102

Childbearing patterns 103
EDUCATIONAL ATTAINMENT
Summary 105
Age and education 106
Sex, race, and ethnicity 107
Householders' education 108
LABOR FORCE
Labor force status 109
Extent of employment 110
Kinds of jobs 111
Labor force, participation rates, 1990–2000 113
INCOME
Household income 114
Individual income 115
Income and age 116
Income of married couples 117
Income of other family households 118
Income of nonfamily households 119
Income and race, families 120
Income and race, nonfamilies 121
Income of Hispanic households 122
Income of dual-earner married couples 123
Income and education 124
Future income 125
EXPENDITURES
Annual expenditures 126
Expenditures by income 128
Weekly shopping 130
Future expenditures 131
WEALTH
Composition of wealth 133
Household savings 134
Owners and renters 135
HEALTH
Health status 136
Height 137
Weight 138
Acute conditions 139
Chronic conditions 141
Activity restrictions 143
Cause of death 144

CHAPTER 5
Consumers Aged 35 to 44

Highlights 145
POPULATION
Share of total population 146

Sex, race, and ethnicity 147
State populations 148
State-by-state changes, 1990–2000 151

HOUSEHOLDS
Number of households 152
Types of households 153
Future household types 154

MARITAL STATUS AND FERTILITY
Marital status 155
Number of marriages and divorces 156
Childbearing patterns 157

EDUCATIONAL ATTAINMENT
Summary 159
Age and education 160
Sex, race, and ethnicity 161
Householders' education 162

LABOR FORCE
Labor force status 163
Extent of employment 164
Kinds of jobs 165
Labor force, participation rates, 1990–2000 167

INCOME
Household income 168
Individual income 169
Income and age 170
Income of married couples 171
Income of other family households 172
Income of nonfamily households 173
Income and race, families 174
Income and race, nonfamilies 175
Income of Hispanic households 176
Income of dual-earner married couples 177
Income and education 178
Future income 179

EXPENDITURES
Annual expenditures 180
Expenditures by income 182
Weekly shopping 184
Future expenditures 185

WEALTH
Composition of wealth 187
Household savings 188
Owners and renters 189

HEALTH
Health status 190
Height 191
Weight 192
Acute conditions 193
Chronic conditions 195

Activity restrictions 197
Cause of death 198

CHAPTER 6
Consumers Aged 45 to 54

Highlights 199

POPULATION
Share of total population 200
Sex, race, and ethnicity 201
State populations 202
State-by-state changes, 1990–2000 205

HOUSEHOLDS
Number of households 206
Types of households 207
Future household types 208

MARITAL STATUS
Marital status 209
Number of marriages and divorces 210

EDUCATIONAL ATTAINMENT
Summary 211
Age and education 212
Sex, race, and ethnicity 213
Householders' education 214

LABOR FORCE
Labor force status 215
Extent of employment 216
Kinds of jobs 217
Labor force, participation rates, 1990–2000 219

INCOME
Household income 220
Individual income 221
Income and age 222
Income of married couples 223
Income of other family households 224
Income of nonfamily households 225
Income and race, families 226
Income and race, nonfamilies 227
Income of Hispanic households 228
Income of dual-earner married couples 229
Income and education 230
Future income 231

EXPENDITURES
Annual expenditures 232
Expenditures by income 234
Weekly shopping 236
Future expenditures 237

WEALTH
Composition of wealth 239
Household savings 240
Owners and renters 241

HEALTH
Health status 242
Height 243
Weight 244
Acute conditions 245
Chronic conditions 247
Activity restrictions 249
Cause of death 250

CHAPTER 7
Consumers Aged 55 to 64

Highlights 251

POPULATION
Share of total population 252
Sex, race, and ethnicity 253
State populations 254
State-by-state changes, 1990–2000 257

HOUSEHOLDS
Number of households 258
Types of households 259
Future household types 260

MARITAL STATUS
Marital status 261
Number of marriages and divorces 262

EDUCATIONAL ATTAINMENT
Summary 263
Age and education 264
Sex, race, and ethnicity 265
Householders' education 266

LABOR FORCE
Labor force status 267
Extent of employment 268
Kinds of jobs 269
Labor force, participation rates, 1990–2000 271

INCOME
Household income 272
Individual income 273
Income and age 274
Income of married couples 275
Income of other family households 276
Income of nonfamily households 277
Income and race, families 278
Income and race, nonfamilies 279

Income of Hispanic households 280
Income of dual-earner married couples 281
Income and education 282
Future income 283

EXPENDITURES
Annual expenditures 284
Expenditures by income 286
Weekly shopping 288
Future expenditures 289

WEALTH
Composition of wealth 291
Household savings 292
Owners and renters 293

HEALTH
Health status 294
Height 295
Weight 296
Acute conditions 297
Chronic conditions 299
Activity restrictions 301
Cause of death 302

CHAPTER 8
Consumers Aged 65 to 74

Highlights 303

POPULATION
Share of total population 304
Sex, race, and ethnicity 305
State populations 306
State-by-state changes, 1990–2000 309

HOUSEHOLDS
Number of households 310
Types of households 311
Future household types 312

MARITAL STATUS
Marital status 313
Number of marriages and divorces 314

EDUCATIONAL ATTAINMENT
Summary 315
Age and education 316
Sex, race, and ethnicity 317
Householders' education 318

LABOR FORCE
Labor force status 319
Extent of employment 320
Kinds of jobs 321
Labor force, participation rates, 1990–2000 323

INCOME
Household income 324
Individual income 325
Income and age 326
Income of married couples 327
Income of other family households 328
Income of nonfamily households 329
Income and race, families 330
Income and race, nonfamilies 331
Income of Hispanic households 332
Income of dual-earner married couples 333
Income and education 334
Future income 335

EXPENDITURES
Annual expenditures 336
Expenditures by income 338
Weekly shopping 340
Future expenditures 341

WEALTH
Composition of wealth 343
Household savings 344
Owners and renters 345

HEALTH
Health status 346
Height 347
Weight 348
Acute conditions 349
Chronic conditions 351
Activity restrictions 353
Cause of death 354

CHAPTER 9
Consumers Aged 75 and Older

Highlights 355

POPULATION
Share of total population 356
Sex, race, and ethnicity 357
State populations 358
State-by-state changes, 1990–2000 361

HOUSEHOLDS
Number of households 362
Types of households 363
Future household types 364

MARITAL STATUS 365

EDUCATIONAL ATTAINMENT
Summary 366
Sex, race, and ethnicity 367
Labor force, participation rates, 1990–2000 368

INCOME
Income and age 369
Income of married couples 370
Income of other family households 371
Income of nonfamily households 372
Income of Hispanic households 373
Income of dual-earner married couples 374
Income and education 375

EXPENDITURES
Annual expenditures 376
Expenditures by income 378
Weekly shopping 380
Future expenditures 381

WEALTH
Owners and renters 383

HEALTH
Health status 384
Acute conditions 385
Chronic conditions 387
Activity restrictions 389
Cause of death 390

APPENDIX 391

INDEX 405

ACKNOWLEDGMENTS

There are several people whose efforts contributed enormously to this book. I would like to thank them for their help.

Penelope Wickham, publisher of American Demographics Press, encouraged me to write this book and assisted with all phases of its production; Jim Madden, the compositor of this almanac, managed the production and also helped with designing, formatting, and editing the tables; Peter Francese, president of American Demographics, Inc., supplied the inspiration to write this book and critiqued it in its early form; Cheryl Russell, editor-in-chief of *American Demographics,* provided on-going technical advice; Diane Crispell, associate national editor of *American Demographics,* fact-checked all the numbers in all the tables and answered many data-related questions.

I would also like to thank Judith Waldrop, research editor of *American Demographics,* for editing the final manuscript, and Jerri Dougherty, administrative assistant at American Demographics Press, for helping produce the tables.

Robert Avery, associate professor of Consumer Economics and Housing at Cornell University, provided special runs of the 1986 Survey of Consumer Finance, and Thomas Exter, research director of *American Demographics,* did the tabulations of the 1988 Current Population Survey. I thank them both for their help.

Anne Kilgore, the designer of the *Almanac,* deserves special thanks for her solution to a challenging design problem.

Finally, I am grateful to my husband, Kells Elmquist, and my son, Dana. Kells encouraged me to assume this project and lent me his quiet faith. Dana was patient while I sat at the Mac and did not develop a case of sibling rivalry with THAT BOOK until it was almost completed. Thanks also go to my parents and my in-laws who were there, of course, at the right moments.

INTRODUCTION

"To separate trends from dead-ends, nothing is more important than a basic knowledge of the age structure of the American population, and an understanding of how the age structure is changing over time."
　　　　　　　　　Cheryl Russell, Editor-in-Chief, American Demographics

Today the demographic identity of consumer markets is more important than ever. As businesses fine-tune their product development and marketing strategies to serve increasingly specific markets, demographic information plays an increasingly essential role. That role is one of providing consistent and reliable measures of the age, sex, racial composition, ethnic background, income, educational attainment, household structure, marital status, labor force participation, wealth, expenditure patterns, and health characteristics of a market or potential market.

This book is designed to give marketers, market researchers, corporate planners, advertising executives, and others interested in the American marketplace the demographic information they need to examine consumer markets. Because current data as well as projections to 2000 are given, users can track each age group through the 1990s and gauge changes occurring in their markets during the decade. The *Almanac* is organized according to age because age is the most consistent predictor of consumer demand. Combining age with other factors like sex, income, education, or household structure increases the predictive power of age, but it is the basic tool for segmenting consumer markets.

Age works because it fixes the timing of life-course events that shape so much of consumption behavior. The appropriate age at which an event occurs may be slowly evolving to a new age-position but we can watch this happen, measure it, and predict its course. We know, for example, that the median age at first marriage, age 23 for women and 25 for men, is at its highest point in 50 years and is expected to stay that way for the rest of the 20th century. And some age-events have a short leash. The baby-boomers are making late motherhood fashionable but, as we all know, there is a limit.

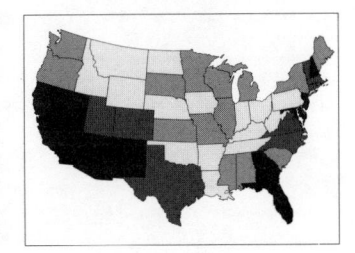

As much as aging is resisted, medicated, and exercised into the background, it still determines a lot of needs. In 1990 the oldest baby boomers will be 44 years old, and no matter how they fight it, many of them will have to start wearing eye glasses and contact lenses. Housing, medical, travel, entertainment, and investment needs all march to the tune of age.

When I look at a population pyramid (like those on the highlight pages of this almanac) I think of it being much the same as a geographer's core of the earth's crust. There is a history, a culture associated with each age layer of the population, because they all lived through the same period of time. Although members of an age group may not react to or remember their time in history in exactly the same way, they were there, and their wants and needs and purchases reflect this. It remains to be seen, for instance, whether the free-spending baby boomers will tighten their belts and save in the manner of their thriftier parents or set a new standard.

HOW TO USE THIS BOOK

The *Almanac* is designed for easy use. Each age group is a separate chapter and, in most cases, all the chapters contain identical tables on a given topic. So you can look up household income data for only 35-to-44-year-olds, or you can compare the numbers with those for 45-to-54-year-olds by simply flipping to the comparable table in the next chapter.

The following tips will help you use the *Almanac*:

• In order to quickly find what you are looking for, consult the detailed table of contents in the beginning of the book or the index in the back.

• If you can't find a comparable table for an age group, look in the next youngest or next oldest age group to see if two age groups have been combined. In cases where data are not available for a certain age group, they may be combined with the next older or younger group. This is most likely to happen with household data for the youngest (under age 25) and oldest (aged 75 and older) householders. The data on asset and debt holdings and savings, for example, are not reliable for households headed by under-25-year-olds because of measurement difficulties so this age group is combined with 25-to-34-year-olds, and those aged 75 and older are included with 65-to-74-year-olds.

• Read the table notes carefully—they will tell you which population is described in the table. If you are unclear about what makes up, for example, the population of male householders, see the glossary.

• In cases where a total for a given population does not appear on the table, you can calculate one by adding up the individual age group totals.

• The appendix includes income tables for all households in each of the household type categories. Also in the appendix are detailed aggregate expenditures tables for 1990 and 2000.

• In those tables with percent distributions instead of numbers, the percentages can be converted to numbers by multiplying the percentages by the total number of persons or households in the category. If, for example, the table says that 80.5 percent of all people aged 45 to 54 are married/spouse present, multiply 80.5 times the number of all people aged 45 to 54 (11,151) to get the number of people who are married/spouse present (.805 x 11,151 = 8,976). Since the numbers are all given in thousands, this means that there are 8,976,000 people aged 45 to 54 who are married and living with their spouses.

GLOSSARY

The *Almanac of Consumer Markets* contains many technical terms that are widely used in demographic work. Most of these terms are defined by government agencies, such as the Bureau of the Census or the Bureau of Labor Statistics.

Baby boom: Those Americans born between 1946 and 1964. Because young people are immigrating to the U.S., the number of baby boomers will peak at 78 million in 1993 and then begin to decline.

Baby bust: The relatively small generation born between 1965 and 1976. There were 42.6 million members of the baby bust in 1988.

Dual-earner couple: A married couple in which both the householder and the householder's spouse are labor force participants.

Employed: All civilians who did any work as a paid employee or farmer/self-employed worker, or who worked 15 hours or more as an unpaid farm worker/in a family-owned business, during the reference period. All those who have jobs but who are temporarily absent from their jobs due to illness, bad weather, vacation, labor management dispute, or personal reasons are considered employed.

Family: A group of two or more persons (one of whom is the householder) related by birth, marriage, or adoption and residing together.

Family household: A household maintained by a family and any unrelated persons who may be residing there. The number of family households is equal to the number of families.

Female/male householder: An unmarried male or female who is the designated householder in a family or nonfamily.

Hispanic: Persons/householders who say that their origin is Mexican, Puerto Rican, Central or South American or some other Hispanic origin.

Household: All the persons who occupy a housing unit. A household includes the related family members and all the unrelated persons, if any, such as lodgers, foster children, wards, or employees who share the housing unit. A person living alone or a group of unrelated persons sharing a housing unit as partners is also counted as a household. Households do not include group quarters.

Household income: The sum of the total money income of all household members.

Household, race/ethnicity of: Households are categorized according to the race or ethnicity of the householder only.

Householder: The householder refers to the person (or one of the persons) in whose name the housing unit is owned or rented (maintained) or, if there is no such person, any adult member. With married couples, the householder may be either the husband or wife. The householder becomes the reference person for the household.

Householder, age of: Only the age of the householder is used to categorize the household into age groups such as those used in the *Almanac*. Married couples, for example, are classified according to either the age of the husband or of the wife.

Householder income: The total money income of the householder only.

Labor force: All the labor force tables in the Almanac are based on the civilian labor force which is made up of all civilians classified as employed or unemployed.

Labor force participation rate: The ratio of the labor force to the population. Labor force participation rates appearing in the *Almanac* are all based on the civilian labor force and civilian population. Labor force participation rates may also be calculated for sex-age groups or other special populations such as mothers of children of a given age.

Median: The median is the measure (of income or years of school completed, for example) which divides the distribution into two equal portions; one below and one above the median.

Nonfamily household: A household maintained by a nonfamily householder.

Nonfamily/nonfamily householder: A householder maintaining a household while living alone or with nonrelatives only.

Percent change: The change (either positive or negative) in a measure that is expressed as a proportion of the starting measure. When the number of persons aged 15 increases from three to four million, for example, this is a 33 percent increase.

Percentage point change: The change (either positive or negative) in a value which is already expressed as a percentage. When a labor force participation rate changes from 70 percent to 75 percent, for example, this is a 5 percentage point increase.

Proportion or share: The value of a part expressed as a percentage of the whole. If the number of persons aged 25 to 43 is 44,321,000 and whites are 32,749,000 of them, the proportion of whites is 74 percent.

Total money income: Total money income is the algebraic sum of gross wages and salaries, net income from self-employment, and income other than earnings, including transfer payments.

Chapter 1

CHILDREN UNDER AGE 5

Businesses in this market will need to keep up with changes during the 1990s. Here are a few reasons why.

The number of children under age 5 will dwindle as their racial and ethnic profile shifts.

■ Between 1990 and 2000 the number of children under age 5 will decline 6 percent.

■ The proportion of white children will drop from 67 to 62 percent of this age group while blacks will bump up from 16 to 17 percent, Hispanics from 13 to 17 percent, and Asians from 3 to 5 percent.

■ Only seven states—Alaska, Arizona, Florida, Georgia, Hawaii, New Mexico, and Utah—will have more under-5-year-olds in 2000 than in 1990.

Some needs will change... some will not.

■ Already over half of the mothers of children under one year old are in the labor force—more than 60 percent of the mothers of 4-year-olds are working.

■ Although 80 percent of these children are in excellent or very good health, they still have over 14 million colds, 12 million cases of flu, and 10 million ear infections a year.

■ These children are chronically plagued by respiratory problems and they spend 90 million whole or half days in bed each year.

■ Infants die most frequently from congenital anomalies and children aged 1 to 4 from accidents and other adverse effects.

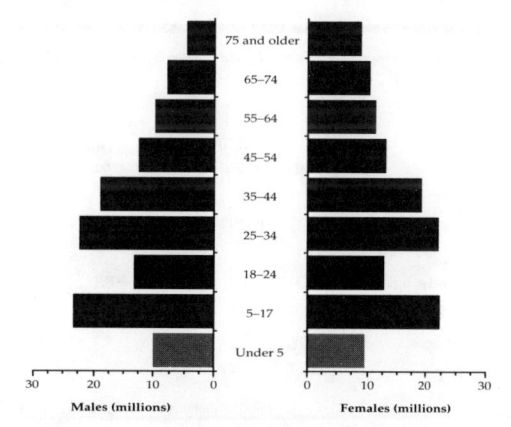

1990

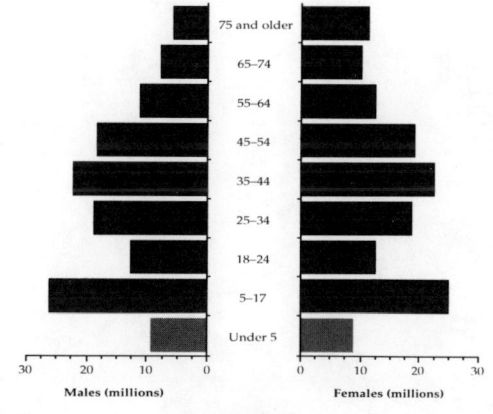

2000

Almanac of Consumer Markets 1

Share of Total Population

POPULATION
under 5

FEWER INFANTS AND TODDLERS

Between 1990 and 2000 the number of infants and toddlers will dwindle as their share of the population shrinks from 8 to 7 percent. Other declining groups will be those aged 18 to 34 and 65 to 74.

(total population and the number of persons under age 5, in thousands, by sex, 1960 to 1980, and projections for 1990 to 2000)

	1960 number	1960 percent of total	1970 number	1970 percent of total	1980 number	1980 percent of total	1990 number	1990 percent of total	1995 number	1995 percent of total	2000 number	2000 percent of total
All ages	180,671	100.0%	205,052	100.0%	227,757	100.0%	252,293	100.0%	264,077	100.0%	274,479	100.0%
All under age 5	20,341	11.3	17,166	8.4	16,458	7.2	19,482	7.7	19,085	7.2	18,243	6.6
Males	10,339	5.7	8,751	4.3	8,411	3.7	9,970	4.0	9,767	3.7	9,336	3.4
Females	10,002	5.5	8,415	4.1	8,040	3.5	9,512	3.8	9,318	3.5	8,907	3.2

Source: Annual Projections of the Population by Age, Sex, and Race, for the United States: 1983 to 2080, *Bureau of the Census, Current Population Reports, Series 17 and the Bureau of the Census*

Note: Total population includes Armed Forces overseas; 1960 to 1980 are based on censuses; projections are based on the Census Bureau's Series 17 projections that incorporate illegal immigration and higher levels of emigration than other Census Bureau projections. Series 17 is consistent with current estimates of illegal aliens living in the United States. Numbers may not add to total due to rounding.

Almanac of Consumer Markets

Sex, Race, and Ethnicity

POPULATION
under 5

MINORITIES GAINING GROUND

Although the total number of very young Americans will drop during the 1990s, there will be more Hispanics and Asians under age 5. White children will slip from 67 to 62 percent of the age group during the decade, while blacks will bump up from 16 to 17 percent, Hispanics from 13 to 17 percent, and Asians from 3 to 5 percent. Nonwhites and Hispanics are projected to increase faster than whites in all age groups.

(projections of the total population and persons under age 5, in thousands, by sex, race, and Hispanic origin, 1990 to 2000)

	1990	1995	2000	percent change 1990–2000
All ages	**252,293**	**264,077**	**274,479**	**8.8%**
White	191,594	195,347	197,634	3.2
Black	30,915	33,237	35,440	14.6
Hispanic	21,854	25,991	30,295	38.6
Asians and other races	7,930	9,502	11,110	40.1
All under age 5	**19,482**	**19,085**	**18,243**	**-6.4**
White	13,148	12,345	11,234	-14.6
Black	3,153	3,123	3,053	-3.2
Hispanic	2,543	2,869	3,120	22.7
Asians and other races	637	748	836	31.2
All males under age 5	**9,970**	**9,767**	**9,336**	**-6.4**
White	6,753	6,342	5,772	-14.5
Black	1,593	1,578	1,543	-3.1
Hispanic	1,300	1,467	1,595	22.7
Asians and other races	324	380	426	31.5
All females under age 5	**9,512**	**9,318**	**8,907**	**-6.4**
White	6,396	6,004	5,461	-14.6
Black	1,560	1,544	1,511	-3.1
Hispanic	1,243	1,403	1,525	22.7
Asians and other races	313	367	410	31.0

Source: Projections of the Population of the United States by Age, Sex, and Race: 1983 to 2080, *Bureau of the Census, Current Population Reports, Series P-25, No. 952, Series 17*

Note: Series 17 projections incorporate illegal immigration and higher levels of emigration than other Census Bureau projections and are consistent with current estimates of illegal aliens living in the United States. Total population includes Armed Forces living overseas. In this table Hispanics have been separated out of the racial groups; categories do not overlap. Numbers may not add to total due to rounding.

State Populations

POPULATION
under 5

GROWTH IN THE SUNBELT

The number of children under age 5 will rise during the 1990s in only seven states—Alaska, Arizona, Florida, Georgia, Hawaii, New Mexico, and Utah. After tapering off in the 1990s, the number of young children will stabilize for the next decade.

(resident population and the number of persons under age 5, in thousands, in Census Bureau divisions and states in 1980 and projections for 1990 to 2010)

Note: Inconsistencies between the data in this table and the preceding two tables are due to different assumptions about immigration and emigration on which the projections are based and the inclusion of Armed Forces overseas in the total population. This table is based on the resident population only.

	census 1980	projections 1990	projections 2000	projections 2010	percent change 1990–2000	percent change 2000–2010
All ages	226,546	249,891	267,747	282,055	7.1%	5.3%
All under age 5	16,348	18,408	16,898	16,899	-8.2	0.0
New England	756	876	789	759	**-9.9**	**-3.8**
Connecticut	185	212	190	179	-10.4	-5.8
Maine	79	87	76	73	-12.6	-3.9
Massachusetts	337	384	344	328	-10.4	-4.7
New Hampshire	63	85	82	82	-3.5	0.0
Rhode Island	57	65	59	58	-9.2	-1.7
Vermont	36	43	38	36	-11.6	-5.3
Middle Atlantic	2,347	2,511	2,214	2,079	**-11.8**	**-6.1**
New Jersey	463	541	504	487	-6.8	-3.4
New York	1,136	1,198	1,078	1,017	-10.0	-5.7
Pennsylvania	747	772	632	575	-18.1	-9.0
East North Central	3,080	3,150	2,681	2,516	**-14.9**	**-6.2**
Illinois	842	889	768	732	-13.6	-4.7
Indiana	419	414	353	330	-14.7	-6.5
Michigan	685	694	588	546	-15.3	-7.1
Ohio	787	790	671	625	-15.1	-6.9
Wisconsin	347	363	300	282	-17.4	-6.0

(continued on next page)

State Populations

POPULATION under 5

(continued from previous page)

(resident population and the number of persons under age 5, in thousands, in Census Bureau divisions and states in 1980 and projections for 1990 to 2010)

	census 1980	projections 1990	projections 2000	projections 2010	percent change 1990–2000	percent change 2000–2010
All ages	226,546	249,891	267,747	282,055	7.1%	5.3%
All under age 5	16,348	18,408	16,898	16,899	-8.2	0.0
West North Central	**1,300**	**1,344**	**1,139**	**1,110**	**-15.3**	**-2.5**
Iowa	222	202	157	143	-22.3	-8.9
Kansas	181	193	166	164	-14.0	-1.2
Minnesota	307	336	289	283	-14.0	-2.1
Missouri	354	382	336	331	-12.0	-1.5
Nebraska	123	124	103	100	-16.9	-2.9
North Dakota	55	50	39	38	-22.0	-2.6
South Dakota	58	58	50	50	-13.8	0.0
South Atlantic	**2,482**	**2,991**	**2,918**	**2,989**	**-2.4**	**2.4**
Delaware	41	49	47	48	-4.1	2.1
District of Columbia	34	31	28	28	9.7	0.0
Florida	570	810	813	863	0.4	6.2
Georgia	415	507	531	561	4.7	5.6
Maryland	272	334	316	316	-5.4	0.0
North Carolina	404	447	431	435	-3.6	0.9
South Carolina	239	263	248	246	-5.7	-0.8
Virginia	361	426	403	404	-5.4	0.2
West Virginia	146	124	101	88	-18.5	-12.9
East South Central	**1,121**	**1,130**	**1,014**	**979**	**-10.3**	**-3.5**
Alabama	296	307	276	271	-10.1	-1.8
Kentucky	283	270	234	218	-13.3	-6.8
Mississippi	215	220	204	198	-7.3	-2.9
Tennessee	326	332	301	291	-9.3	-3.3
West South Central	**1,939**	**2,281**	**2,157**	**2,220**	**-5.4**	**2.9**
Arkansas	176	174	154	150	-11.5	-2.6
Louisiana	362	377	320	309	-15.1	-3.4
Oklahoma	233	241	212	215	-12.0	1.4
Texas	1,169	1,488	1,471	1,546	-1.1	5.1

(continued on next page)

Almanac of Consumer Markets

State Populations

POPULATION
under 5

(continued from previous page)

(resident population and the number of persons under age 5, in thousands, in Census Bureau divisions and states in 1980 and projections for 1990 to 2010)

	census 1980	projections 1990	projections 2000	2010	percent change 1990–2000	percent change 2000–2010
All ages	226,546	249,891	267,747	282,055	7.1%	5.3%
All under age 5	16,348	18,408	16,898	16,899	-8.2	0.0
Mountain	**994**	**1,183**	**1,150**	**1,225**	**-2.8**	**6.5**
Arizona	214	306	313	343	2.3	9.6
Colorado	216	256	238	246	-7.0	3.4
Idaho	94	86	77	77	-10.5	0.0
Montana	64	60	50	50	-16.7	0.0
Nevada	56	73	72	78	-1.4	8.3
New Mexico	115	146	151	167	3.4	10.6
Utah	190	210	211	228	0.5	8.1
Wyoming	45	44	37	36	-15.9	-2.7
Pacific	**2,329**	**2,943**	**2,836**	**3,026**	**-3.6**	**6.7**
Alaska	39	54	59	64	9.3	8.5
California	1,708	2,289	2,242	2,412	-2.1	7.6
Hawaii	78	72	74	83	2.8	12.2
Oregon	198	196	170	172	-13.3	1.2
Washington	306	332	291	297	-12.3	2.1

Source: Projections of the Population of States by Age, Sex and Race: 1988 to 2010, *Bureau of the Census, Current Population Reports, Series P-25, No. 1017*

Note: Numbers may not add to total due to rounding.

State-by-State Changes

POPULATION
under 5

MIDWEST LOSSES

Iowa and North Dakota will see the greatest slump in the number of children under age 5 during the 1990s, reflecting overall shrinkage, especially in the East North Central and West North Central states.

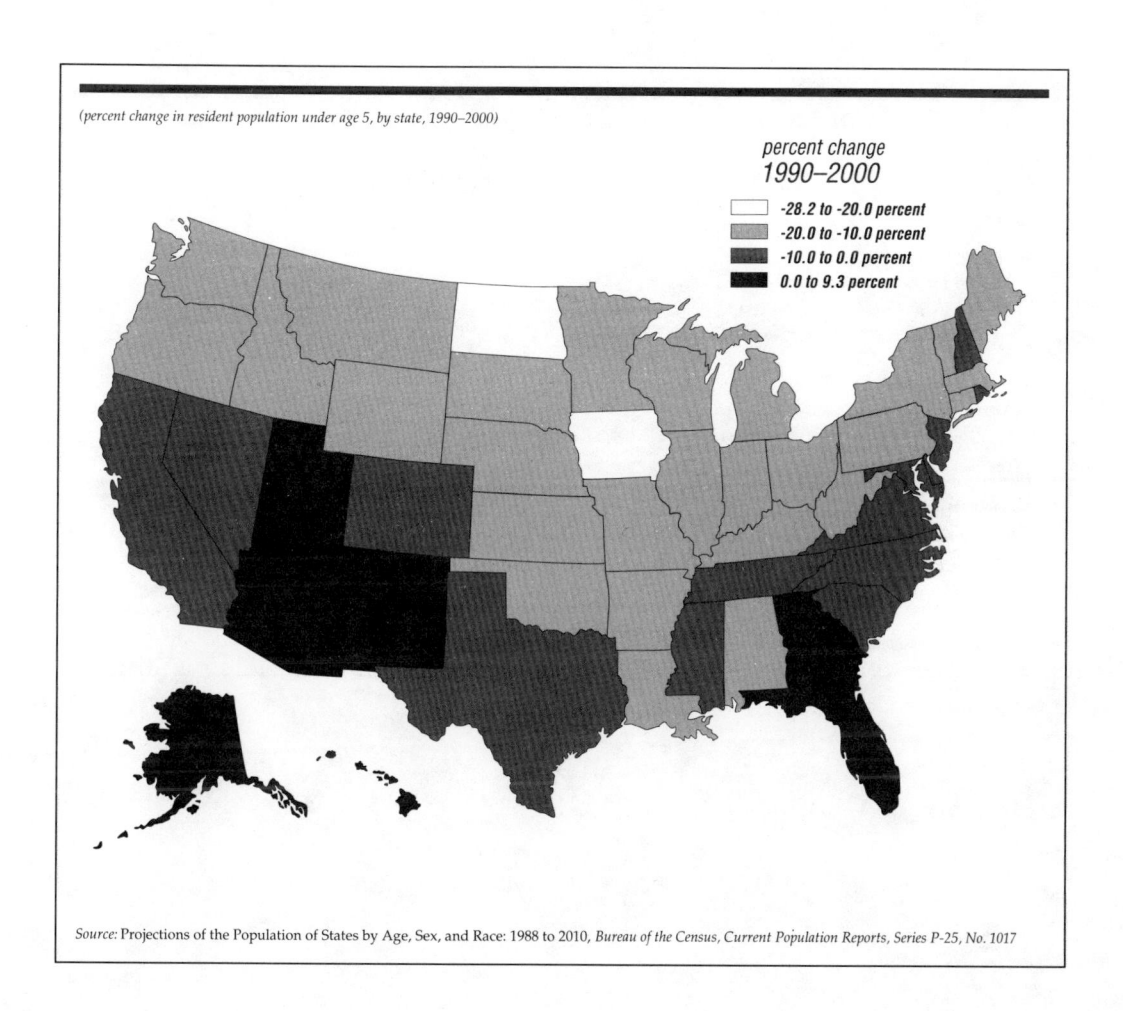

(percent change in resident population under age 5, by state, 1990–2000)

percent change
1990–2000
- -28.2 to -20.0 percent
- -20.0 to -10.0 percent
- -10.0 to 0.0 percent
- 0.0 to 9.3 percent

Source: Projections of the Population of States by Age, Sex, and Race: 1988 to 2010, *Bureau of the Census, Current Population Reports,* Series P-25, No. 1017

Mothers Who Work

WORKING MOTHERS under 5

WORKING MAJORITY

Just over half of the mothers of children under one year old are in the labor force. Labor force participation rises quickly for both married and single-parent mothers as their youngest child grows up.

(labor force participation rates* of married and single-parent mothers by age of youngest child, for children age 5 and under, 1978 to 1988)

	\multicolumn{5}{c}{age of youngest child}
	1 year or younger	2 years old	3 years old	4 years old	5 years old
1978					
All mothers	35.7	47.0	48.0	50.2	53.1
Married mothers	34.8	45.6	47.0	47.7	49.8
Single-parent mothers	43.2	54.4	53.2	60.4	66.7
1983					
All mothers	44.5	51.1	56.3	58.2	59.4
Married mothers	44.6	50.4	56.1	57.2	56.6
Single-parent mothers	44.0	54.6	57.2	61.7	69.0
1988					
All mothers	50.8	60.3	59.3	61.3	63.6
Married mothers	51.9	61.7	59.3	61.4	63.6
Single-parent mothers	44.9	52.5	59.0	60.8	63.5

*Labor force participation rates are the ratio of mothers in the labor force to the total number of mothers with the same marital status and same age children.

Source: Bureau of Labor Statistics

Health Status

HEALTH
under 5

STARTING OUT WELL

Girls under age 5 have a slight health advantage over the boys. Fifty-five percent of the girls and 53 percent of the boys are described by their parents as having excellent health. The proportion of children with excellent health is considerably higher in households with a household income of $35,000 and more than in lower-income households.

(parental-assessed health status of persons under age 5, by sex, race and household income, number of persons in thousands)

	all persons	all health statuses	excellent	very good	good	fair	poor
Both sexes, all races	18,174	100.0%	53.8%	26.5%	16.9%	2.2%	0.6%
Male	9,300	100.0	53.2	26.6	17.6	2.0	0.7
Female	8,875	100.0	54.5	26.4	16.2	2.4	0.5
White	14,729	100.0	55.9	27.0	14.8	1.8	0.5
Black	2,735	100.0	42.2	25.0	27.7	4.5	0.7
Asian and other	647	100.0	54.6	22.3	20.6	1.9	0.6
Household income							
Less than $10,000	2,935	100.0%	40.9%	26.2%	29.2%	2.9%	0.8%
$10,000 to $19,999	3,812	100.0	51.0	26.0	18.5	3.6	1.0
$20,000 to $34,999	5,314	100.0	56.9	27.8	13.3	1.6	0.4
$35,000 and over	4,260	100.0	63.9	25.3	9.3	1.0	0.5

Source: The 1986 National Health Interview Survey, National Center for Health Statistics

Note: All persons includes those of unknown health status, all health statuses includes only those with known health status. Household income includes only those persons with known household income. Numbers may not add to total due to rounding.

Acute Conditions

HEALTH
under 5

COMMON, COMMON COLD

Colds, flus, and ear infections are the three most common acute illnesses among these young children. For both boys and girls, the common cold and other respiratory problems account for about half of all acute conditions reported in a year.

(number of acute conditions reported in a year for all persons and those under age 5, by sex, numbers in thousands)

	males all ages	males under age 5	females all ages	females under age 5
All acute conditions	191,369	34,423	257,177	31,077
Infective and parasitic diseases	23,122	5,112	31,244	4,981
Common childhood diseases	2,565	918	1,876	897
Intestinal virus, unspecified	4,244	982	5,288	666
Viral infections, unspecified	9,621	1,885	14,273	2,060
Other	6,692	1,327	9,807	1,358
Respiratory conditions	99,216	17,093	129,626	15,246
Common cold	30,445	7,786	32,983	6,253
Other acute upper respiratory infections	8,472	1,934	13,320	1,582
Influenza	55,256	5,610	75,295	6,011
Acute bronchitis	1,960	555	4,315	596
Pneumonia	1,365	549	1,277	220
Other respiratory conditions	1,718	659	2,435	584
Digestive system conditions	5,860	601	9,112	888
Dental conditions	1,059	302	1,955	308
Indigestion, nausea and vomiting	3,299	118	4,670	465
Other digestive conditions	1,502	182	2,487	115
Injuries	34,588	2,707	29,706	1,554
Fractures and dislocations	4,367	175	3,978	97
Sprains and strains	6,127	0	6,208	0
Open wounds and lacerations	11,153	1,583	5,094	310
Contusions and superficial injuries	7,986	610	7,191	605
Other current injuries	4,955	339	7,235	543

(continued next page)

Acute Conditions

HEALTH
under 5

(continued from previous page)

(number of acute conditions reported in a year for all persons and those under age 5, by sex, numbers in thousands)

	males		females	
	all ages	under age 5	all ages	under age 5
Selected other acute conditions	**21,183**	**7,266**	**40,385**	**7,663**
Eye conditions	1,072	378	2,080	286
Acute ear infections	8,689	4,385	10,116	5,245
Other ear conditions	1,884	678	2,193	624
Acute urinary conditions	989	0	4,399	194
Skin conditions	2,065	686	3,597	554
Acute musculoskeletal conditions	3,038	97	3,972	0
Headache, excluding migraine	1,253	103	2,461	0
Fever, unspecified	2,192	940	2,675	759
All other acute conditions	**7,400**	**1,644**	**17,104**	**744**

Source: The 1986 National Health Interview Survey, National Center for Health Statistics

Note: An acute condition is defined by The National Health Interview Survey as an illness or injury that usually lasts less than three months and was first noticed less than three months before the respondent's interview. The acute condition must also have caused the person to restrict activities for at least a half a day or to have contacted a physician. The data are based only on information given by the respondent and are subject to recall and selective reporting error. Numbers may not add to total due to rounding.

Chronic Conditions

HEALTH
under 5

BREATHING DIFFICULTIES

Respiratory problems, and especially bronchitis, are the most common chronic conditions plaguing very young children. After bronchitis, asthma, hay fever, and sinusitis, dermatitis is the next most frequently reported condition among under-5-year-olds.

(number of selected chronic conditions reported in a year for all persons and those under age 5, by sex, numbers in thousands)

	males all ages	males under age 5	females all ages	females under age 5
Selected skin and musculoskeletal conditions				
Arthritis	10,751	14	20,160	23
Gout, including gouty arthritis	1,515	0	713	0
Intervertebral disc disorders	2,522	0	1,645	0
Bone spur or tendonitis, unspecified	781	0	898	0
Disorders of bone or cartilage	449	0	943	0
Trouble with bunions	594	0	2,321	0
Bursitis, unclassified	1,641	0	2,464	35
Sebaceous skin cyst	640	0	881	0
Trouble with acne	2,193	0	2,116	0
Psoriasis	1,069	0	1,262	0
Dermatitis	3,851	233	5,696	280
Trouble with dry, itching skin, unclassified	1,994	23	2,606	29
Trouble with ingrown nails	2,352	18	3,030	21
Trouble with corns and calluses	1,669	0	3,164	0
Impairments				
Visual impairment	4,994	0	3,358	47
Color blindness	2,694	0	272	0
Cataracts	1,534	28	3,497	0
Glaucoma	735	0	967	25
Hearing impairment	11,727	88	9,004	88
Tinnitus	3,388	0	2,927	0
Speech impairment	1,924	70	871	70
Absence of extremity(s)	374	0	24	0
Paralysis, entire body, one side of body, or both legs	200	0	152	22
Partial paralysis of body or legs	236	0	99	0
Deformity of back	6,812	0	9,676	123
Deformity of upper extremities	1,622	0	1,475	54
Deformity of lower extremities	6,454	53	5,739	25
Selected digestive conditions				
Ulcer	2,116	0	2,378	0
Hernia of abdominal cavity	2,300	84	2,283	58
Gastritis or duodenitis	1,080	39	1,813	42

(continued next page)

Chronic Conditions

HEALTH
under 5

(ontinued from previous page)

(number of selected chronic conditions reported in a year for all persons and those under age 5, by sex, numbers in thousands)

	males		females	
	all ages	under age 5	all ages	under age 5
Frequent indigestion	2,504	0	2,811	30
Enteritis or colitis	574	0	1,820	62
Spastic colon	264	0	1,377	22
Diverticula of intestines	404	0	1,508	0
Frequent constipation	1,002	35	3,537	92
Selected conditions of the genitourinary, nervous, endocrine, metabolic, and blood system				
Goiter or other disorders of the thyroid	420	0	2,789	0
Diabetes	2,949	44	3,635	0
Anemias	570	104	2,617	102
Epilepsy	656	44	863	27
Migraine headache	2,068	0	6,448	0
Neuralgia or neuritis, unspecified	215	0	364	0
Kidney trouble	1,305	21	2,662	108
Bladder disorders	516	23	3,253	0
Diseases of prostate	1,281	0	–	–
Inflammatory female genital diseases	–	–	427	0
Noninflammatory female genital diseases	–	–	1,095	0
Menstrual disorders	–	–	2,097	0
Selected circulatory conditions				
Ischemic heart disease	4,091	0	2,809	0
Tachycardia or rapid heart	700	22	1,226	34
Heart murmurs	1,310	214	2,583	93
Other heart rhythm disorders	499	0	800	34
Other heart diseases	1,482	11	2,265	24
High blood pressure (hypertension)	12,512	0	16,457	24
Cerebrovascular disease	1,156	0	1,646	34
Hardening of the arteries	1,428	0	1,225	0
Varicose veins	1,042	0	5,814	0
Hemorrhoids	4,568	0	5,341	0
Selected respiratory conditions				
Chronic bronchitis	4,707	596	6,671	849
Asthma	4,670	393	5,019	101
Hay fever or allergic rhinitis without asthma	10,136	379	11,566	237
Chronic sinusitis	14,636	369	19,749	222
Deviated nasal septum	825	0	465	0
Chronic disease of tonsils or adenoids	1,071	140	2,068	264
Emphysema	1,201	0	796	0

Source: The 1986 National Health Interview Survey, National Center for Health Statistics

Note: Chronic conditions are defined by the National Health Interview Survey as conditions that either a) were first noticed three months or more before the date of the interview or b) belong to a group of conditions (such as heart disease or diabetes) that are considered chronic regardless of when they began. Totals for all chronic conditions are not shown because the National Health Interview Survey does not measure the total number of chronic conditions for each person. The data are based only on information given by the respondent and are subject to recall and selective reporting error.

Activity Restrictions

HEALTH
under 5

COMMON CURE

Children under age 5 collectively spend nearly 90 million whole or half days in bed each year because of an illness or injury. Each boy and girl in this age group can expect to have about five such bed days a year which is lower than the number for Americans in general.

(number of days of activity restriction reported in a year and per person due to acute and chronic conditions, by type of restriction and sex, race, and household income, for all persons and those under age 5, numbers in thousands)

	number of days per year		number of days per person	
	bed day	work-loss day	bed day	work-loss day
All ages	1,547,980	833,396	6.5	5.4
Male	613,113	401,503	5.4	4.8
Female	934,867	431,892	7.7	6.0
White	1,298,039	716,187	6.5	5.4
Black	220,102	99,332	7.7	5.4
Household income				
Less than $10,000	384,962	90,268	11.5	6.1
$10,000 to $19,999	346,115	162,604	7.7	6.1
$20,000 to $34,999	326,166	254,563	5.2	5.7
$35,000 and over	275,957	232,139	4.3	4.6
All under age 5	89,762	–	4.9	–
Male	49,443	–	5.3	–
Female	40,320	–	4.5	–
White	72,937	–	4.9	–
Black	13,869	–	5.1	–
Household income				
Less than $10,000	16,791	–	5.7	–
$10,000 to $19,999	22,848	–	6.0	–
$20,000 to $34,999	25,816	–	4.9	–
$35,000 and over	21,375	–	5.0	–

Source: The 1986 National Health Interview Survey, National Center for Health Statistics

Note: Numbers may not add to total due to rounding. A bed day is one during which a person stayed in bed more than half a day because of illness or injury. All hospital days for inpatients are considered bed days even if the patient was not in bed more than half a day. A work-loss day is one on which a currently employed person aged 18 or older missed more than half a day of work. The data are based only on information given by the respondent and are subject to recall and selective reporting error.

Cause of Death

HEALTH
under 5

UNTIMELY DEATHS

More than one-third of all infant deaths are due to congenital anomalies (21 percent) and the sudden infant death syndrome (14 percent). Infant mortality reached a record low in 1986 and the average life expectancy at birth rose to a record high of 74.8 years (78.3 years for females and 71.3 for males). Children aged 1 to 4 are more likely to die from accidents and adverse effects (39 percent) than from any other single cause.

(ten leading causes of death among infants—persons under age 1—and persons aged 1 to 4)

	number of infant deaths	number of deaths all ages	percent accounted for by infants
All causes	38,891	2,105,361	1.8%
Congenital anomalies	8,244	12,638	65.2
Sudden infant death syndrome	5,278	–	–
Respiratory distress syndrome	3,403	–	–
Disorders relating to short gestation and unspecified low birthweight	3,245	–	–
Newborn affected by maternal complications of pregnancy	1,355	–	–
Intrauterine hypoxia and birth asphyxia	983	–	–
Infections specific to the perinatal period	918	–	–
Accidents and adverse effects	909	95,277	1.0
Newborn affected by complications of placenta, cord, and membranes	836	–	–
Pneumonia and influenza	663	69,812	0.9
All other causes	13,057	1,927,634	0.7

	number of deaths persons aged 1 to 4	number of deaths all ages	percent accounted for by persons aged 1 to 4
All causes	7,480	2,105,361	0.4%
Accidents and adverse effects	2,934	95,277	3.1
Congenital anomalies	879	12,638	7.0
Malignant neoplasms (cancers)	569	469,376	0.1
Homicide and legal intervention	382	21,731	1.8
Heart diseases	366	765,490	0.0
Pneumonia and influenza	199	69,812	0.3
Meningitis	144	1,160	12.4
Certain conditions originating in the perinatal period	132	18,391	0.7
Septicemia (infections of the blood stream)	90	18,795	0.5
Meningococcal infection	64	286	22.4
All other causes	1,721	632,414	0.3

Source: Advance Report of Final Mortality Statistics, 1986, *National Center for Health Statistics, Vol. 37, No. 6*

Chapter 2

CHILDREN AGED 5 TO 17

This is one of the growth groups of the 1990s. Here's what to expect.

There will be more 5-to-17-year-olds and they'll be a more diverse lot.

■ There will be 12 percent more young people aged 5 to 17 in 2000 than in 1990.

■ The share of black and Hispanic children will climb from 27 to 31 percent of the age group while the share of white children will fall from 70 to 65 percent.

■ Enrollment in public high schools will be up 16 percent between 1990 and 1997.

■ Their mothers will probably be in the work force—60 percent of women with children aged 6 to 13 and 75 percent of those with children aged 14 to 17 are already working.

■ In 1990, 46 percent of 16-and-17-year-olds are in the work force—by 2000, 49 percent of these young men and 50 percent of the women will be workers.

■ Most of them work part-time; 85 percent of employed 16-and-17-year-olds hold part-time jobs.

■ Over 60 percent of 16-and-17-year-olds who work are employed in service and sales occupations; 26 percent are in food service alone.

■ Although nearly 80 percent of 5-to-17-year-olds are in excellent or very good health, they account for some 28 percent of all reported cases of flu.

■ They are prone to chronic respiratory problems and miss more than 226 million whole or half days of school each year.

■ Accidents, mostly motor vehicle-related, are the number one cause of death in this age group.

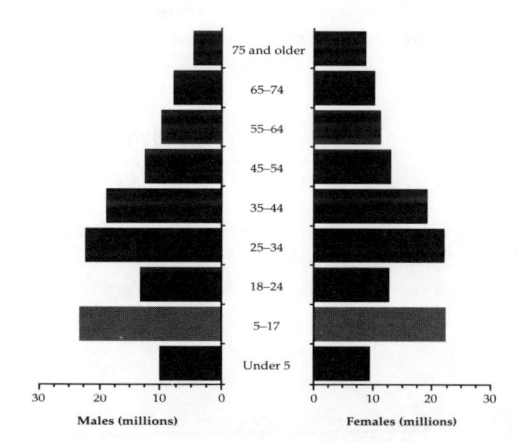

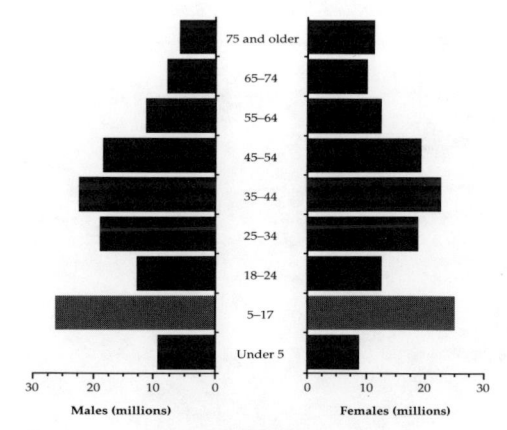

Share of Total Population

POPULATION
5–17

UPWARD TREND

Although growth in this age group will be strong during the 1990s, its share of the population will increase only slightly. By the turn of the century the proportion of 5-to-17-year-olds will drop 6 percentage points from its 1970 high of 26 percent of all Americans.

(total population and the number of persons aged 5 to 17, in thousands, by sex, 1960 to 1980, and projections for 1990 to 2000)

	1960 number	1960 percent of total	1970 number	1970 percent of total	1980 number	1980 percent of total	1990 number	1990 percent of total	1995 number	1995 percent of total	2000 number	2000 percent of total
All ages	180,671	100.0%	205,052	100.0%	227,757	100.0%	252,293	100.0%	264,077	100.0%	274,479	100.0%
All aged 5 to 17	44,184	24.5	52,596	25.7	47,237	20.7	45,703	18.1	49,502	18.7	51,216	18.7
Males	22,445	12.4	26,795	13.1	24,140	10.6	23,369	9.3	25,311	9.6	26,192	9.5
Females	21,739	12.0	25,801	12.6	23,098	10.1	22,335	8.9	24,191	9.2	25,024	9.1

Source: Annual Projections of the Population by Age, Sex, and Race, for the United States: 1983 to 2080, Bureau of the Census, Current Population Reports, Series 17 and the Bureau of the Census

Note: Total population includes Armed Forces overseas; 1960 to 1980 are based on censuses; projections are based on the Census Bureau's Series 17 projections that incorporate illegal immigration and higher levels of emigration than other Census Bureau projections. Series 17 is consistent with current estimates of illegal aliens living in the United States. Numbers may not add to total due to rounding.

Sex, Race, and Ethnicity

POPULATION
5-17

RACIAL DIVERSITY

The number of 5-to-17-year-olds will climb faster than the population as a whole during the 1990s. The share of black and Hispanic children will increase from 27 to 31 percent of the age group while the share of white children will fall from 70 to 65 percent. Nonwhites and Hispanics are projected to increase faster than whites in all age groups.

(projections of the total population and persons aged 5 to 17, in thousands, by sex, race, and Hispanic origin, 1990 to 2000)

	1990	1995	2000	percent change 1990–2000
All ages	252,293	264,077	274,479	8.8%
White	191,594	195,347	197,634	3.2
Black	30,915	33,237	35,440	14.6
Hispanic	21,854	25,991	30,295	38.6
Asians and other races	7,930	9,502	11,110	40.1
All aged 5 to 17	45,703	49,503	51,217	12.1
White	31,852	33,458	33,391	4.8
Black	6,915	7,745	8,217	18.8
Hispanic	5,297	6,419	7,526	42.1
Asians and other races	1,639	1,881	2,083	27.1
All males aged 5 to 17	23,368	25,312	26,193	12.1
White	16,337	17,162	17,133	4.9
Black	3,489	3,908	4,149	18.9
Hispanic	2,705	3,281	3,848	42.3
Asians and other races	837	961	1,063	27.0
All females aged 5 to 17	22,335	24,191	25,024	12.0
White	15,515	16,296	16,259	4.8
Black	3,429	3,837	4,069	18.7
Hispanic	2,592	3,138	3,678	41.9
Asians and other races	800	921	1,018	27.3

Source: Projections of the Population of the United States by Age, Sex, and Race: 1983 to 2080, Bureau of the Census, Current Population Reports, Series P-25, No. 952, Series 17

Note: Series 17 projections incorporate illegal immigration and higher levels of emigration than other Census Bureau projections and are consistent with current estimates of illegal aliens living in the United States. Total population includes Armed Forces living overseas. In this table Hispanics have been separated out of the racial groups so categories do not overlap. Numbers may not add to total due to rounding.

Almanac of Consumer Markets

State Populations

POPULATION
5-17

NATIONAL EXPANSION

About three-quarters of the states will see more 5-to-17-year-olds in the 1990s, with growth concentrated in the South Atlantic, Pacific, Mountain, and New England states.

(resident population and the number of persons aged 5 to 17, in thousands, in Census Bureau divisions and states in 1980 and projections for 1990 to 2010)

Note: Inconsistencies between the data in this table and the preceding two tables are due to different assumptions about immigration and emigration on which the projections are based and the inclusion of Armed Forces overseas in the total population. This table is based on the resident population only.

	census 1980	1990	projections 2000	2010	percent change 1990–2000	percent change 2000–2010
All ages	226,546	249,891	267,747	282,055	7.1%	5.3%
All aged 5 to 17	47,406	45,629	48,815	45,747	7.0	-6.3
New England	**2,525**	**2,151**	**2,384**	**2,187**	**10.8**	**-8.3**
Connecticut	638	539	590	536	9.5	-9.2
Maine	243	218	233	211	6.9	-9.4
Massachusetts	1,153	932	1,024	939	9.9	-8.3
New Hampshire	196	199	247	235	24.1	-4.9
Rhode Island	186	163	177	164	8.6	-7.3
Vermont	110	101	111	102	9.9	-8.1
Middle Atlantic	**7,455**	**6,362**	**6,620**	**5,979**	**4.1**	**-9.7**
New Jersey	1,528	1,321	1,533	1,448	16.0	-5.5
New York	3,552	3,048	3,111	2,845	2.1	-8.6
Pennsylvania	2,376	1,993	1,977	1,685	-0.8	-14.8
East North Central	**8,985**	**7,824**	**7,835**	**6,920**	**0.1**	**-11.7**
Illinois	2,401	2,142	2,178	1,952	1.7	-10.4
Indiana	1,199	1,042	1,029	912	-1.2	-11.4
Michigan	2,067	1,747	1,759	1,548	0.7	-12.0
Ohio	2,308	1,994	1,960	1,724	-1.7	-12.0
Wisconsin	1,011	899	908	785	1.0	-13.5

(continued on next page)

State Populations

POPULATION 5-17

(continued from previous page)

(resident population and the number of persons aged 5 to 17, in thousands, in Census Bureau divisions and states in 1980 and projections for 1990 to 2010)

	census 1980	projections 1990	projections 2000	2010	percent change 1990–2000	percent change 2000–2010
All ages	226,546	249,891	267,747	282,055	7.1%	5.3%
All aged 5 to 17	47,406	45,629	48,815	45,747	7.0	-6.3
West North Central	**3,553**	**3,291**	**3,333**	**2,959**	**1.3**	**-11.2**
Iowa	604	513	465	386	-9.4	-17.0
Kansas	468	461	467	421	1.3	-9.9
Minnesota	865	796	849	759	6.7	-10.6
Missouri	1,008	948	995	905	5.0	-9.0
Nebraska	324	300	295	258	-1.7	-12.5
North Dakota	136	132	118	100	-10.6	-15.3
South Dakota	147	142	144	130	1.4	-9.7
South Atlantic	**7,635**	**7,591**	**8,637**	**8,406**	**13.8**	**-2.7**
Delaware	125	116	132	129	13.8	-2.3
District of Columbia	109	90	84	77	-6.7	-8.3
Florida	1,789	1,998	2,431	2,407	21.7	-1.0
Georgia	1,231	1,297	1,526	1,555	17.7	1.9
Maryland	896	815	950	904	16.6	-4.8
North Carolina	1,254	1,189	1,292	1,249	8.7	-3.3
South Carolina	703	683	719	685	5.3	-4.7
Virginia	1,113	1,060	1,204	1,145	13.6	-4.9
West Virginia	414	345	300	256	-13.0	-14.7
East South Central	**3,237**	**3,005**	**2,997**	**2,761**	**-0.3**	**-7.9**
Alabama	866	812	835	775	2.8	-7.2
Kentucky	800	709	671	600	-5.4	-10.6
Mississippi	599	581	587	551	1.0	-6.1
Tennessee	972	905	904	834	-0.1	-7.7
West South Central	**5,223**	**5,625**	**5,945**	**5,689**	**5.7**	**-4.3**
Arkansas	495	468	466	426	-0.4	-8.6
Louisiana	968	947	909	809	-4.0	-11.0
Oklahoma	621	632	626	580	-0.9	-7.3
Texas	3,137	3,577	3,944	3,872	10.3	-1.8

(continued on next page)

State Populations

POPULATION
5–17

(continued from previous page)

(resident population and the number of persons aged 5 to 17, in thousands, in Census Bureau divisions and states in 1980 and projections for 1990 to 2010)

	census 1980	1990	projections 2000	2010	percent change 1990–2000	percent change 2000–2010
All ages	226,546	249,891	267,747	282,055	7.1%	5.3%
All aged 5 to 17	47,406	45,629	48,815	45,747	7.0	-6.3
Mountain	**2,464**	**2,818**	**3,162**	**3,101**	**12.2**	**-1.9**
Arizona	578	709	879	886	24.0	0.8
Colorado	592	629	686	647	9.1	-5.7
Idaho	213	223	214	198	-4.0	-7.5
Montana	167	160	147	131	-8.1	-10.9
Nevada	160	184	214	210	16.3	-1.9
New Mexico	303	342	418	428	22.2	2.4
Utah	350	463	504	512	8.9	1.6
Wyoming	101	107	100	89	-6.5	-11.0
Pacific	**6,328**	**6,963**	**7,903**	**7,746**	**13.5**	**-2.0**
Alaska	91	123	141	144	14.6	2.1
California	4,681	5,292	6,159	6,108	16.4	-0.8
Hawaii	197	212	222	227	4.7	2.3
Oregon	525	497	506	465	1.8	-8.1
Washington	834	841	872	801	3.7	-8.1

Source: Projections of the Population of States by Age, Sex and Race: 1988 to 2010, *Bureau of the Census, Current Population Reports, Series P-25, No. 1017*

Note: Numbers may not add to total due to rounding.

State-by-State Changes

POPULATION
5–17

BIG LOSSES IN TWO STATES

Arizona, California, Florida, Georgia, Maryland, Nevada, New Hampshire, New Jersey, and New Mexico will have the largest increases in the number of children aged 5 to 17 during the 1990s. The biggest drops are forecasted for North Dakota and West Virginia.

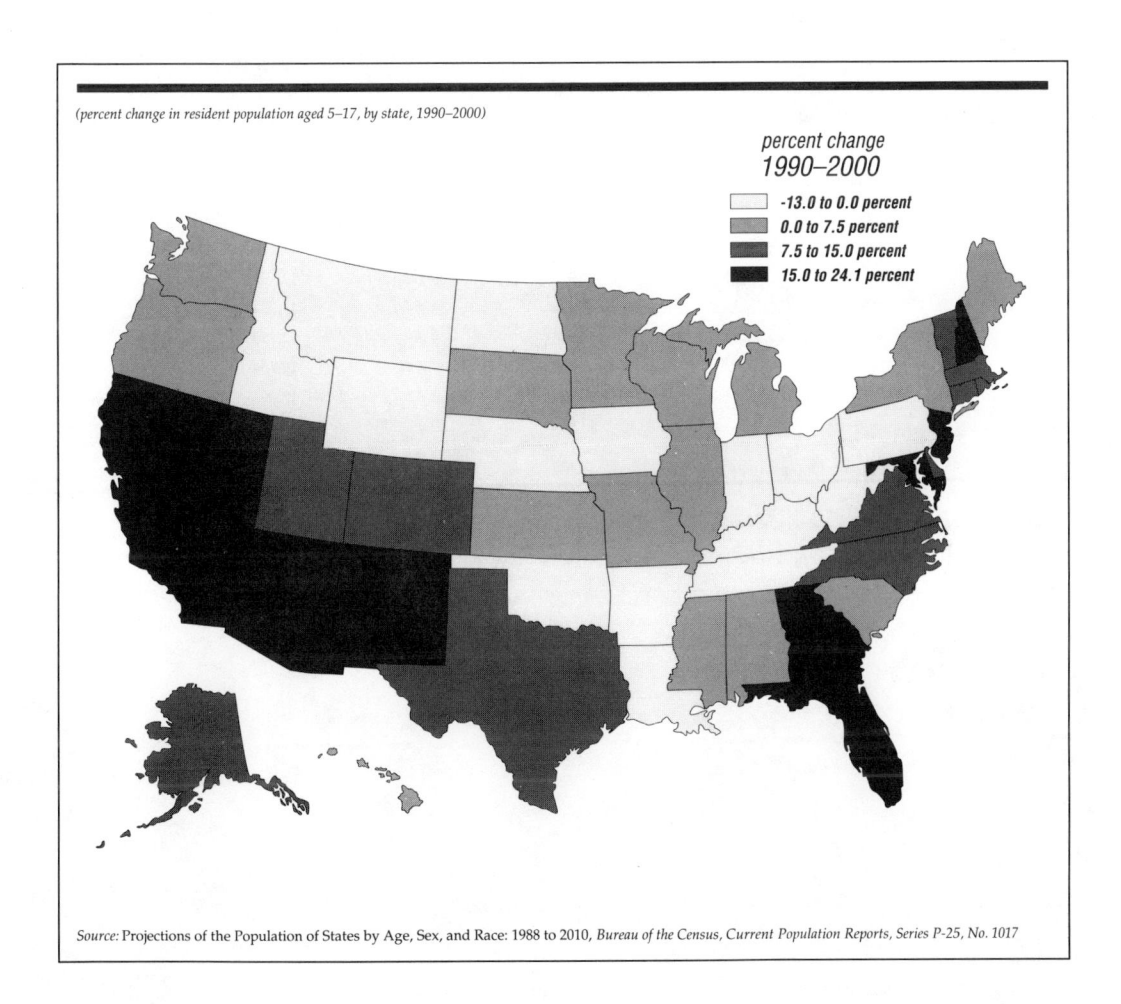

(percent change in resident population aged 5–17, by state, 1990–2000)

percent change
1990–2000

- -13.0 to 0.0 percent
- 0.0 to 7.5 percent
- 7.5 to 15.0 percent
- 15.0 to 24.1 percent

Source: Projections of the Population of States by Age, Sex, and Race: 1988 to 2010, *Bureau of the Census, Current Population Reports,* Series P-25, No. 1017

School Enrollment

EXPANDING HIGH SCHOOLS

Between 1990 and 1997, the biggest enrollment growth will be in the public high schools. Their student body will increase by 16 percent while the number of children in kindergarten through eighth grade will climb only 5 percent.

(projected enrollment in grades K-8* and 9-12 of public elementary and secondary schools for the 50 states and District of Columbia, 1990 to 1997, numbers in thousands)

	K-12*	K-8*	9-12
1990	40,752	29,366	11,386
1991	41,306	29,794	11,512
1992	41,879	30,178	11,701
1993	42,444	30,460	11,984
1994	43,014	30,624	12,390
1995	43,442	30,738	12,704
1996	43,775	30,772	13,003
1997	43,960	30,754	13,206
Percent change 1990-1997	7.9%	4.7%	16.0%

*Includes most kindergarten and some nursery school enrollment.

Source: Projections of Educational Statistics to 1997-1998, *National Center for Education Statistics, Department of Education*

Mothers Who Work

MOSTLY WORKING

In 1978, 60 percent of women with children aged 6 to 13 were labor force participants; that share rose to 73 percent in 1988. Three-quarters of women with high-school-aged-children are in the work force.

(labor force participation rates* of women with children aged 6 to 17, by marital status, 1978 to 1988)

	total	age of youngest child aged 6 to 13	aged 14 to 17
1978			
All women with children aged 6 to 17	60.0%	60.2%	59.6%
Married, spouse present	57.2	57.0	57.5
Other marital status	71.2	72.2	67.7
1983			
All women with children aged 6 to 17	66.3	65.8	67.3
Married, spouse present	63.8	63.3	64.9
Other marital status	74.1	73.5	75.3
1988			
All women with children aged 6 to 17	73.3	72.7	74.5
Married, spouse present	72.5	72.2	73.0
Other marital status	75.5	74.1	78.8

*Labor force participation rates are the ratio of women in the labor force to the total number of women with the same marital status and same age children.

Source: Bureau of Labor Statistics

Note: Other marital status includes women who are divorced, never-married, separated, and widowed.

Labor Force Status

LABOR FORCE
5–17

FEWER THAN HALF WORKERS

Fewer than half of all 16-and-17-year-olds are in the labor force. Forty-six percent of the boys in this age group and 45 percent of the girls are labor force participants.

(labor force status of all persons aged 16 and older, aged 18 to 64, and those aged 16 and 17, by sex and race, numbers in thousands)

	total population	total in labor force	percent of population in labor force	number employed	number unemployed	percent of labor force unemployed	not in labor force
Males aged 16 and older	86,899	66,207	76.2	62,107	4,101	6.2	20,692
White	75,189	57,779	76.8	54,647	3,132	5.4	17,410
Black	9,128	6,486	71.1	5,661	826	12.7	2,642
Males aged 18 to 64	71,443	62,563	87.6	58,864	3,699	5.9	8,880
White	61,583	54,522	88.5	51,705	2,818	5.2	7,061
Black	7,615	6,179	81.1	5,427	750	12.1	1,437
Males aged 16 and 17	3,824	1,745	45.6	1,393	353	20.2	2,079
White	3,125	1,524	48.8	1,252	272	17.9	1,601
Black	566	179	31.7	109	70	39.0	387
Females aged 16 and older	95,853	53,658	56.0	50,334	3,324	6.2	42,195
White	81,769	45,510	55.7	43,142	2,369	5.2	36,258
Black	11,224	6,507	58.0	5,648	858	13.2	4,717
Females aged 18 to 64	75,700	50,799	67.1	47,801	3,000	5.9	24,901
White	63,964	42,999	67.2	40,878	2,120	4.9	20,965
Black	9,262	6,227	67.2	5,438	791	12.7	3,035
Females aged 16 and 17	3,677	1,638	44.6	1,343	295	18.0	2,039
White	2,985	1,439	48.2	1,216	223	15.5	1,546
Black	557	157	28.2	93	64	40.5	400

Source: Annual averages from Employment and Earnings, 1987, Bureau of Labor Statistics

Note: The population here includes all civilian, noninstitutionalized people aged 16 and older.

Extent of Employment

LABOR FORCE
5–17

MOSTLY PART-TIME

Although they're a traditional source of part-time workers, fewer than half of teenagers aged 16 and 17 hold down jobs. Eighty-five percent of employed 16-and-17-year-olds are part-timers, and two-thirds of those workers are on the job just 1 to 26 weeks a year.

(work experience in 1987 of workers aged 16 and older and aged 16 to 17, by sex, numbers in thousands)

	\multicolumn{4}{c	}{worked at full-time jobs}	\multicolumn{4}{c	}{worked at part-time jobs}	non-workers
	total	50-52 weeks	27-49 weeks	1-26 weeks	total	50-52 weeks	27-49 weeks	1-26 weeks	total
Males									
Aged 16 and older	59,740	47,106	7,489	5,143	9,280	3,175	2,165	3,940	18,582
Aged 16 and 17	384	33	29	322	1,582	251	270	1,060	1,811
Females									
Aged 16 and older	40,398	29,882	5,788	4,727	18,538	7,774	4,301	6,463	37,580
Aged 16 and 17	186	17	13	157	1,617	288	281	1,048	1,812

Source: The 1988 Current Population Survey, Bureau of Labor Statistics

Note: Numbers may not add to total due to rounding. The categories in this table are not mutually exclusive. Workers may, for example, be counted as both a full-time and a part-time worker if they held jobs of both kinds during the year. For this reason, the total number of workers will be higher and the number of nonworkers lower than in the previous table that uses annual averages of the number of workers in each category. Civilians only.

Kinds of Jobs

LABOR FORCE
5–17

BEHIND THE COUNTERS

Over 60 percent of 16-and-17-year-olds who work are employed in service and sales occupations; fully 26 percent work in food service alone. Another 17 percent of these teenagers work as operators, fabricators and laborers.

(occupations of employed persons aged 16 and older, and those aged 16 and 17, by sex, numbers in thousands)

	aged 16+	aged 16 and 17	males aged 16 and 17	females aged 16 and 17	percent aged 16+	percent aged 16 and 17
All employed persons	112,440	2,736	1,393	1,343	100.0	100.0
Managerial and professional	27,742	62	31	31	24.7	2.3
Executive, administrative and managerial	13,316	16	8	8	11.8	0.6
Officials & administrators, public admin.	549	0	0	0	0.5	0.0
Other executive, admin., & managerial	9,190	14	8	6	8.2	0.5
Management-related occupations	3,577	3	1	2	3.2	0.1
Professional specialty occupations	14,426	46	23	23	12.8	1.7
Engineers	1,731	0	0	0	1.5	0.0
Math & computer scientists	685	0	0	0	0.6	0.0
Natural scientists	388	0	0	0	0.3	0.0
Health diagnosing occupations	793	0	0	0	0.7	0.0
Health assessment & treating	2,148	0	0	0	1.9	0.0
Teachers, college & university	661	1	0	1	0.6	0.0
Teachers, except college & university	3,587	23	13	10	3.2	0.8
Lawyers & judges	707	0	0	0	0.6	0.0
Other professional specialty occupations	3,727	72	60	12	3.3	2.6
Technical, sales, admin. support	35,082	856	229	627	31.2	31.3
Technicians & related support occupations	3,346	9	6	3	3.0	0.3
Health technologists & technicians	1,142	1	0	1	1.0	0.0
Engineering & science technicians	1,100	3	2	1	1.0	0.1
Techs., except health, engineering, science	1,104	5	3	2	1.0	0.2
Sales occupations	13,480	606	160	446	12.0	22.1
Supervisors & proprietors	3,572	5	2	3	3.2	0.2

(continued next page)

Kinds of Jobs

LABOR FORCE
5-17

(continued from previous page)
(occupations of employed persons aged 16 and older, and those aged 16 and 17, by sex, numbers in thousands)

	aged 16+	aged 16 and 17	males aged 16 and 17	females aged 16 and 17	percent aged 16+	percent aged 16 and 17
Sales reps., finance & business service	2,330	21	5	16	2.1%	0.8%
Sales reps., commodities except retail	1,544	6	3	3	1.4	0.2
Sales, retail and personal	5,973	572	150	422	5.3	20.9
Sales-related occupations	60	2	0	2	0.1	0.1
Administrative support including clerical	**18,256**	**241**	**63**	**178**	**16.2**	**8.8**
Supervisors	723	1	1	0	0.6	0.0
Computer equipment operators	914	11	4	7	0.8	0.4
Secretaries, stenographers, & typists	5,004	49	4	45	4.5	1.8
Financial records processing	2,469	11	1	10	2.2	0.4
Mail & message distributing	961	13	9	4	0.9	0.5
Other admin. support including clerical	8,185	156	46	110	7.3	5.7
Service occupations	**15,054**	**1,080**	**492**	**588**	**13.4**	**39.5**
Private household	934	140	9	131	0.8	5.1
Protective services	1,907	21	11	10	1.7	0.8
Service, except private hhld. & protective	12,213	918	471	447	10.9	33.6
Food service	5,204	703	360	343	4.6	25.7
Health service	1,873	31	8	23	1.7	1.1
Cleaning & building service	2,886	107	74	33	2.6	3.9
Personal service	2,249	78	30	48	2.0	2.9
Precision production, craft, repair	**13,568**	**75**	**68**	**7**	**12.1**	**2.7**
Mechanics & repairers	445	21	20	1	0.4	0.8
Construction trades	5,011	36	36	0	4.5	1.3
Other production, craft, repair	4,112	17	11	6	3.7	0.6
Operators, fabricators, laborers	**17,486**	**476**	**410**	**66**	**15.6**	**17.4**
Machine operators, assemblers, inspectors	7,994	56	35	21	7.1	2.0
Transportation, material moving	4,712	38	34	4	4.2	1.4
Handlers, equip. cleaners, helpers, laborers	4,779	383	341	42	4.3	14.0
Farming, forestry, fishing	**3,507**	**187**	**163**	**24**	**3.1**	**6.8**
Farm operators & managers	1,317	5	4	1	1.2	0.2
Farm workers & related occupations	2,013	177	154	23	1.8	6.5
Forestry and fishing occupations	177	4	4	0	0.2	0.1

Source: Unpublished annual data for 1987, Bureau of Labor Statistics

Note: Numbers may not add to total due to rounding. Civilian, noninstitutionalized employees only.

Almanac of Consumer Markets

Workers in the 1990s

LABOR FORCE
5–17

WORKERS ON THE RISE

Unlike male workers in general, there will be proportionately more 16-and-17-year-old men—and women—in the labor force in the 1990s. The participation rate of young black men will climb the most—up almost 5 percentage points by 2000.

(labor force and labor force participation rates* for persons aged 16 and older and those aged 16 and 17, by sex, race, and ethnicity, in 1990 and 2000, numbers in thousands)

	1990 number	1990 participation rate	2000 number	2000 participation rate	1990-2000 percent change
Both sexes, aged 16 and older	124,457	66.2%	138,775	67.8%	11.5%
White	106,648	66.5	116,701	68.2	9.4
Black	13,788	64.6	16,334	66.0	18.5
Hispanic	9,718	65.9	14,086	67.1	44.9
Asian and other	4,021	64.8	5,740	65.8	42.8
Males, aged 16 and older	67,909	75.8	73,136	74.7	7.7
Males, aged 16 and 17	1,544	46.1	1,871	48.7	21.2
White	1,335	49.8	1,589	52.5	19.0
Black	168	31.9	224	36.6	33.3
Hispanic	136	36.6	203	38.1	49.3
Asian and other	41	29.1	58	29.1	41.5
Females, aged 16 and older	56,548	57.4	65,639	61.5	16.1
Females, aged 16 and 17	1,481	46.1	1,829	49.7	23.5
White	1,280	50.0	1,561	54.0	22.0
Black	164	31.7	220	37.2	34.1
Hispanic	107	29.5	173	33.7	61.7
Asian and other	37	27.6	48	24.7	29.7

*Labor force participation rates are the ratio of people in the labor force to the total population of a given sex, age and race or ethnicity.

Source: Unpublished data from the Bureau of Labor Statistics

Note: The labor force here includes civilians who are working or looking for work. Hispanics are of any race.

Health Status

HEALTH
5-17

WHAT MONEY CAN BUY

Boys aged 5 to 17 are more likely to have excellent health (55 percent) than girls in this age group (50 percent). The proportion of children with excellent or very good health is considerably higher in households with a household income of $35,000 or more than in lower-income households.

(parental-assessed health status of persons aged 5 to 17, by sex, race and household income, number of persons in thousands)

	all persons	all health statuses	excellent	very good	good	fair	poor
Both sexes, all races	44,957	100.0%	52.2%	27.0%	18.2%	2.3%	0.3%
Male	22,992	100.0	54.6	25.8	17.1	2.2	0.2
Female	21,966	100.0	49.8	28.1	19.3	2.3	0.4
White	36,584	100.0	54.6	27.5	15.9	1.7	0.3
Black	6,914	100.0	39.3	25.1	30.1	5.2	0.4
Asian and other	1,459	100.0	54.5	23.2	19.4	2.4	0.5
Household income							
Less than $10,000	6,106	100.0%	38.1%	24.0%	32.5%	4.8%	0.6%
$10,000 to $19,999	8,056	100.0	43.2	30.2	22.7	3.5	0.4
$20,000 to $34,999	12,410	100.0	56.6	26.3	15.4	1.4	0.3
$35,000 and over	13,068	100.0	62.9	26.5	9.6	0.8	0.2

Source: The 1986 National Health Interview Survey, National Center for Health Statistics

Note: All persons includes those of unknown health status, all health statuses includes only those with known health status. Household income includes only those persons with known household income. Numbers may not add to total due to rounding.

Acute Conditions

HOME WITH A FLU

Influenza accounts for one in every three acute conditions suffered by 5-to-17-year-olds. In addition to flu and colds, the other leading acute condition for boys in this age group is wounds and cuts. Girls are most likely to have have flu, colds, and other respiratory infections.

(number of acute conditions reported in a year for all persons and those aged 5 to 17, by sex, numbers in thousands)

	males all ages	males aged 5 to 17	females all ages	females aged 5 to 17
All acute conditions	191,369	53,501	257,177	63,409
Infective and parasitic diseases	23,122	8,112	31,244	9,807
Common childhood diseases	2,565	1,368	1,876	979
Intestinal virus, unspecified	4,244	1,021	5,288	1,731
Viral infections, unspecified	9,621	3,302	14,273	4,750
Other	6,692	2,421	9,807	2,347
Respiratory conditions	99,216	28,772	129,626	33,925
Common cold	30,445	7,659	32,983	8,660
Other acute upper respiratory infections	8,472	2,378	13,320	4,334
Influenza	55,256	17,793	75,295	19,223
Acute bronchitis	1,960	571	4,315	868
Pneumonia	1,365	182	1,277	87
Other respiratory conditions	1,718	189	2,435	754
Digestive system conditions	5,860	1,652	9,112	2,091
Dental conditions	1,059	102	1,955	427
Indigestion, nausea and vomiting	3,299	1,381	4,670	1,578
Other digestive conditions	1,502	170	2,487	87
Injuries	34,588	8,948	29,706	6,561
Fractures and dislocations	4,367	1,622	3,978	1,022
Sprains and strains	6,127	1,473	6,208	753
Open wounds and lacerations	11,153	3,626	5,094	1,742
Contusions and superficial injuries	7,986	1,598	7,191	1,736
Other current injuries	4,955	629	7,235	1,308

(continued next page)

Acute Conditions

(continued from previous page)

(number of acute conditions reported in a year for all persons and those aged 5 to 17, by sex, numbers in thousands)

	males all ages	males aged 5 to 17	females all ages	females aged 5 to 17
Selected other acute conditions	21,183	4,911	40,385	8,104
Eye conditions	1,072	85	2,080	213
Acute ear infections	8,689	2,550	10,116	2,006
Other ear conditions	1,884	374	2,193	790
Acute urinary conditions	989	0	4,399	610
Disorders of menstruation	–	–	2,251	436
Other disorders of female genital tract	–	–	2,174	348
Delivery and other conditions of pregnancy	–	–	4,466	97
Skin conditions	2,065	239	3,597	645
Acute musculoskeletal conditions	3,038	268	3,972	528
Headache, excluding migraine	1,253	230	2,461	817
Fever, unspecified	2,192	1,166	2,675	1,614
All other acute conditions	7,400	1,106	17,104	2,920

Source: The 1986 National Health Interview Survey, National Center for Health Statistics

Note: An acute condition is defined by The National Health Interview Survey as an illness or injury that usually lasts less than three months and was first noticed less than three months before the respondent's interview. The acute condition must also have caused the person to restrict activities for at least a half a day or to have contacted a physician. The data are based only on information given by the respondent and are subject to recall and selective reporting error. Numbers may not add to total due to rounding.

Chronic Conditions

HEALTH
5–17

AGE OF THE CHRONIC SKIN PROBLEM

After sinusitis, hay fever, asthma, and bronchitis, boys and girls aged 5 to 17 are most likely to be chronically bothered by dermatitis. Boys in this age group account for over 30 percent of all reported cases of chronic dermatitis among males and girls aged 5 to 17 account for 17 percent of all the females' cases.

(number of selected chronic conditions reported in a year for all persons and those aged 5 to 17, by sex, numbers in thousands)

	males all ages	males aged 5 to 17	females all ages	females aged 5 to 17
Selected skin and musculoskeletal conditions				
Arthritis	10,751	27	20,160	62
Gout, including gouty arthritis	1,515	0	713	0
Intervertebral disc disorders	2,522	0	1,645	0
Bone spur or tendonitis, unspecified	781	0	898	0
Disorders of bone or cartilage	449	46	943	0
Trouble with bunions	594	0	2,321	70
Bursitis, unclassified	1,641	0	2,464	22
Sebaceous skin cyst	640	0	881	50
Trouble with acne	2,193	767	2,116	582
Psoriasis	1,069	83	1,262	55
Dermatitis	3,851	1,191	5,696	948
Trouble with dry, itching skin, unclassified	1,994	232	2,606	289
Trouble with ingrown nails	2,352	313	3,030	258
Trouble with corns and calluses	1,669	46	3,164	56
Impairments				
Visual impairment	4,994	465	3,358	257
Color blindness	2,694	344	272	0
Cataracts	1,534	13	3,497	0
Glaucoma	735	15	967	0
Hearing impairment	11,727	438	9,004	655
Tinnitus	3,388	52	2,927	176
Speech impairment	1,924	656	871	351
Absence of extremity(s)	374	0	24	0
Paralysis, entire body, one side of body, or both legs	200	0	152	0
Partial paralysis of body or legs	236	0	99	0
Deformity of back	6,812	266	9,676	688
Deformity of upper extremities	1,622	42	1,475	47
Deformity of lower extremities	6,454	580	5,739	423
Selected digestive conditions				
Ulcer	2,116	18	2,378	19
Hernia of abdominal cavity	2,300	128	2,283	25
Gastritis or duodenitis	1,080	0	1,813	97

(continued next page)

34 *Almanac of Consumer Markets*

Chronic Conditions

HEALTH 5-17

(continued from previous page)

(number of selected chronic conditions reported in a year for all persons and those aged 5 to 17, by sex, numbers in thousands)

	males all ages	males aged 5 to 17	females all ages	females aged 5 to 17
Frequent indigestion	2,504	101	2,811	113
Enteritis or colitis	574	37	1,820	79
Spastic colon	264	0	1,377	29
Diverticula of intestines	404	0	1,508	0
Frequent constipation	1,002	153	3,537	76
Selected conditions of the genitourinary, nervous, endocrine, metabolic, and blood system				
Goiter or other disorders of the thyroid	420	13	2,789	151
Diabetes	2,949	51	3,635	59
Anemias	570	153	2,617	101
Epilepsy	656	102	863	220
Migraine headache	2,068	398	6,448	523
Neuralgia or neuritis, unspecified	215	0	364	0
Kidney trouble	1,305	52	2,662	97
Bladder disorders	516	41	3,253	87
Diseases of prostate	1,281	0	–	–
Inflammatory female genital diseases	–	–	427	0
Noninflammatory female genital diseases	–	–	1,095	24
Menstrual disorders	–	–	2,097	167
Selected circulatory conditions				
Ischemic heart disease	4,091	0	2,809	0
Tachycardia or rapid heart	700	0	1,226	24
Heart murmurs	1,310	177	2,583	434
Other heart rhythm disorders	499	8	800	0
Other heart diseases	1,482	73	2,265	0
High blood pressure (hypertension)	12,512	0	16,457	99
Cerebrovascular disease	1,156	16	1,646	0
Hardening of the arteries	1,428	0	1,225	0
Varicose veins	1,042	0	5,814	0
Hemorrhoids	4,568	40	5,341	15
Selected respiratory conditions				
Chronic bronchitis	4,707	1,261	6,671	1,282
Asthma	4,670	1,464	5,019	1,265
Hay fever or allergic rhinitis without asthma	10,136	1,757	11,566	1,690
Chronic sinusitis	14,636	1,879	19,749	1,687
Deviated nasal septum	825	77	465	22
Chronic disease of tonsils or adenoids	1,071	565	2,068	906
Emphysema	1,201	0	796	0

Source: The 1986 National Health Interview Survey, National Center for Health Statistics

Note: Chronic conditions are defined by the National Health Interview Survey as conditions that either a) were first noticed three months or more before the date of the interview or b) belong to a group of conditions (such as heart disease or diabetes) that are considered chronic regardless of when they began. Totals for all chronic conditions are not shown because the National Health Interview Survey does not measure the total number of chronic conditions for each person. The data are based only on information given by the respondent and are subject to recall and selective reporting error.

Activity Restrictions

HEALTH
5–17

LOST LESSONS

Because of an illness or injury, children aged 5 to 17 will miss five whole or half days of school each year and they will each spend about four and one-half days in bed. Girls in this age group tend to miss more days of school because of illness or injury than boys. Together, the boys and girls accumulate more than 226 million school-loss days a year.

(number of days of activity restriction reported in a year and per person due to acute and chronic conditions, by type of restriction and sex, race, and household income, for persons of all ages and aged 5 to 17, numbers in thousands)

	number of days per year		number of days per person	
	bed day	school-loss or work-loss day	bed day	school-loss or work-loss day
All ages	1,547,980	833,396	6.5	5.4
Male	613,113	401,503	5.4	4.8
Female	934,867	431,892	7.7	6.0
White	1,298,039	716,187	6.5	5.4
Black	220,102	99,332	7.7	5.4
Household income				
Less than $10,000	384,962	90,268	11.5	6.1
$10,000 to $19,999	346,115	162,604	7.7	6.1
$20,000 to $34,999	326,166	254,563	5.2	5.7
$35,000 and over	275,957	232,139	4.3	4.6
All aged 5 to 17	200,350	226,369	4.5	5.0
Male	84,636	99,472	3.7	4.3
Female	115,715	126,897	5.3	5.8
White	172,685	193,846	4.7	5.3
Black	23,595	27,652	3.4	4.0
Household income				
Less than $10,000	26,518	35,209	4.3	5.8
$10,000 to $19,999	35,566	36,543	4.4	4.5
$20,000 to $34,999	55,856	63,697	4.5	5.1
$35,000 and over	61,460	67,523	4.7	5.2

Source: The 1986 National Health Interview Survey, National Center for Health Statistics

Note: Numbers may not add to total due to rounding. A bed day is one during which a person stayed in bed more than half a day because of illness or injury. All hospital days for inpatients are considered bed days even if the patient was not in bed more than half a day. A work-loss day is one on which a currently employed person aged 18 or older missed more than half a day of work. A school-loss day is one in which a student aged 5 to 17 missed more than a half a day of school. The data are based only on information given by the respondent and are subject to recall and selective reporting error.

Cause of Death

LETHAL MOVEMENTS

Almost half—48 percent—of all deaths among persons aged 5 to 14 are caused by accidents and adverse effects. Fifty-six percent of those accidents are motor vehicle-related. Cancer, the second leading cause of death for 5-to-14-year-olds, accounts for 13 percent of the deaths in this age group.

(ten leading causes of death among persons aged 5 to 14)

	number of deaths persons aged 5 to 14	number of deaths all ages	percent accounted for by persons aged 5 to 14
All causes	8,788	2,105,361	0.4%
Accidents and adverse effects	4,226	95,277	4.4
Malignant neoplasms (cancer)	1,165	469,376	0.2
Congenital anomalies	453	12,638	3.6
Homicide and legal intervention	379	21,731	1.7
Heart diseases	310	765,490	0.0
Suicide	255	30,904	0.8
Pneumonia and influenze	147	69,812	0.2
Chronic obstructive pulmonary diseases and allied conditions	106	76,559	0.1
Benign, uncertain, and unspecified neoplasms	90	6,730	1.3
Cerebrovascular diseases	73	149,643	0.0
All other causes	1,584	407,201	0.4

Source: Advance Report of Final Mortality Statistics, 1986, *National Center for Health Statistics, Vol. 37, No. 6*

Chapter 3

CONSUMERS AGED 18 TO 24

This market will be shrinking and changing during the 1990s. Here are some factors to watch.

There will be fewer young adults and fewer households headed by young adults.

■ Between 1990 and 2000 the number of 18-to-24-year-olds will drop 3 percent.

■ The number of households headed by under-25-year-olds will fall 5 percent during the 1990s.

■ In 1990 married couples head 33 percent of these youngest households; that share will be only 24 percent in 2000.

■ Eighty-three percent of men and 69 percent of women aged 18 to 24 have never married.

■ Seventy percent of these young women and 80 percent of the men are in the labor force. Most of the workers hold full-time jobs.

■ Twenty-seven percent of households headed by an under-25-year-old have household incomes between $20,000 and $35,000 and 13 percent have incomes of more than $35,000. But 60 percent of these households bring in less than $20,000.

■ Married couples have the highest median household income—$21,000—in this age group. The median income of dual-earner married couples is $4,100 higher than that.

■ These young households devote more of their spending dollar to food away from home, alcoholic beverages, shelter, apparel, and transportation than the average household.

■ Because of their dwindling numbers, households headed by under-25-year-olds will be spending an estimated three billion dollars less in 2000 than in 1990.

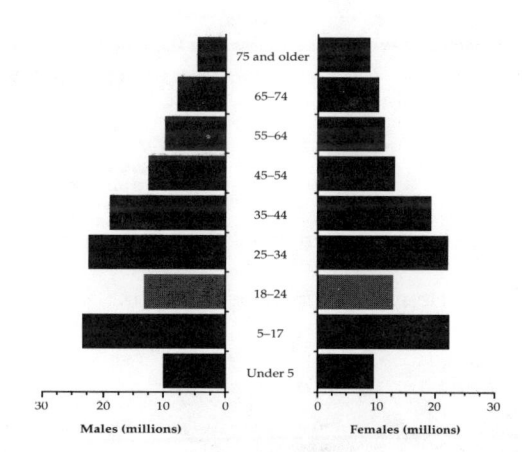

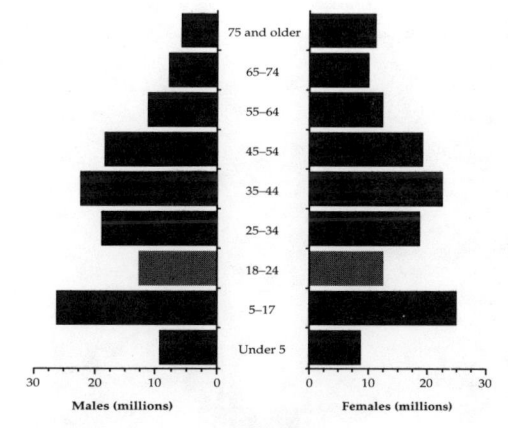

1990

2000

Almanac of Consumer Markets 39

Share of Total Population

POPULATION
18–24

FEWER YOUNG ADULTS

The number of 18-to-24-year-olds will plummet from a 1980 high of 13 percent of the population to only 9 percent by 2000.

(total population and the number of persons aged 18 to 24, in thousands, by sex, 1960 to 1980, and projections for 1990 to 2000)

	1960 number	1960 percent of total	1970 number	1970 percent of total	1980 number	1980 percent of total	1990 number	1990 percent of total	1995 number	1995 percent of total	2000 number	2000 percent of total
All ages	180,671	100.0%	205,052	100.0%	227,757	100.0%	252,293	100.0%	264,077	100.0%	274,479	100.0%
All aged 18 to 24	16,128	8.9	24,711	12.1	30,350	13.3	26,134	10.4	24,227	9.2	25,315	9.2
Males	8,094	4.5	12,451	6.1	15,327	6.7	13,281	5.3	12,321	4.7	12,874	4.7
Females	8,034	4.4	12,261	6.0	15,023	6.6	12,853	5.1	11,906	4.5	12,442	4.5

Source: Annual Projections of the Population by Age, Sex, and Race, for the United States: 1983 to 2080, *Bureau of the Census, Current Population Reports, Series 17 and the Bureau of the Census*

Note: Total population includes Armed Forces overseas; 1960 to 1980 are based on censuses; projections are based on the Census Bureau's Series 17 projections that incorporate illegal immigration and higher levels of emigration than other Census Bureau projections. Series 17 is consistent with current estimates of illegal aliens living in the United States. Numbers may not add to total due to rounding.

Sex, Race, and Ethnicity

POPULATION
18–24

NONWHITES AND HISPANICS GAINING

During the 1990s the number of young adults in this age group will fall 3 percent despite increases among Hispanics and Asians. Whites will drop from 72 to 67 percent of those aged 18 to 24, while blacks will increase from 14 to 15 percent, Hispanics from 11 to 14 percent, and Asians from 3 to 5 percent. Nonwhites and Hispanics are projected to increase faster than whites in all age groups.

(projections of the total population and persons aged 18 to 24, in thousands, by sex, race, and Hispanic origin, 1990 to 2000)

	1990	1995	2000	percent change 1990–2000
All ages	252,293	264,077	274,479	8.8%
White	191,594	195,347	197,634	3.2
Black	30,915	33,237	35,440	14.6
Hispanic	21,854	25,991	30,295	38.6
Asians and other races	7,930	9,502	11,110	40.1
All aged 18 to 24	26,134	24,227	25,315	-3.1
White	18,700	16,657	16,909	-9.6
Black	3,756	3,525	3,755	0.0
Hispanic	2,811	3,068	3,497	24.4
Asians and other races	867	977	1,154	33.1
All males aged 18 to 24	13,281	12,321	12,874	-3.1
White	9,521	8,482	8,607	-9.6
Black	1,879	1,768	1,883	0.2
Hispanic	1,456	1,591	1,813	24.5
Asians and other races	424	480	571	34.7
All females aged 18 to 24	12,853	11,906	12,442	-3.2
White	9,179	8,176	8,301	-9.6
Black	1,877	1,757	1,872	-0.3
Hispanic	1,354	1,477	1,684	24.4
Asians and other races	443	496	585	32.1

Source: Projections of the Population of the United States by Age, Sex, and Race: 1983 to 2080, Bureau of the Census, Current Population Reports, Series P-25, No. 952, Series 17

Note: Series 17 projections incorporate illegal immigration and higher levels of emigration than other Census Bureau projections and are consistent with current estimates of illegal aliens living in the United States. Total population includes Armed Forces living overseas. In this table Hispanics have been separated out of the racial groups; categories do not overlap. Numbers may not add to total due to rounding.

State Populations

POPULATION 18–24

TRENDING DOWNWARD

Thirty states will have fewer people aged 18 to 24 at the turn of the century than in 1990. Large declines in the number of 18-to-24-year-olds will occur in the Northeast while most western states will gain more young adults.

(resident population and the number of persons aged 18 to 24, in thousands, in Census Bureau divisions and states in 1980 and projections for 1990 to 2010)

Note: Inconsistencies between the data in this table and the preceding two tables are due to different assumptions about immigration and emigration on which the projections are based and the inclusion of Armed Forces overseas in the total population. This table is based on the resident population only.

	census 1980	projections 1990	projections 2000	2010	percent change 1990–2000	percent change 2000–2010
All ages	226,546	249,891	267,747	282,055	7.1%	5.3%
All aged 18 to 24	30,022	25,897	24,987	26,911	-3.5	7.7
New England	**1,632**	**1,369**	**1,184**	**1,331**	**-13.5**	**12.4**
Connecticut	385	328	277	307	-15.5	10.8
Maine	141	124	109	119	-12.1	9.2
Massachusetts	784	627	534	602	-14.8	12.7
New Hampshire	121	122	114	136	-6.6	19.3
Rhode Island	129	108	97	106	-10.2	9.3
Vermont	71	60	54	60	-10.0	11.1
Middle Atlantic	**4,531**	**3,753**	**3,237**	**3,446**	**-13.7**	**6.5**
New Jersey	872	773	677	789	-12.4	16.5
New York	2,158	1,821	1,594	1,666	-12.5	4.5
Pennsylvania	1,502	1,159	966	992	-16.7	2.7
East North Central	**5,559**	**4,362**	**3,852**	**3,944**	**-11.7**	**2.4**
Illinois	1,508	1,190	1,081	1,119	-9.2	3.5
Indiana	737	581	514	521	-11.5	1.4
Michigan	1,258	1,000	855	883	-14.5	3.3
Ohio	1,414	1,107	962	970	-13.1	0.8
Wisconsin	643	484	440	451	-9.1	2.5

(continued on next page)

State Populations

POPULATION 18–24

(continued from previous page)

(resident population and the number of persons aged 18 to 24, in thousands, in Census Bureau divisions and states in 1980 and projections for 1990 to 2010)

	census 1980	projections 1990	projections 2000	2010	percent change 1990–2000	percent change 2000–2010
All ages	226,546	249,891	267,747	282,055	7.1%	5.3%
All aged 18 to 24	30,022	25,897	24,987	26,911	-3.8	7.7
West North Central	**2,313**	**1,749**	**1,683**	**1,724**	**-3.8**	**2.4**
Iowa	388	265	237	222	-10.6	-6.3
Kansas	327	251	252	259	0.4	2.8
Minnesota	558	430	412	439	-4.2	6.6
Missouri	636	510	492	519	-3.5	5.5
Nebraska	211	156	148	149	-5.1	0.7
North Dakota	97	68	68	64	0.0	-5.9
South Dakota	95	68	72	72	5.9	0.0
South Atlantic	**4,858**	**4,595**	**4,547**	**5,109**	**-1.0**	**12.4**
Delaware	83	71	67	76	-5.6	13.4
District of Columbia	97	69	66	69	-4.3	4.5
Florida	1,140	1,162	1,210	1,416	4.1	17.0
Georgia	732	749	785	903	4.8	15.0
Maryland	552	498	459	526	-7.8	14.6
North Carolina	822	761	742	810	-2.5	9.2
South Carolina	447	407	403	429	-1.0	6.5
Virginia	742	693	662	738	-4.5	11.5
West Virginia	243	185	154	142	-16.8	-7.8
East South Central	**1,947**	**1,663**	**1,585**	**1,616**	**-4.7**	**2.0**
Alabama	515	441	421	444	-4.5	5.5
Kentucky	492	403	368	360	-8.7	-2.2
Mississippi	339	295	297	303	0.7	2.0
Tennessee	601	525	498	509	-5.1	2.2
West South Central	**3,261**	**2,989**	**3,095**	**3,288**	**3.5**	**6.2**
Arkansas	278	238	230	234	-3.4	1.7
Louisiana	595	485	468	460	-3.5	-1.7
Oklahoma	402	330	336	344	1.8	2.4
Texas	1,986	1,936	2,060	2,250	6.4	9.2

(continued on next page)

State Populations

POPULATION
18–24

(continued from previous page)

(resident population and the number of persons aged 18 to 24, in thousands, in Census Bureau divisions and states in 1980 and projections for 1990 to 2010)

	census 1980	projections 1990	projections 2000	2010	percent change 1990–2000	percent change 2000–2010
All ages	226,546	249,891	267,747	282,055	7.1%	5.3%
All aged 18 to 24	30,022	25,897	24,987	26,911	-3.8	7.7
Mountain	**1,583**	**1,443**	**1,602**	**1,759**	**11.0**	**9.8**
Arizona	369	385	434	508	12.7	17.1
Colorado	418	361	377	407	4.4	8.0
Idaho	123	99	103	101	4.0	-1.9
Montana	104	75	75	72	0.0	-4.0
Nevada	105	108	121	136	12.0	12.4
New Mexico	178	168	188	220	11.9	17.0
Utah	216	196	251	265	28.1	5.6
Wyoming	69	50	52	51	4.0	-1.9
Pacific	**4,339**	**3,972**	**4,204**	**4,693**	**5.8**	**11.6**
Alaska	60	70	76	85	8.6	11.8
California	3,252	3,036	3,242	3,687	6.8	13.7
Hawaii	142	137	154	160	12.4	3.9
Oregon	331	259	257	266	-0.8	3.5
Washington	554	470	475	495	1.1	4.2

Source: Projections of the Population of States by Age, Sex and Race: 1988 to 2010, *Bureau of the Census, Current Population Reports, Series P-25, No. 1017*

Note: Numbers may not add to total due to rounding.

State-by-State Changes

POPULATION
18–24

RISING IN THE WEST

Major drops in the number of 18-to-24-year-olds during the 1990s will be concentrated in the Northeast and Midwest. Large projected increases will occur in the western states of Arizona, Hawaii, Nevada, New Mexico, and Utah.

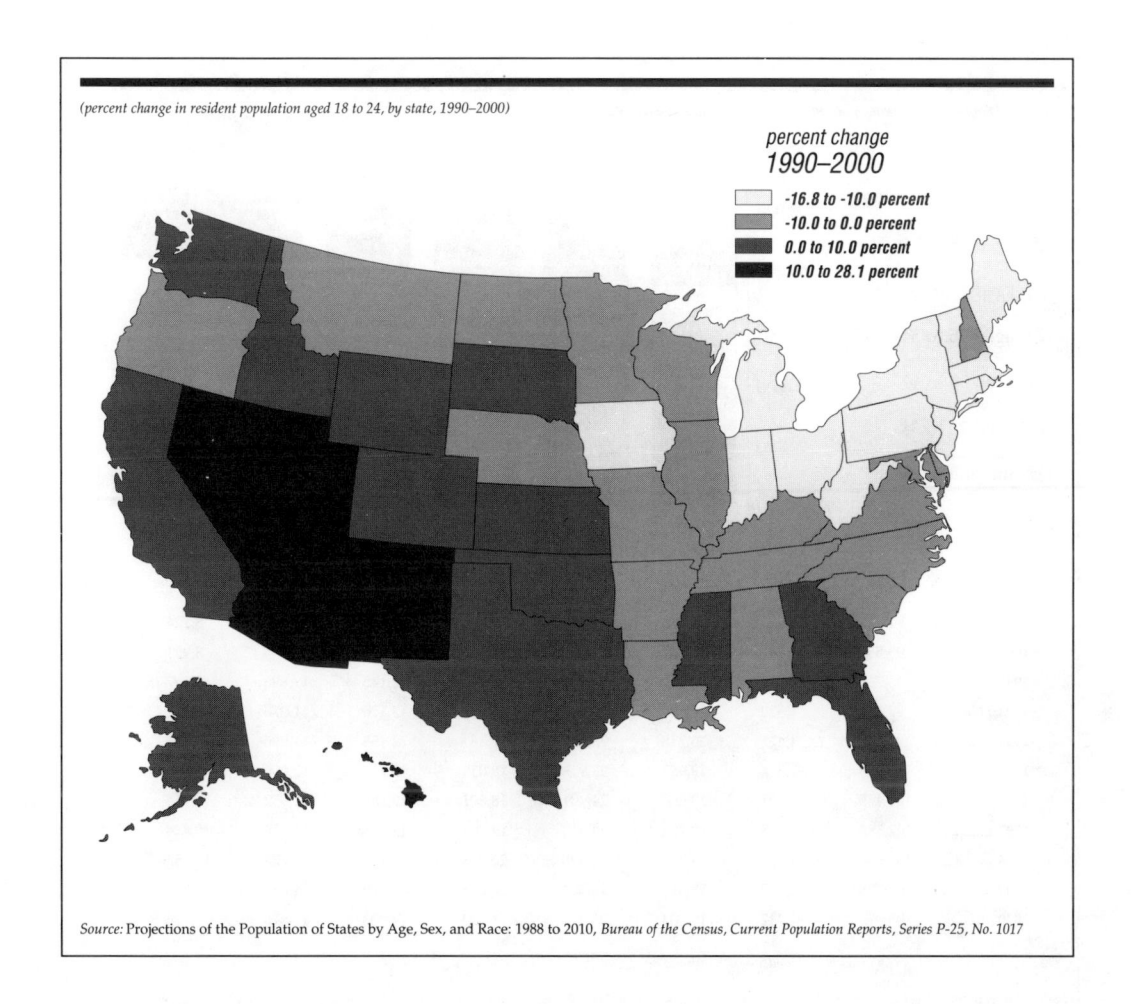

(percent change in resident population aged 18 to 24, by state, 1990–2000)

percent change
1990–2000

- -16.8 to -10.0 percent
- -10.0 to 0.0 percent
- 0.0 to 10.0 percent
- 10.0 to 28.1 percent

Source: Projections of the Population of States by Age, Sex, and Race: 1988 to 2010, *Bureau of the Census, Current Population Reports, Series P-25, No. 1017*

Number of Households

**HOUSEHOLDS
18–24**

FEWER HOUSEHOLDS

During the 1990s the number of households headed by members of this age group* will drop 5 percent. Married couples will be the most rapidly declining household type among under-25-year-olds.

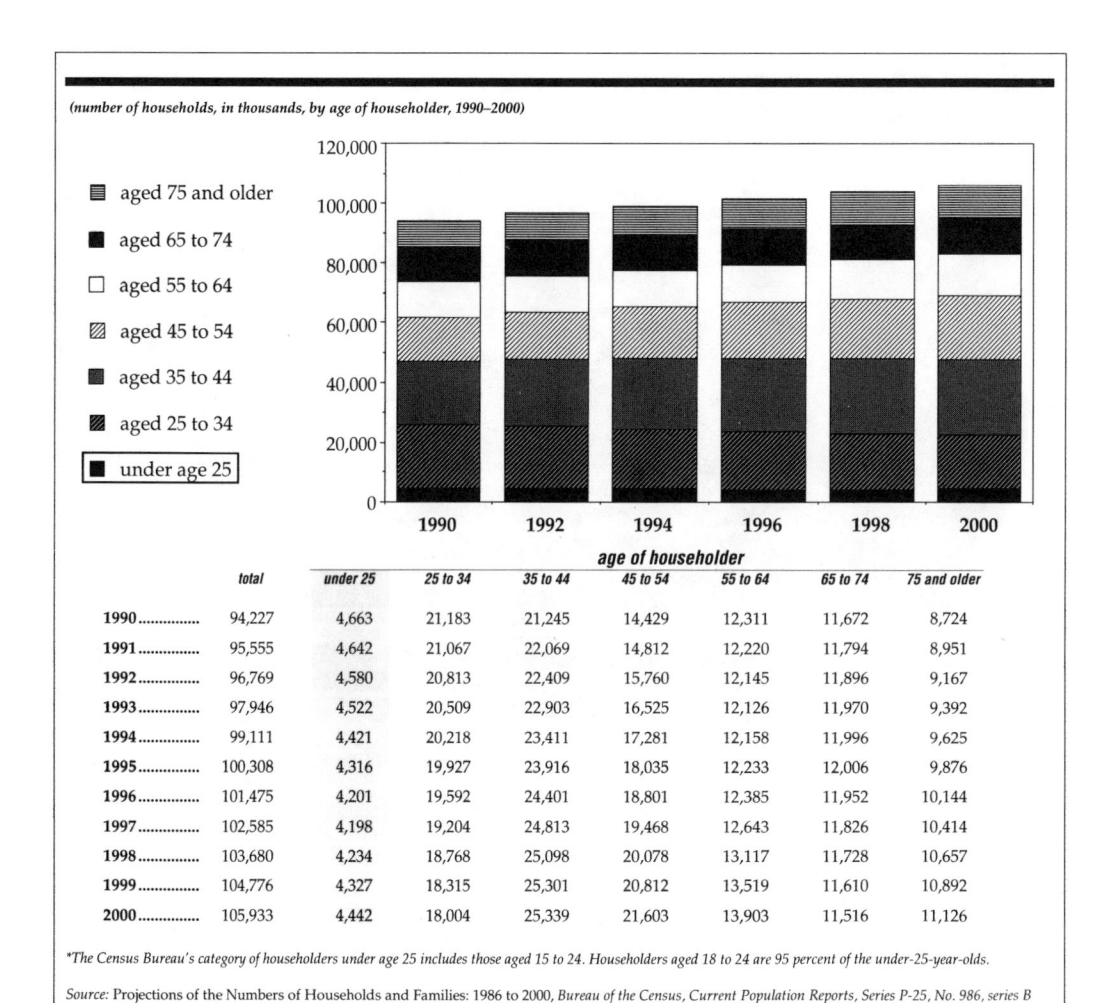

(number of households, in thousands, by age of householder, 1990–2000)

	total	under 25	25 to 34	35 to 44	45 to 54	55 to 64	65 to 74	75 and older
1990	94,227	4,663	21,183	21,245	14,429	12,311	11,672	8,724
1991	95,555	4,642	21,067	22,069	14,812	12,220	11,794	8,951
1992	96,769	4,580	20,813	22,409	15,760	12,145	11,896	9,167
1993	97,946	4,522	20,509	22,903	16,525	12,126	11,970	9,392
1994	99,111	4,421	20,218	23,411	17,281	12,158	11,996	9,625
1995	100,308	4,316	19,927	23,916	18,035	12,233	12,006	9,876
1996	101,475	4,201	19,592	24,401	18,801	12,385	11,952	10,144
1997	102,585	4,198	19,204	24,813	19,468	12,643	11,826	10,414
1998	103,680	4,234	18,768	25,098	20,078	13,117	11,728	10,657
1999	104,776	4,327	18,315	25,301	20,812	13,519	11,610	10,892
2000	105,933	4,442	18,004	25,339	21,603	13,903	11,516	11,126

*The Census Bureau's category of householders under age 25 includes those aged 15 to 24. Householders aged 18 to 24 are 95 percent of the under-25-year-olds.

Source: Projections of the Numbers of Households and Families: 1986 to 2000, Bureau of the Census, Current Population Reports, Series P-25, No. 986, series B
Note: Numbers may not add to total due to rounding.

Types of Households

HOUSEHOLDS
18–24

JUST 6 PERCENT OF HOUSEHOLDS

Only 5 million strong, the under-25-year-olds* are just 6 percent of all householders. At 44 percent, nonfamily households top those headed by married couples, which are 35 percent of households in this age group.

(household types for all households and for householders under age 25, numbers in thousands)

	all households		householder under age 25	
	total	percent of households in category	total	percent of households in category
All households	91,066	100.0%	5,228	100.0%
Family households	65,133	71.5	2,926	56.0
Married couple	51,809	56.9	1,807	34.6
With children under age 18 at home	24,600	27.0	931	17.8
Without children under age 18 at home	27,209	29.9	876	16.8
Female householder	10,608	11.6	843	16.1
With children under age 18 at home	6,273	6.9	730	14.0
Without children under age 18 at home	4,335	4.8	114	2.2
Male householder	2,715	3.0	275	5.3
With children under age 18 at home	1,047	1.1	78	1.5
Without children under age 18 at home	1,669	1.8	197	3.8
Nonfamily households	25,993	28.5	2,302	44.0
Living alone	21,889	24.0	1,245	23.8
Female householder	13,101	14.4	592	11.3
Male householder	8,788	9.7	654	12.5
Living with others	4,044	4.4	1,057	20.2
Female householder	1,523	1.7	445	8.5
Male householder	2,521	2.8	611	11.7

*The Census Bureau's category of householders under age 25 includes those aged 15 to 24. Householders aged 18 to 24 are 95 percent of the under-25-year-olds.

Source: The 1988 Current Population Survey, Bureau of the Census

Note: Numbers may not add to total due to rounding.

Almanac of Consumer Markets 47

Future Household Types

HOUSEHOLDS
18–24

FEWER FAMILIES

The number of households headed by under-25-year-olds* will drop during the 1990s, with the greatest decline—32 percent—seen among married couples. By 2000 more than half of these young households will be nonfamilies.

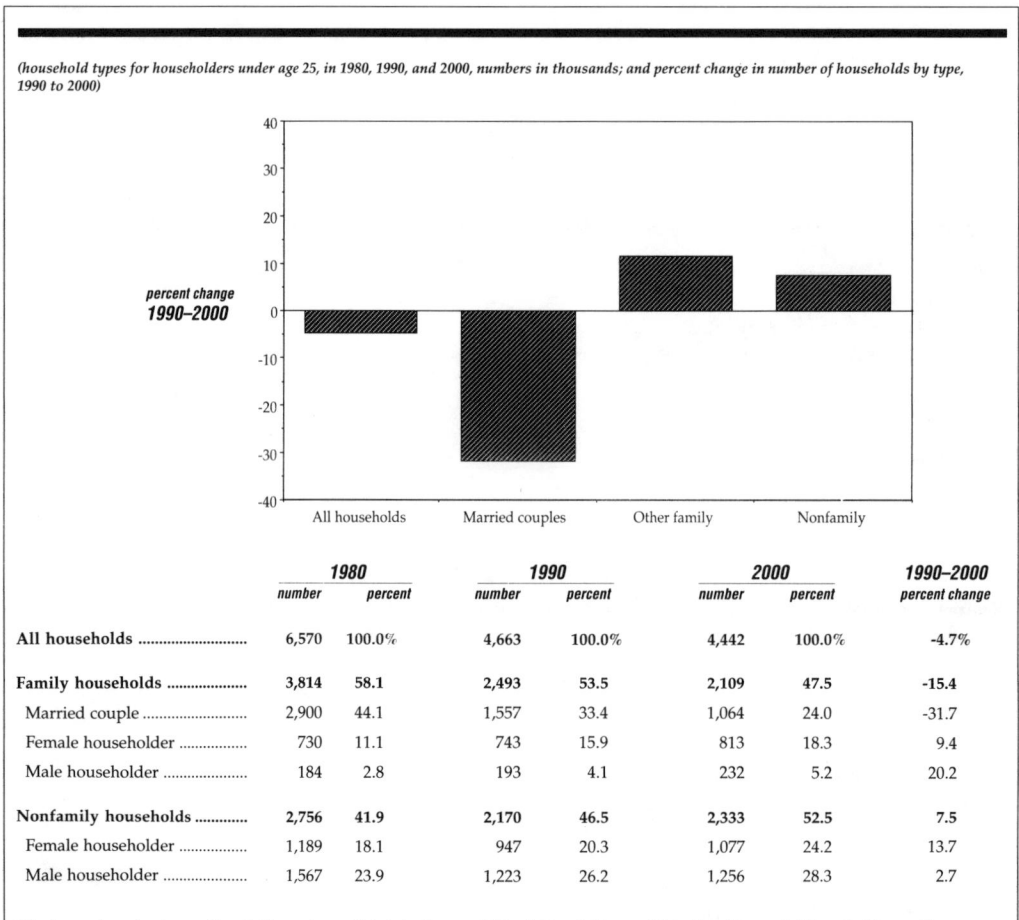

(household types for householders under age 25, in 1980, 1990, and 2000, numbers in thousands; and percent change in number of households by type, 1990 to 2000)

	1980		1990		2000		1990–2000
	number	percent	number	percent	number	percent	percent change
All households	6,570	100.0%	4,663	100.0%	4,442	100.0%	-4.7%
Family households	3,814	58.1	2,493	53.5	2,109	47.5	-15.4
Married couple	2,900	44.1	1,557	33.4	1,064	24.0	-31.7
Female householder	730	11.1	743	15.9	813	18.3	9.4
Male householder	184	2.8	193	4.1	232	5.2	20.2
Nonfamily households	2,756	41.9	2,170	46.5	2,333	52.5	7.5
Female householder	1,189	18.1	947	20.3	1,077	24.2	13.7
Male householder	1,567	23.9	1,223	26.2	1,256	28.3	2.7

*The Census Bureau's category of householders under age 25 includes those aged 15 to 24. Householders aged 18 to 24 are 95 percent of the under-25-year-olds.
Source: The 1980 Current Population Survey and Bureau of the Census
Note: Numbers may not add to total due to rounding.

Almanac of Consumer Markets

Marital Status

MARITAL STATUS AND FERTILITY
18–24

YOUNG HISPANIC BRIDES

Seventy-six percent of 18-to-24-year-olds are unmarried. However, young women, especially those who are Hispanic, are more likely than young men to have taken the step.

(marital status of persons aged 15 and older and those 18 to 24, by sex, race and Hispanic origin, numbers in thousands)

	all	total	single never married	married spouse present	married spouse absent	divorced	widowed
Males all ages							
All races/ethnicities	89,368	100.0%	30.0%	58.5%	2.9%	6.3%	2.4%
White	77,212	100.0	28.2	60.9	2.5	6.2	2.3
Black	9,472	100.0	42.9	40.4	6.0	7.5	3.3
Hispanic origin	6,517	100.0	36.4	49.9	6.2	5.8	1.6
Males aged 18 to 24							
All races/ethnicities	13,029	100.0	82.9	14.6	1.3	1.1	–
White	10,905	100.0	81.2	16.1	1.4	1.2	–
Black	1,708	100.0	91.1	6.9	1.1	0.6	0.3
Hispanic origin	1,399	100.0	77.4	18.2	3.6	0.9	–
Females all ages							
All races	97,320	100.0	23.0	53.7	3.6	8.3	11.4
White	83,003	100.0	21.0	56.6	2.7	8.0	11.6
Black	11,447	100.0	36.5	32.7	9.2	10.4	11.2
Hispanic origin	6,588	100.0	26.6	51.2	7.7	8.3	6.2
Females aged 18 to 24							
All races	13,433	100.0	68.5	26.5	2.6	2.4	–
White	11,096	100.0	65.5	29.3	2.4	2.8	–
Black	1,954	100.0	83.7	11.8	3.9	0.6	–
Hispanic origin	1,263	100.0	56.6	35.1	5.6	2.6	–

Source: Marital Status and Living Arrangements: March 1987, Bureau of the Census, Current Population Reports, Series P-20, No. 423

Note: Nearly 100 percent of men and 98 percent of women aged 15 to 17 have never married. Hispanics may be of any race. Numbers may not add to total due to rounding.

Number of Marriages and Divorces

MARITAL STATUS AND FERTILITY
18–24

YOUTHFUL BRIDES AND GROOMS

Nearly half of all brides in 1985 were under age 25, and a full 93 percent of those women were between the ages of 18 and 24. Thirty-five percent of grooms were under age 25—99 percent of them were 18 to 24 years old.

(number of marriages and divorces for all persons and for those under age 25, by sex)

	all persons male	all persons female	persons under age 25 male	persons under age 25 female	percent involving persons under age 25 male	percent involving persons under age 25 female
All marriages	1,858,783	1,858,783	658,301	899,261	35.4%	48.4%
First marriages	1,185,904	1,196,119	610,527	802,660	51.5	67.7
Remarriages	635,086	623,867	32,033	74,991	5.0	11.8
Previously divorced	499,735	485,848	27,213	63,107	5.4	12.6
Divorces	577,713	577,713	55,730	97,354	9.6	16.9

Source: Advance Report of Final Marriage Statistics, 1985 and Advance Report of Final Divorce Statistics, 1985, *National Center for Health Statistics*

Note: Numbers will not add to total because all divorces include those not stating their age and all marriages include those not stating whether they were previously married.

Childbearing Patterns

MARITAL STATUS AND FERTILITY
18–24

RACIAL DIFFERENCES

The proportion of childless women aged 18 to 24 climbed from 69 to 74 percent between 1976 and 1988. Ninety-two percent of white women aged 18 and 19 are childless as are 88 percent of Hispanic women that age and 73 percent of black women. By ages 20 to 24, half of all black women have had one child or more, as have 46 percent of Hispanic and 29 percent of white women.

(number of children ever born to women aged 18 to 44 and those aged 18 to 24, by race and marital status, number of women in thousands)

	all women	total	none	one	two	three	four	five and six	seven or more
All races									
All marital statuses									
Aged 18 to 44	52,586	100.0%	38.0%	18.6%	25.2%	11.8%	4.2%	2.0%	0.3%
Aged 18 and 19	3,628	100.0	89.3	8.5	2.1	0.1	–	–	–
Aged 20 to 24	9,539	100.0	68.5	17.6	10.4	2.6	0.6	0.3	–
Women ever married									
Aged 18 to 44	36,847	100.0	19.6	22.0	33.8	16.0	5.7	2.5	0.4
Aged 18 and 19	297	100.0	55.7	34.0	9.0	1.3	–	–	–
Aged 20 to 24	3,616	100.0	41.7	31.2	20.8	4.8	1.3	0.2	–
Women never married									
Aged 18 to 44	15,739	100.0	81.0	10.5	5.0	2.0	0.8	0.6	0.1
Aged 18 and 19	3,330	100.0	92.3	6.3	1.4	–	–	–	–
Aged 20 to 24	5,923	100.0	84.8	9.4	4.1	1.3	0.2	0.3	–
White women									
All marital statuses									
Aged 18 to 44	43,870	100.0	39.2	17.8	25.4	11.8	3.9	1.6	0.3
Aged 18 and 19	2,990	100.0	92.1	6.7	1.1	0.1	–	–	–
Aged 20 to 24	7,807	100.0	71.4	16.3	9.5	2.1	0.5	0.1	–
Women ever married									
Aged 18 to 44	31,909	100.0	20.3	22.1	34.0	15.8	5.2	2.1	0.4
Aged 18 and 19	276	100.0	56.3	34.1	8.2	1.4	–	–	–
Aged 20 to 24	3,194	100.0	43.1	31.5	19.9	4.2	1.1	0.1	–
Women never married									
Aged 18 to 44	11,960	100.0	89.4	6.5	2.6	1.0	0.4	0.2	–
Aged 18 and 19	2,714	100.0	95.7	3.9	0.4	–	–	–	–
Aged 20 to 24	4,613	100.0	91.0	5.7	2.3	0.7	0.1	0.1	–

(continued next page)

Childbearing Patterns

MARITAL STATUS AND FERTILITY
18–24

(continued from previous page)

(number of children ever born to women aged 18 to 44 and those aged 18 to 24, by race and marital status, number of women in thousands)

	all women	total	\multicolumn{7}{c}{number of children ever born}
			none	one	two	three	four	five and six	seven or more
Black women									
All marital statuses									
Aged 18 to 44	6,835	100.0%	30.3%	23.9%	23.1%	12.0%	6.0%	4.1%	0.7%
Aged 18 and 19	542	100.0	72.9	19.9	7.2	–	–	–	–
Aged 20 to 24	1,374	100.0	50.2	26.1	15.6	5.5	1.5	1.2	–
Women ever married									
Aged 18 to 44	3,611	100.0	13.6	22	31.3	17.4	9.2	5.7	0.8
Aged 18 and 19	16	100.0	B	B	B	B	B	B	B
Aged 20 to 24	322	100.0	29.7	29.1	25.6	10.0	4.2	1.4	–
Women never married									
Aged 18 to 44	3,225	100.0	48.9	26.1	14.0	5.9	2.4	2.2	0.5
Aged 18 and 19	526	100.0	73.6	19.3	7.1	–	–	–	–
Aged 20 to 24	1,052	100.0	56.4	25.1	12.6	4.1	0.7	1.1	–
Hispanic women									
All marital statuses									
Aged 18 to 44	4,326	100.0	33.6	17.0	22.7	15.6	5.6	4.4	1.0
Aged 18 and 19	273	100.0	88.3	8.8	2.8	–	–	–	–
Aged 20 to 24	956	100.0	54.4	24.2	14.6	5.7	1.2	–	–
Women ever married									
Aged 18 to 44	3,012	100.0	17.2	19.4	28.9	20.3	7.0	5.8	1.5
Aged 18 and 19	32	100.0	B	B	B	B	B	B	B
Aged 20 to 24	449	100.0	29.5	38.0	23.3	7.5	1.7	–	–
Women never married									
Aged 18 to 44	1,314	100.0	71.3	11.5	8.6	4.9	2.4	1.3	–
Aged 18 and 19	241	100.0	94.4	5.6	–	–	–	–	–
Aged 20 to 24	507	100.0	76.4	11.9	6.8	4.1	0.8	–	–

Source: Fertility of American Women: June 1988, *Bureau of the Census, Current Population Reports, Series P-20, No. 436*

Note: The symbol "B" means that the base number of women was too small to calculate a reliable percent distribution. Hispanic women are of any race.

Age and Education

EDUCATIONAL ATTAINMENT
18–24

IN PROGRESS

Fifty-two percent of men and women aged 19 are just high school graduates but that percentage declines rapidly from age 20 to age 24 as the proportion of those attending college rises. By age 24, one in five has completed four or more years of college.

(years of school completed by persons aged 18 to 24, by sex and single year of age, numbers in thousands)

	number	total	not high school graduate	high school graduate	1 to 3 years of college	4 or more years of college	median years
Males aged 18 and 19	3,530	100.0%	46.0%	42.7%	11.2%	0.0%	12.1
Age 18	1,845	100.0	63.9	34.4	1.7	0.0	11.7
Age 19	1,685	100.0	26.6	51.8	21.6	0.0	12.5
Males aged 20 to 24	9,499	100.0	16.7	41.5	32.1	9.7	12.8
Age 20	1,824	100.0	16.4	45.4	37.8	0.4	12.7
Age 21	1,751	100.0	17.0	41.6	40.3	1.1	12.8
Age 22	1,961	100.0	16.1	43.1	33.1	7.6	12.8
Age 23	1,936	100.0	16.1	39.1	27.4	17.4	12.9
Age 24	2,027	100.0	17.8	38.5	23.4	20.3	12.8
Females aged 18 and 19	3,574	100.0	34.9	49.1	15.7	0.2	12.3
Age 18	1,801	100.0	51.3	46.5	1.9	0.2	12.0
Age 19	1,773	100.0	18.3	51.8	29.7	0.2	12.6
Females aged 20 to 24	9,859	100.0	14.0	42.1	33.3	10.6	12.9
Age 20	1,876	100.0	15.2	41.7	42.9	0.2	12.8
Age 21	1,880	100.0	14.5	42.3	41.4	1.7	12.8
Age 22	1,866	100.0	13.6	44.8	34.8	12.6	12.9
Age 23	2,088	100.0	13.3	42.8	26.0	18.0	12.9
Age 24	2,040	100.0	14.4	41.2	24.7	19.7	12.9

Source: Educational Attainment in the United States: March 1987 and 1986, *Bureau of the Census, Current Population Reports, Series P-20, No. 428*

Note: Numbers may not add to total due to rounding.

Enrollment in Higher Education

EDUCATIONAL ATTAINMENT
18–24

FEWER TRADITIONAL STUDENTS

Between 1987 and 1997, the number of these traditionally aged college students will drop, with those aged 22 to 24 falling 19 percent. In 1977, men and women aged 18 to 24 accounted for 60 percent of the enrollment in institutions of higher education—that figure will be 53 percent in 1997.

(estimated and projected enrollment in all institutions of higher education for all persons aged 14 and older and for those aged 18 to 24, by sex and attendance status, in 1987 and 1997, numbers in thousands)

	1987 total	1987 full-time	1987 part-time	1997 total	1997 full-time	1997 part-time	1987-1997 percent change total enrollment
All ages	12,544	7,219	5,325	12,173	6,750	5,423	-3.0%
Men	5,881	3,611	2,270	5,688	3,423	2,265	-3.3
Women	6,663	3,608	3,055	6,485	3,327	3,158	-2.7
All aged 18 to 19	2,764	2,450	314	2,746	2,425	321	-0.7
Men	1,309	1,174	135	1,367	1,223	144	4.4
Women	1,455	1,276	179	1,379	1,202	177	-5.2
All aged 20 to 21	2,224	1,847	377	2,051	1,705	346	-7.8
Men	1,089	927	162	1,008	860	148	-7.4
Women	1,135	920	215	1,043	845	198	-8.1
All aged 22 to 24	2,048	1,308	740	1,652	1,049	603	-19.3
Men	1,080	728	352	878	591	287	-18.7
Women	968	580	388	774	458	316	-20.0

Note: Institutions of higher education include all four-year and two-year colleges and universities. Projections are based on the National Center for Education Statistics' middle alternative. Numbers may not add to total due to rounding.

Source: Projections of Educational Statistics to 1997-1998, *National Center for Education Statistics, Department of Education*

Sex, Race, and Ethnicity

EDUCATIONAL ATTAINMENT
18–24

PULLING AHEAD

The share of women aged 18 to 24 with some college (29 percent) and with four or more years of college (8 percent) is higher than that of the men (26 percent and 7 percent, respectively). All women in this age group—white, black, and Hispanic—are more likely than the men to have completed one to three years of college.

(years of school completed by persons aged 25 and older and those aged 18 to 24, by sex, race, and Hispanic origin, numbers in thousands)

	number	total	not high school graduate	high school graduate	1 to 3 years of college	4 or more years of college
All persons aged 25 and older	149,144	100.0%	24.4%	38.7%	17.1%	19.9%
White	129,170	100.0	23.0	39.2	17.2	20.5
Black	15,580	100.0	36.6	37.1	15.7	10.7
Hispanic origin	9,449	100.0	49.1	29.0	13.3	8.6
All persons aged 18 to 24	26,463	100.0	22.1	42.9	27.5	7.5
White	22,001	100.0	20.7	43.1	28.0	8.1
Black	3,663	100.0	30.1	43.6	22.5	3.8
Hispanic origin	2,662	100.0	44.2	35.3	17.3	3.1
Males aged 25 and older	70,677	100.0	24.0	35.4	17.1	23.6
White	61,678	100.0	22.7	35.6	17.2	24.5
Black	6,919	100.0	37.0	36.5	15.5	11.0
Hispanic origin	4,614	100.0	48.2	28.0	14.2	9.7
Males aged 18 to 24	13,029	100.0	24.6	41.8	26.4	7.1
White	10,905	100.0	23.2	42.4	26.7	7.6
Black	1,708	100.0	34.3	40.5	21.6	3.7
Hispanic origin	1,399	100.0	46.8	33.3	16.3	3.5
Females aged 25 and older	78,467	100.0	24.7	41.6	17.1	16.5
White	67,492	100.0	23.3	42.6	17.3	16.9
Black	8,661	100.0	36.2	37.5	15.8	10.4
Hispanic origin	4,835	100.0	50.0	30.0	12.5	7.5
Females aged 18 to 24	13,433	100.0	19.6	44.0	28.6	7.9
White	11,096	100.0	18.3	43.8	29.3	8.6
Black	1,954	100.0	26.5	46.4	23.3	3.9
Hispanic origin	1,263	100.0	41.3	37.6	18.4	2.6

Source: Educational Attainment in the United States: March 1987 and March 1986, Bureau of the Census, Current Population Reports, Series P-20, No. 428

Note: Hispanics are of any race. Numbers may not add to total due to rounding.

Householders

EDUCATIONAL ATTAINMENT
18–24

EDUCATIONAL SEGMENTS

One-quarter of all male and female householders under age 25* have completed one to three years of college while 11 percent of the men and 13 percent of the women have four or more years of college. White householders are more than twice as likely to have finished four years of college than black or Hispanic householders in this age group.

(years of school completed by householders under age 25, by sex, race, and Hispanic origin, numbers in thousands)

	number	total	not high school graduate	high school graduate	1 to 3 years of college	4 or more years of college	median years
Male householders	**3,083**	**100.0%**	**17.4%**	**46.6%**	**24.8%**	**11.3%**	**12.7**
White	2,768	100.0	17.7	46.9	23.4	11.9	12.7
Black	233	100.0	13.3	51.1	30.9	4.7	12.7
Hispanic	325	100.0	47.7	31.7	16.0	4.3	12.1
Female householders	**2,114**	**100.0**	**19.3**	**42.5**	**24.9**	**13.3**	**12.7**
White	1,628	100.0	16.8	41.5	25.9	15.8	12.8
Black	437	100.0	28.6	47.1	19.5	5.0	12.5
Hispanic	199	100.0	51.3	33.2	11.1	4.5	11.9

*The Census Bureau's category of householders under age 25 includes those aged 15 to 24. Householders aged 18 to 24 are 95 percent of the under-25-year-olds.

Source: Educational Attainment in the United States: March 1987 and March 1986, *Bureau of the Census, Current Population Reports, Series P-20, No. 428*

Note: Hispanics are of any race. Numbers may not add to total due to rounding.

Labor Force Status

LABOR FORCE
18–24

MOSTLY WORKERS

A full 70 percent of 18-to-24-year-old women are in the labor force, as opposed to 67 percent of all women aged 18 to 64. The reverse is true for men: 80 percent of 18-to-24-year-olds are labor force participants, versus 88 percent of all men aged 18 to 64. In this age group, blacks and whites show wide differences in their labor force participation and unemployment rates.

(labor force status of all persons aged 16 and older, aged 18 to 64, and those aged 18 to 24, by sex and race, numbers in thousands)

	total population	total in labor force	percent of population in labor force	number employed	number unemployed	percent of labor force unemployed	not in labor force
Males aged 16 and older	86,899	66,207	76.2%	62,107	4,101	6.2%	20,692
White	75,189	57,779	76.8	54,647	3,132	5.4	17,410
Black	9,128	6,486	71.1	5,661	826	12.7	2,642
Males aged 18 to 64	71,443	62,563	87.6	58,864	3,699	5.9	8,880
White	61,583	54,522	88.5	51,705	2,818	5.2	7,061
Black	7,615	6,179	81.1	5,427	750	12.1	1,437
Males aged 18 to 24	12,705	10,204	80.3	9,046	1,158	11.3	2,501
White	10,619	8,740	82.3	7,897	844	9.7	1,879
Black	1,672	1,198	71.7	923	276	23.0	474
Females aged 16 and older	95,853	53,658	56.0%	50,334	3,324	6.2%	42,195
White	81,769	45,510	55.7	43,142	2,369	5.2	36,258
Black	11,224	6,507	58.0	5,648	858	13.2	4,717
Females aged 18 to 64	75,700	50,799	67.1	47,801	3,000	5.9	24,901
White	63,964	42,999	67.2	40,878	2,120	4.9	20,965
Black	9,262	6,227	67.2	5,438	791	12.7	3,035
Females aged 18 to 24	13,370	9,377	70.1	8,383	995	10.6	3,993
White	11,018	7,955	72.2	7,282	673	8.5	3,063
Black	1,946	1,182	60.7	883	299	25.3	764

Source: Annual averages from Employment and Earnings, 1987, Bureau of Labor Statistics

Note: The population here includes all civilian, noninstitutionalized people aged 16 and older.

Extent of Employment

LABOR FORCE
18–24

MOSTLY FULL-TIME

Among working men in this age group, 70 percent hold full-time jobs and over half of those full-timers work year-round. Fifty-eight percent of working women aged 18 to 24 work full-time and a majority of them (56 percent) work all year.

(work experience in 1987 of workers aged 16 and older, and those aged 18 to 24, by sex, numbers in thousands)

	\multicolumn{4}{c}{worked at full-time jobs}	\multicolumn{4}{c}{worked at part-time jobs}	non-workers
	total	50-52 weeks	27-49 weeks	1-26 weeks	total	50-52 weeks	27-49 weeks	1-26 weeks	total
Males									
Aged 16 and older	59,740	47,106	7,489	5,143	9,280	3,175	2,165	3,940	18,582
Aged 18 to 24	7,568	4,210	1,485	1,872	3,316	1,113	798	1,405	1,702
Females									
Aged 16 and older	40,398	29,882	5,788	4,727	18,538	7,774	4,301	6,463	37,580
Aged 18 to 24	6,103	3,417	1,135	1,553	4,340	1,469	1,081	1,789	2,782

Source: The 1988 Current Population Survey, Bureau of Labor Statistics

Note: Numbers may not add to total due to rounding. The categories in this table are not mutually exclusive. Workers may, for example, be counted as both a full-time and a part-time worker if they held jobs of both kinds during the year. For this reason, the total number of workers will be higher and the number of nonworkers lower than in the previous table that uses annual averages of the number of workers in each category. Civilians only.

Kinds of Jobs

LABOR FORCE
18–24

FOUR BIG OCCUPATIONS

Nearly three-quarters of all 18-to-24-year-olds who work have service, sales, administrative support, and operator, fabricator or laborer jobs. Higher proportions of people aged 18 to 24 are employed in each of these occupations than are workers in general.

(occupations of employed persons aged 16 and older, and those aged 18 to 24, by sex, numbers in thousands)

	aged 16+	aged 18-24	males aged 18-24	females aged 18-24	percent aged 16+	percent aged 18-24
All employed persons	112,440	17,429	9,046	8,383	100.0%	100.0%
Managerial and professional	27,742	1,978	876	1,102	24.7	11.3
Executive, administrative and managerial	13,316	936	443	493	11.8	5.4
Officials & administrative, public admin.	549	15	7	8	0.5	0.1
Other executive, admin., & managerial	9,190	600	316	284	8.2	3.4
Management related occupations	3,577	321	120	201	3.2	1.8
Professional specialty occupations	14,426	1,043	435	608	12.8	6.0
Engineers	1,731	126	105	21	1.5	0.7
Math & computer scientists	685	56	32	24	0.6	0.3
Natural scientists	388	25	15	10	0.3	0.1
Health diagnosing occupations	793	8	5	3	0.7	0.0
Health assessment & treating	2,148	171	21	150	1.9	1.0
Teachers, college & university	661	47	24	23	0.6	0.3
Teachers, except college & university	3,587	225	44	181	3.2	1.3
Lawyers & judges	707	14	9	5	0.6	0.1
Other professional specialty occupations.	3,727	371	179	192	3.3	2.1
Technical, sales, administrative support	35,082	6,440	1,918	4,522	31.2	36.9
Technicians & related support occupations.	3,346	475	244	231	3.0	2.7
Health technologists & technicians	1,142	130	22	108	1.0	0.7
Engineering & science technicians	1,100	177	137	40	1.0	1.0
Techs., except health, engineering, science	1,104	167	85	82	1.0	1.0
Sales occupations	13,480	2,524	945	1,579	12.0	14.5
Supervisors & proprietors	3,572	339	194	145	3.2	1.9

(continued next page)

Almanac of Consumer Markets 59

Kinds of Jobs

LABOR FORCE 18–24

(continued from previous page)

(occupations of employed persons aged 16 and older, and those aged 18 to 24, by sex, numbers in thousands)

	aged 16+	aged 18-24	males aged 18-24	females aged 18-24	percent aged 16+	percent aged 18-24
Sales reps., finance & business service	2,330	212	109	103	2.1%	1.2%
Sales reps., commodities except retail	1,544	112	77	35	1.4	0.6
Sales, retail and personal	5,973	1,855	563	1,292	5.3	10.6
Sales-related occupations	60	7	2	5	0.1	0.0
Administrative support including clerical	**18,256**	**3,441**	**729**	**2,712**	**16.2**	**19.7**
Supervisors	723	45	15	30	0.6	0.3
Computer equipment operators	914	210	75	135	0.8	1.2
Secretaries, stenographers, & typists	5,004	931	20	911	4.5	5.3
Financial records processing	2,469	312	43	269	2.2	1.8
Mail & message distributing	961	127	81	46	0.9	0.7
Other admin. support including clerical	8,185	1,817	495	1,322	7.3	10.4
Service occupations	**15,054**	**3,270**	**1,392**	**1,878**	**13.4**	**18.8**
Private household	934	156	7	149	0.8	0.9
Protective services	1,907	259	201	58	1.7	1.5
Service, except private hhld. & protective	**12,213**	**2,854**	**1,183**	**1,671**	**10.9**	**16.4**
Food service	5,204	1,643	749	894	4.6	9.4
Health service	1,873	344	50	294	1.7	2.0
Cleaning & building service	2,886	436	298	138	2.6	2.5
Personal service	2,249	431	88	343	2.0	2.5
Precision production, craft, repair	**13,568**	**1,780**	**1,640**	**140**	**12.1**	**10.2**
Mechanics & repairers	4,445	543	528	15	4.0	3.1
Construction trades	5,011	808	792	16	4.5	4.6
Other production, craft, repair	4,112	428	319	109	3.7	2.5
Operators, fabricators, laborers	**17,486**	**3,366**	**2,694**	**672**	**15.6**	**19.3**
Machine operators, assemblers, inspectors	7,994	1,236	794	442	7.1	7.1
Transportation, material moving	4,712	628	585	43	4.2	3.6
Handlers, equip. cleaners, helpers, laborers	4,779	1,503	1,315	188	4.3	8.6
Farming, forestry, fishing	**3,507**	**594**	**526**	**68**	**3.1**	**3.4**
Farm operators & managers	1,317	59	52	7	1.2	0.3
Farm workers & related occupations	2,013	513	455	58	1.8	2.9
Forestry and fishing occupations	177	22	19	3	0.2	0.1

Source: Unpublished annual data for 1987, Bureau of Labor Statistics

Note: Numbers may not add to total due to rounding. Civilian, noninstitutionalized employees only.

Workers in the 1990s

LABOR FORCE
18–24

CONFLICTING RATES

Although there will be fewer of them in 2000 than in 1990, proportionately more 18-to-24-year-olds will be in the labor force by 2000. The women's participation rate will jump from 71 to 75 percent, an increase more dramatic than that expected for the men.

(labor force and labor force participation rates* for persons aged 16 and older and those aged 18 to 24, by sex, race, and ethnicity, in 1990 and 2000, numbers in thousands)

	1990 number	1990 participation rate	2000 number	2000 participation rate	1990-2000 percent change
Both sexes, aged 16 and older	124,457	66.2%	138,775	67.8%	11.5%
White	106,648	66.5	116,701	68.2	9.4
Black	13,788	64.6	16,334	66.0	18.5
Hispanic	9,718	65.9	14,086	67.1	44.9
Asian and other	4,021	64.8	5,740	65.8	42.8
Males, aged 16 and older	67,909	75.8	73,136	74.7	7.7
Males, aged 18 to 24	9,842	81.3	9,635	82.7	-2.1
White	8,334	83.3	7,963	85.2	-4.5
Black	1,203	73.8	1,273	75.1	5.8
Hispanic	1,164	83.1	1,485	84.8	27.6
Asian and other	305	64.9	399	65.0	30.8
Females, aged 16 and older	56,548	57.4	65,639	61.5	16.1
Females, aged 18 to 24	9,116	71.3	9,296	75.4	2.0
White	7,665	73.6	7,630	78.3	-0.5
Black	1,169	61.8	1,270	65.7	8.6
Hispanic	770	57.0	1,033	61.5	34.2
Asian and other	282	58.5	396	61.7	40.4

*Labor force participation rates are the ratio of people in the labor force to the total population of a given sex, age and race or ethnicity.

Source: Unpublished data from the Bureau of Labor Statistics

Note: The labor force here includes civilians who are working or looking for work. Hispanics are of any race.

Household Income

INCOME
18-24

SMALLEST SLICE OF THE PIE

Households headed by under-25-year-olds* are 6 percent of households, but they command only 4 percent of all household income. Despite their relatively small size— 2.32 persons per household—their income per household member is the lowest of any age group.

(household income and income per household member, for all households and for households by age of householder, numbers for 1988 in thousands, income is for 1987)

	households		persons in household			total household income		
	number	percent	number	percent	persons per household	$ billions	percent	per household member
All households	91,066	100.0%	240,722	100.0%	2.64	$2,927.2	100.0%	$12,160
Age of householder								
under 25	5,228	5.7	12,117	5.0	2.32	102.0	3.5	8,415
25 to 34	20,583	22.6	58,724	24.4	2.85	621.6	21.2	10,586
35 to 44	19,323	21.2	64,351	26.7	3.33	763.8	26.1	11,870
45 to 54	13,630	15.0	41,379	17.2	3.04	597.0	20.4	14,426
55 to 64	12,846	14.1	30,151	12.5	2.35	447.3	15.3	14,835
65 and older	19,456	21.4	33,999	14.1	1.75	395.6	13.5	11,635

*The Census Bureau's category of householders under age 25 includes those aged 15 to 24. Householders aged 18 to 24 are 95 percent of the under-25-year-olds.

Source: The 1988 Current Population Survey, Bureau of the Census

Individual Income

UPHILL BATTLE

Considering how many Americans under age 25* hold part-time jobs, it is not surprising that 78 percent of the income-producing women, and 69 percent of the men, make less than $10,000.

(income distribution and median income for males and females aged 15 and older and under age 25, numbers for 1988 in thousands, income is for 1987)

	males aged 15 and older		males under age 25	
	number	percent	number	percent
All males	90,284	–	18,343	–
All males with income	85,623	100.0%	14,874	100.0%
Less than $5,000	13,025	15.2	7,183	48.3
$5,000 to $9,999	12,066	14.1	3,089	20.8
$10,000 to $14,999	11,708	13.7	2,161	14.5
$15,000 to $19,999	9,887	11.5	1,232	8.3
$20,000 to $24,999	8,714	10.2	633	4.3
$25,000 to $29,999	7,266	8.5	303	2.0
$30,000 to $34,999	6,124	7.2	101	0.7
$35,000 to $49,999	9,941	11.6	111	0.7
$50,000 to $74,999	4,669	5.5	53	0.4
$75,000 and over	2,225	2.6	7	–
Median income, all with income		$17,752		$5,316

	females aged 15 and older		females under age 25	
	number	percent	number	percent
All females	98,168	–	18,493	–
All females, with income	89,279	100.0%	14,676	100.0%
Less than $5,000	30,715	34.4	8,146	55.5
$5,000 to $9,999	19,782	22.2	3,231	22.0
$10,000 to $14,999	13,313	14.9	1,785	12.2
$15,000 to $19,999	9,470	10.6	887	6.0
$20,000 to $24,999	6,321	7.1	390	2.7
$25,000 to $29,999	3,768	4.2	136	0.9
$30,000 to $34,999	2,331	2.6	46	0.3
$35,000 to $49,999	2,602	2.9	42	0.3
$50,000 to $74,999	708	0.8	7	–
$75,000 and over	268	0.3	7	–
Median income, all with income		$8,101		$4,200

*Men and women under age 25 are aged 15 to 24.
Source: Money Income and Poverty Status in the United States: 1987, Bureau of the Census, Current Population Reports, Series P-20, No. 161
Note: Numbers may not add to total due to rounding.

Income and Age

INCOME
18–24

LOW END OF THE SCALE

Sixty percent of households headed by someone under age 25* bring in less than $20,000, a percentage topped only by people aged 75 and older. On the brighter side, 27 percent of these young households have household incomes between $20,000 and $35,000 and 13 percent have more than $35,000.

(household income by age of householder, numbers for 1988 in thousands, income is for 1987)

				age of householder					
	total	under 25	25 to 34	35 to 44	45 to 54	55 to 64	65 to 74	75+
All households	91,066	5,228	20,583	19,323	13,630	12,846	11,410	8,045
All households	100.0%	100.0%	100.0%	100.0%	100.0%	100.0%	100.0%	100.0%
Less than $10,000	18.4	30.3	13.6	10.3	10.4	17.4	27.1	44.6
$10,000 to $14,999	10.6	15.8	9.6	6.6	6.6	9.5	17.3	18.5
$15,000 to $19,999	10.0	14.1	11.1	7.4	6.8	9.7	13.8	11.8
$20,000 to $24,999	9.2	11.5	11.1	8.3	7.2	9.1	10.1	7.5
$25,000 to $29,999	8.4	9.0	10.6	8.5	7.6	8.0	8.3	4.3
$30,000 to $34,999	7.7	6.8	9.7	9.0	7.8	7.2	6.0	3.2
$35,000 to $39,999	6.8	4.5	8.6	9.0	7.2	6.3	4.2	2.4
$40,000 to $44,999	5.8	2.3	6.7	7.9	7.4	6.0	3.0	1.7
$45,000 to $49,999	4.6	1.3	5.1	6.6	5.9	4.7	2.4	1.5
$50,000 to $59,999	6.7	2.1	6.7	9.6	10.1	7.5	2.7	1.9
$60,000 to $74,999	5.5	1.5	4.2	7.9	9.9	6.3	2.1	1.2
$75,000 and over	6.3	0.9	3.0	8.9	13.1	8.3	3.0	1.4
Median household income	$25,986	$16,204	$26,923	$34,926	$37,250	$27,538	$16,906	$11,261

*The Census Bureau's category of householders under age 25 includes householders aged 15 to 24. Householders aged 18 to 24 are 95 percent of the under-25-year-olds.

Source: The 1988 Current Population Survey, Bureau of the Census

Note: Numbers may not add to total due to rounding.

Income of Married Couples

MARRIAGE AND MONEY

Among families headed by someone under age 25*, those with a married couple at the helm have the highest median household income—$21,000. Thirty-nine percent of these young married couples bring in between $20,000 and $35,000, and 15 percent have incomes over $35,000. Families without children at home have consistently higher incomes than those with children.

(household income of married-couple householder families with and without children under 18 at home, householders under age 25, numbers for 1988 in thousands, income is for 1987)

	\multicolumn{3}{c}{married-couple householder under age 25}
	total	with children under 18 at home	without children under 18 at home
All households	1,807	931	876
All households	100.0%	100.0%	100.0%
Less than $10,000	14.2	17.0	11.1
$10,000 to $14,999	15.2	18.5	11.6
$15,000 to $19,999	16.6	17.3	15.9
$20,000 to $24,999	14.6	17.1	12.0
$25,000 to $29,999	13.4	12.2	14.6
$30,000 to $34,999	10.9	7.8	14.2
$35,000 to $39,999	5.6	3.5	7.8
$40,000 to $44,999	3.5	1.7	5.4
$45,000 to $49,999	1.4	1.5	1.4
$50,000 to $59,999	2.4	1.4	3.4
$60,000 to $74,999	1.6	1.4	1.8
$75,000 and over	0.7	0.5	0.8
Median household income	$21,070	$19,005	$24,546

*The Census Bureau's category of householders under age 25 includes those aged 15 to 24. Householders aged 18 to 24 are 95 percent of the under-25-year-olds.

Source: The 1988 Current Population Survey, Bureau of the Census

Note: Numbers may not add to total due to rounding.

Income of Other Family Households

INCOME
18–24

THE CHILD FACTOR

Children have a negative effect on the incomes of young women* who head family households—those without children in their homes can claim a median income that is $16,000 more than the median for those with children. Whether they have children or not, 87 percent of these female-headed families have incomes below $20,000, while a full 68 percent do not even bring in $10,000.

(household income of unmarried female- and male-householder families with and without children under 18 at home, householders under age 25, numbers for 1988, in thousands, income is for 1987)

	female householder under age 25			male householder under age 25		
	total	with children under 18 at home	without children under 18 at home	total	with children under 18 at home	without children under 18 at home
All households	843	730	114	275	78	197
All households	100.0%	100.0%	100.0%	100.0%	100.0%	100.0%
Less than $10,000	66.7	73.8	20.2	19.6	26.9	16.2
$10,000 to $14,999	12.7	13.0	9.6	17.8	25.6	14.7
$15,000 to $19,999	7.1	6.0	14.0	12.0	7.7	13.7
$20,000 to $24,999	5.0	3.3	15.8	16.0	24.4	12.7
$25,000 to $29,999	3.8	1.9	15.8	12.4	6.4	14.7
$30,000 to $34,999	0.9	0.4	4.4	7.3	2.6	9.1
$35,000 to $39,999	0.9	0.8	1.8	5.1	1.3	6.6
$40,000 to $44,999	0.4	0.0	2.6	2.9	2.6	3.0
$45,000 to $49,999	0.2	0.1	0.9	1.5	2.6	1.0
$50,000 to $59,999	1.1	0.0	7.9	2.5	–	3.6
$60,000 to $74,999	0.7	0.0	5.3	2.2	–	3.0
$75,000 and over	0.4	0.1	1.8	0.7	–	1.0
Median household income	$6,167	$5,553	$21,481	$20,027	$13,161	$21,514

*The Census Bureau's category of householders under age 25 includes those aged 15 to 24. Householders aged 18 to 24 are 95 percent of the under-25-year-olds.

Source: The 1988 Current Population Survey, Bureau of the Census

Note: Numbers may not add to total due to rounding.

Income of Nonfamily Households

INCOME
18–24

POWER IN NUMBERS

More than half of the 2.3 million nonfamily householders under age 25* live alone and have a median income that is less than half that of their counterparts who live with unrelated others. At $24,300, male householders who live with others have the highest median income in this category.

(household income of nonfamily households by household type, householders under age 25, numbers for 1988 in thousands, income is for 1987)

	total number	living alone — total	living alone — male householder	living alone — female householder	living with others — total	living with others — male householder	living with others — female householder
All nonfamily households	2,302	1,245	654	592	1,057	611	445
All nonfamily households	100.0%	100.0%	100.0%	100.0%	100.0%	100.0%	100.0%
Less than $10,000	31.0	46.8	44.6	49.2	12.4	12.3	12.6
$10,000 to $14,999	17.3	19.5	19.9	19.1	14.7	11.8	18.7
$15,000 to $19,999	14.8	15.2	14.2	16.0	14.4	13.1	16.2
$20,000 to $24,999	10.9	10.1	11.8	8.3	11.7	13.9	8.8
$25,000 to $29,999	7.0	4.0	4.4	3.5	10.4	8.8	12.4
$30,000 to $34,999	5.7	1.8	1.7	2.0	10.2	9.8	10.8
$35,000 to $39,999	4.8	1.4	1.8	0.8	8.8	9.3	8.1
$40,000 to $44,999	2.1	0.4	0.3	0.7	4.2	4.4	3.6
$45,000 to $49,999	1.5	0.2	0.3	0.0	3.0	3.6	2.2
$50,000 to $59,999	2.1	0.2	0.3	0.2	4.4	5.4	2.9
$60,000 to $74,999	1.7	0.4	0.8	0.0	3.3	3.8	2.7
$75,000 and over	1.3	0.0	0.0	0.0	2.7	3.8	1.3
Median household income	$15,196	$10,727	$10,973	$10,017	$23,158	$24,276	$21,309

*The Census Bureau's category of householders under age 25 includes those aged 15 to 24. Householders aged 18 to 24 are 95 percent of the under-25-year-olds.

Source: The 1988 Current Population Survey, Bureau of the Census

Note: Nonfamilies are either people living alone or living with an individual (or individuals) unrelated to the householder. Numbers may not add to total due to rounding.

Income and Race, Families

INCOME
18–24

KEEPING IT TOGETHER

Young married couples of both races are better off than are other types of families with a householder under age 25*. Twenty-five percent of the white couples and 21 percent of the black couples have incomes of $30,000 or more.

(household income of family households by race and household type for householders under age 25, numbers for 1988 in thousands, income is for 1987)

	\multicolumn{4}{c}{**white family households**}
	total	married couple	male householder	female householder
All households	2,348	1,613	209	526
Total	100.0%	100.0%	100.0%	100.0%
Less than $10,000	26.5	14.3	21.1	66.2
$10,000 to $19,999	30.5	32.8	35.4	21.1
$20,000 to $29,999	22.8	27.8	22.5	7.8
$30,000 to $39,999	12.2	15.8	11.0	1.3
$40,000 to $49,999	3.9	4.6	3.8	1.7
$50,000 to $59,999	2.0	2.2	2.4	1.1
$60,000 to $74,999	1.6	1.8	2.9	0.4
$75,000 and over	0.6	0.5	1.0	0.6
Median household income	$17,574	$20,813	$18,231	$6,724

	\multicolumn{4}{c}{**black family households**}
	total	married couple	male householder	female householder
All households	502	154	54	294
Total	100.0%	100.0%	100.0%	100.0%
Less than $10,000	58.2	15.6	48.1	82.0
$10,000 to $19,999	21.7	33.1	22.2	15.3
$20,000 to $29,999	12.9	29.9	20.4	2.4
$30,000 to $39,999	5.4	14.3	9.3	–
$40,000 to $49,999	0.8	2.6	–	–
$50,000 to $59,999	0.6	1.9	–	–
$60,000 to $74,999	–	–	–	–
$75,000 and over	0.6	1.9	–	–
Median household income	$7,747	$20,364	–	$4,416

*The Census Bureau's category of householders under age 25 includes those aged 15 to 24. Householders aged 18 to 24 are 95 percent of the under-25-year-olds.

Source: Money Income of Households, Families, and Persons in the United States: 1987, Bureau of the Census, Current Population Reports, Series P-60, No. 162
Note: Numbers may not add to total due to rounding. Median income is unreliable and is therefore not given when the category contains fewer than 75,000 households.

Almanac of Consumer Markets

Income and Race, Nonfamilies

RACIAL DIFFERENCES

At $13,900, the median income for all white nonfamily householders is $5,700 higher than that of all black nonfamily householders. Among the youngest householders* that difference is less than $4,000.

(householder income of nonfamily householders by race and household type for householders under age 25, numbers for 1988 in thousands, income is for 1987)

	white householder			black householder		
	total	male householder	female householder	total	male householder	female householder
All households	2,049	1,120	929	171	98	72
Total	100.0%	100.0%	100.0%	100.0%	100.0%	100.0%
Less than $10,000	43.5	39.7	48.0	61.4	62.2	62.5
$10,000 to $19,999	37.4	37.3	37.5	29.8	31.6	27.8
$20,000 to $24,999	10.2	11.5	8.6	2.3	2.0	2.8
$25,000 to $29,999	4.1	5.2	2.7	5.8	4.1	6.9
$30,000 to $34,999	2.0	2.2	1.8	–	–	–
$35,000 to $49,999	2.2	3.1	1.2	–	–	–
$50,000 and over	0.6	0.9	0.3	–	–	–
Median householder income	$11,250	$11,753	$10,457	$7,422	$6,892	–

*The Census Bureau's category of householders under age 25 includes those aged 15 to 24. Householders aged 18 to 24 are 95 percent of the under-25-year-olds.

Source: Money Income of Households, Families, and Persons in the United States: 1987, Bureau of the Census, Current Population Reports, Series P-60, No. 162

Note: Numbers may not add to total due to rounding. Householder income is the total money income of the householder only. Median income is unreliable and is therefore not given when the category contains fewer than 75,000 households.

Income of Hispanic Households

INCOME 18–24

INDEPENDENT INCOMES

Fewer nonfamily than family households headed by Hispanics under age 25* are in the lowest income category. Fifty-four percent of these families and 42 percent of the nonfamilies have incomes of $15,000 or less.

(household income of Hispanic households, by household type, for householders under age 25, numbers for 1988 in thousands, income is for 1987)

family households

	total	married couple	male householder	female householder
All households	416	216	63	137
Total	100.0%	100.0%	100.0%	100.0%
Less than $15,000	54.0	40.6	41.5	81.1
$15,000 to $24,999	21.6	24.9	27.6	13.7
$25,000 and over	24.4	34.6	30.9	5.2
Median household income	$13,747	$18,879	–	$6,986

nonfamily households

	total	male householder living alone	male householder living with others	female householder living alone	female householder living with others
All households	144	45	55	21	22
Total	100.0%	100.0%	100.0%	100.0%	100.0%
Less than $15,000	41.8	74.8	18.0	56.4	20.3
$15,000 to $24,999	29.9	22.2	21.1	43.6	54.7
$25,000 and over	28.3	3.0	60.9	–	25.1
Median household income	–	–	–	–	–

*The Census Bureau's category of householders under age 25 includes those aged 15 to 24. Householders aged 18 to 24 are 95 percent of the under-25-year-olds.

Source: The 1988 Current Population Survey, Bureau of the Census

Note: Numbers may not add to total due to rounding. Hispanics are of any race. Median income is unreliable and is therefore not given when the category contains fewer than 75,000 households.

Income of Dual-Earner Couples

INCOME 18–24

TWO-INCOME NORM

Sixty-two percent of married couples under age 25* are dual earners with a median household income of $25,200—$4,100 higher than the median income for all married couples in this age group.

(household income for all dual-earner married couples and for those with married-couple householders under age 25, numbers for 1988 in thousands, income is for 1987)

	householder all ages			householder under age 25		
	total	with children under 18 at home	without children under 18 at home	total	with children under 18 at home	without children under 18 at home
All households	26,227	14,989	11,238	1,112	453	659
All households	100.0%	100.0%	100.0%	100.3%	100.2%	100.2%
Less than $15,000	5.7	6.0	5.4	17.1	18.8	15.9
$15,000 to $19,999	5.1	5.4	4.7	16.6	18.5	15.2
$20,000 to $24,999	7.3	7.8	6.6	15.5	20.8	11.8
$25,000 to $29,999	8.3	9.0	7.5	17.4	19.9	15.6
$30,000 to $34,999	9.4	10.2	8.3	13.8	10.2	16.2
$35,000 to $39,999	10.3	11.2	9.0	8.0	5.3	9.9
$40,000 to $44,999	9.6	9.8	9.3	4.5	1.3	6.7
$45,000 to $49,999	8.1	8.2	7.9	1.3	1.5	1.2
$50,000 to $59,999	13.0	12.5	13.6	3.1	1.1	4.4
$60,000 to $74,999	11.2	10.2	12.5	2.0	1.8	2.1
$75,000 and over	12.1	9.6	15.3	1.1	1.1	1.1
Median household income	$41,904	$40,044	$44,508	$25,153	$22,940	$27,788

*The Census Bureau's category of householders under age 25 includes those aged 15 to 24. Householders aged 18 to 24 are 95 percent of the under-25-year-olds.

Source: The 1988 Current Population Survey, Bureau of the Census

Note: Numbers may not add to total due to rounding.

Income and Education

INCOME
18–24

STILL IN PROGRESS

Sixty percent of young householders* with one to three years of college and 58 percent of those who are high school graduates have household incomes under $20,000. Additional college improves the economic picture of householders under age 25. Among those who completed four or more years of college, 33 percent bring in $30,000 or more.

(household income of householders under age 25, by years of school completed by householder, numbers for 1988 in thousands, income is for 1987)

	total	not high school graduate	high school graduate	1 to 3 years of college	4 or more years of college
All households	5,228	1,016	2,219	1,297	696
All households	100.0%	100.0%	100.0%	100.0%	100.0%
Less than $10,000	30.3	51.6	26.9	26.6	17.0
$10,000 to $19,999	29.9	23.3	31.2	33.4	28.9
$20,000 to $29,999	20.4	15.1	22.6	20.1	22.0
$30,000 to $39,999	11.3	6.0	12.0	12.3	14.8
$40,000 to $49,999	3.6	2.4	3.2	4.0	6.2
$50,000 to $59,999	2.1	0.5	1.5	2.1	5.9
$60,000 to $74,999	1.5	0.8	1.8	0.5	4.0
$75,000 and over	0.9	0.4	0.8	0.8	1.9

*The Census Bureau's category of householders under age 25 includes those aged 15 to 24. Householders aged 18 to 24 are 95 percent of the under-25-year-olds.

Source: The 1988 Current Population Survey, Bureau of the Census.

Note: Numbers may not add to total due to rounding.

Future Income

INCOME
18–24

MORE HIGH INCOMES

As the number of householders under age 25* declines over the next five years, so will the number of low-income households among them. The biggest change forecasted for this age category is that more households will have incomes between $60,000 and $75,000.

(projections of the number of households with householders under age 25, by household income, 1990 and 1995, numbers in thousands, income is in 1985 dollars)

	1990 number	1990 percent	1995 number	1995 percent	percent change 1990-1995
All households	4,663	100.0%	4,316	100.0%	-7.4%
Less than $10,000	1,315	28.2	1,165	27.0	-11.4
$10,000 to $19,999	1,501	32.2	1,349	31.2	-10.1
$20,000 to $29,999	1,046	22.4	972	22.5	-7.1
$30,000 to $39,999	486	10.4	498	11.5	2.5
$40,000 to $49,999	174	3.7	185	4.3	6.3
$50,000 to $59,999	72	1.5	73	1.7	1.4
$60,000 to $74,999	43	0.9	49	1.1	14.0
$75,000 and over	25	0.5	26	0.6	4.0
Median household income	$16,770		$17,367		

*The Census Bureau's category of householders under age 25 includes those aged 15 to 24. Householders aged 18 to 24 are 95 percent of the under-25-year-olds.

Source: American Demographics, *May to August, 1986*, based on the national econometric model of Wharton Economic Forecasting Association and on household projections from the Bureau of the Census

Note: Numbers may not add to total due to rounding.

Annual Expenditures

EXPENDITURES
18–24

SUPPORTING YOUNG LIFESTYLES

These young households devote more of their spending dollar to food away from home, alcoholic beverages, shelter (especially rent), apparel, and transportation than the average household. Their share of expenditures going to education and to televisions, radios, and sound equipment is also above average.

(average annual expenditure and percent distribution of expenditures for all households and for householders under age 25, number of households in thousands)

	all households		householder under age 25	
	average annual expenditure	percent of all expenditures	average annual expenditure	percent of all expenditures
Number of households	93,741		8,840	
Total expenditure	$22,710	100.0%	$13,763	100.0%
Food	3,363	14.8	2,026	14.7
Food at home	2,313	10.2	1,262	9.2
Food away from home	1,049	4.6	763	5.5
Alcoholic beverages	273	1.2	335	2.4
Housing	6,888	30.3	4,122	29.9
Shelter	3,986	17.6	2,654	19.3
Owned dwellings	2,305	10.1	393	2.9
Mortgage interest and charges	1,428	6.3	271	2.0
Property taxes	417	1.8	35	0.3
Maintenance, repairs, insurance, and other expenses	460	2.0	87	0.6
Rented dwellings	1,269	5.6	2,047	14.9
Other lodging	412	1.8	213	1.5
Fuels, utilities, and public services	1,646	7.2	795	5.8
Natural gas	248	1.1	82	0.6
Electricity	674	3.0	303	2.2
Fuel oil and other fuels	107	0.5	28	0.2
Telephone	471	2.1	342	2.5
Water and other public services	145	0.6	40	0.3
Household operations	353	1.6	148	1.1
Domestic services	288	1.3	121	0.9
Other household expenses	65	0.3	27	0.2
Household furnishings, equipment	903	4.0	524	3.8
Household textiles	83	0.4	36	0.3
Furniture	303	1.3	196	1.4
Floor coverings	51	0.2	14	0.1
Major appliances	155	0.7	100	0.7

(continued next page)

Annual Expenditures

EXPENDITURES 18–24

(continued from previous page)

(average annual expenditure and percent distribution of expenditures for all households and for householders under age 25, number of households in thousands)

	all households		householder under age 25	
	average annual expenditure	percent of all expenditures	average annual expenditure	percent of all expenditures
Small appliances, miscellaneous housewares	55	0.2	40	0.3
Miscellaneous household equipment	256	1.1	138	1.0
Apparel	**1,149**	**5.1**	**871**	**6.3**
Men and boys	283	1.2	206	1.5
Men, 16 and over	228	1.0	193	1.4
Boys, 2 to 15	55	0.2	13	0.1
Women and girls	462	2.0	299	2.2
Women, 16 and over	396	1.7	286	2.1
Girls, 2 to 15	66	0.3	14	0.1
Children under 2	45	0.2	61	0.4
Footwear	123	0.5	84	0.6
Other apparel products and services	237	1.0	220	1.6
Transportation	**4,815**	**21.2**	**3,335**	**24.2**
Cars and trucks, new (net outlay)	1,414	6.2	740	5.4
Cars and trucks, used (net outlay)	897	3.9	864	6.3
Other vehicles	29	0.1	72	0.5
Vehicle finance charges	270	1.2	172	1.2
Gasoline and motor oil	916	4.0	655	4.8
Maintenance and repairs	458	2.0	319	2.3
Vehicle insurance	420	1.8	262	1.9
Public transportation	248	1.1	155	1.1
Vehicle rental, licenses, other charges	163	0.7	97	0.7
Health care	**1,062**	**4.7**	**336**	**2.4**
Health insurance	371	1.6	108	0.8
Medical services	502	2.2	174	1.3
Medicines and medical supplies	189	0.8	54	0.4
Entertainment	**1,087**	**4.8**	**672**	**4.9**
Fees and admissions	308	1.4	207	1.5
Television, radios, sound equipment	373	1.6	273	2.0
Other equipment and services	406	1.8	192	1.4
Personal care	207	0.9	122	0.9
Reading	140	0.6	67	0.5
Education	298	1.3	582	4.2
Tobacco and smoking supplies	230	1.0	174	1.3
Miscellaneous	323	1.4	137	1.0
Contributions and support payments	746	3.3	143	1.0
Personal insurance and pensions	**2,129**	**9.4**	**840**	**6.1**
Life insurance and other personal insurance	293	1.3	63	0.5
Retirement, pensions, Social Security	1,836	8.1	777	5.6

Source: The 1986 Consumer Expenditure Survey, Bureau of Labor Statistics

Expenditures by Income

EXPENDITURES
18–24

CHANGING SHARES

With the exception of education, expenditures for all categories increase with household income in this age group. The share of each spending dollar going to different categories also changes as income increases. Food, for example, takes 18 percent of each dollar among households bringing in under $10,000, but 12 percent of the budgets of households with $40,000 or more. On the other hand, those high-income households allocate 29 percent of their spending dollar to transportation while their low-income counterparts devote 20 percent to this item.

(annual average expenditure of households with householders under age 25, by household income, number of households in thousands)

	all households	under $10,000	$10-14,999	$15-19,999	$20-29,999	$30-39,999	$40,000+
Number of households	7,688	4,109	1,198	829	991	336	226
Total expenditure	$13,736	$8,356	$14,507	$17,847	$21,552	$29,279	$33,948
Food	2,012	1,468	2,063	2,548	2,836	3,359	3,907
Food at home	1,237	895	1,258	1,547	1,814	2,066	2,329
Food away from home	774	572	805	1,001	1,021	1,294	1,578
Alcoholic beverages	314	266	327	344	381	408	551
Housing	3,919	2,296	4,003	5,682	6,224	8,101	9,882
Shelter	2,507	1,475	2,547	3,695	3,888	5,166	6,503
Owned dwellings	404	67	140	482	910	2,230	2,691
Rented dwellings	1,908	1,190	2,256	3,111	2,858	2,705	3,138
Other lodging	196	218	150	102	120	231	673
Fuels, utilities, public services	769	493	857	1,044	1,211	1,353	1,448
Household operations	133	55	134	239	246	272	425
Household furnishings, equipment	511	274	466	705	879	1,310	1,507
Apparel and services	848	631	795	1,017	1,208	1,615	1,696
Transportation	3,495	1,691	4,052	4,340	6,137	9,176	9,788
Vehicles	1,835	794	2,264	2,020	3,396	5,342	5,448
Gasoline and motor oil	685	419	775	936	1,057	1,314	1,508
Other vehicle expenses	832	371	870	1,245	1,438	2,286	2,547
Public transportation	145	108	143	139	246	234	285
Health care	383	243	397	511	609	901	554
Entertainment	684	466	637	799	1,066	1,199	2,026
Personal care	117	87	114	133	163	221	266

(continued next page)

Expenditures by Income

(continued from previous page)

(annual average expenditure of households with householders under age 25, by household income, number of households in thousands)

	all households	under $10,000	$10-14,999	$15-19,999	$20-29,999	$30-39,999	$40,000+
Reading	68	47	64	80	98	172	134
Education	556	728	506	361	249	206	335
Tobacco and smoking supplies	161	120	198	221	211	147	272
Miscellaneous	163	49	186	368	256	548	395
Cash contributions	137	39	241	160	266	353	388
Personal insurance and pensions	879	225	924	1,285	1,850	2,872	3,754
Life and other insurance	64	17	80	98	135	235	136
Retirement, pensions, Social Security	815	207	844	1,186	1,715	2,638	3,618

Source: *The 1986 Consumer Expenditure Survey, Bureau of Labor Statistics*

Note: All households include complete income reporters only. Total expenditure exceeds total income in some income categories due to a number of factors including the underreporting of income, borrowing, and the use of savings.

Weekly Shopping

EXPENDITURES
18–24

SPENDING MORE ON ALCOHOLIC BEVERAGES

Households headed by an under-25-year-old spend 10 percent more each week on alcoholic beverages than the average household. On all other frequently purchased items, however, they tend to spend less. These young households spend at least 60 percent less than the average household on fresh fruits, fats and oils, and pet food.

(average weekly expenditure for all households and for householders under age 25)

	all households	index all households	householders under age 25	index householders under age 25
Food, total	$59.60	100	$36.46	61
Food at home, total	37.73	100	19.18	51
Cereals and cereal products	1.78	100	1.02	57
Bakery products	3.51	100	1.69	48
Beef	3.63	100	1.72	47
Pork	2.23	100	0.95	43
Other meats	1.52	100	0.77	51
Poultry	1.64	100	0.71	43
Fish and seafood	1.22	100	0.51	42
Eggs	0.57	100	0.28	49
Fresh milk and cream	2.35	100	1.56	66
Other dairy products	2.47	100	1.16	47
Fresh fruits	1.96	100	0.70	36
Fresh vegetables	1.77	100	0.75	42
Processed fruits	1.38	100	0.65	47
Processed vegetables	1.03	100	0.52	50
Sugar and other sweets	1.42	100	0.72	51
Fats and oils	0.99	100	0.39	39
Miscellaneous foods	4.53	100	2.84	63
Nonalcoholic beverages	3.71	100	2.26	61
Food away from home	21.87	100	17.28	79
Nonfood items				
Alcoholic beverages	4.84	100	5.31	110
Tobacco products and smoking supplies	3.60	100	2.49	69
Pet food	1.09	100	0.39	36
Personal care products and services	5.01	100	2.65	53
Non-prescription drugs and supplies	2.31	100	1.13	49
Housekeeping supplies	6.07	100	2.82	46

Source: The 1986 Consumer Expenditure Survey, Bureau of Labor Statistics

Note: An index of 100 represents the average. An index of 132 means that the average weekly expenditure of the subgroup is 32 percent above the average for all households. An index of 68 indicates spending that is 32 percent below average. Numbers may not add to total due to rounding.

Future Expenditures

EXPENDITURES
18–24

DROPPING BY $3 BILLION

In 2000 these young households will be spending an estimated three billion dollars less than in 1990. This drop in spending is due to the declining number of households headed by under-25-year-olds during the decade.

(projected aggregate expenditures in 1990 and 2000 for all households and for households by age of householder, in billions of dollars)

	all households	under 25	25-34	35-44	45-54	55-64	65-74	75+
Number of households (in thousands)	94,227	4,663	21,183	21,245	14,429	12,311	11,672	8,724
Total expenditures (in billions of dollars)	$2,203.1	$64.2	$476.6	$628.6	$441.2	$292.8	$197.2	$102.5
Food	330.8	9.4	70.3	93.7	64.1	43.9	32.3	17.2
Food at home	225.1	5.9	44.8	64.9	41.8	30.9	23.0	13.7
Food away from home	101.5	3.6	21.2	28.8	22.2	13.0	9.3	3.5
Alcoholic beverages	25.4	1.6	7.5	6.4	4.7	3.0	1.8	0.6
Housing	667.6	19.2	158.3	193.5	121.9	80.8	58.3	35.6
Shelter	385.6	12.4	97.2	115.7	71.7	42.4	28.8	17.5
Owned dwellings	229.7	1.8	50.3	75.8	46.9	28.2	17.9	8.7
Rented dwellings	115.2	9.5	41.6	27.6	13.1	8.4	7.2	7.6
Other lodging	40.8	1.0	5.2	12.2	11.6	5.8	3.7	1.2
Fuels, utilities, and public services	160.0	3.7	32.0	41.2	29.6	23.2	18.6	11.8
Household operations	34.2	0.7	9.6	10.2	3.8	3.7	2.9	3.3
Household furnishings, equipment	87.8	2.4	19.5	26.5	16.8	11.6	8.0	3.0
Apparel and services	111.0	4.1	24.6	33.7	22.8	13.8	8.3	3.6
Transportation	464.9	15.6	107.0	130.7	98.7	61.1	37.7	14.2
Health care	103.7	1.6	14.5	21.4	16.9	16.0	17.9	15.4
Entertainment	106.0	3.1	23.3	35.2	20.6	13.0	8.0	2.6
Personal care	20.1	0.6	3.7	5.2	3.8	3.1	2.3	1.3
Reading	13.6	0.3	2.6	3.8	2.6	1.9	1.6	0.8
Education	27.6	2.7	3.9	8.3	8.8	2.9	0.8	0.1
Tobacco and smoking supplies	22.0	0.8	4.9	5.8	4.5	3.3	2.0	0.7
Miscellaneous	31.5	0.6	6.5	8.1	5.9	4.5	3.6	2.3
Contributions and support payments	74.2	0.7	7.3	17.7	17.4	12.9	12.5	5.7
Personal insurance and pensions	208.9	3.9	46.4	65.2	48.5	32.6	10.0	2.3

(continued next page)

Future Expenditures

EXPENDITURES
18–24

(continued from previous page)

(projected aggregate expenditures in 2000 for all households and for households by age of householder, in billions of dollars)

	\multicolumn{8}{c}{*2000 aggregate annual expenditures in billions*}
	all households	under 25	25-34	35-44	45-54	55-64	65-74	75+
Number of households (in thousands)	105,933	4,442	18,004	25,339	21,603	13,903	11,516	11,126
Total expenditures (in billions of dollars)	$2,532.4	$61.1	$405.1	$749.7	$660.6	$330.6	$194.6	$130.7
Food	379.7	9.0	59.7	111.7	95.9	49.5	31.9	22.0
Food at home	258.9	5.6	38.1	77.4	62.6	34.9	22.7	17.5
Food away from home	117.2	3.4	18.0	34.3	33.2	14.7	9.1	4.5
Alcoholic beverages	28.3	1.5	6.4	7.6	7.0	3.4	1.7	0.7
Housing	760.3	18.3	134.5	230.8	182.5	91.3	57.5	45.3
Shelter	438.2	11.8	82.6	137.9	107.3	47.9	28.4	22.3
Owned dwellings	265.8	1.7	42.8	90.4	70.3	31.9	17.6	11.1
Rented dwellings	123.4	9.1	35.4	32.9	19.7	9.5	7.2	9.7
Other lodging	49.1	0.9	4.4	14.6	17.4	6.5	3.7	1.5
Fuels, utilities, and public services	183.6	3.5	27.2	49.1	44.3	26.2	18.3	15.0
Household operations	38.0	0.7	8.2	12.2	5.7	4.1	2.9	4.2
Household furnishings, equipment	100.5	2.3	16.6	31.6	25.2	13.1	7.9	3.8
Apparel and services	127.6	3.9	20.9	40.2	34.2	15.6	8.2	4.6
Transportation	533.7	14.8	90.9	155.9	147.7	69.0	37.2	18.1
Health care	120.0	1.5	12.4	25.5	25.3	18.1	17.7	19.6
Entertainment	121.7	3.0	19.8	42.0	30.9	14.7	7.9	3.3
Personal care	23.1	0.5	3.2	6.2	5.7	3.5	2.3	1.7
Reading	15.7	0.3	2.2	4.5	3.9	2.2	1.6	1.0
Education	33.2	2.6	3.3	10.0	13.1	3.3	0.8	0.2
Tobacco and smoking supplies	25.2	0.8	4.2	6.9	6.8	3.7	2.0	0.9
Miscellaneous	36.2	0.6	5.5	9.7	8.9	5.0	3.5	2.9
Contributions and support payments	88.2	0.6	6.2	21.1	26.0	14.5	12.3	7.3
Personal insurance and pensions	243.2	3.7	39.4	77.7	72.7	36.8	9.9	2.9

Source: *The 1986 Consumer Expenditure Survey, Bureau of Labor Statistics* and Projections of the Number of Households and Families:1986 to 2000, *Bureau of the Census, Series P-25, No. 986*

Note: Aggregate expenditures are the sum of the total expenditures of all households in the nation or of all households in an age group. Projections are based on the average annual expenditures in 1986 and have not been adjusted for inflation. Projections show how total annual expenditures would change as the number of households in the age group changes during the 1990s. All other factors such as price and expenditure pattern are held constant and are not accounted for in these projections.

Owners and Renters

WEALTH
18–24

PASSING THROUGH

Only 15 percent of these young householders live in their own home. The largest proportion (59 percent) of homeowners under age 25* are married couples and another 19 percent are men who live alone or with unrelated others. As in all the age groups, whites are more likely to be homeowners than are blacks or Hispanics.

(owner- and renter-occupied households by race of householder and household type, for householders under age 25, numbers in thousands, ownership status as of March 1988)

	total	white	black	Hispanic origin
All households	5,228	4,398	673	560
Owner households	809	737	52	57
Family households				
Married-couple	476	447	22	27
Male householder	48	40	8	7
Female householder	68	53	15	4
Nonfamily households				
Male householder	150	137	5	16
Female householder	65	60	2	3
Renter households	4,419	3661	622	504
Family households				
Married-couple	1,331	1,166	132	189
Male householder	226	170	47	56
Female householder	775	473	280	133
Nonfamily households				
Male householder	1,114	983	93	84
Female householder	971	869	70	40

*The Census Bureau's category of householders under age 25 includes those aged 15 to 24. Householders aged 18 to 24 are 95 percent of the under-25-year-olds.

Source: Household and Family Characteristics: March 1988, Bureau of the Census, Current Population Reports, Series P-20, No. 424

Note: Hispanics are of any race. Numbers may not add to total due to rounding.

Health Status

HEALTH
18–24

SO FAR, SO GOOD

Seventy-seven percent of men and 72 percent of women aged 18 to 24 rate their health as excellent or very good. The proportion of 18-to-24-year-olds with excellent or very good health is considerably higher in households with a household income of $35,000 or more than in lower-income households.

(self-assessed health status of persons aged 18 to 24, by sex, race and household income, number of persons in thousands)

	all persons	all health statuses	excellent	very good	good	fair	poor
Both sexes, all races	26,721	100.0%	44.6%	30.1%	21.5%	3.2%	0.5%
Male	13,020	100.0	49.1	28.1	19.8	2.5	0.5
Female	13,701	100.0	40.4	32.0	23.2	3.8	0.6
White	22,077	100.0	46.3	30.9	19.5	2.7	0.5
Black	3,673	100.0	35.6	25.3	32.4	6.2	0.6
Asian and other	971	100.0	40.4	30.5	26.7	2.0	0.4
Household income							
Less than $10,000	5,870	100.0%	37.6%	32.2%	25.3%	3.9%	0.9%
$10,000 to $19,999	5,232	100.0	39.4	30.4	25.2	4.6	0.5
$20,000 to $34,999	6,169	100.0	48.3	29.7	19.3	2.5	0.2
$35,000 and over	5,948	100.0	55.4	27.5	15.3	1.2	0.6

Source: The 1986 National Health Interview Survey, National Center for Health Statistics

Note: All persons includes those of unknown health status, all health statuses includes only those with known health status. Household income includes only those persons with known household income. Numbers may not add to total due to rounding.

Height

STANDING TALL

Men and women are at their peak height when they are aged 18 to 24; then they begin to shrink. The average man aged 18 to 24 is nearly 5'10" tall and the average woman in this age group stands 5'4" tall.

(cumulative percentage of height of males and females aged 18 to 24 and their average height, by race)

height, males	cumulative percentage	height, females	cumulative percentage
Less than 60 inches	0.2%	Less than 55 inches	0.1%
Less than 61 inches	0.2	Less than 56 inches	0.1
Less than 62 inches	0.3	Less than 57 inches	0.4
Less than 63 inches	0.6	Less than 58 inches	0.9
Less than 64 inches	2.4	Less than 59 inches	2.2
Less than 65 inches	3.8	Less than 60 inches	4.2
Less than 66 inches	8.2	Less than 61 inches	9.1
Less than 67 inches	16.2	Less than 62 inches	17.8
Less than 68 inches	26.7	Less than 63 inches	29.1
Less than 69 inches	38.9	Less than 64 inches	41.8
Less than 70 inches	53.7	Less than 65 inches	58.1
Less than 71 inches	68.2	Less than 66 inches	74.8
Less than 72 inches	80.1	Less than 67 inches	85.4
Less than 73 inches	88.5	Less than 68 inches	92.3
Less than 74 inches	92.7	Less than 69 inches	96.2
Less than 75 inches	96.2	Less than 70 inches	98.3
Less than 76 inches	98.4	Less than 71 inches	99.4
All height categories	100.0%	All height categories	100.0%
Average height, all races	**69.7 inches**	**Average height, all races**	**64.3 inches**
White	69.8	White	64.4
Black	69.6	Black	64.3

Source: Anthropometric Reference Data and Prevalence of Overweight: United States, 1976-80, *National Center for Health Statistics, National Health Survey Series 11, No. 238.*

Note: Height is without shoes.

Weight

HEALTH 18–24

WEIGHING IN

The average woman aged 18 to 24 weighs 134 pounds and the average man in this age group weighs 163 pounds. Twelve percent of men and 11 percent of women aged 20 to 24 are overweight and about 4 percent of all 20-to-24-year-olds are severely overweight.

(cumulative percentage of weight of males and females aged 18 to 24 and their average weight, by race)

weight, males	cumulative percentage	weight, females	cumulative percentage
Less than 100 pounds	0.2%	Less than 90 pounds	0.7%
Less than 110 pounds	0.6	Less than 100 pounds	3.6
Less than 120 pounds	2.3	Less than 110 pounds	12.7
Less than 130 pounds	7.7	Less than 120 pounds	30.6
Less than 140 pounds	20.4	Less than 130 pounds	52.7
Less than 150 pounds	35.9	Less than 140 pounds	69.7
Less than 160 pounds	52.4	Less than 150 pounds	80.8
Less than 170 pounds	66.7	Less than 160 pounds	86.8
Less than 180 pounds	78.7	Less than 170 pounds	91.7
Less than 190 pounds	86.2	Less than 180 pounds	94.2
Less than 200 pounds	90.3	Less than 190 pounds	96.2
Less than 210 pounds	93.3	Less than 200 pounds	97.5
Less than 220 pounds	95.2	Less than 220 pounds	98.4
Less than 230 pounds	97.0	Less than 240 pounds	99.0
Less than 240 pounds	98.8	Less than 260 pounds	99.6
Less than 250 pounds	99.2	Less than 280 pounds	100.0
All weight categories	100.0%	All weight categories	100.0%
Average weight, all races	**162.7 pounds**	**Average weight, all races**	**133.6 pounds**
White	163.5	White	133.2
Black	159.3	Black	139.2

Source: Anthropometric Reference Data and Prevalence of Overweight: United States, 1976-80, *National Center for Health Statistics, National Health Survey Series 11, No. 238.*

Notes: Weight includes clothing weight, estimated as ranging from 0.20 to 0.62 pounds. Overweight is defined in terms of a body mass index which is determined by dividing weight in kilograms by height in meters squared. Overweight people have a body mass index equal to or greater than that at the 85th percentile of men and women aged 20 to 29. Severe overweight means a body mass index equal to or greater than at the 95th percentile of men and women aged 20 to 29. Data on overweight are not available for persons aged 18 and 19.

Acute Conditions

HEALTH
18–24

SUFFERING FROM FLUS

Flus are the most common ailment of 18-to-24-year-olds, accounting for about 30 percent of their acute conditions. Men in this age group suffer most frequently from flus, colds, and bruises and superficial injuries while the women are most prone to flus, colds, and other respiratory infections.

(number of acute conditions reported in a year for all persons and those aged 18 to 24, by sex, numbers in thousands)

	males all ages	males aged 18 to 24	females all ages	females aged 18 to 24
All acute conditions	191,369	20,311	257,177	31,818
Infective and parasitic diseases	**23,122**	**1,768**	**31,244**	**3,457**
Common childhood diseases	2,565	0	1,876	0
Intestinal virus, unspecified	4,244	658	5,288	509
Viral infections, unspecified	9,621	604	14,273	1,000
Other	6,692	505	9,807	1,948
Respiratory conditions	**99,216**	**10,337**	**129,626**	**15,977**
Common cold	30,445	3,387	32,983	3,757
Other acute upper respiratory infections	8,472	1,182	13,320	1,772
Influenza	55,256	5,531	75,295	9,702
Acute bronchitis	1,960	237	4,315	180
Pneumonia	1,365	0	1,277	0
Other respiratory conditions	1,718	0	2,435	565
Digestive system conditions	**5,860**	**680**	**9,112**	**1,240**
Dental conditions	1,059	0	1,955	461
Indigestion, nausea and vomiting	3,299	501	4,670	442
Other digestive conditions	1,502	179	2,487	336
Injuries	**34,588**	**5,148**	**29,706**	**3,651**
Fractures and dislocations	4,367	279	3,978	247
Sprains and strains	6,127	1,125	6,208	1,100
Open wounds and lacerations	11,153	1,424	5,094	513
Contusions and superficial injuries	7,986	1,671	7,191	787
Other current injuries	4,955	649	7,235	1,003

(continued next page)

Acute Conditions

HEALTH
18–24

(continued from previous page)

(number of acute conditions reported in a year for all persons and those aged 18 to 24, by sex, numbers in thousands)

	males		females	
	all ages	aged 18 to 24	all ages	aged 18 to 24
Selected other acute conditions	**21,183**	**1,403**	**40,385**	**5,751**
Eye conditions	1,072	0	2,080	305
Acute ear infections	8,689	97	10,116	406
Other ear conditions	1,884	110	2,193	177
Acute urinary conditions	989	206	4,399	1,152
Disorders of menstruation	–	–	2,251	821
Other disorders of female genital tract	–	–	2,174	701
Delivery and other conditions of pregnancy	–	–	4,466	1,513
Skin conditions	2,065	301	3,597	149
Acute musculoskeletal conditions	3,038	312	3,972	419
Headache, excluding migraine	1,253	291	2,461	0
Fever, unspecified	2,192	87	2,675	107
All other acute conditions	**7,400**	**975**	**17,104**	**1,742**

Source: The 1986 National Health Interview Survey, National Center for Health Statistics

Note: An acute condition is defined by The National Health Interview Survey as an illness or injury that usually lasts less than three months and was first noticed less than three months before the respondent's interview. The acute condition must also have caused the person to restrict activities for at least a half a day or to have contacted a physician. The data are based only on information given by the respondent and are subject to recall and selective reporting error. Numbers may not add to total due to rounding.

Chronic Conditions

HAY FEVER, SKIN PROBLEMS, AND ACCIDENTS

The chronic conditions that are most likely to plague women aged 18 to 24 are sinusitis, hay fever, back deformities, migraine headaches, and acne. Men in this age group most frequently report problems with hay fever, sinusitis, acne, back deformities, and leg deformities.

(number of selected chronic conditions reported in a year for all persons and those aged 18 to 24, by sex, numbers in thousands)

	males all ages	males aged 18 to 24	females all ages	females aged 18 to 24
Selected skin and musculoskeletal conditions				
Arthritis	10,751	122	20,160	494
Gout, including gouty arthritis	1,515	0	713	21
Intervertebral disc disorders	2,522	104	1,645	69
Bone spur or tendonitis, unspecified	781	56	898	25
Disorders of bone or cartilage	449	48	943	102
Trouble with bunions	594	10	2,321	87
Bursitis, unclassified	1,641	147	2,464	0
Sebaceous skin cyst	640	36	881	85
Trouble with acne	2,193	860	2,116	667
Psoriasis	1,069	23	1,262	128
Dermatitis	3,851	395	5,696	603
Trouble with dry, itching skin, unclassified	1,994	163	2,606	250
Trouble with ingrown nails	2,352	285	3,030	342
Trouble with corns and calluses	1,669	120	3,164	193
Impairments				
Visual impairment	4,994	402	3,358	104
Color blindness	2,694	290	272	0
Cataracts	1,534	0	3,497	0
Glaucoma	735	0	967	0
Hearing impairment	11,727	395	9,004	559
Tinnitus	3,388	74	2,927	232
Speech impairment	1,924	200	871	86
Absence of extremity(s)	374	0	24	0
Paralysis, entire body, one side of body, or both legs	200	0	152	0
Partial paralysis of body or legs	236	0	99	0
Deformity of back	6,812	800	9,676	1,093
Deformity of upper extremities	1,622	269	1,475	79
Deformity of lower extremities	6,454	747	5,739	350
Selected digestive conditions				
Ulcer	2,116	296	2,378	196
Hernia of abdominal cavity	2,300	0	2,283	48
Gastritis or duodenitis	1,080	30	1,813	160

(continued next page)

Chronic Conditions

HEALTH 18–24

(continued from previous page)

(number of selected chronic conditions reported in a year for all persons and those aged 18 to 24, by sex, numbers in thousands)

	males		females	
	all ages	aged 18 to 24	all ages	aged 18 to 24
Frequent indigestion	2,504	81	2,811	148
Enteritis or colitis	574	67	1,820	82
Spastic colon	264	0	1,377	55
Diverticula of intestines	404	0	1,508	0
Frequent constipation	1,002	71	3,537	173
Selected conditions of the genitourinary, nervous, endocrine, metabolic, and blood system				
Goiter or other disorders of the thyroid	420	0	2,789	186
Diabetes	2,949	0	3,635	144
Anemias	570	22	2,617	280
Epilepsy	656	99	863	154
Migraine headache	2,068	291	6,448	726
Neuralgia or neuritis, unspecified	215	24	364	0
Kidney trouble	1,305	73	2,662	365
Bladder disorders	516	30	3,253	554
Diseases of prostate	1,281	0	–	–
Inflammatory female genital diseases	–	–	427	79
Noninflammatory female genital diseases	–	–	1,095	104
Menstrual disorders	–	–	2,097	519
Selected circulatory conditions				
Ischemic heart disease	4,091	0	2,809	53
Tachycardia or rapid heart	700	0	1,226	24
Heart murmurs	1,310	155	2,583	229
Other heart rhythm disorders	499	0	800	24
Other heart diseases	1,482	85	2,265	81
High blood pressure (hypertension)	12,512	320	16,457	613
Cerebrovascular disease	1,156	0	1,646	0
Hardening of the arteries	1,428	0	1,225	0
Varicose veins	1,042	23	5,814	263
Hemorrhoids	4,568	163	5,341	228
Selected respiratory conditions				
Chronic bronchitis	4,707	440	6,671	626
Asthma	4,670	701	5,019	547
Hay fever or allergic rhinitis without asthma	10,136	1,350	11,566	1,286
Chronic sinusitis	14,636	1,340	19,749	1,863
Deviated nasal septum	825	57	465	59
Chronic disease of tonsils or adenoids	1,071	172	2,068	357
Emphysema	1,201	0	796	0

Source: The 1986 National Health Interview Survey, National Center for Health Statistics

Note: Chronic conditions are defined by the National Health Interview Survey as conditions that either a) were first noticed three months or more before the date of the interview or b) belong to a group of conditions (such as heart disease or diabetes) that are considered chronic regardless of when they began. Totals for all chronic conditions are not shown because the National Health Interview Survey does not measure the total number of chronic conditions for each person. The data are based only on information given by the respondent and are subject to recall and selective reporting error.

Activity Restrictions

HEALTH
18–24

REGULAR EMPLOYEES

Men and women aged 18 to 24 spend fewer days in bed and miss fewer work days because of illness or injury than Americans in general. Working women in this age group have seven work-loss days a year and men who work miss four such days.

(number of days of activity restriction reported in a year and per person due to acute and chronic conditions, by type of restriction and sex, race, and household income, for all persons and those aged 18 to 24, numbers in thousands)

	number of days per year		number of days per person	
	bed day	work-loss day	bed day	work-loss day
All ages	1,547,980	833,396	6.5	5.4
Male	613,113	401,503	5.4	4.8
Female	934,867	431,892	7.7	6.0
White	1,298,039	716,187	6.5	5.4
Black	220,102	99,332	7.7	5.4
Household income				
Less than $10,000	384,962	90,268	11.5	6.1
$10,000 to $19,999	346,115	162,604	7.7	6.1
$20,000 to $34,999	326,166	254,563	5.2	5.7
$35,000 and over	275,957	232,139	4.3	4.6
All aged 18 to 24	111,208	91,140	4.2	5.0
Male	39,655	33,405	3.0	3.5
Female	71,553	57,735	5.2	6.6
White	92,772	80,538	4.2	5.1
Black	14,884	6,951	4.1	3.5
Household income				
Less than $10,000	26,219	14,123	4.5	4.9
$10,000 to $19,999	26,680	19,167	5.1	5.3
$20,000 to $34,999	23,702	33,280	3.8	7.1
$35,000 and over	22,134	18,932	3.7	4.0

Source: The 1986 National Health Interview Survey, National Center for Health Statistics

Note: Numbers may not add to total due to rounding. A bed day is one during which a person stayed in bed more than half a day because of illness or injury. All hospital days for inpatients are considered bed days even if the patient was not in bed more than half a day. A work-loss day is one on which a currently employed person aged 18 or older missed more than half a day of work. The data are based only on information given by the respondent and are subject to recall and selective reporting error.

Cause of Death

HEALTH
18–24

DEATH IN THE FAST LANE

Although deaths among people aged 15 to 24 account for only 2 percent of all deaths, they are 21 percent of all accident-related deaths and 25 percent of all deaths involving homicide and illegal interventions. Seventy-six percent of the accidental deaths among 15-to-24-year-olds are linked to motor vehicle accidents.

(ten leading causes of death among persons aged 15 to 24)

	number of deaths persons aged 15 to 24	number of deaths all ages	percent accounted for by persons aged 15 to 24
All causes	39,929	2,105,361	1.9%
Accidents and adverse effects	19,975	95,277	21.0
Homicide and illegal interventions	5,522	21,731	25.4
Suicide	5,120	30,904	16.6
Malignant neoplasms (cancer)	2,115	469,376	0.5
Heart diseases	1,096	765,490	0.1
Congenital anomalies	511	12,638	4.0
Pneumonia and influenza	276	69,812	0.4
Cerebrovascular diseases	263	149,643	0.2
Chronic obstructive pulmonary diseases and allied conditions	191	76,559	0.2
Diabetes mellitus	140	37,184	0.4
All other causes	4,720	376,747	1.3

Source: Advance Report of Final Mortality Statistics, 1986, *National Center for Health Statistics, Vol. 37, No. 6*

Chapter 4

CONSUMERS AGED 25 TO 34

Marketers beware. This age group will shrink the most and change a lot during the 1990s.

There will be fewer 25-to-34-year-olds in the next decade and they will head fewer households.

■ Between 1990 and 2000, the number of Americans aged 25 to 34 will fall 15 percent.

■ There will be 3 million fewer households headed by 25-to-34-year-olds in 2000 than in 1990.

■ During the 1990s, the number of family households will plunge 23 percent as the number of non-families will trend upward by 4 percent.

■ Men and women in this age group account for the largest share of all divorces and remarriages.

■ In 1987, 95 percent of men aged 25 to 34 were in the labor force; that share will decline slightly to 94 percent in 2000. In 1987, 72 percent of women in this age group were in the labor force; that share will climb to 82 percent in 2000.

■ Compared with other age groups, 25-to-34-year-olds head the largest proportion—31 percent—of households with incomes between $20,000 and $35,000. Of those remaining, an even 34 percent are above and below that range.

■ The median household income of these households is $26,900. Households headed by married couples have a median income of $32,800 and dual-earner married couples have the highest median income in the age group—$36,400.

■ This is the age group with the largest chunk of their spending dollar—33 percent—going to housing.

■ Between 1990 and 2000, the aggregate spending of these households will drop off by 72 billion dollars.

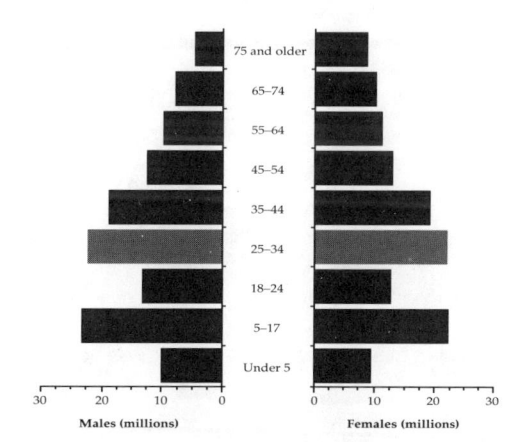

1990

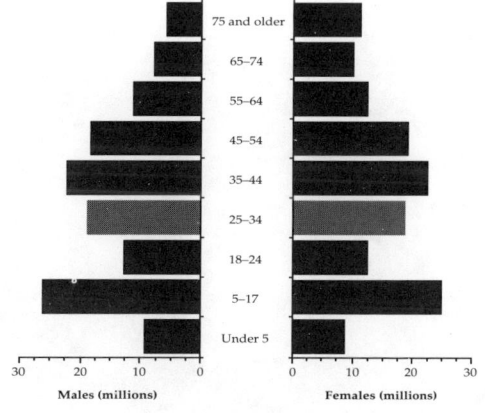

2000

Almanac of Consumer Markets 91

Share of Total Population

POPULATION
25–34

ANOTHER SHRINKING AGE GROUP

By the turn of the century the number of 25-to-34-year-olds will drop to 14 percent of the population as members of the baby bust enter this age group. Other age groups that will shrink during the 1990s are children under age 5, 18-to-24-year-olds and 65-to-74-year-olds.

(total population and the number of persons aged 25 to 34, in thousands, by sex, 1960 to 1980, and projections for 1990 to 2000)

	1960 number	1960 percent of total	1970 number	1970 percent of total	1980 number	1980 percent of total	1990 number	1990 percent of total	1995 number	1995 percent of total	2000 number	2000 percent of total
All ages	180,671	100.0%	205,052	100.0%	227,757	100.0%	252,293	100.0%	264,077	100.0%	274,479	100.0%
All aged 25 to 34	22,919	12.7	25,323	12.3	37,626	16.5	44,321	17.6	41,653	15.8	37,823	13.8
Males	11,327	6.3	12,537	6.1	18,742	8.2	22,256	8.8	20,947	7.9	19,026	6.9
Females	11,591	6.4	12,787	6.2	18,883	8.3	22,065	8.7	20,706	7.8	18,796	6.8

Source: Annual Projections of the Population by Age, Sex, and Race, for the United States: 1983 to 2080, *Bureau of the Census, Current Population Reports, Series 17* and the Bureau of the Census

Note: Total population includes Armed Forces overseas; 1960 to 1980 are based on censuses; projections are based on the Census Bureau's Series 17 projections that incorporate illegal immigration and higher levels of emigration than other Census Bureau projections. Series 17 is consistent with current estimates of illegal aliens living in the United States. Numbers may not add to total due to rounding.

Sex, Race, and Ethnicity

POPULATION
25–34

WHITES ON THE DECLINE

Between 1990 and 2000, the number of Americans aged 25 to 34 will fall 15 percent. But the number of Hispanics and Asians will increase in this, as well as in all the other age groups. During the decade, the proportion of white 25-to-34-year-olds will drop from 74 percent to 68 percent while blacks will increase from 13 to 14 percent, Hispanics from 10 to 14 percent and Asians from 3 to 5 percent.

(projections of the total population and persons aged 25 to 34, in thousands, by sex, race, and Hispanic origin, 1990 to 2000)

	1990	1995	2000	percent change 1990–2000
All ages	**252,293**	**264,077**	**274,479**	**8.8%**
White	191,594	195,347	197,634	3.2
Black	30,915	33,237	35,440	14.6
Hispanic	21,854	25,991	30,295	38.6
Asians and other races	7,930	9,502	11,110	40.1
All aged 25 to 34	**44,321**	**41,653**	**37,823**	**-14.7**
White	32,749	29,450	25,550	-22.0
Black	5,782	5,725	5,319	-8.0
Hispanic	4,241	4,779	5,126	20.9
Asians and other races	1,549	1,699	1,829	18.1
All males aged 25 to 34	**22,256**	**20,947**	**19,026**	**-14.5**
White	16,459	14,806	12,845	-22.0
Black	2,821	2,825	2,630	-6.8
Hispanic	2,248	2,539	2,717	20.9
Asians and other races	727	777	835	14.9
All females aged 25 to 34	**22,065**	**20,706**	**18,796**	**-14.8**
White	16,289	14,645	12,705	-22.0
Black	2,962	2,900	2,690	-9.2
Hispanic	1,994	2,240	2,409	20.8
Asians and other races	820	921	992	21.0

Source: Projections of the Population of the United States by Age, Sex, and Race: 1983 to 2080, *Bureau of the Census, Current Population Reports, Series P-25, No. 952, Series 17*

Note: Series 17 projections incorporate illegal immigration and higher levels of emigration than other Census Bureau projections and are consistent with current estimates of illegal aliens living in the United States. Total population includes Armed Forces living overseas. In this table Hispanics have been separated out of the racial groups; categories do not overlap. Numbers may not add to total due to rounding.

State Populations

POPULATION
25–34

ONLY TWO GAINERS

Only Alaska and Hawaii will have more 25-to-34-year-olds in 2000 than in 1990. Generally the sunbelt states—California, Nevada, Arizona, New Mexico, Texas, Florida, and Georgia—will show the least shrinkage.

(resident population and the number of persons aged 25 to 34, in thousands, in Census Bureau divisions and states in 1980 and projections for 1990 to 2010)

Note: Inconsistencies between the data in this table and the preceding two tables are due to different assumptions about immigration and emigration on which the projections are based and the inclusion of Armed Forces overseas in the total population. This table is based on the resident population only.

	census 1980	1990	projections 2000	2010	percent change 1990–2000	percent change 2000–2010
All ages	226,546	249,891	267,747	282,055	7.1%	5.3%
All aged 25 to 34	37,082	43,728	36,952	37,375	-15.5	1.1
New England	**1,996**	**2,357**	**1,952**	**1,865**	**-17.2**	**-4.5**
Connecticut	491	561	471	444	-16.0	-5.7
Maine	179	207	171	162	-17.4	-5.3
Massachusetts	935	1,089	890	852	-18.3	-4.3
New Hampshire	157	214	190	186	-11.2	-2.1
Rhode Island	146	180	147	143	-18.3	-2.7
Vermont	87	106	82	80	-22.6	-2.4
Middle Atlantic	**5,711**	**6,362**	**5,231**	**4,952**	**-17.8**	**-5.3**
New Jersey	1,138	1,334	1,170	1,125	-12.3	-3.8
New York	2,780	3,052	2,598	2,488	-14.9	-4.2
Pennsylvania	1,793	1,976	1,465	1,339	-25.9	-8.6
East North Central	**6,718**	**7,335**	**5,686**	**5,366**	**-22.5**	**-5.6**
Illinois	1,855	2,043	1,620	1,568	-20.7	-3.2
Indiana	875	966	736	688	-23.8	-6.5
Michigan	1,515	1,648	1,293	1,193	-21.5	-7.7
Ohio	1,724	1,844	1,429	1,330	-22.5	-6.9
Wisconsin	750	833	608	587	-27.0	-3.5

(continued on next page)

Almanac of Consumer Markets

State Populations

(continued from previous page)

(resident population and the number of persons aged 25 to 34, in thousands, in Census Bureau divisions and states in 1980 and projections for 1990 to 2010)

	census 1980	1990	projections 2000	2010	percent change 1990–2000	percent change 2000–2010
All ages	226,546	249,891	267,747	282,055	7.1%	5.3%
All aged 25 to 34	37,082	43,728	36,952	37,375	-15.5	1.1
West North Central	**2,709**	**3,039**	**2,270**	**2,283**	**-25.3**	**0.6**
Iowa	449	458	304	289	-33.6	-4.9
Kansas	375	425	323	331	-24.0	2.5
Minnesota	676	774	592	597	-23.5	0.8
Missouri	752	879	686	693	-22.0	1.0
Nebraska	249	271	200	199	-26.2	-0.5
North Dakota	104	114	80	83	-29.8	3.8
South Dakota	103	117	86	92	-26.5	7.0
South Atlantic	**5,999**	**7,546**	**6,846**	**7,020**	**-9.3**	**2.5**
Delaware	95	124	105	105	-15.3	0.0
District of Columbia	122	130	115	119	-11.5	3.5
Florida	1,412	1,982	1,844	1,943	-7.0	5.4
Georgia	930	1,201	1,184	1,250	-1.4	5.6
Maryland	725	871	779	784	-10.6	0.6
North Carolina	964	1,175	1,051	1,062	-10.6	1.0
South Carolina	517	629	545	553	-13.4	1.5
Virginia	928	1,136	1,013	1,017	-10.8	0.4
West Virginia	306	299	214	188	-28.4	-12.1
East South Central	**2,299**	**2,640**	**2,143**	**2,112**	**-18.8**	**-1.4**
Alabama	598	710	578	577	-18.6	-0.2
Kentucky	585	637	489	463	-23.2	-5.3
Mississippi	369	442	367	376	-17.0	2.5
Tennessee	745	852	708	696	-16.9	-1.7
West South Central	**3,918**	**4,914**	**4,264**	**4,490**	**-13.2**	**5.3**
Arkansas	335	381	303	305	-20.5	0.7
Louisiana	681	794	604	612	-23.9	1.3
Oklahoma	476	547	424	447	-22.5	5.4
Texas	2,426	3,192	2,932	3,125	-8.1	6.6

(continued on next page)

State Populations

POPULATION
25–34

(continued from previous page)

(resident population and the number of persons aged 25 to 34, in thousands, in Census Bureau divisions and states in 1980 and projections for 1990 to 2010)

	census 1980	projections 1990	2000	2010	percent change 1990–2000	percent change 2000–2010
All ages	226,546	249,891	267,747	282,055	7.1%	5.3%
All aged 25 to 34	37,082	43,728	36,952	37,375	-15.5	1.1
Mountain	**1,993**	**2,484**	**2,168**	**2,369**	**-12.7**	**9.3**
Arizona	444	644	604	670	-6.2	10.9
Colorado	570	664	564	596	-15.1	5.7
Idaho	155	162	127	134	-21.6	5.5
Montana	133	133	100	103	-24.8	3.0
Nevada	145	206	190	208	-7.8	9.5
New Mexico	216	287	271	304	-5.6	12.2
Utah	241	296	245	286	-17.2	16.7
Wyoming	88	94	66	69	-29.8	4.5
Pacific	**5,739**	**7,051**	**6,393**	**6,918**	**-9.3**	**8.2**
Alaska	91	117	128	140	9.4	9.4
California	4,243	5,425	4,997	5,428	-7.9	8.6
Hawaii	179	205	217	252	5.9	16.1
Oregon	482	477	377	389	-21.0	3.2
Washington	745	826	676	708	-18.2	4.7

Source: Projections of the Population of States by Age, Sex and Race: 1988 to 2010, *Bureau of the Census, Current Population Reports, Series P-25, No. 1017*

Note: Numbers may not add to total due to rounding.

State-by-State Changes

POPULATION
25–34

ON THE DOWNWARD PATH

No other age group will lose as much ground during the 1990s as young adults aged 25 to 34, with the biggest losses occurring in the East North Central and West North Central divisions—traditional farming and manufacturing states.

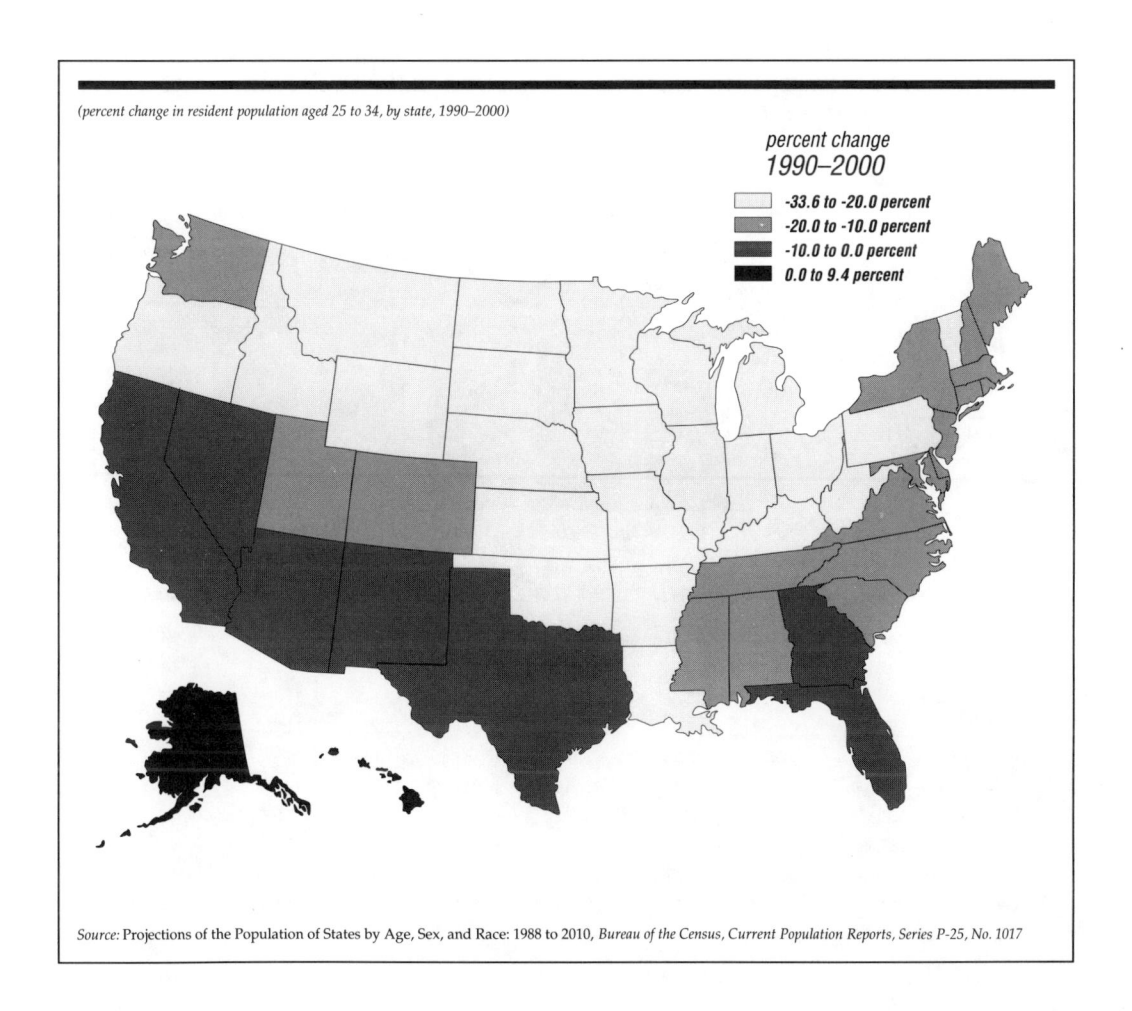

(percent change in resident population aged 25 to 34, by state, 1990–2000)

percent change
1990–2000

- -33.6 to -20.0 percent
- -20.0 to -10.0 percent
- -10.0 to 0.0 percent
- 0.0 to 9.4 percent

Source: Projections of the Population of States by Age, Sex, and Race: 1988 to 2010, *Bureau of the Census, Current Population Reports, Series P-25, No. 1017*

Almanac of Consumer Markets 97

Number of Households

HOUSEHOLDS
25–34

DOWNTURNING MARKET

As the small baby bust generation starts turning 25, this age group will see a sharp 15 percent decline, spelling big changes ahead for a formerly booming market.

(number of households, in thousands, by age of householder, 1990–2000)

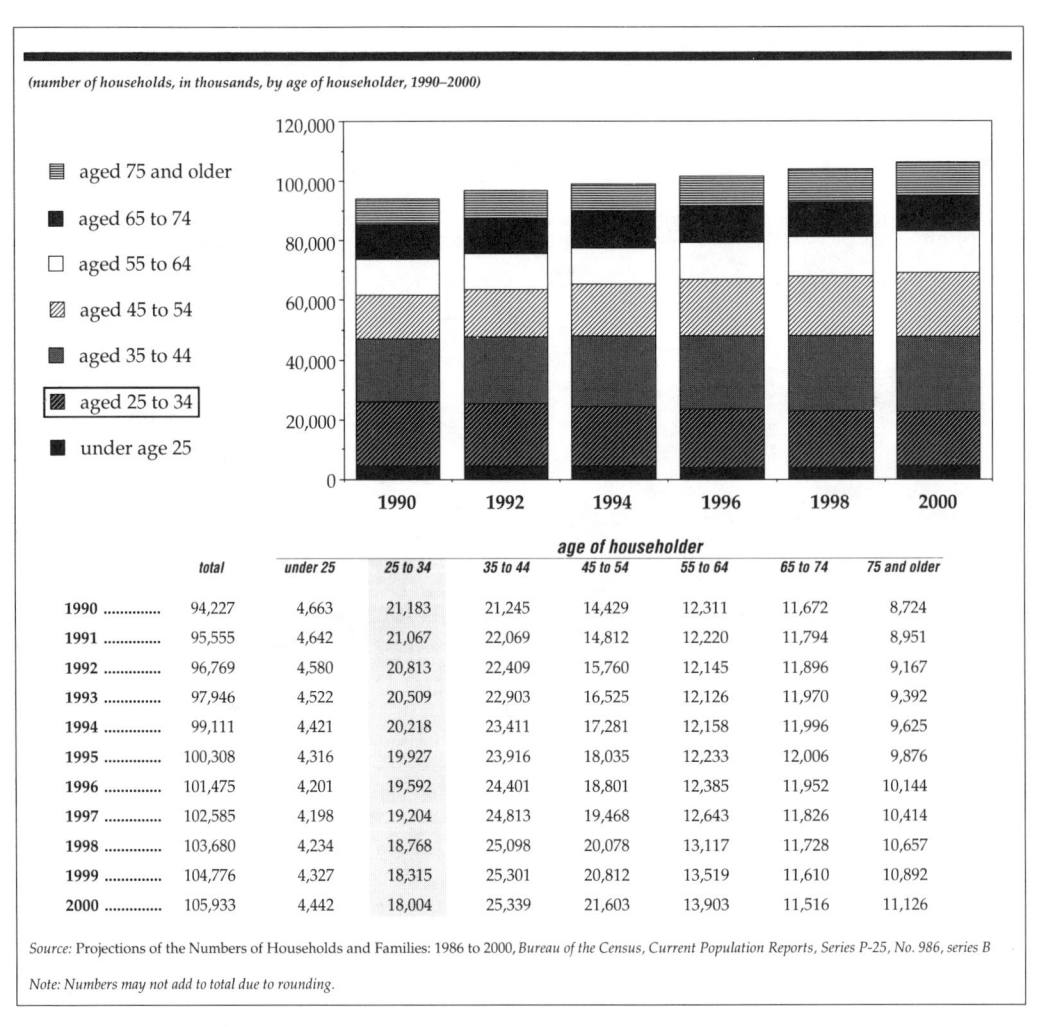

Legend:
- aged 75 and older
- aged 65 to 74
- aged 55 to 64
- aged 45 to 54
- aged 35 to 44
- aged 25 to 34
- under age 25

	total	under 25	25 to 34	35 to 44	45 to 54	55 to 64	65 to 74	75 and older
1990	94,227	4,663	21,183	21,245	14,429	12,311	11,672	8,724
1991	95,555	4,642	21,067	22,069	14,812	12,220	11,794	8,951
1992	96,769	4,580	20,813	22,409	15,760	12,145	11,896	9,167
1993	97,946	4,522	20,509	22,903	16,525	12,126	11,970	9,392
1994	99,111	4,421	20,218	23,411	17,281	12,158	11,996	9,625
1995	100,308	4,316	19,927	23,916	18,035	12,233	12,006	9,876
1996	101,475	4,201	19,592	24,401	18,801	12,385	11,952	10,144
1997	102,585	4,198	19,204	24,813	19,468	12,643	11,826	10,414
1998	103,680	4,234	18,768	25,098	20,078	13,117	11,728	10,657
1999	104,776	4,327	18,315	25,301	20,812	13,519	11,610	10,892
2000	105,933	4,442	18,004	25,339	21,603	13,903	11,516	11,126

Source: Projections of the Numbers of Households and Families: 1986 to 2000, *Bureau of the Census, Current Population Reports, Series P-25, No. 986, series B*

Note: Numbers may not add to total due to rounding.

Types of Households

HOUSEHOLDS
25–34

FAMILY HEADS

Seventy-three percent of householders aged 25 to 34 are family heads. This age group accounts for 22 percent of all married couples, and a full 35 percent of all couples with children under age 18 living at home.

(household types for all households and for householders aged 25 to 34, numbers in thousands)

	all households total	all households percent of households in category	householder aged 25 to 34 total	householder aged 25 to 34 percent of households in category
All households	91,066	100.0%	20,583	100.0%
Family households	65,133	71.5	15,008	72.9
Married couple	51,809	56.9	11,638	56.5
With children under age 18 at home	24,600	27.0	8,665	42.1
Without children under age 18 at home	27,209	29.9	2,972	14.4
Female householder	10,608	11.6	2,736	13.3
With children under age 18 at home	6,273	6.9	2,549	12.4
Without children under age 18 at home	4,335	4.8	187	0.9
Male householder	2,715	3.0	634	3.1
With children under age 18 at home	1,047	1.1	326	1.6
Without children under age 18 at home	1,669	1.8	308	1.5
Nonfamily households	25,993	28.5	5,575	27.1
Living alone	21,889	24.0	4,019	19.5
Female householder	13,101	14.4	1,650	8.0
Male householder	8,788	9.7	2,369	11.5
Living with others	4,044	4.4	1,556	7.6
Female householder	1,523	1.7	515	2.5
Male householder	2,521	2.8	1,041	5.1

Source: The 1988 Current Population Survey, Bureau of the Census

Note: Numbers may not add to total due to rounding.

Almanac of Consumer Markets

Future Household Types

HOUSEHOLDS
25–34

SHARP DROP AHEAD

The number of households headed by 25-to-34-year-olds is scheduled for a sharp decline—a dip of over 3 million—during the 1990s. Family households will plunge 23 percent while the number of nonfamilies will trend upward by 4 percent.

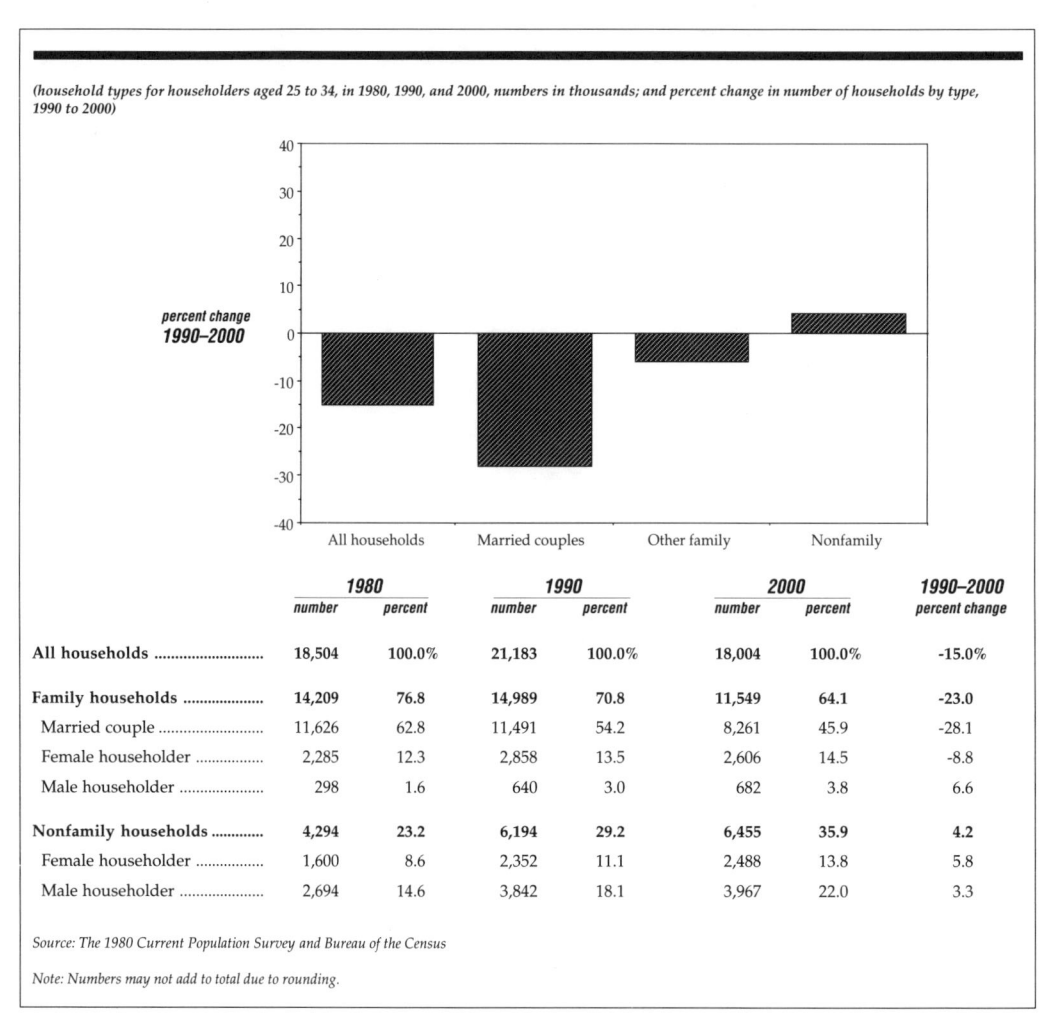

(household types for householders aged 25 to 34, in 1980, 1990, and 2000, numbers in thousands; and percent change in number of households by type, 1990 to 2000)

	1980		1990		2000		1990–2000
	number	percent	number	percent	number	percent	percent change
All households	18,504	100.0%	21,183	100.0%	18,004	100.0%	-15.0%
Family households	14,209	76.8	14,989	70.8	11,549	64.1	-23.0
Married couple	11,626	62.8	11,491	54.2	8,261	45.9	-28.1
Female householder	2,285	12.3	2,858	13.5	2,606	14.5	-8.8
Male householder	298	1.6	640	3.0	682	3.8	6.6
Nonfamily households	4,294	23.2	6,194	29.2	6,455	35.9	4.2
Female householder	1,600	8.6	2,352	11.1	2,488	13.8	5.8
Male householder	2,694	14.6	3,842	18.1	3,967	22.0	3.3

Source: The 1980 Current Population Survey and Bureau of the Census

Note: Numbers may not add to total due to rounding.

Marital Status

SIXTY PERCENT MARRIED

Among 25-to-34-year-olds, 33 percent of the men and 22 percent of the women have never married; 7 percent of the men and 9 percent of the women are divorced. But 60 percent of all Americans in this age group are married and living with their spouses.

(marital status of persons aged 15 and older and those aged 25 to 34, by sex, race and Hispanic origin, numbers in thousands)

	all	total	single never married	married spouse present	married spouse absent	divorced	widowed
Males all ages							
All races/ethnicities	89,368	100.0%	30.0%	58.5%	2.9%	6.3%	2.4%
White	77,212	100.0	28.2	60.9	2.5	6.2	2.3
Black	9,472	100.0	42.9	40.4	6.0	7.5	3.3
Hispanic origin	6,517	100.0	36.4	49.9	6.2	5.8	1.6
Males aged 25 to 34							
All races/ethnicities	21,142	100.0	32.8	56.9	3.6	6.7	0.1
White	18,017	100.0	30.4	59.4	3.2	7.0	0.1
Black	2,393	100.0	47.6	40.7	5.9	5.8	0.1
Hispanic origin	1,859	100.0	31.0	55.4	7.8	5.0	-
Females all ages							
All races/ethnicities	97,320	100.0	23.0	53.7	3.6	8.3	11.4
White	83,003	100.0	21.0	56.6	2.7	8.0	11.6
Black	11,447	100.0	36.5	32.7	9.2	10.4	11.2
Hispanic origin	6,588	100.0	26.6	51.2	7.7	8.3	6.2
Females aged 25 to 34							
All races/ethnicities	21,494	100.0	21.9	63.3	5.0	9.3	0.6
White	17,871	100.0	19.0	66.9	3.9	9.7	0.5
Black	2,803	100.0	39.7	39.9	11.1	8.2	1.1
Hispanic origin	1,754	100.0	19.3	61.8	9.7	8.3	0.9

Source: Marital Status and Living Arrangements: March 1987, *Bureau of the Census, Current Population Reports, Series P-20, No. 423*

Note: Hispanics may be of any race. Numbers may not add to total due to rounding.

Number of Marriages and Divorces

MARITAL STATUS AND FERTILITY
25–34

THE MOST DIVORCES AND REMARRIAGES

Men and women aged 25 to 34 account for the largest proportion of all divorces and remarriages. Forty-three percent of women and 37 percent of men who remarry are in this age group.

(number of marriages and divorces for all persons and for those aged 25 to 34, by sex)

	all persons male	all persons female	persons aged 25 to 34 male	persons aged 25 to 34 female	percent involving persons aged 25 to 34 male	percent involving persons aged 25 to 34 female
All marriages	1,858,783	1,858,783	752,944	634,327	40.5%	34.1%
First marriages	1,185,904	1,196,119	504,738	351,144	42.6	29.6
Remarriages	635,086	623,867	232,459	270,850	36.6	42.6
Previously divorced	499,735	485,848	198,362	227,287	39.7	45.5
Divorces	577,713	577,713	215,823	221,109	37.4	38.3

Source: Advance Report of Final Marriage Statistics, 1985 and Advance Report of Final Divorce Statistics, 1985, *National Center for Health Statistics*

Note: Numbers will not add to total because all divorces include those not stating their age and all marriages include those not stating whether they were previously married.

Childbearing Patterns

MARITAL STATUS AND FERTILITY
25–34

MORE OLDER MOTHERS

By the time they are aged 25 to 29, 71 percent of all ever-married women have had at least one child; that proportion climbs to 83 percent among 30-to-34-year-olds. Over half of childless wives aged 30 to 34 say they expect to have a baby. If those women do become mothers they will be following the trend of later childbearing. One-third of the children born in 1988 were born to mothers in their thirties, up from 19 percent in 1976.

(number of children ever born to women aged 18 to 44 and those aged 25 to 34, by race and marital status, number of women in thousands)

	all women	total	none	one	two	three	four	five and six	seven or more
All races									
All marital statuses									
Aged 18 to 44	52,586	100.0%	38.0%	18.6%	25.2%	11.8%	4.2%	2.0%	0.3%
Aged 25 to 29	10,839	100.0	42.2	23.0	22.6	8.9	2.2	0.9	0.1
Aged 30 to 34	10,838	100.0	25.1	21.5	32.8	13.9	4.9	1.7	0.2
Women ever married									
Aged 18 to 44	36,847	100.0	19.6	22.0	33.8	16.0	5.7	2.5	0.4
Aged 25 to 29	7,682	100.0	29.1	27.4	29.1	11.0	2.5	1.0	0.1
Aged 30 to 34	9,121	100.0	16.6	22.8	37.5	15.8	5.5	1.7	0.2
Women never married									
Aged 18 to 44	15,739	100.0	81.0	10.5	5.0	2.0	0.8	0.6	0.1
Aged 25 to 29	3,157	100.0	74.2	12.5	6.8	3.8	1.7	0.9	0.1
Aged 30 to 34	1,717	100.0	70.1	14.6	8.0	3.8	1.6	1.8	0.1
White women									
All marital statuses									
Aged 18 to 44	43,870	100.0	39.2	17.8	25.4	11.8	3.9	1.6	0.3
Aged 25 to 29	9,003	100.0	43.8	23.0	22.5	8.2	1.9	0.6	–
Aged 30 to 34	9,015	100.0	26.4	20.5	33.4	13.5	4.6	1.4	0.1
Women ever married									
Aged 18 to 44	31,909	100.0	20.3	22.1	34.0	15.8	5.2	2.1	0.4
Aged 25 to 29	6,725	100.0	30.0	27.7	28.8	10.4	2.3	0.7	–
Aged 30 to 34	7,801	100.0	17.5	22.3	38.0	15.3	5.1	1.5	0.1
Women never married									
Aged 18 to 44	11,960	100.0	89.4	6.5	2.6	1.0	0.4	0.2	–
Aged 25 to 29	2,278	100.0	84.5	8.9	3.9	1.8	0.9	0.1	–
Aged 30 to 34	1,214	100.0	83.3	8.8	4.1	2.0	1.1	0.7	–

(continued next page)

Childbearing Patterns

MARITAL STATUS AND FERTILITY
25–34

(continued from previous page)

(number of children ever born to women aged 18 to 44 and those aged 25 to 34, by race and marital status, number of women in thousands)

	all women	total	none	one	two	three	four	five and six	seven or more
Black women									
All marital statuses									
Aged 18 to 44	6,835	100.0%	30.3%	23.9%	23.1%	12.0%	6.0%	4.1%	0.7%
Aged 25 to 29	1,463	100.0	30.4	25.6	24.0	12.3	4.1	3.3	0.5
Aged 30 to 34	1,401	100.0	17.9	27.4	29.1	14.6	7.2	3.5	0.3
Women ever married									
Aged 18 to 44	3,611	100.0	13.6	22	31.3	17.4	9.2	5.7	0.8
Aged 25 to 29	698	100.0	17.5	26.7	33.0	14.9	4.0	3.3	0.6
Aged 30 to 34	957	100.0	11.2	25.7	33.7	17.3	9.0	2.9	0.3
Women never married									
Aged 18 to 44	3,225	100.0	48.9	26.1	14.0	5.9	2.4	2.2	0.5
Aged 25 to 29	765	100.0	42.1	24.6	15.7	9.9	4.2	3.2	0.4
Aged 30 to 34	444	100.0	32.4	31.2	19.2	8.7	3.2	4.9	0.5
Hispanic women									
All marital statuses									
Aged 18 to 44	4,326	100.0	33.6	17.0	22.7	15.6	5.6	4.4	1.0
Aged 25 to 29	975	100.0	35.0	19.3	25.2	14.4	3.9	2.0	0.2
Aged 30 to 34	828	100.0	20.4	17.5	30.7	19.0	8.5	3.9	–
Women ever married									
Aged 18 to 44	3,012	100.0	17.2	19.4	28.9	20.3	7.0	5.8	1.5
Aged 25 to 29	717	100.0	25.1	21.9	29.5	16.7	4.1	2.5	0.3
Aged 30 to 34	685	100.0	13.3	18.9	35.0	21.2	8.1	3.5	–
Women never married									
Aged 18 to 44	1,314	100.0	71.3	11.5	8.6	4.9	2.4	1.3	–
Aged 25 to 29	258	100.0	62.7	12.2	13.2	7.9	3.2	0.8	–
Aged 30 to 34	143	100.0	54.6	11.1	9.9	8.3	10.1	6.0	–

Source: Fertility of American Women: June 1988, Bureau of the Census, Current Population Reports, Series P-20, No. 436

Note: Hispanic women are of any race.

Summary of Educational Attainment

EDUCATIONAL ATTAINMENT
25–34

THE BIG PICTURE

Data from the Census Bureau indicate that we have reached a plateau—the current generation of young adults is no better educated than its predecessors. Men are still more likely to have completed one or more years of college than women. Asians are better educated than whites, blacks, or Hispanics.

(years of school completed by persons aged 25 and over, by selected characteristics, numbers in thousands)

	number	4 years of high school or more	1 or more years of college	4 or more years of college
All persons	149,144	75.6%	37.0%	19.9%
Age groups:				
25 to 34	42,635	86.5	45.4	23.9
35 to 44	33,632	85.9	46.8	26.5
45 to 54	23,018	77.6	35.6	19.5
55 to 64	21,883	67.8	28.0	14.9
65 to 74	17,232	56.9	21.9	10.6
75 years and older	10,743	42.0	18.0	8.9
Sex:				
Male	70,677	76.0	40.6	23.6
Female	78,476	75.3	33.6	16.5
Race:				
White	129,170	77.0	37.8	20.5
Black	15,580	63.4	26.4	10.7
Asian and other	4,394	78.4	50.9	33.4
Hispanic origin:				
Hispanic	9,449	50.9	21.9	8.6
Non-Hispanic	139,695	77.3	38.0	20.6
Region:				
Northeast	32,030	76.5	36.8	22.2
Midwest	36,322	77.4	33.7	17.6
South	50,848	70.8	34.1	18.3
West	29,943	80.6	45.9	22.8
Metropolitan residence:				
Metropolitan area	115,614	77.6	40.0	22.1
Nonmetropolitan area	33,529	68.7	26.5	12.6

Source: Educational Attainment in the United States: March 1987 and March 1986, *Bureau of the Census, Current Population Reports, Series P-20, No. 428*

Age and Education

EDUCATIONAL ATTAINMENT
25–34

A HIGHER DEGREE

The share of men with four or more years of college is 6 percentage points higher for the older members of this age group (aged 30 to 34) than for the younger ones (aged 25 to 29). Likewise, the proportion of women with four or more years of college increases from 22 percent to 24 percent for those age groups.

(years of school completed by persons aged 25 to 34, by sex and single year of age, numbers in thousands)

	number	total	not high school graduate	high school graduate	1 to 3 years of college	4 or more years of college	median years
Males aged 25 to 29	10,694	100.0%	14.5%	42.4%	20.7%	22.3%	12.8
Age 25	2,199	100.0	16.5	42.8	19.2	21.5	12.8
Age 26	2,262	100.0	14.1	44.1	20.8	20.9	12.8
Age 27	2,129	100.0	14.7	41.5	21.8	22.0	12.9
Age 28	2,075	100.0	14.3	43.1	19.8	22.8	12.8
Age 29	2,028	100.0	12.6	40.4	22.1	24.8	12.9
Males aged 30 to 34	10,448	100.0	13.4	38.3	20.7	27.5	13.0
Age 30	2,283	100.0	13.7	39.8	20.8	25.7	12.9
Age 31	2,085	100.0	13.8	38.4	21.5	26.3	12.9
Age 32	2,074	100.0	11.4	38.9	20.1	29.8	13.0
Age 33	2,013	100.0	14.3	37.1	20.1	28.6	13.0
Age 34	1,993	100.0	13.8	37.2	21.3	27.5	13.0
Females aged 25 to 29	10,942	100.0	13.6	42.4	22.3	21.8	12.9
Age 25	2,168	100.0	13.3	41.9	22.6	22.2	12.9
Age 26	2,239	100.0	15.2	41.6	22.7	20.5	12.8
Age 27	2,302	100.0	13.5	41.5	22.3	22.7	12.9
Age 28	2,095	100.0	12.9	44.5	21.2	21.4	12.8
Age 29	2,138	100.0	12.9	42.6	22.7	21.8	12.9
Females aged 30 to 34	10,552	100.0	12.4	41.3	22.1	24.2	12.9
Age 30	2,168	100.0	13.0	40.3	23.8	22.9	12.9
Age 31	2,132	100.0	12.4	43.7	21.1	22.7	12.9
Age 32	2,071	100.0	12.1	43.4	20.9	23.7	12.9
Age 33	2,174	100.0	11.2	41.1	23.2	24.5	12.9
Age 34	2,007	100.0	13.5	37.9	21.4	27.2	13.0

Source: Educational Attainment in the United States: March 1987 and 1986, Bureau of the Census, Current Population Reports, Series P-20, No. 428

Note: Numbers may not add to total due to rounding.

Sex, Race, and Ethnicity

EDUCATIONAL ATTAINMENT
25–34

FALLING BEHIND

Although this age group has the second highest proportion of people with four or more years of college (24 percent for 25-to-34-year-olds versus 27 percent for 35-to-44-year-olds), the educational attainment of whites, blacks, and Hispanics is very different.

(years of school completed by persons aged 25 and older and those aged 25 to 34, by sex, race, and Hispanic origin, numbers in thousands)

	number	total	not high school graduate	high school graduate	1 to 3 years of college	4 or more years of college
All persons aged 25 and older	149,144	100.0%	24.4%	38.7%	17.1%	19.9%
White	129,170	100.0	23.0	39.2	17.2	20.5
Black	15,580	100.0	36.6	37.1	15.7	10.7
Hispanic origin	9,449	100.0	49.1	29.0	13.3	8.6
All persons aged 25 to 34	42,635	100.0	13.5	41.1	21.5	23.9
White	35,888	100.0	12.8	41.0	21.2	25.1
Black	5,196	100.0	18.4	46.7	22.7	12.3
Hispanic origin	3,613	100.0	39.6	33.2	17.4	9.8
Males aged 25 and older	70,677	100.0	24.0	35.4	17.1	23.6
White	61,678	100.0	22.7	35.6	17.2	24.5
Black	6,919	100.0	37.0	36.5	15.5	11.0
Hispanic origin	4,614	100.0	48.2	28.0	14.2	9.7
Males aged 25 to 34	21,142	100.0	14.0	40.4	20.7	24.9
White	18,017	100.0	13.6	39.8	20.4	26.2
Black	2,393	100.0	16.8	49.6	21.5	12.1
Hispanic origin	1,859	100.0	40.6	32.1	17.4	10.0
Females aged 25 and older	78,467	100.0	24.7	41.6	17.1	16.5
White	67,492	100.0	23.3	42.6	17.3	16.9
Black	8,661	100.0	36.2	37.5	15.8	10.4
Hispanic origin	4,835	100.0	50.0	30.0	12.5	7.5
Females aged 25 to 34	21,494	100.0	13.0	41.8	22.2	22.9
White	17,871	100.0	11.9	42.1	21.9	24.0
Black	2,803	100.0	19.6	44.2	23.7	12.6
Hispanic origin	1,754	100.0	38.9	34.3	17.3	9.5

Source: Educational Attainment in the United States: March 1987 and March 1986, Bureau of the Census, Current Population Reports, Series P-20, No. 428

Note: Hispanics are of any race. Numbers may not add to total due to rounding.

Householders

EDUCATIONAL ATTAINMENT
25–34

HEAD OF THE CLASS

This age group has the highest proportion of highly educated householders. Twenty-two percent of male and female householders aged 25 to 34 completed at least one year of college. Another 27 percent of the men and 24 percent of the women finished four or more years of college.

(years of school completed by householders aged 25 to 34, by sex, race, and Hispanic origin, numbers in thousands)

	number	total	not high school graduate	high school graduate	1 to 3 years of college	4 or more years of college	median years
Male householders	14,821	100.0%	11.8%	39.7%	21.5%	27.0%	13.0
White	13,147	100.0	11.8	39.3	21.2	27.7	13.0
Black	1,240	100.0	13.0	47.7	23.7	15.4	12.8
Hispanic origin	1,131	100.0	39.9	30.9	18.4	10.9	12.3
Female householders	5,682	100.0	16.1	37.8	22.0	24.0	12.9
White	4,195	100.0	13.8	36.7	21.6	27.9	13.0
Black	1,300	100.0	23.9	43.4	22.8	9.8	12.6
Hispanic origin	519	100.0	39.7	33.9	17.9	8.7	12.3

Source: Educational Attainment in the United States: March 1987 and March 1986, *Bureau of the Census, Current Population Reports, Series P-20, No. 428*

Note: Hispanics are of any race. Numbers may not add to total due to rounding.

Labor Force Status

LABOR FORCE
25-34

TOP LABOR FORCE PARTICIPATION

No other age group can top the 95 percent labor force participation of men aged 25 to 34 and 35 to 44. Among women, 72 percent of those aged 25 to 34 are labor force participants, a proportion bested only by 35-to-44-year-old women. Black 25-to-34-year-old women are more likely to be in the labor force than white women of the same age.

(labor force status of all persons aged 16 and older, aged 18 to 64, and those aged 25 to 34, by sex and race, numbers in thousands)

	total population	total in labor force	percent of population in labor force	number employed	number unemployed	percent of labor force unemployed	not in labor force
Males aged 16 and older	**86,899**	**66,207**	**76.2%**	**62,107**	**4,101**	**6.2%**	**20,692**
White	75,189	57,779	76.8	54,647	3,132	5.4	17,410
Black	9,128	6,486	71.1	5,661	826	12.7	2,642
Males aged 18 to 64	**71,443**	**62,563**	**87.6**	**58,864**	**3,699**	**5.9**	**8,880**
White	61,583	54,522	88.5	51,705	2,818	5.2	7,061
Black	7,615	6,179	81.1	5,427	750	12.1	1,437
Males aged 25 to 34	**20,781**	**19,656**	**94.6**	**18,487**	**1,169**	**5.9**	**1,125**
White	17,754	16,963	95.5	16,084	879	5.2	792
Black	2,320	2,074	89.4	1,821	253	12.2	246
Females aged 16 and older	**95,853**	**53,658**	**56.0%**	**50,334**	**3,324**	**6.2%**	**42,195**
White	81,769	45,510	55.7	43,142	2,369	5.2	36,258
Black	11,224	6,507	58.0	5,648	858	13.2	4,717
Females aged 18 to 64	**75,700**	**50,799**	**67.1**	**47,801**	**3,000**	**5.9**	**24,901**
White	63,964	42,999	67.2	40,878	2,120	4.9	20,965
Black	9,262	6,227	67.2	5,438	791	12.7	3,035
Females aged 25 to 34	**21,516**	**15,577**	**72.4**	**14,617**	**960**	**6.2**	**5,938**
White	17,913	12,993	72.5	12,345	648	5.0	4,920
Black	2,819	2,073	73.5	1,793	280	13.5	746

Source: Annual averages from Employment and Earnings, 1987, *Bureau of Labor Statistics*

Note: The population here includes all civilian, noninstitutionalized people aged 16 and older.

Extent of Employment

LABOR FORCE
25–34

HIGH EMPLOYMENT

Full-time employment is the norm for workers aged 25 to 34—94 percent of the men and 76 percent of the women who work are at it full time. Among those full-time workers, 75 percent of the women and 80 percent of the men work year-round.

(work experience in 1987 of workers aged 16 and older and aged 25 to 34, by sex, numbers in thousands)

	\multicolumn{4}{c	}{worked at full-time jobs}	\multicolumn{4}{c	}{worked at part-time jobs}	non-workers
	total	50-52 weeks	27-49 weeks	1-26 weeks	total	50-52 weeks	27-49 weeks	1-26 weeks	total
Males									
Aged 16 and older	59,740	47,106	7,489	5,143	9,280	3,175	2,165	3,940	18,582
Aged 25 to 34	18,518	14,899	2,479	1,139	1,196	453	361	382	1,192
Females									
Aged 16 and older	40,398	29,882	5,788	4,727	18,538	7,774	4,301	6,463	37,580
Aged 25 to 34	12,747	9,569	1,866	1,313	3,937	1,594	1,008	1,335	4,965

Source: The 1988 Current Population Survey, Bureau of Labor Statistics

Note: Numbers may not add to total due to rounding. The categories in this table are not mutually exclusive. Workers may, for example, be counted as both a full-time and a part-time worker if they held jobs of both kinds during the year. For this reason, the total number of workers will be higher and the number of nonworkers lower than in the previous table that uses annual averages of the number of workers in each category. Civilians only.

Kinds of Jobs

LABOR FORCE
25–34

AVERAGE WORKERS

Like workers in general, 25 percent of employed 25-to-34-year-olds hold managerial and professional jobs, while 31 percent are in technical, sales, and administrative support work.

(occupations of employed persons aged 16 and older and those aged 25 to 34, by sex, numbers in thousands)

	aged 16+	aged 25-34	males aged 25-34	females aged 25-34	percent aged 16+	percent aged 25-34
All employed persons	112,440	33,105	18,488	14,617	100.0%	100.0%
Managerial and professional	27,742	8,295	4,248	4,047	24.7	25.1
Executive, administrative and managerial ...	13,316	3,748	2,101	1,647	11.8	11.3
Officials & administrators, public admin.	549	91	45	46	0.5	0.3
Other executive, admin., & managerial	9,190	2,422	1,484	938	8.2	7.3
Management-related occupations	3,577	1,235	572	663	3.2	3.7
Professional specialty occupations	14,426	4,546	2,146	2,400	12.8	13.7
Engineers	1,731	578	518	60	1.5	1.7
Math & computer scientists	685	266	167	99	0.6	0.8
Natural scientists	388	144	101	43	0.3	0.4
Health diagnosing occupations	793	213	156	57	0.7	0.6
Health assessment & treating	2,148	838	118	720	1.9	2.5
Teachers, college & university	661	144	87	57	0.6	0.4
Teachers, except college & university	3,587	962	232	730	3.2	2.9
Lawyers & judges	707	241	170	71	0.6	0.7
Other professional specialty occupations .	3,727	1,161	598	563	3.3	3.5
Technical, sales, administrative support	35,082	10,335	3,812	6,523	31.2	31.2
Technicians & related support occupations .	3,346	1,340	677	663	3.0	4.0
Health technologists & technicians	1,142	465	86	379	1.0	1.4
Engineering & science technicians	1,100	398	311	87	1.0	1.2
Techs., except health, engineering, science	1,104	478	280	198	1.0	1.4
Sales occupations	13,480	3,623	2,032	1,591	12.0	10.9
Supervisors & proprietors	3,572	1,067	721	346	3.2	3.2
Sales reps., finance & business service	2,330	668	386	282	2.1	2.0

(continued next page)

Almanac of Consumer Markets

Kinds of Jobs

LABOR FORCE 25–34

(continued from previous page)
(occupations of employed persons aged 16 and older and those aged 25 to 34, by sex, numbers in thousands)

	aged 16+	aged 25-34	males aged 25-34	females aged 25-34	percent aged 16+	percent aged 25-34
Sales reps., commodities except retail	1,544	556	444	112	1.4%	1.7%
Sales, retail and personal	5,973	1,318	479	839	5.3	4.0
Sales-related occupations	60	15	4	11	0.1	0.0
Administrative support including clerical	18,256	5,372	1,103	4,269	16.2	16.2
Supervisors	723	200	76	124	0.6	0.6
Computer equipment operators	914	341	123	218	0.8	1.0
Secretaries, stenographers, & typists	5,004	1,424	31	1,393	4.5	4.3
Financial records processing	2,469	721	61	660	2.2	2.2
Mail & message distributing	961	290	163	127	0.9	0.9
Other admin. support including clerical	8,185	2,396	649	1,747	7.3	7.2
Service occupations	15,054	3,808	1,541	2,267	13.4	11.5
Private household	934	145	5	140	0.8	0.4
Protective services	1,907	589	502	87	1.7	1.8
Service, except private hhld. & protective	12,213	3,074	1,034	2,040	10.9	9.3
Food service	5,204	1,225	476	749	4.6	3.7
Health service	1,873	543	64	479	1.7	1.6
Cleaning & building service	2,886	681	402	279	2.6	2.1
Personal service	2,249	624	90	534	2.0	1.9
Precision production, craft, repair	13,568	4,476	4,143	333	12.1	13.5
Mechanics & repairers	4,445	1,461	1,408	53	0.4	4.4
Construction trades	5,011	1,786	1,748	38	4.5	5.4
Other production, craft, repair	4,112	1,229	987	242	3.7	3.7
Operators, fabricators, laborers	17,486	5,339	4,021	1,318	15.6	16.1
Machine operators, assemblers, inspectors	7,994	2,569	1,600	969	7.1	7.8
Transportation, material moving	4,712	1,420	1,300	120	4.2	4.3
Handlers, equip. cleaners, helpers, laborers	4,779	1,351	1,121	230	4.3	4.1
Farming, forestry, fishing	3,507	852	723	129	3.1	2.6
Farm operators & managers	1,317	242	212	30	1.2	0.7
Farm workers & related occupations	2,013	553	457	96	1.8	1.7
Forestry and fishing occupations	177	57	54	3	0.2	0.2

Source: Unpublished annual data for 1987, Bureau of Labor Statistics
Note: Numbers may not add to total due to rounding. Civilian, noninstitutionalized employees only.

Workers in the 1990s

LABOR FORCE
25–34

WOMEN'S RATES CLIMBING

Men aged 25 to 34—like men in general—are less likely to be working in 2000 than in 1990. But the share of 25-to-34-year-old women that will be in the labor force will climb from 75 to 82 percent.

(labor force and labor force participation rates* for persons aged 16 and older and those aged 25 to 34, by sex, race, and ethnicity, in 1990 and 2000, numbers in thousands)

	1990 number	1990 participation rate	2000 number	2000 participation rate	1990-2000 percent change
Both sexes, aged 16 and older	124,457	66.2%	138,775	67.8%	11.5%
White	106,648	66.5	116,701	68.2	9.4
Black	13,788	64.6	16,334	66.0	18.5
Hispanic	9,718	65.9	14,086	67.1	44.9
Asian and other	4,021	64.8	5,740	65.8	42.8
Males, aged 16 and older	67,909	75.8	73,136	74.7	7.7
Males, aged 25 to 34	19,832	94.1	16,559	93.6	-16.5
White	16,991	95.1	13,784	94.8	-18.9
Black	2,177	89.5	2,002	88.9	-8.0
Hispanic	2,069	94.2	2,491	93.7	20.4
Asian and other	664	86.3	773	86.1	16.4
Females, aged 16 and older	56,548	57.4	65,639	61.5	16.1
Females, aged 25 to 34	16,318	75.2	15,098	82.3	-7.5
White	13,591	75.7	12,282	83.6	-9.6
Black	2,191	74.5	2,109	78.0	-3.7
Hispanic	1,224	61.6	1,636	68.1	33.7
Asian and other	536	66.5	707	74.4	31.9

*Labor force participation rates are the ratio of people in the labor force to the total population of a given sex, age and race or ethnicity.

Source: Unpublished data from the Bureau of Labor Statistics

Note: The labor force here includes civilians who are working or looking for work. Hispanics are of any race.

Household Income

INCOME
25–34

ALMOST EQUAL

This age group accounts for 23 percent of all householders and 21 percent of total household income. Income per household member in this age group is $10,600.

(household income and income per household member, for all households and for households by age of householder, numbers for 1988 in thousands, income is for 1987)

	households		persons in household			total household income		
	number	percent	number	percent	persons per household	$ billions	percent	per household member
All households	91,066	100.0%	240,722	100.0%	2.64	$2,927.2	100.0%	$12,160
Age of householder								
under 25	5,228	5.7	12,117	5.0	2.32	102.0	3.5	8,415
25 to 34	20,583	22.6	58,724	24.4	2.85	621.6	21.2	10,586
35 to 44	19,323	21.2	64,351	26.7	3.33	763.8	26.1	11,870
45 to 54	13,630	15.0	41,379	17.2	3.04	597.0	20.4	14,426
55 to 64	12,846	14.1	30,151	12.5	2.35	447.3	15.3	14,835
65 and older	19,456	21.4	33,999	14.1	1.75	395.6	13.5	11,635

Source: The 1988 Current Population Survey, Bureau of the Census

Individual Income

INCOME
25–34

A BALANCING ACT

Compared with all income-producing people, 25-to-34-year-olds are more likely to have incomes between $20,000 and $35,000—a full 34 percent of the men and 18 percent of the women have incomes in that middle range.

(income distribution and median income for males and females aged 15 and older and aged 25 to 34, numbers for 1988 in thousands, income is for 1987)

	males aged 15 and older		males aged 25 to 34	
	number	percent	number	percent
All males	90,284	–	21,321	–
All males with income	85,623	100.0%	20,844	100.0%
Less than $5,000	13,025	15.2	1,762	8.5
$5,000 to $9,999	12,066	14.1	2,239	10.7
$10,000 to $14,999	11,708	13.7	3,171	15.2
$15,000 to $19,999	9,887	11.5	3,164	15.2
$20,000 to $24,999	8,714	10.2	2,905	13.9
$25,000 to $29,999	7,266	8.5	2,369	11.4
$30,000 to $34,999	6,124	7.2	1,866	9.0
$35,000 to $49,999	9,941	11.6	2,419	11.6
$50,000 to $74,999	4,669	5.5	739	3.5
$75,000 and over	2,225	2.6	208	1.0
Median income, all with income		$17,752		$20,112
Median income, year-round, full-time workers		$26,722		$23,804

	females aged 15 and older		females aged 25 to 34	
	number	percent	number	percent
All females	98,168	–	21,649	–
All females with income	89,279	100.0%	20,092	100.0%
Less than $5,000	30,715	34.4	5,616	28.0
$5,000 to $9,999	19,782	22.2	3,577	17.8
$10,000 to $14,999	13,313	14.9	3,532	17.6
$15,000 to $19,999	9,470	10.6	2,942	14.6
$20,000 to $24,999	6,321	7.1	1,955	9.7
$25,000 to $29,999	3,768	4.2	1,076	5.4
$30,000 to $34,999	2,331	2.6	662	3.3
$35,000 to $49,999	2,602	2.9	561	2.8
$50,000 to $74,999	708	0.8	130	0.6
$75,000 and over	268	0.3	41	0.2
Median income, all with income		$8,101		$11,049
Median income, year-round, full-time workers		$17,504		$17,583

Source: Money Income and Poverty Status in the United States: 1987, Bureau of the Census, Current Population Reports, Series P-20, No. 161
Note: Numbers may not add to total due to rounding.

Income and Age

INCOME
25–34

CHUNK OF THE MIDDLE

Compared with other age groups, 25-to-34-year-olds head the largest proportion—31 percent—of households with incomes between $20,000 and $35,000. Of those remaining, an even 34 percent are above and below that range.

(household income by age of householder, numbers for 1988 in thousands, income is for 1987)

	total	under 25	25 to 34	35 to 44	45 to 54	55 to 64	65 to 74	75 +
All households	91,066	5,228	20,583	19,323	13,630	12,846	11,410	8,045
All households	100.0%	100.0%	100.0%	100.0%	100.0%	100.0%	100.0%	100.0%
Less than $10,000	18.4	30.3	13.6	10.3	10.4	17.4	27.1	44.6
$10,000 to $14,999	10.6	15.8	9.6	6.6	6.6	9.5	17.3	18.5
$15,000 to $19,999	10.0	14.1	11.1	7.4	6.8	9.7	13.8	11.8
$20,000 to $24,999	9.2	11.5	11.1	8.3	7.2	9.1	10.1	7.5
$25,000 to $29,999	8.4	9.0	10.6	8.5	7.6	8.0	8.3	4.3
$30,000 to $34,999	7.7	6.8	9.7	9.0	7.8	7.2	6.0	3.2
$35,000 to $39,999	6.8	4.5	8.6	9.0	7.2	6.3	4.2	2.4
$40,000 to $44,999	5.8	2.3	6.7	7.9	7.4	6.0	3.0	1.7
$45,000 to $49,999	4.6	1.3	5.1	6.6	5.9	4.7	2.4	1.5
$50,000 to $59,999	6.7	2.1	6.7	9.6	10.1	7.5	2.7	1.9
$60,000 to $74,999	5.5	1.5	4.2	7.9	9.9	6.3	2.1	1.2
$75,000 and over	6.3	0.9	3.0	8.9	13.1	8.3	3.0	1.4
Median household income	$25,986	$16,204	$26,923	$34,926	$37,250	$27,538	$16,906	$11,261

Source: The 1988 Current Population Survey, Bureau of the Census

Note: Numbers may not add to total due to rounding.

Income of Married Couples

MIDDLE-INCOME FAMILIES

Married couples in this age group who don't have children under age 18 in the home have a median income that is nearly $7,000 greater than the median for those with children. Forty-five percent of married couples aged 25 to 34 have incomes between $20,000 and $40,000.

(household income of married-couple householder families with and without children under 18 at home, householders aged 25 to 34, numbers for 1988 in thousands, income is for 1987)

		married-couple householder aged 25 to 34	
	total	with children under 18 at home	without children under 18 at home
All households	11,638	8,665	2,972
All households	100.0%	100.0%	100.0%
Less than $10,000	5.1	5.7	3.1
$10,000 to $14,999	6.9	7.9	3.9
$15,000 to $19,999	9.0	9.7	6.7
$20,000 to $24,999	10.1	11.0	7.7
$25,000 to $29,999	11.7	12.0	10.9
$30,000 to $34,999	11.5	12.1	9.8
$35,000 to $39,999	11.2	10.8	12.3
$40,000 to $44,999	9.1	8.8	10.1
$45,000 to $49,999	6.7	6.2	7.9
$50,000 to $59,999	9.1	7.6	13.3
$60,000 to $74,999	5.7	4.9	8.2
$75,000 and over	3.9	3.2	6.1
Median household income	$32,813	$31,111	$37,893

Source: The 1988 Current Population Survey, Bureau of the Census

Note: Numbers may not add to total due to rounding.

Income of Other Family Households

INCOME
25–34

MIXED BAG

Twenty-eight percent of male-headed families and 8 percent of female-headed families with householders aged 25 to 34 bring in $35,000 or more. Another 31 percent of the men and 17 percent of the women head households with incomes between $20,000 and $35,000. Households with children under 18 at home have a median income that is substantially less than that of the childless households.

(household income of unmarried female- and male-householder families with and without children under 18 at home, householders aged 25 to 34, numbers for 1988, in thousands, income is for 1987)

	female householder aged 25 to 34			male householder aged 25 to 34		
	total	with children under 18 at home	without children under 18 at home	total	with children under 18 at home	without children under 18 at home
All households	2,736	2,549	187	634	326	308
All households	100.0%	100.0%	100.0%	100.0%	100.0%	100.0%
Less than $10,000	48.9	51.4	15.0	16.6	25.2	7.5
$10,000 to $14,999	15.5	16.1	7.5	9.3	13.2	5.2
$15,000 to $19,999	11.5	11.8	8.0	15.1	14.4	15.9
$20,000 to $24,999	8.4	7.8	16.6	11.7	11.7	11.7
$25,000 to $29,999	5.1	4.7	9.6	11.5	10.7	12.3
$30,000 to $34,999	3.0	2.5	9.6	7.6	4.9	10.4
$35,000 to $39,999	2.0	1.5	8.6	7.6	6.7	8.4
$40,000 to $44,999	1.6	1.3	5.3	4.7	4.6	5.2
$45,000 to $49,999	0.8	0.5	4.3	5.5	3.7	7.5
$50,000 to $59,999	1.5	1.0	7.5	5.2	2.8	7.8
$60,000 to $74,999	1.1	1.0	2.7	2.7	1.2	4.2
$75,000 and over	0.6	0.2	5.3	2.7	0.9	4.5
Median household income	$10,289	$9,469	$27,122	$23,010	$18,903	$28,269

Source: The 1988 Current Population Survey, Bureau of the Census

Note: Numbers may not add to total due to rounding.

Income of Nonfamily Households

INCOME 25–34

MOVING ON UP

The median household income of nonfamily households headed by members of this age group is $8,000 more than that of nonfamily households in general. Only nonfamilies headed by 35- to-44-year-olds have a higher median income than these households.

(household income of nonfamily households by household type, householders aged 25 to 34, numbers for 1988 in thousands, income is for 1987)

	total number	living alone — total	living alone — male householder	living alone — female householder	living with others — total	living with others — male householder	living with others — female householder
All nonfamily households	5,575	4,019	2,369	1,650	1,556	1,041	515
All nonfamily households	100.0%	100.0%	100.0%	100.0%	100.0%	100.0%	100.0%
Less than $10,000	13.7	16.5	16.4	16.6	6.4	6.6	6.0
$10,000 to $14,999	12.4	14.9	15.4	14.1	6.2	6.0	6.8
$15,000 to $19,999	14.8	17.4	16.3	19.0	8.2	9.2	6.2
$20,000 to $24,999	14.5	16.2	15.2	17.7	9.8	10.2	9.3
$25,000 to $29,999	10.8	11.3	11.1	11.6	9.5	8.9	10.7
$30,000 to $34,999	9.4	9.3	8.5	10.5	9.8	8.1	13.2
$35,000 to $39,999	6.5	5.9	6.7	4.7	8.0	8.1	8.0
$40,000 to $44,999	4.4	3.5	4.1	2.5	6.9	7.3	6.2
$45,000 to $49,999	3.8	1.7	2.1	1.3	9.3	8.9	10.1
$50,000 to $59,999	4.3	1.7	2.1	1.0	11.2	10.4	12.6
$60,000 to $74,999	2.8	1.0	1.4	0.4	7.5	7.8	7.0
$75,000 and over	2.4	0.6	0.8	0.5	7.1	8.6	3.9
Median household income	$22,694	$20,035	$20,076	$19,985	$34,952	$35,495	$33,918

Source: The 1988 Current Population Survey, Bureau of the Census

Note: Nonfamilies are either people living alone or living with an individual (or individuals) unrelated to the householder. Numbers may not add to total due to rounding.

Income and Race, Families

INCOME
25–34

MAJOR GAP

At $15,300, the median household income of black families with a householder aged 25 to 34 is only half that of white families. Married couples of both races are better off than are other types of families. Sixty-one percent of white couples and 57 percent of black couples with a householder in this age group have household incomes between $20,000 and $50,000.

(household income of family households by race and household type for householders aged 25 to 34, numbers for 1988 in thousands, income is for 1987)

white family households

	total	married couple	male householder	female householder
All households	12,547	10,353	513	1,681
Total	100.0%	100.0%	100.0%	100.0%
Less than $10,000	10.2	4.4	16.4	44.3
$10,000 to $19,999	17.6	14.8	25.7	32.5
$20,000 to $29,999	21.2	22.0	24.2	15.0
$30,000 to $39,999	20.2	23.0	16.2	4.3
$40,000 to $49,999	13.9	16.2	8.4	1.7
$50,000 to $59,999	8.2	9.5	4.9	1.5
$60,000 to $74,999	5.0	6.0	1.9	0.4
$75,000 and over	3.5	4.0	1.9	0.4
Median household income	$30,403	$33,599	$22,368	$11,308

black family households

	total	married couple	male householder	female householder
All households	1,984	920	87	977
Total	100.0%	100.0%	100.0%	100.0%
Less than $10,000	38.0	9.7	31.0	65.4
$10,000 to $19,999	23.3	24.9	35.6	20.9
$20,000 to $29,999	16.7	23.8	18.4	9.7
$30,000 to $39,999	11.4	21.0	4.6	3.1
$40,000 to $49,999	5.9	12.2	2.3	0.4
$50,000 to $59,999	2.1	4.1	3.4	0.1
$60,000 to $74,999	1.3	2.1	3.4	0.3
$75,000 and over	1.2	2.3	2.3	0.1
Median household income	$15,313	$25,713	$15,549	$7,303

Source: Money Income of Households, Families, and Persons in the United States: 1987, Bureau of the Census, Current Population Reports, Series P-60, No. 162
Note: Numbers may not add to total due to rounding.

Income and Race, Nonfamilies

INCOME
25–34

PULLING AHEAD

At $21,400, white male householders aged 25 to 34 have the highest median householder income in this age group. White female householders follow with a median income of $19,800. Twenty-five percent of these white householders and 10 percent of their black counterparts have an income of $30,000 or more.

(householder income of nonfamily householders by race and household type for householders aged 25 to 34, numbers for 1988 in thousands, income is for 1987)

	white householder			black householder		
	total	male householder	female householder	total	male householder	female householder
All householders	4,817	2,931	1,887	608	368	241
Total	100.0%	100.0%	100.0%	100.0%	100.0%	100.0%
Less than $10,000	15.6	15.1	16.2	31.6	31.3	31.5
$10,000 to $19,999	31.4	29.3	34.6	34.9	38.0	29.5
$20,000 to $24,999	16.4	16.4	16.4	19.1	14.1	26.6
$25,000 to $29,999	11.8	11.3	12.5	5.4	6.8	3.3
$30,000 to $34,999	9.7	9.7	9.8	4.4	4.3	4.6
$35,000 to $49,999	11.3	13.3	8.2	4.6	4.3	5.0
$50,000 and over	3.8	4.9	2.2	0.5	0.8	–
Median householder income	$20,718	$21,382	$19,778	$15,063	$14,260	$16,158

Source: Money Income of Households, Families, and Persons in the United States: 1987, *Bureau of the Census, Current Population Reports, Series P-60, No. 162*

Note: Numbers may not add to total due to rounding. Householder income is the total money income of the householder only.

Income of Hispanic Households

INCOME
25–34

NECK AND NECK

The median income of Hispanic family households headed by 25-to-34-year-olds ($20,100) falls between that of white ($30,400) and black ($15,300) family households, and the same is true for nonfamilies in this age group.

(household income of Hispanic households, by household type, for householders aged 25 to 34, numbers for 1988 in thousands, income is for 1987)

family households

	total	married couple	male householder	female householder
All households	1,435	1,028	91	316
Total	100.0%	100.0%	100.0%	100.0%
less than $15,000	38.5	29.1	28.6	72.2
$15,000 to $24,999	21.0	21.7	28.6	16.5
$25,000 and over	40.6	49.2	42.9	11.4
Median household income	$20,091	$24,041	$22,285	$7,922

nonfamily households

	total	male householder living alone	male householder living with others	female householder living alone	female householder living with others
All households	301	112	87	70	32
Total	100.0%	100.0%	100.0%	100.0%	100.0%
less than $15,000	37.9	41.1	25.3	45.7	43.8
$15,000 to $24,999	27.6	31.3	29.9	27.1	6.3
$25,000 and over	34.9	26.8	46.0	27.1	50.0
Median household income	$20,061	$17,981	$21,820	–	–

Source: The 1988 Current Population Survey, Bureau of the Census

Note: Numbers may not add to total due to rounding. Hispanics are of any race. Median income is unreliable and is therefore not given when the category contains fewer than 75,000 households.

Income of Dual-Earner Couples

INCOME
25–34

TWO-THIRDS DUAL EARNERS

Sixty-four percent of married couples in this age group are dual earners, with a median household income of $36,400. Thirty-two percent of them bring in between $35,000 and $50,000, and another 23 percent have household incomes of $50,000 or more.

(household income for all dual-earner married couples and for those with married-couple householders aged 25 to 34, numbers for 1988 in thousands, income is for 1987)

	householder all ages			householder aged 25 to 34		
	total	with children under 18 at home	without children under 18 at home	total	with children under 18 at home	without children under 18 at home
All households	26,227	14,989	11,238	7,458	5,022	2,435
All households	100.0%	100.0%	100.0%	100.0%	100.0%	100.0%
Less than $15,000	5.7	6.0	5.4	7.1	8.4	4.3
$15,000 to $19,999	5.1	5.4	4.7	6.5	7.4	4.7
$20,000 to $24,999	7.3	7.8	6.6	9.3	10.3	7.1
$25,000 to $29,999	8.3	9.0	7.5	11.4	12.0	10.3
$30,000 to $34,999	9.4	10.2	8.3	11.6	12.8	9.2
$35,000 to $39,999	10.3	11.2	9.0	12.8	12.7	12.9
$40,000 to $44,999	9.6	9.8	9.3	10.7	10.6	11.0
$45,000 to $49,999	8.1	8.2	7.9	8.1	7.8	8.6
$50,000 to $59,999	13.0	12.5	13.6	11.1	9.1	15.2
$60,000 to $74,999	11.2	10.2	12.5	7.0	5.7	9.7
$75,000 and over	12.1	9.6	15.3	4.5	3.3	6.9
Median household income	$41,904	$40,044	$44,508	$36,356	$34,659	$40,185

Source: The 1988 Current Population Survey, Bureau of the Census

Note: Numbers may not add to total due to rounding.

Income and Education

INCOME
25–34

DIRECT CONNECTION

The more college a 25-to-34-year-old householder has completed, the higher his or her household income is likely to be. Fourteen percent of those with one to three years of college, and a full 28 percent of the group that completed four or more years have household incomes of $50,000 or more.

(household income of householders aged 25 to 34 by years of school completed by householder, numbers for 1988 in thousands, income is for 1987)

	total	not high school graduate	high school graduate	1 to 3 years of college	4 or more years of college
All households	20,583	2,759	8,200	4,266	5,356
All households	100.0%	100.0%	100.0%	100.0%	100.0%
Less than $10,000	13.6	34.6	14.5	9.5	4.6
$10,000 to $19,999	20.7	28.6	24.4	20.0	11.3
$20,000 to $29,999	21.7	19.0	23.3	23.2	19.6
$30,000 to $39,999	18.3	11.4	18.8	20.4	19.5
$40,000 to $49,999	11.8	4.1	10.8	12.8	16.6
$50,000 to $59,999	6.7	1.2	4.9	7.9	11.1
$60,000 to $74,999	4.2	0.7	2.2	4.5	9.0
$75,000 and over	3.0	0.5	1.1	1.8	8.3

Source: The 1988 Current Population Survey, Bureau of the Census.

Note: Numbers may not add to total due to rounding.

Future Income

INCOME
25–34

AFFLUENCE PREVAILS

Although the number of households headed by 25-to-34-year-olds will decline between 1990 and 1995, the good news is that more of them will have incomes between $50,000 and $60,000. The biggest drop will be in the number of households with household incomes under $20,000.

(projections of the number of households with householders aged 25 to 34, by household income, 1990 and 1995, numbers in thousands, income is in 1985 dollars)

	1990 number	1990 percent	1995 number	1995 percent	percent change 1990-1995
All households	21,183	100.0%	19,927	100.0%	-5.9%
Less than $10,000	3,072	14.5	2,826	14.2	-8.0
$10,000 to $19,999	4,921	23.2	4,493	22.5	-8.7
$20,000 to $29,999	5,389	25.4	4,990	25.0	-7.4
$30,000 to $39,999	3,822	18.0	3,670	18.4	-4.0
$40,000 to $49,999	2,069	9.8	2,011	10.1	-2.8
$50,000 to $59,999	943	4.5	981	4.9	4.0
$60,000 to $74,999	530	2.5	524	2.6	-1.1
$75,000 and over	436	2.1	435	2.2	-0.2
Median household income	$24,823		$25,300		

Source: American Demographics, *May to August, 1986, based on the national econometric model of Wharton Economic Forecasting Association and on household projections from the Bureau of the Census*

Note: Numbers may not add to total due to rounding.

Annual Expenditures

EXPENDITURES
25–34

ONE-THIRD FOR HOUSING

One-third of all the dollars spent by households headed by a 25-to-34-year-old go to housing. This is the age group with the largest chunk of their spending dollar devoted to housing.

(average annual expenditure and percent distribution of expenditures for all households and for householders aged 25 to 34, number of households in thousands)

	all households		householder aged 25 to 34	
	average annual expenditure	percent of all expenditures	average annual expenditure	percent of all expenditures
Number of households	93,741		21,733	
Total expenditure	$22,710	100.0%	$22,500	100.0%
Food	3,363	14.8	3,117	13.9
Food at home	2,313	10.2	2,116	9.4
Food away from home	1,049	4.6	1,001	4.4
Alcoholic beverages	273	1.2	354	1.6
Housing	6,888	30.3	7,473	33.2
Shelter	3,986	17.6	4,588	20.4
Owned dwellings	2,305	10.1	2,375	10.6
Mortgage interest and charges	1,428	6.3	1,854	8.2
Property taxes	417	1.8	225	1.0
Maintenance, repairs, insurance, and other expenses	460	2.0	297	1.3
Rented dwellings	1,269	5.6	1,965	8.7
Other lodging	412	1.8	247	1.1
Fuels, utilities, and public services	1,646	7.2	1,510	6.7
Natural gas	248	1.1	217	1.0
Electricity	674	3.0	616	2.7
Fuel oil and other fuels	107	0.5	76	0.3
Telephone	471	2.1	484	2.2
Water and other public services	145	0.6	117	0.5
Household operations	353	1.6	454	2.0
Domestic services	288	1.3	399	1.8
Other household expenses	65	0.3	55	0.2
Household furnishings, equipment	903	4.0	921	4.1
Household textiles	83	0.4	67	0.3
Furniture	303	1.3	354	1.6
Floor coverings	51	0.2	34	0.2
Major appliances	155	0.7	150	0.7

(continued next page)

Annual Expenditures

EXPENDITURES 25–34

(continued from previous page)

(average annual expenditure and percent distribution of expenditures for all households and for householders aged 25 to 34, number of households in thousands)

	all households		householder aged 25 to 34	
	average annual expenditure	percent of all expenditures	average annual expenditure	percent of all expenditures
Small appliances, miscellaneous housewares	55	0.2	43	0.2
Miscellaneous household equipment	256	1.1	274	1.2
Apparel	**1,149**	**5.1**	**1,161**	**5.2**
Men and boys	283	1.2	284	1.3
Men, 16 and over	228	1.0	223	1.0
Boys, 2 to 15	55	0.2	61	0.3
Women and girls	462	2.0	406	1.8
Women, 16 and over	396	1.7	331	1.5
Girls, 2 to 15	66	0.3	74	0.3
Children under 2	45	0.2	81	0.4
Footwear	123	0.5	119	0.5
Other apparel products and services	237	1.0	273	1.2
Transportation	**4,815**	**21.2**	**5,051**	**22.4**
Cars and trucks, new (net outlay)	1,414	6.2	1,498	6.7
Cars and trucks, used (net outlay)	897	3.9	1,054	4.7
Other vehicles	29	0.1	34	0.2
Vehicle finance charges	270	1.2	321	1.4
Gasoline and motor oil	916	4.0	919	4.1
Maintenance and repairs	458	2.0	442	2.0
Vehicle insurance	420	1.8	388	1.7
Public transportation	248	1.1	226	1.0
Vehicle rental, licenses, other charges	163	0.7	169	0.8
Health care	**1,062**	**4.7**	**686**	**3.0**
Health insurance	371	1.6	231	1.0
Medical services	502	2.2	367	1.6
Medicines and medical supplies	189	0.8	89	0.4
Entertainment	**1,087**	**4.8**	**1,101**	**4.9**
Fees and admissions	308	1.4	276	1.2
Television, radios, sound equipment	373	1.6	386	1.7
Other equipment and services	406	1.8	439	2.0
Personal care	207	0.9	177	0.8
Reading	140	0.6	124	0.6
Education	298	1.3	186	0.8
Tobacco and smoking supplies	230	1.0	231	1.0
Miscellaneous	323	1.4	305	1.4
Contributions and support payments	746	3.3	345	1.5
Personal insurance and pensions	**2,129**	**9.4**	**2,190**	**9.7**
Life insurance and other personal insurance	293	1.3	223	1.0
Retirement, pensions, Social Security	1,836	8.1	1,967	8.7

Source: The 1986 Consumer Expenditure Survey, Bureau of Labor Statistics

Expenditures by Income

EXPENDITURES
25–34

WHERE THE MONEY GOES

Although expenditures of households in this age group tend to rise along with income, there are exceptions—the amount spent on rent, for instance, peaks among households with incomes of $15,000 to $20,000. Food takes a smaller chunk out of the budgets of high-income than low-income households, but households at the high end devote 40 percent of their food budget to food away from home while those at the low end use only 22 percent of their food budget in this way.

(annual average expenditure of households with householders aged 25 to 34, by household income, number of households in thousands)

	all households	under $10,000	$10-14,999	$15-19,999	$20-29,999	$30-39,999	$40,000+
Number of households	19,249	3,603	2,480	2,324	4,483	3,003	3,357
Total expenditure	$22,667	$12,390	$14,826	$17,430	$22,184	$27,529	$39,422
Food	3,114	2,342	2,385	2,600	3,024	3,538	4,580
Food at home	2,087	1,825	1,714	1,742	2,017	2,358	2,731
Food away from home	1,028	517	672	857	1,008	1,180	1,849
Alcoholic beverages	357	213	263	334	361	387	566
Housing	7,448	4,364	4,916	5,732	7,116	8,757	13,093
Shelter	4,569	2,665	2,994	3,576	4,405	5,240	8,085
Owned dwellings	2,412	618	721	989	2,008	3,319	6,304
Rented dwellings	1,913	1,960	2,182	2,418	2,171	1,652	1,206
Other lodging	244	88	92	169	226	270	575
Fuels, utilities, public services	1,478	1,106	1,174	1,287	1,468	1,730	2,024
Household operations	459	193	285	267	416	590	947
Household furnishings, equipment	942	400	463	602	827	1,196	2,038
Apparel and services	1,191	622	713	897	1,140	1,343	2,291
Transportation	4,955	2,706	3,155	3,915	5,117	6,153	8,130
Vehicles	2,405	1,404	1,303	1,746	2,412	2,997	4,213
Gasoline and motor oil	975	599	794	890	1,053	1,200	1,267
Other vehicle expenses	1,325	548	867	1,078	1,438	1,761	2,130
Public transportation	249	155	192	202	216	193	520
Health care	707	353	555	526	787	819	1,121
Entertainment	1,181	520	733	902	1,099	1,545	2,200
Personal care	171	100	118	137	167	204	284

(continued next page)

Expenditures by Income

EXPENDITURES 25–34

(continued from previous page)

(annual average expenditure of households with householders aged 25 to 34, by household income, number of households in thousands)

	all households	under $10,000	$10-14,999	$15-19,999	$20-29,999	$30-39,999	$40,000+
Reading	129	62	83	107	128	148	238
Education	195	199	238	97	210	147	246
Tobacco and smoking supplies	227	234	251	202	222	242	214
Miscellaneous	314	189	209	250	286	445	490
Cash contributions	357	93	178	268	316	627	649
Personal insurance and pensions	2,320	392	1,029	1,463	2,209	3,174	5,321
Life and other insurance	226	95	143	148	225	309	408
Retirement, pensions, Social Security	2,094	297	886	1,315	1,984	2,864	4,912

Source: The 1986 Consumer Expenditure Survey, Bureau of Labor Statistics

Note: All households include complete income reporters only. Total expenditure exceeds total income in some income categories due to a number of factors including the underreporting of income, borrowing, and the use of savings.

Weekly Shopping

EXPENDITURES
25–34

AVERAGE SHOPPERS

The weekly food purchases of householders aged 25 to 34 are close to the average for all households—they spend just 1 percent less than households in general. But their expenditure on alcoholic beverages is 34 percent above average.

(average weekly expenditure for all households and for householders aged 25 to 34)

	all households	index all households	householders aged 25 to 34	index householders aged 25 to 34
Food, total	$59.60	100	$59.01	99
Food at home, total	**37.73**	**100**	**35.63**	**94**
Cereals and cereal products	1.78	100	1.71	96
Bakery products	3.51	100	3.21	91
Beef	3.63	100	3.28	90
Pork	2.23	100	1.94	87
Other meats	1.52	100	1.39	91
Poultry	1.64	100	1.60	98
Fish and seafood	1.22	100	1.04	85
Eggs	0.57	100	0.51	89
Fresh milk and cream	2.35	100	2.41	103
Other dairy products	2.47	100	2.33	94
Fresh fruits	1.96	100	1.66	85
Fresh vegetables	1.77	100	1.54	87
Processed fruits	1.38	100	1.28	93
Processed vegetables	1.03	100	0.99	96
Sugar and other sweets	1.42	100	1.30	92
Fats and oils	0.99	100	0.88	89
Miscellaneous foods	4.53	100	5.14	113
Nonalcoholic beverages	3.71	100	3.43	92
Food away from home	**21.87**	**100**	**23.37**	**107**
Nonfood items				
Alcoholic beverages	4.84	100	6.48	134
Tobacco products and smoking supplies	3.60	100	3.71	103
Pet food	1.09	100	1.10	101
Personal care products and services	5.01	100	4.68	93
Non-prescription drugs and supplies	2.31	100	1.54	67
Housekeeping supplies	6.07	100	5.56	92

Source: The 1986 Consumer Expenditure Survey, Bureau of Labor Statistics

Note: An index of 100 represents the average. An index of 132 means that the average weekly expenditure of the subgroup is 32 percent above the average for all households. An index of 68 indicates spending that is 32 percent below average. Numbers may not add to total due to rounding.

Future Expenditures

EXPENDITURES
25–34

SPENDING $72 BILLION LESS

These households will be spending an estimated 72 billion dollars less in 2000 than in 1990. This spending drop is due to the 15 percent decline in the number of households headed by 25-to-34-year-olds during the decade.

(projected aggregate expenditures in 1990 and 2000 for all households and for households by age of householder, in billions of dollars)

	all households	under 25	25-34	35-44	45-54	55-64	65-74	75+
			1990 aggregate annual expenditures in billions					
Number of households (in thousands)	94,227	4,663	21,183	21,245	14,429	12,311	11,672	8,724
Total expenditures (in billions of dollars)	$2,203.1	$64.2	$476.6	$628.6	$441.2	$292.8	$197.2	$102.5
Food	330.8	9.4	70.3	93.7	64.1	43.9	32.3	17.2
Food at home	225.1	5.9	44.8	64.9	41.8	30.9	23.0	13.7
Food away from home	101.5	3.6	21.2	28.8	22.2	13.0	9.3	3.5
Alcoholic beverages	25.4	1.6	7.5	6.4	4.7	3.0	1.8	0.6
Housing	667.6	19.2	158.3	193.5	121.9	80.8	58.3	35.6
Shelter	385.6	12.4	97.2	115.7	71.7	42.4	28.8	17.5
Owned dwellings	229.7	1.8	50.3	75.8	46.9	28.2	17.9	8.7
Rented dwellings	115.2	9.5	41.6	27.6	13.1	8.4	7.2	7.6
Other lodging	40.8	1.0	5.2	12.2	11.6	5.8	3.7	1.2
Fuels, utilities, and public services	160.0	3.7	32.0	41.2	29.6	23.2	18.6	11.8
Household operations	34.2	0.7	9.6	10.2	3.8	3.7	2.9	3.3
Household furnishings, equipment	87.8	2.4	19.5	26.5	16.8	11.6	8.0	3.0
Apparel and services	111.0	4.1	24.6	33.7	22.8	13.8	8.3	3.6
Transportation	464.9	15.6	107.0	130.7	98.7	61.1	37.7	14.2
Health care	103.7	1.6	14.5	21.4	16.9	16.0	17.9	15.4
Entertainment	106.0	3.1	23.3	35.2	20.6	13.0	8.0	2.6
Personal care	20.1	0.6	3.7	5.2	3.8	3.1	2.3	1.3
Reading	13.6	0.3	2.6	3.8	2.6	1.9	1.6	0.8
Education	27.6	2.7	3.9	8.3	8.8	2.9	0.8	0.1
Tobacco and smoking supplies	22.0	0.8	4.9	5.8	4.5	3.3	2.0	0.7
Miscellaneous	31.5	0.6	6.5	8.1	5.9	4.5	3.6	2.3
Contributions and support payments	74.2	0.7	7.3	17.7	17.4	12.9	12.5	5.7
Personal insurance and pensions	208.9	3.9	46.4	65.2	48.5	32.6	10.0	2.3

(continued next page)

Future Expenditures

EXPENDITURES
25–34

(continued from previous page)

(projected aggregate expenditures in 2000 for all households and for households by age of householder, in billions of dollars)

	\multicolumn{8}{c}{**2000 aggregate annual expenditures in billions**}
	all households	under 25	25-34	35-44	45-54	55-64	65-74	75+
Number of households (in thousands)	105,933	4,442	18,004	25,339	21,603	13,903	11,516	11,126
Total expenditures (in billions of dollars)	$2,532.4	$61.1	$405.1	$749.7	$660.6	$330.6	$194.6	$130.7
Food	379.7	9.0	59.7	111.7	95.9	49.5	31.9	22.0
Food at home	258.9	5.6	38.1	77.4	62.6	34.9	22.7	17.5
Food away from home	117.2	3.4	18.0	34.3	33.2	14.7	9.1	4.5
Alcoholic beverages	28.3	1.5	6.4	7.6	7.0	3.4	1.7	0.7
Housing	760.3	18.3	134.5	230.8	182.5	91.3	57.5	45.3
Shelter	438.2	11.8	82.6	137.9	107.3	47.9	28.4	22.3
Owned dwellings	265.8	1.7	42.8	90.4	70.3	31.9	17.6	11.1
Rented dwellings	123.4	9.1	35.4	32.9	19.7	9.5	7.2	9.7
Other lodging	49.1	0.9	4.4	14.6	17.4	6.5	3.7	1.5
Fuels, utilities, and public services	183.6	3.5	27.2	49.1	44.3	26.2	18.3	15.0
Household operations	38.0	0.7	8.2	12.2	5.7	4.1	2.9	4.2
Household furnishings, equipment	100.5	2.3	16.6	31.6	25.2	13.1	7.9	3.8
Apparel and services	127.6	3.9	20.9	40.2	34.2	15.6	8.2	4.6
Transportation	533.7	14.8	90.9	155.9	147.7	69.0	37.2	18.1
Health care	120.0	1.5	12.4	25.5	25.3	18.1	17.7	19.6
Entertainment	121.7	3.0	19.8	42.0	30.9	14.7	7.9	3.3
Personal care	23.1	0.5	3.2	6.2	5.7	3.5	2.3	1.7
Reading	15.7	0.3	2.2	4.5	3.9	2.2	1.6	1.0
Education	33.2	2.6	3.3	10.0	13.1	3.3	0.8	0.2
Tobacco and smoking supplies	25.2	0.8	4.2	6.9	6.8	3.7	2.0	0.9
Miscellaneous	36.2	0.6	5.5	9.7	8.9	5.0	3.5	2.9
Contributions and support payments	88.2	0.6	6.2	21.1	26.0	14.5	12.3	7.3
Personal insurance and pensions	243.2	3.7	39.4	77.7	72.7	36.8	9.9	2.9

Source: *The 1986 Consumer Expenditure Survey, Bureau of Labor Statistics* and *Projections of the Number of Households and Families:1986 to 2000, Bureau of the Census, Series P-25, No. 986*

Note: Aggregate expenditures are the sum of the total expenditures of all households in the nation or of all households in an age group. Projections are based on the average annual expenditures in 1986 and have not been adjusted for inflation. Projections show how total annual expenditures would change as the number of households in the age group changes during the 1990s. All other factors such as price and expenditure pattern are held constant and are not accounted for in these projections.

Composition of Wealth

EARLY INVESTMENTS

Although they account for 21 percent of all household income, households headed by people aged 35 and under have only about 7 percent of all household wealth. A larger proportion of these households own automobiles (88 percent) and have employer accounts such as profit sharing and thrifts (20 percent) than households in general.

(percentage of households with assets and debts and the mean value of owners' holdings in 1986 dollars, for all households and householders under age 35, numbers in thousands)

	percent owning		mean holdings of owners	
	all households	householder under age 35	all households	householder under age 35
Number of households	83,042	20,198	83,042	20,198
Assets				
Home	65.7%	43.6%	$80,650	$66,266
Other real estate	22.4	14.4	118,892	51,113
Public stock	19.3	15.0	81,367	3,786
Bonds	20.2	16.3	28,116	3,137
Checking and saving accounts	89.2	88.5	7,445	3,215
IRA's and Keoghs	27.3	17.7	18,752	4,537
CD's and money market	27.9	17.8	31,575	9,277
Business assets (net)	12.4	10.1	210,310	72,724
Automobiles	85.9	88.0	7,964	7,151
Employer accounts	14.8	19.5	26,704	5,274
Other*	45.7	35.6	22,282	14,211
Debts				
Mortgage, principle residence	38.40%	39.90%	$34,564	$40,855
Other debts	64.6	78.8	15,881	7,624

*Cash value of life insurance, trusts, and notes owned by individuals.

Source: The 1986 Survey of Consumer Finances, Federal Reserve Board

Note: Wealth here accounts for all major household assets and liabilities except for non-auto consumer durables, collectibles such as artwork, and the present value of expected future benefits from pensions or social security. Wealth is not given separately for householders under age 25 because the measures are not reliable.

Household Savings

WEALTH
25–34

STARTING TO SAVE

In the three-year period, 1983 to 1986, households headed by someone under age 35 had an increase in their net worth of $17,912. This savings is 7 percent of the total household income they received from 1983 to 1985 and represents about 19 percent of all household savings accumulated during those years.

(average household savings 1983 to 1986 in current dollars, share of total savings and percentage of 1983 to 1985 total household income that is savings for households, by age of householder, marital status, race and Hispanic origin, homeownership status, and household income)

	average savings for 3 year period	share of total savings	median 3-year savings as a percentage of 1983-1985 median income
All households	$24,402	100.0%	9.7%
Age of householder			
under age 35	17,912	18.7	7.1
35 to 44	23,301	16.8	12.6
45 to 54	46,606	22.4	16.1
55 to 64	39,392	20.9	9.8
65 and older	33,867	21.3	5.9
Marital status			
Married	40,392	91.8	13.8
Singe male	9,242	3.2	3.1
Single female	6,405	5.0	2.8
Race			
White	34,913	97.8	11.4
Black/Hispanic	3,679	2.2	2.4
Homeownership status			
Homeowner	39,426	88.2	16.1
Renter	10,107	11.8	4.0
Household income			
Less than $10,000	871	0.5	0.0
$10,000 to $20,000	6,633	5.9	4.8
$20,000 to $50,000	18,835	27.2	15.8
$50,000 to $100,000	70,545	27.3	22.8
$100,000 and over	455,294	39.2	44.2

Source: The 1986 Survey of Consumer Finances, Federal Reserve Board

Note: Household savings is the difference in household net worth between 1986 and 1983, expressed in 1986 dollars. Net worth (wealth) is defined as gross assets minus gross debts. Net worth here accounts for all major household assets and liabilities except for non-auto consumer durables, collectibles such as artwork, and the present value of expected future benefits from pensions or social security. Savings is not given separately for householders under age 25 because the measure is not reliable.

Owners and Renters

WEALTH
25–34

ON HOLD

Forty-five percent of householders aged 25 to 34 live in their own home and three in four of those homeowners are married couples. The proportion of white householders that are homeowners (49 percent) is nearly double the figure for both black (23 percent)and Hispanic (26 percent)householders.

(owner- and renter-occupied households by race of householder and household type, for householders aged 25 to 34, numbers in thousands, ownership status as of March 1988)

	total	white	black	Hispanic origin
All households	20,583	17,365	2,592	1,736
Owner households	9,256	8,478	600	449
Family households				
Married-couple	7,017	6,531	370	353
Male householder	253	216	28	17
Female householder	581	431	136	38
Nonfamily households				
Male householder	917	846	42	23
Female householder	487	456	24	18
Renter households	11,327	8,886	1,992	1,287
Family households				
Married-couple	4,621	3,821	551	676
Male householder	381	298	58	73
Female householder	2,155	1,250	841	278
Nonfamily households				
Male householder	2,492	2,085	326	176
Female householder	1,678	1,431	216	84

Source: Household and Family Characteristics: March 1988, *Bureau of the Census, Current Population Reports, Series P-20, No. 424*

Note: Hispanics are of any race. Numbers may not add to total due to rounding.

Health Status

HEALTH
25–34

BEING WELL

Seventy-seven percent of men and 70 percent of women aged 25 to 34 rate their health as excellent or very good. The proportion of 25-to-34-year-olds with excellent or very good health is considerably higher in households with a household income of $35,000 or more than in lower-income households.

(self-assessed health status of persons aged 25 to 34, by sex, race and household income, number of persons in thousands)

	all persons	all health statuses	excellent	very good	good	fair	poor
Both sexes, all races	41,712	100.0%	43.8%	30.0%	21.0%	4.4%	0.9%
Male	20,494	100.0	48.8	28.6	18.1	3.7	0.9
Female	21,218	100.0	38.9	31.4	23.8	5.1	0.9
White	35,101	100.0	45.3	30.9	19.3	3.8	0.7
Black	5,026	100.0	33.7	24.7	31.3	8.7	1.6
Asian and other	1,585	100.0	42.9	26.3	25.3	4.5	1.0
Household income							
Less than $10,000	4,589	100.0%	30.3%	23.8%	31.0%	11.9%	3.1%
$10,000 to $19,999	8,341	100.0	37.5	31.3	25.1	5.3	0.9
$20,000 to $34,999	13,594	100.0	46.9	31.4	18.2	3.3	0.2
$35,000 and over	10,792	100.0	53.2	30.3	14.4	1.6	0.4

Source: The 1986 National Health Interview Survey, National Center for Health Statistics

Note: All persons includes those of unknown health status, all health statuses includes only those with known health status. Household income includes only those persons with known household income. Numbers may not add to total due to rounding.

Height

JUST AVERAGE

Three out of every five women aged 25 to 34 are under 5'5" tall and 95 percent of the men in this age group are over 5'5" tall. The average 25-to-34-year-old woman stands 5'4", the same height as the average American woman. The average man aged 25 to 34 is nearly 5'10" tall—one inch taller than the average man.

(cumulative percentage of height of males and females aged 25 to 34 and their average height, by race)

height, males	cumulative percentage	height, females	cumulative percentage
Less than 60 inches	0.1%	Less than 55 inches	–
Less than 61 inches	0.3	Less than 56 inches	–
Less than 62 inches	0.4	Less than 57 inches	0.2%
Less than 63 inches	0.5	Less than 58 inches	0.6
Less than 64 inches	1.5	Less than 59 inches	1.7
Less than 65 inches	4.4	Less than 60 inches	3.7
Less than 66 inches	9.5	Less than 61 inches	8.6
Less than 67 inches	15.2	Less than 62 inches	19.1
Less than 68 inches	26.7	Less than 63 inches	33.0
Less than 69 inches	39.7	Less than 64 inches	47.4
Less than 70 inches	55.4	Less than 65 inches	61.4
Less than 71 inches	69.7	Less than 66 inches	74.9
Less than 72 inches	81.6	Less than 67 inches	85.7
Less than 73 inches	90.0	Less than 68 inches	93.3
Less than 74 inches	95.6	Less than 69 inches	97.2
Less than 75 inches	98.0	Less than 70 inches	99.5
Less than 76 inches	99.2	Less than 71 inches	99.7
All height categories	100.0%	All height categories	100.0%
Average height, all races	**69.6 inches**	**Average height, all races**	**64.2 inches**
White	69.7	White	64.3
Black	69.6	Black	63.9

Source: Anthropometric Reference Data and Prevalence of Overweight: United States, 1976-80, *National Center for Health Statistics, National Health Survey Series 11, No. 238.*

Note: *Height is without shoes.*

Weight

HEALTH
25–34

THIRTY-SOMETHING AND COUNTING

One-fifth of all men and women aged 25 to 34 weigh more than the weight to height (overweight) standard used by the National Center for Health Statistics. The average woman aged 25 to 34 weighs 142 pounds and the average man in this age group tips the scales at 173 pounds.

(cumulative percentage of weight of males and females aged 25 to 34, and their average weight and percent overweight, by race)

weight, males	cumulative percentage	weight, females	cumulative percentage
Less than 100 pounds	–	Less than 90 pounds	0.4%
Less than 110 pounds	0.2%	Less than 100 pounds	3.3
Less than 120 pounds	1.0	Less than 110 pounds	10.7
Less than 130 pounds	4.1	Less than 120 pounds	25.6
Less than 140 pounds	10.9	Less than 130 pounds	41.3
Less than 150 pounds	21.8	Less than 140 pounds	59.1
Less than 160 pounds	35.1	Less than 150 pounds	71.7
Less than 170 pounds	48.0	Less than 160 pounds	79.1
Less than 180 pounds	62.1	Less than 170 pounds	84.2
Less than 190 pounds	77.5	Less than 180 pounds	88.6
Less than 200 pounds	84.6	Less than 190 pounds	91.3
Less than 210 pounds	90.1	Less than 200 pounds	94.1
Less than 220 pounds	93.5	Less than 220 pounds	96.9
Less than 230 pounds	95.4	Less than 240 pounds	98.7
Less than 240 pounds	96.5	Less than 260 pounds	99.2
Less than 250 pounds	97.8	Less than 280 pounds	99.4
All weight categories	100.0%	All weight categories	100.0%
Average weight, all races	**173.4 pounds**	**Average weight, all races**	**141.6 pounds**
White	174.3	White	140.2
Black	172.5	Black	152.7
Percent overweight, all races	**20.4%**	**Percent overweight, all races**	**20.0%**
White	20.9	White	17.9
Black	17.5	Black	33.5
Percent severely overweight, all races	**6.7%**	**Percent severely overweight, all races**	**8.8%**
White	6.7	White	7.5
Black	6.5	Black	16.9

Source: Anthropometric Reference Data and Prevalence of Overweight: United States, 1976-80, *National Center for Health Statistics, National Health Survey Series 11, No. 238.*

Notes: Weight includes clothing weight, estimated as ranging from 0.20 to 0.62 pounds. Overweight is defined in terms of a body mass index which is determined by dividing weight in kilograms by height in meters squared. Overweight people have a body mass index equal to or greater than that at the 85th percentile of men and women aged 20 to 29. Severe overweight means a body mass index equal to or greater than at the 95th percentile of men and women aged 20 to 29.

Acute Conditions

HEALTH
25–34

FLUS AND OTHER AILMENTS

Men and women aged 25 to 34 are more likely to suffer from flus than from any other acute condition. Colds are the second most common ailment of men this age, followed by open wounds and cuts. Along with common colds, the other top conditions affecting 25-to-34-year-old women are delivery and other conditions of pregnancy.

(number of acute conditions reported in a year for all persons and those aged 25 to 34, by sex, numbers in thousands)

	males all ages	males aged 25 to 34	females all ages	females aged 25 to 34
All acute conditions	191,369	32,137	257,177	47,170
Infective and parasitic diseases	**23,122**	**3,706**	**31,244**	**5,526**
Common childhood diseases	2,565	279	1,876	0
Intestinal virus, unspecified	4,244	697	5,288	785
Viral infections, unspecified	9,621	1,333	14,273	2,813
Other	6,692	1,397	9,807	1,928
Respiratory conditions	**99,216**	**15,667**	**129,626**	**24,188**
Common cold	30,445	3,452	32,983	5,792
Other acute upper respiratory infections	8,472	1,569	13,320	1,781
Influenza	55,256	10,414	75,295	15,184
Acute bronchitis	1,960	0	4,315	842
Pneumonia	1,365	126	1,277	199
Other respiratory conditions	1,718	106	2,435	390
Digestive system conditions	**5,860**	**1,187**	**9,112**	**1,437**
Dental conditions	1,059	554	1,955	484
Indigestion, nausea and vomiting	3,299	531	4,670	677
Other digestive conditions	1,502	102	2,487	276
Injuries	**34,588**	**8,422**	**29,706**	**4,716**
Fractures and dislocations	4,367	1,181	3,978	776
Sprains and strains	6,127	1,783	6,208	1,025
Open wounds and lacerations	11,153	2,109	5,094	470
Contusions and superficial injuries	7,986	1,997	7,191	1,321
Other current injuries	4,955	1,352	7,235	1,124

(continued next page)

Acute Conditions

HEALTH
25–34

(continued from previous page)

(number of acute conditions reported in a year for all persons and those aged 25 to 34, by sex, numbers in thousands)

	males		females	
	all ages	aged 25 to 34	all ages	aged 25 to 34
Selected other acute conditions	**21,183**	**2,505**	**40,385**	**8,220**
Eye conditions	1,072	0	2,080	215
Acute ear infections	8,689	706	10,116	1,322
Other ear conditions	1,884	111	2,193	42
Acute urinary conditions	989	98	4,399	672
Disorders of menstruation	–	–	2,251	644
Other disorders of female genital tract	–	–	2,174	849
Delivery and other conditions of pregnancy	–	–	4,466	2,659
Skin conditions	2,065	239	3,597	582
Acute musculoskeletal conditions	3,038	989	3,972	527
Headache, excluding migraine	1,253	361	2,461	515
Fever, unspecified	2,192	0	2,675	195
All other acute conditions	**7,400**	**652**	**17,104**	**3,083**

Source: The 1986 National Health Interview Survey, National Center for Health Statistics

Note: An acute condition is defined by The National Health Interview Survey as an illness or injury that usually lasts less than 3 months and was first noticed less than 3 months before the respondent's interview. The acute condition must also have caused the person to restrict activities for at least a half a day or to have contacted a physician. The data are based only on information given by the respondent and are subject to recall and selective reporting error. Numbers may not add to total due to rounding.

Chronic Conditions

HEALTH
25–34

SUFFERING FROM SINUSES

Men aged 25 to 34 are most likely to report chronic problems with sinusitis, hay fever, leg deformities, high blood pressure, and back deformities. Women in this age group list sinusitis, hay fever, back deformities, dermatitis, and migraine headaches as their most common chronic conditions.

(number of selected chronic conditions reported in a year for all persons and those aged 25 to 34, by sex, numbers in thousands)

	males all ages	males aged 25 to 34	females all ages	females aged 25 to 34
Selected skin and musculoskeletal conditions				
Arthritis	10,751	586	20,160	1,046
Gout, including gouty arthritis	1,515	68	713	15
Intervertebral disc disorders	2,522	454	1,645	228
Bone spur or tendonitis, unspecified	781	101	898	95
Disorders of bone or cartilage	449	137	943	54
Trouble with bunions	594	76	2,321	185
Bursitis, unclassified	1,641	230	2,464	211
Sebaceous skin cyst	640	196	881	170
Trouble with acne	2,193	447	2,116	414
Psoriasis	1,069	206	1,262	199
Dermatitis	3,851	694	5,696	1,416
Trouble with dry, itching skin, unclassified	1,994	452	2,606	511
Trouble with ingrown nails	2,352	279	3,030	387
Trouble with corns and calluses	1,669	348	3,164	362
Impairments				
Visual impairment	4,994	923	3,358	433
Color blindness	2,694	637	272	76
Cataracts	1,534	47	3,497	5
Glaucoma	735	28	967	0
Hearing impairment	11,727	1,168	9,004	710
Tinnitus	3,388	237	2,927	261
Speech impairment	1,924	349	871	79
Absence of extremity(s)	374	47	24	0
Paralysis, entire body, one side of body, or both legs	200	63	152	0
Partial paralysis of body or legs	236	50	99	0
Deformity of back	6,812	1,257	9,676	1,931
Deformity of upper extremities	1,622	281	1,475	270
Deformity of lower extremities	6,454	1,401	5,739	900
Selected digestive conditions				
Ulcer	2,116	312	2,378	540
Hernia of abdominal cavity	2,300	301	2,283	76
Gastritis or duodenitis	1,080	209	1,813	374

(continued next page)

Chronic Conditions

HEALTH 25–34

(continued from previous page)

(number of selected chronic conditions reported in a year for all persons and those aged 25 to 34, by sex, numbers in thousands)

	males all ages	males aged 25 to 34	females all ages	females aged 25 to 34
Frequent indigestion	2,504	626	2,811	661
Enteritis or colitis	574	148	1,820	339
Spastic colon	264	169	1,377	323
Diverticula of intestines	404	0	1,508	0
Frequent constipation	1,002	173	3,537	634
Selected conditions of the genitourinary, nervous, endocrine, metabolic, and blood system				
Goiter or other disorders of the thyroid	420	38	2,789	414
Diabetes	2,949	77	3,635	348
Anemias	570	24	2,617	789
Epilepsy	656	158	863	145
Migraine headache	2,068	468	6,448	1,403
Neuralgia or neuritis, unspecified	215	0	364	0
Kidney trouble	1,305	244	2,662	613
Bladder disorders	516	50	3,253	514
Diseases of prostate	1,281	74	–	–
Inflammatory female genital diseases	–	–	427	225
Noninflammatory female genital diseases	–	–	1,095	476
Menstrual disorders	–	–	2,097	660
Selected circulatory conditions				
Ischemic heart disease	4,091	160	2,809	68
Tachycardia or rapid heart	700	135	1,226	185
Heart murmurs	1,310	256	2,583	692
Other heart rhythm disorders	499	0	800	84
Other heart diseases	1,482	21	2,265	179
High blood pressure (hypertension)	12,512	1,335	16,457	1,023
Cerebrovascular disease	1,156	0	1,646	23
Hardening of the arteries	1,428	22	1,225	26
Varicose veins	1,042	51	5,814	1,033
Hemorrhoids	4,568	735	5,341	1,387
Selected respiratory conditions				
Chronic bronchitis	4,707	425	6,671	709
Asthma	4,670	423	5,019	699
Hay fever or allergic rhinitis without asthma	10,136	2,322	11,566	2,715
Chronic sinusitis	14,636	2,778	19,749	3,904
Deviated nasal septum	825	51	465	99
Chronic disease of tonsils or adenoids	1,071	129	2,068	293
Emphysema	1,201	22	796	0

Source: The 1986 National Health Interview Survey, National Center for Health Statistics

Note: Chronic conditions are defined by the National Health Interview Survey as conditions that either a) were first noticed 3 months or more before the date of the interview or b) belong to a group of conditions (such as heart disease or diabetes) that are considered chronic regardless of when they began. Totals for all chronic conditions are not shown because the National Health Interview Survey does not measure the total number of chronic conditions for each person. The data are based only on information given by the respondent and are subject to recall and selective reporting error.

Activity Restrictions

HEALTH
25–34

HIGHER INCOME, FEWER ABSENCES

Men and women aged 25 to 34 miss five whole or half days of work each year because of illness and injury. As with American workers in general, workers from higher-income households miss work less frequently than those from households with lower incomes.

(number of days of activity restriction reported in a year and per person due to acute and chronic conditions, by type of restriction and sex, race, and household income, for all persons and those aged 25 to 34, numbers in thousands)

	number of days per year		number of days per person	
	bed day	work-loss day	bed day	work-loss day
All ages	1,547,980	833,396	6.5	5.4
Male	613,113	401,503	5.4	4.8
Female	934,867	431,892	7.7	6.0
White	1,298,039	716,187	6.5	5.4
Black	220,102	99,332	7.7	5.4
Household income				
Less than $10,000	384,962	90,268	11.5	6.1
$10,000 to $19,999	346,115	162,604	7.7	6.1
$20,000 to $34,999	326,166	254,563	5.2	5.7
$35,000 and over	275,957	232,139	4.3	4.6
All aged 25 to 34	197,726	165,695	4.7	5.0
Male	85,259	88,125	4.2	4.8
Female	112,467	77,570	5.3	5.3
White	160,960	136,941	4.6	4.9
Black	32,213	25,502	6.4	6.9
Household income				
Less than $10,000	43,491	13,844	9.5	5.6
$10,000 to $19,999	40,619	33,377	4.9	5.2
$20,000 to $34,999	51,840	50,928	3.8	4.5
$35,000 and over	39,886	43,342	3.7	4.6

Source: The 1986 National Health Interview Survey, National Center for Health Statistics

Note: Numbers may not add to total due to rounding. A bed day is one during which a person stayed in bed more than half a day because of illness or injury. All hospital days for inpatients are considered bed days even if the patient was not in bed more than half a day. A work-loss day is one on which a currently employed person aged 18 or older missed more than half a day of work. The data are based only on information given by the respondent and are subject to recall and selective reporting error.

Cause of Death

HEALTH
25–34

SOCIAL DISEASES

The three leading causes of death among people aged 25 to 34—accidents, homicide and illegal interventions, and suicide—account for 54 percent of all deaths in this age group. Although deaths of 24-to-34-year-olds account for only 3 percent of all deaths, they are 18 percent of accident-related deaths, 32 percent of all homicides and illegal interventions, and 22 percent of all suicides.

(ten leading causes of death among persons aged 25 to 34)

	number of deaths persons aged 25 to 34	number of deaths all ages	percent accounted for by persons aged 25 to 34
All causes	56,530	2,105,361	2.7%
Accidents and adverse effects	16,906	95,277	17.7
Homicide and illegal interventions	6,904	21,731	31.8
Suicide	6,711	30,904	21.7
Malignant neoplasms (cancer)	5,604	469,376	1.2
Heart diseases	3,691	765,490	0.5
Chronic liver disease and cirrhosis	1,182	26,159	4.5
Cerebrovascular diseases	960	149,643	0.6
Diabetes mellitus	634	37,184	1.7
Pneumonia and influenza	736	69,812	1.1
Congenital anomalies	398	12,638	3.1
All other causes	12,804	427,147	3.0

Source: Advance Report of Final Mortality Statistics, 1986, *National Center for Health Statistics, Vol. 37, No. 6*

35–44

Chapter 5

CONSUMERS AGED 35 TO 44

They will be 16 percent of all Americans in 2000, they are gaining economic clout, and their demographic profile is changing.

More people and households
...and nontraditional households.

- Between 1990 and 2000, baby boomers will hike the number of 35-to-44-year-olds by 18 percent.

- There will be a 19 percent increase in the number of households headed by members of this age group during the 1990s.

- During those 10 years, family households will grow 12 percent; nonfamilies by 50 percent.

- They are the most highly educated group of Americans—47 percent of them completed one to three years of college and 27 percent finished four or more years.

- Women aged 35 to 44 are more likely to be in the work force than women in any other age group. Seventy-five percent of them were workers in 1987, a proportion that will increase to 84 percent by 2000.

- They head 21 percent of all households but account for 26 percent of all household income.

- Married couples in this age group have a median household income of $41,300. Median income is higher—$44,600—among the 68 percent of married couples that are dual-earners.

- They devote a bigger share of their spending dollar to food, housing, apparel, entertainment, and insurance and pensions than the average American household.

- Households headed by 35-to-44-year-olds will spend an estimated 121 billion dollars more in 2000 than in 1990.

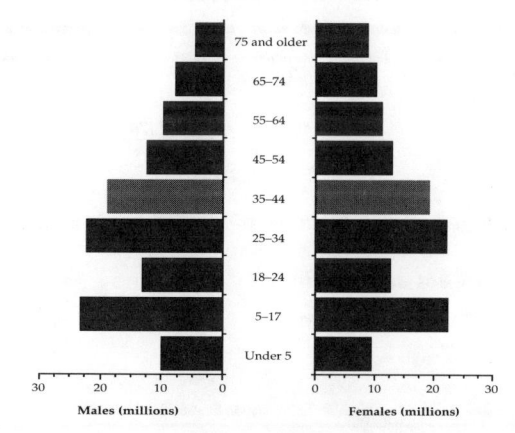

1990

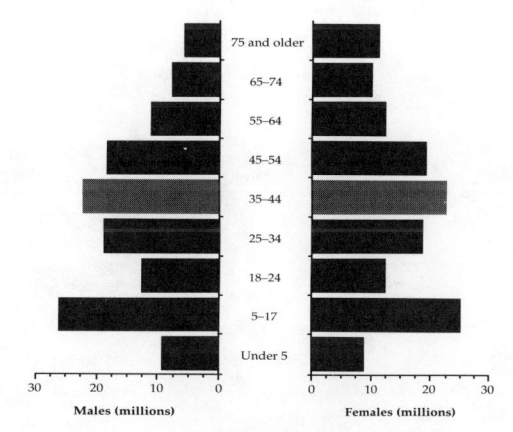

2000

Almanac of Consumer Markets 145

Share of Total Population

POPULATION 35–44

GAINING THIS DECADE

Between 1990 and 2000, the baby boomers will hike the number of 35-to-44-year-olds by 18 percent, making them a full 16 percent of the population by the turn of the century.

(total population and the number of persons aged 35 to 44, in thousands, by sex, 1960 to 1980, and projections for 1990 to 2000)

	1960 number	1960 percent of total	1970 number	1970 percent of total	1980 number	1980 percent of total	1990 number	1990 percent of total	1995 number	1995 percent of total	2000 number	2000 percent of total
All ages	180,671	100.0%	205,052	100.0%	227,757	100.0%	252,293	100.0%	264,077	100.0%	274,479	100.0%
All aged 35 to 44	24,221	13.4	23,150	11.3	25,868	11.4	38,212	15.1	42,830	16.2	45,059	16.4
Males	11,872	6.6	11,322	5.5	12,720	5.6	18,917	7.5	21,299	8.1	22,495	8.2
Females	12,349	6.8	11,828	5.8	13,148	5.8	19,295	7.6	21,532	8.2	22,565	8.2

Source: Annual Projections of the Population by Age, Sex, and Race, for the United States: 1983 to 2080, *Bureau of the Census, Current Population Reports, Series 17 and the Bureau of the Census*

Note: Total population includes Armed Forces overseas; 1960 to 1980 are based on censuses; projections are based on the Census Bureau's Series 17 projections that incorporate illegal immigration and higher levels of emigration than other Census Bureau projections. Series 17 is consistent with current estimates of illegal aliens living in the United States. Numbers may not add to total due to rounding.

Sex, Race, and Ethnicity

POPULATION
35-44

A NATIONAL TREND

As with all other age groups, the white share of the population will decline during the 1990s. Whites aged 35 to 44 will decrease from 78 to 73 percent of the age group while blacks will increase from 11 to 13 percent, Hispanics from 8 to 10 percent and Asians from 3 to 4 percent. Overall, the number of Americans aged 35 to 44 will jump 18 percent during the decade.

(projections of the total population and persons aged 35 to 44, in thousands, by sex, race, and Hispanic origin, 1990 to 2000)

	1990	1995	2000	percent change 1990–2000
All ages	252,293	264,077	274,479	8.8%
White	191,594	195,347	197,634	3.2
Black	30,915	33,237	35,440	14.6
Hispanic	21,854	25,991	30,295	38.6
Asians and other races	7,930	9,502	11,110	40.1
All aged 35 to 44	38,212	42,830	45,059	17.9
White	29,761	32,306	32,796	10.2
Black	4,233	5,120	5,781	36.6
Hispanic	2,899	3,768	4,582	58.1
Asians and other races	1,319	1,636	1,900	44.0
All males aged 35 to 44	18,917	21,299	22,495	18.9
White	14,871	16,155	16,399	10.3
Black	1,968	2,423	2,797	42.1
Hispanic	1,457	1,948	2,415	65.8
Asians and other races	621	773	884	42.4
All females aged 35 to 44	19,295	21,532	22,565	16.9
White	14,891	16,151	16,397	10.1
Black	2,265	2,696	2,984	31.7
Hispanic	1,442	1,821	2,168	50.3
Asians and other races	699	864	1,016	45.5

Source: Projections of the Population of the United States by Age, Sex, and Race: 1983 to 2080, *Bureau of the Census, Current Population Reports, Series P-25, No. 952, Series 17*

Note: Series 17 projections incorporate illegal immigration and higher levels of emigration than other Census Bureau projections and are consistent with current estimates of illegal aliens living in the United States. Total population includes Armed Forces living overseas. In this table Hispanics have been separated out of the racial groups; categories do not overlap. Numbers may not add to total due to rounding.

Almanac of Consumer Markets

State Populations

POPULATION
35–44

WHAT GOES UP...

All but four states will see growth in the number of 35-to-44-year-olds during the 1990s, with the greatest gains in the South Atlantic and New England states. As the baby bust moves into this age category in the first decade of the new century, the number of 35-to-44-year-olds will tumble.

(resident population and the number of persons aged 35 to 44, in thousands, in Census Bureau divisions and states in 1980 and projections for 1990 to 2010)

Note: Inconsistencies between the data in this table and the preceding two tables are due to different assumptions about immigration and emigration on which the projections are based and the inclusion of Armed Forces overseas in total population. This table is based on the resident population only.

	census 1980	projections 1990	projections 2000	projections 2010	percent change 1990–2000	percent change 2000–2010
All ages	226,546	249,891	267,747	282,055	7.1%	5.3%
All aged 35 to 44	25,634	37,827	43,841	37,131	15.9	-15.3
New England	**1,383**	**2,006**	**2,387**	**1,987**	**19.0**	**-16.8**
Connecticut	369	510	595	499	16.7	-16.1
Maine	123	185	214	177	15.7	-17.3
Massachusetts	628	893	1,056	875	18.3	-17.1
New Hampshire	107	185	241	207	30.3	-14.1
Rhode Island	98	146	177	146	21.2	-17.5
Vermont	57	88	104	82	18.2	-21.2
Middle Atlantic	**4,197**	**5,575**	**6,283**	**5,229**	**12.7**	**-16.8**
New Jersey	880	1,213	1,457	1,272	20.1	-12.7
New York	2,043	2,638	2,935	2,523	11.3	-14.0
Pennsylvania	1,274	1,724	1,892	1,434	9.7	-24.2
East North Central	**4,638**	**6,233**	**6,815**	**5,353**	**9.3**	**-21.5**
Illinois	1,294	1,723	1,879	1,512	9.1	-19.5
Indiana	614	816	900	694	10.3	-22.9
Michigan	1,029	1,396	1,539	1,218	10.2	-20.9
Ohio	1,200	1,591	1,723	1,353	8.3	-21.5
Wisconsin	502	708	777	577	9.7	-25.7

(continued on next page)

State Populations

POPULATION
35–44

(continued from previous page)

(resident population and the number of persons aged 35 to 44, in thousands, in Census Bureau divisions and states in 1980 and projections for 1990 to 2010)

	census 1980	projections 1990	projections 2000	2010	percent change 1990–2000	percent change 2000–2010
All ages	226,546	249,891	267,747	282,055	7.1%	5.3%
All aged 35 to 44	25,634	37,827	43,841	37,131	15.9	-15.3
West North Central	**1,835**	**2,596**	**2,854**	**2,180**	**9.9**	**-23.6**
Iowa	302	397	399	276	0.5	-30.8
Kansas	249	363	395	308	8.8	-22.0
Minnesota	449	665	748	577	12.5	-22.9
Missouri	541	750	865	684	15.3	-20.9
Nebraska	163	228	241	182	5.7	-24.5
North Dakota	63	96	98	71	2.1	-27.6
South Dakota	66	97	108	82	11.3	-24.1
South Atlantic	**4,259**	**6,554**	**8,156**	**7,260**	**24.4**	**-11.0**
Delaware	68	96	123	106	28.1	-13.8
District of Columbia	74	97	114	103	17.5	-9.6
Florida	1,039	1,765	2,297	2,063	30.1	-10.2
Georgia	647	1,029	1,340	1,262	30.2	-5.8
Maryland	527	760	930	824	22.4	-11.4
North Carolina	682	1,005	1,233	1,088	22.7	-11.8
South Carolina	350	528	638	552	20.8	-13.5
Virginia	663	993	1,204	1,055	21.2	-12.4
West Virginia	208	282	277	206	-1.8	-25.6
East South Central	**1,629**	**2,279**	**2,623**	**2,151**	**15.1**	**-18.0**
Alabama	430	603	711	589	17.9	-17.2
Kentucky	405	558	599	467	7.3	-22.0
Mississippi	260	360	438	367	21.7	-16.2
Tennessee	534	758	874	728	15.3	-16.7
West South Central	**2,638**	**4,197**	**4,920**	**4,248**	**17.2**	**-13.7**
Arkansas	248	341	390	316	14.4	-19.0
Louisiana	450	655	708	557	8.1	-21.3
Oklahoma	337	492	536	433	8.9	-19.2
Texas	1,603	2,711	3,286	2,942	21.2	-10.5

(continued on next page)

State Populations

POPULATION
35–44

(continued from previous page)

(resident population and the number of persons aged 35 to 44, in thousands, in Census Bureau divisions and states in 1980 and projections for 1990 to 2010)

	census 1980	projections 1990	projections 2000	projections 2010	percent change 1990–2000	percent change 2000–2010
All ages	226,546	249,891	267,747	282,055	7.1%	5.3%
All aged 35 to 44	25,634	37,827	43,841	37,131	15.9	-15.3
Mountain	**1,284**	**2,183**	**2,576**	**2,221**	**18.0**	**-13.8**
Arizona	298	544	710	637	30.5	-3.2
Colorado	347	603	672	567	11.4	-15.6
Idaho	105	160	164	133	2.5	-18.9
Montana	88	129	128	100	-0.8	-21.9
Nevada	105	182	232	206	27.5	-11.2
New Mexico	145	247	316	291	27.9	-7.9
Utah	143	231	269	224	16.5	-16.7
Wyoming	53	88	84	63	-4.5	-25.0
Pacific	**3,772**	**6,203**	**7,225**	**6,502**	**16.5**	**-10.0**
Alaska	54	105	122	120	16.2	-1.6
California	2,814	4,635	5,572	5,075	20.2	-8.9
Hawaii	111	178	212	221	19.1	4.2
Oregon	304	479	476	385	-0.6	-19.1
Washington	487	804	844	701	5.0	-16.9

Source: Projections of the Population of States by Age, Sex and Race: 1988 to 2010, *Bureau of the Census, Current Population Reports, Series P-25, No. 1017*

Note: Numbers may not add to total due to rounding.

State-by-State Changes

POPULATION
35–44

LOSSES IN ONLY FOUR STATES

The number of 35-to-44-year-olds will shrink during the 1990s only in Montana, Oregon, West Virginia, and Wyoming. Gains are forecasted for every other state during the last decade of the century.

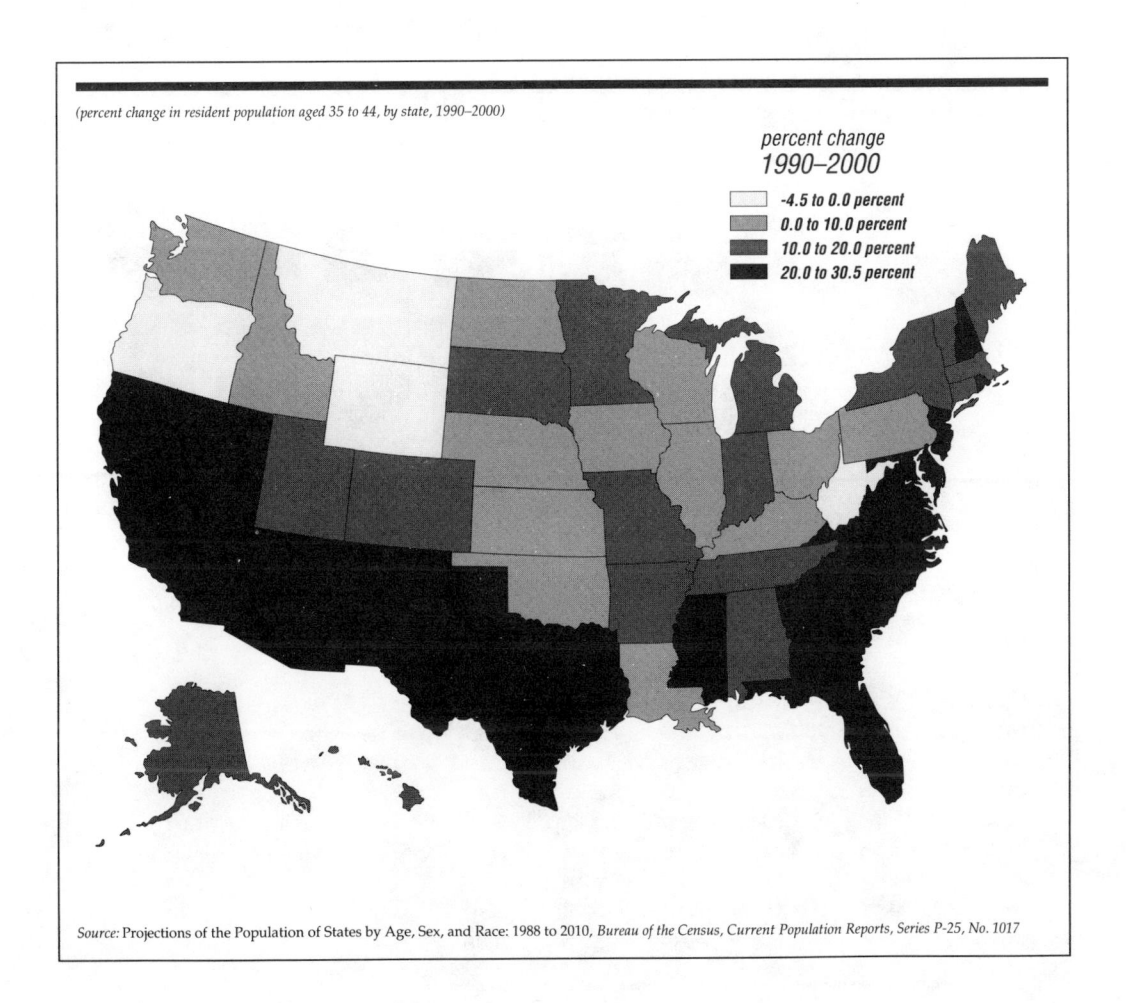

(percent change in resident population aged 35 to 44, by state, 1990–2000)

percent change
1990–2000

- -4.5 to 0.0 percent
- 0.0 to 10.0 percent
- 10.0 to 20.0 percent
- 20.0 to 30.5 percent

Source: Projections of the Population of States by Age, Sex, and Race: 1988 to 2010, *Bureau of the Census, Current Population Reports,* Series P-25, No. 1017

Number of Households

HOUSEHOLDS
35–44

BOOMING NUMBERS

Younger baby boomers starting out and older boomers starting over will contribute to a 19 percent rise in the number of households headed by 35-44-year-olds during the 1990s. Family households will grow 12 percent, while nonfamilies will zoom up a full 50 percent.

(number of households, in thousands, by age of householder, 1990–2000)

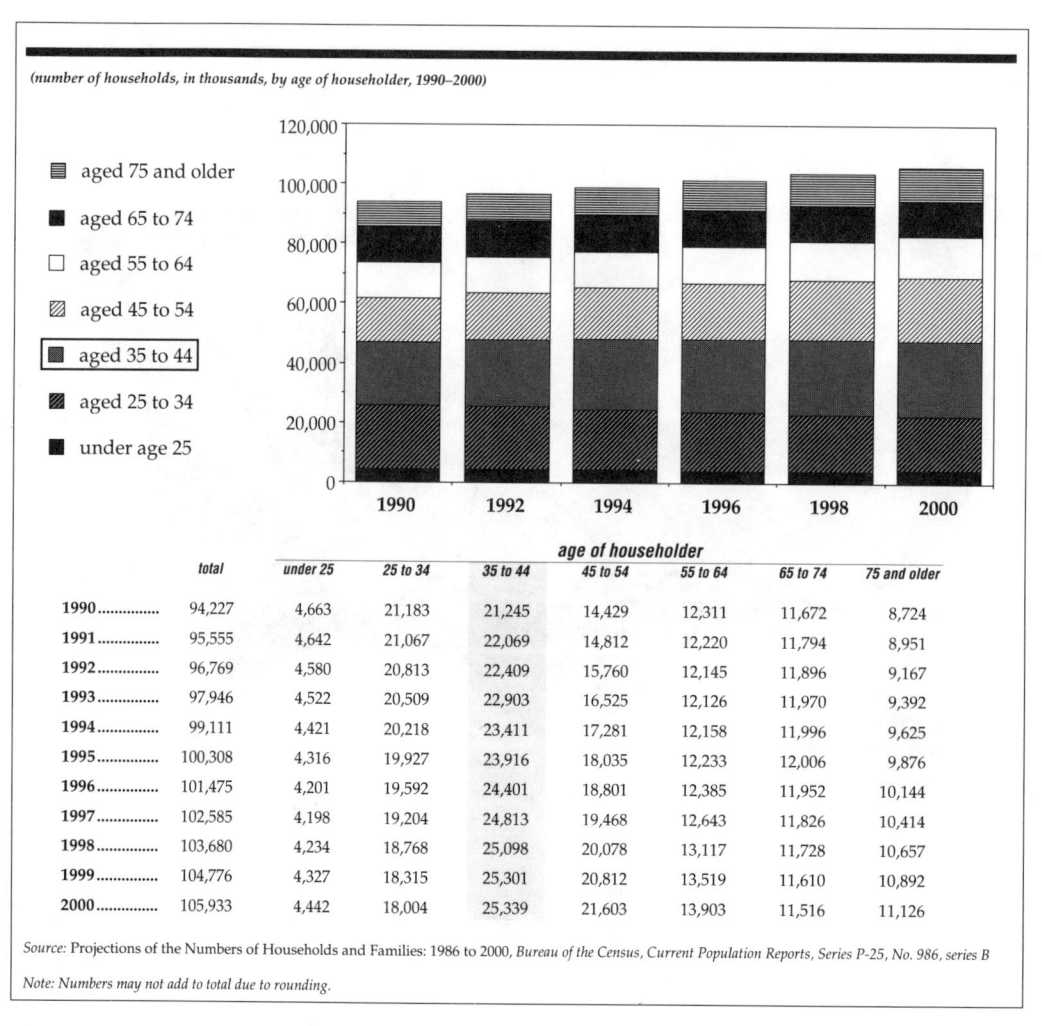

- aged 75 and older
- aged 65 to 74
- aged 55 to 64
- aged 45 to 54
- aged 35 to 44
- aged 25 to 34
- under age 25

	total	under 25	25 to 34	35 to 44	45 to 54	55 to 64	65 to 74	75 and older
1990	94,227	4,663	21,183	21,245	14,429	12,311	11,672	8,724
1991	95,555	4,642	21,067	22,069	14,812	12,220	11,794	8,951
1992	96,769	4,580	20,813	22,409	15,760	12,145	11,896	9,167
1993	97,946	4,522	20,509	22,903	16,525	12,126	11,970	9,392
1994	99,111	4,421	20,218	23,411	17,281	12,158	11,996	9,625
1995	100,308	4,316	19,927	23,916	18,035	12,233	12,006	9,876
1996	101,475	4,201	19,592	24,401	18,801	12,385	11,952	10,144
1997	102,585	4,198	19,204	24,813	19,468	12,643	11,826	10,414
1998	103,680	4,234	18,768	25,098	20,078	13,117	11,728	10,657
1999	104,776	4,327	18,315	25,301	20,812	13,519	11,610	10,892
2000	105,933	4,442	18,004	25,339	21,603	13,903	11,516	11,126

Source: Projections of the Numbers of Households and Families: 1986 to 2000, Bureau of the Census, Current Population Reports, Series P-25, No. 986, series B

Note: Numbers may not add to total due to rounding.

Types of Households

HOUSEHOLDS
35–44

MANY FAMILIES

A vast majority—82 percent—of householders aged 35 to 44 are family heads, a proportion that no other age group can top. The 10 million married couples with children under age 18 living at home account for 41 percent of all such families in the nation.

(household types for all households and for householders aged 35 to 44, numbers in thousands)

	all households total	all households percent of households in category	householder aged 35 to 44 total	householder aged 35 to 44 percent of households in category
All households	91,066	100.0%	19,323	100.0%
Family households	65,133	71.5	15,852	82.0
Married couple	51,809	56.9	12,448	64.4
With children under age 18 at home	24,600	27.0	10,121	52.4
Without children under age 18 at home	27,209	29.9	2,327	12.0
Female householder	10,608	11.6	2,765	14.3
With children under age 18 at home	6,273	6.9	2,281	11.8
Without children under age 18 at home	4,335	4.8	484	2.5
Male householder	2,715	3.0	639	3.3
With children under age 18 at home	1,047	1.1	416	2.2
Without children under age 18 at home	1,669	1.8	223	1.2
Nonfamily households	25,993	28.5	3,471	18.0
Living alone	21,889	24.0	2,837	14.7
Female householder	13,101	14.4	1,061	5.5
Male householder	8,788	9.7	1,776	9.2
Living with others	4,044	4.4	635	3.3
Female householder	1,523	1.7	204	1.1
Male householder	2,521	2.8	431	2.2

Source: The 1988 Current Population Survey, Bureau of the Census

Note: Numbers may not add to total due to rounding.

Future Household Types

GAINS AMONG NONFAMILIES

Aging baby boomers will continue to swell the number of 35-to-44-year-old householders during the 1990s. Like the older boomers who came before them, these householders will be increasingly likely to live in nonfamily units.

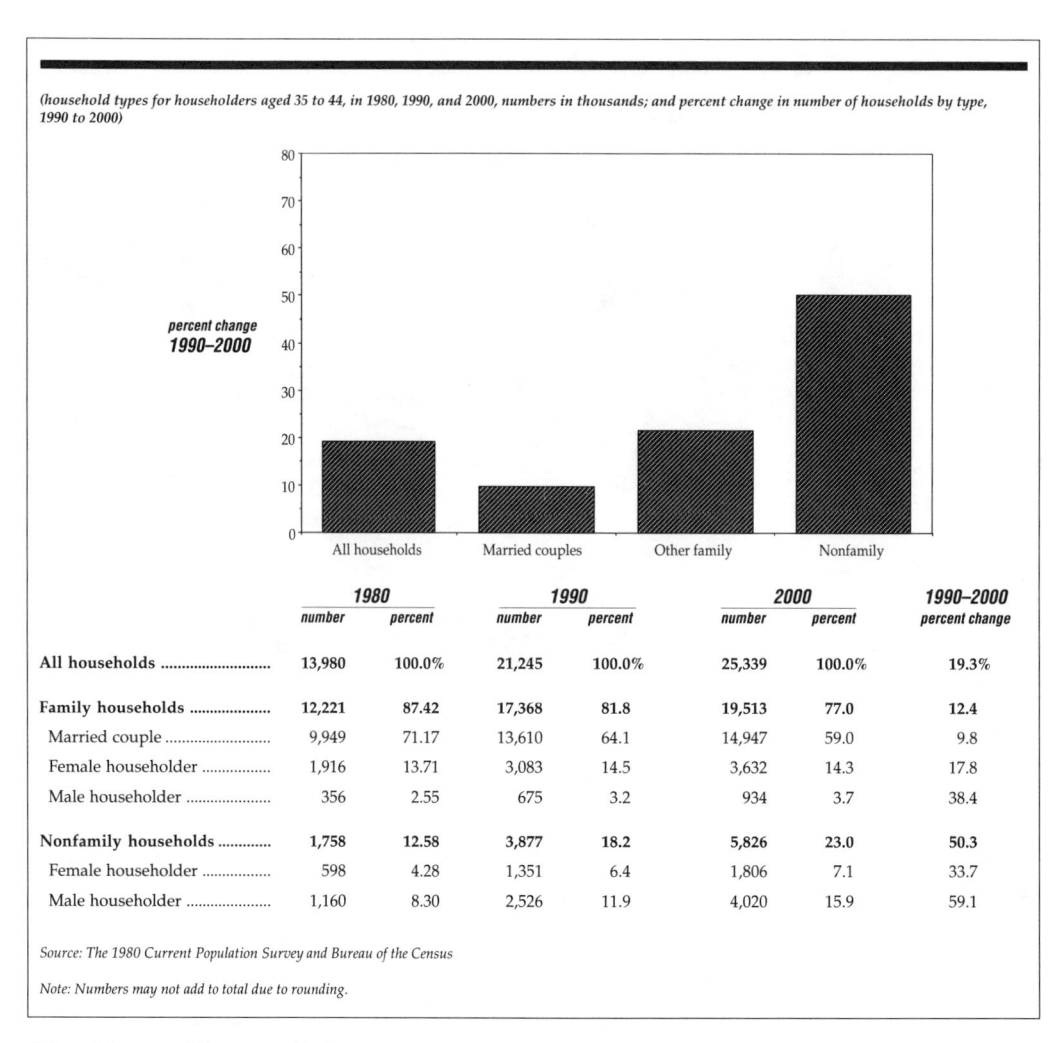

(household types for householders aged 35 to 44, in 1980, 1990, and 2000, numbers in thousands; and percent change in number of households by type, 1990 to 2000)

percent change 1990–2000

	1980 number	1980 percent	1990 number	1990 percent	2000 number	2000 percent	1990–2000 percent change
All households	13,980	100.0%	21,245	100.0%	25,339	100.0%	19.3%
Family households	12,221	87.42	17,368	81.8	19,513	77.0	12.4
Married couple	9,949	71.17	13,610	64.1	14,947	59.0	9.8
Female householder	1,916	13.71	3,083	14.5	3,632	14.3	17.8
Male householder	356	2.55	675	3.2	934	3.7	38.4
Nonfamily households	1,758	12.58	3,877	18.2	5,826	23.0	50.3
Female householder	598	4.28	1,351	6.4	1,806	7.1	33.7
Male householder	1,160	8.30	2,526	11.9	4,020	15.9	59.1

Source: The 1980 Current Population Survey and Bureau of the Census

Note: Numbers may not add to total due to rounding.

Almanac of Consumer Markets

Marital Status

MARITAL STATUS AND FERTILITY
35–44

MOSTLY MARRIED

People aged 35 to 44 top the overall figures when it comes to the likelihood of being married—75 percent of the men and 72 percent of the women are married and living with their spouses. Nine percent of the members of this age group have never married, and another 12 percent are divorced.

(marital status of persons aged 15 and older and those aged 35 to 44, by sex, race and Hispanic origin, numbers in thousands)

	all	total	single never married	married spouse present	married spouse absent	divorced	widowed
Males all ages							
All races/ethnicities	89,368	100.0%	30.0%	58.5%	2.9%	6.3%	2.4%
White	77,212	100.0	28.2	60.9	2.5	6.2	2.3
Black	9,472	100.0	42.9	40.4	6.0	7.5	3.3
Hispanic origin	6,517	100.0	36.4	49.9	6.2	5.8	1.6
Males aged 35 to 44							
All races/ethnicities	16,528	100.0	10.0	74.7	4.2	10.8	0.3
White	14,389	100.0	9.2	76.5	3.5	10.7	0.3
Black	1,601	100.0	17.1	57.4	10.8	14.1	0.6
Hispanic origin	1,202	100.0	10.1	69.5	9.6	10.5	0.4
Females all ages							
All races/ethnicities	97,320	100.0	23.0	53.7	3.6	8.3	11.4
White	83,003	100.0	21.0	56.6	2.7	8.0	11.6
Black	11,447	100.0	36.5	32.7	9.2	10.4	11.2
Hispanic origin	6,588	100.0	26.6	51.2	7.7	8.3	6.2
Females aged 35 to 44							
All races/ethnicities	17,103	100.0	7.5	71.5	5.2	14.0	1.8
White	14,571	100.0	6.3	74.8	4.0	13.4	1.5
Black	1,952	100.0	16.6	46.1	14.2	19.5	3.6
Hispanic origin	1,235	100.0	8.6	67.6	9.2	12.7	1.9

Source: Marital Status and Living Arrangements: March 1987, Bureau of the Census, Current Population Reports, Series P-20, No. 423

Note: Hispanics may be of any race. Numbers may not add to total due to rounding.

Number of Marriages and Divorces

MARITAL STATUS AND FERTILITY
35–44

MARRIAGE AND REMARRIAGE

Women aged 35 to 44 account for over one-quarter of remarriages but only 3 percent of first-time weddings. Men in this age group account for 5 percent of first-time marriages and 32 percent of remarriages.

(number of marriages and divorces for all persons and for those aged 35 to 44, by sex)

	all persons male	all persons female	persons aged 35 to 44 male	persons aged 35 to 44 female	percent involving persons aged 35 to 44 male	percent involving persons aged 35 to 44 female
All marriages	1,858,783	1,858,783	260,123	206,079	14.0%	11.1%
First marriages	1,185,904	1,196,119	56,104	33,832	4.7	2.9
Remarriages	635,086	623,867	200,403	169,203	31.6	26.6
Previously divorced	499,735	485,848	168,278	138,173	33.7	27.6
Divorces	577,713	577,713	151,273	132,406	26.2	22.9

Source: Advance Report of Final Marriage Statistics, 1985 and Advance Report of Final Divorce Statistics, 1985, *National Center for Health Statistics*

Note: Numbers will not add to total because all divorces include those not stating their age and all marriages include those not stating whether they were previously married.

Childbearing Patterns

MARITAL STATUS AND FERTILITY
35–44

ONE IN TEN CHILDLESS

Twelve percent of all ever-married women aged 35 to 39 are childless as are 10 percent of those aged 40 to 44. The largest share—37 percent—of women in this age group have had two children; the next most popular number is three children.

(number of children ever born to women aged 18 to 44 and those aged 35 to 44, by race and marital status, number of women in thousands)

	all women	total	none	one	two	three	four	five and six	seven or more
All races									
All marital statuses									
Aged 18 to 44	52,586	100.0%	38.0	18.6	25.2	11.8	4.2	2.0	0.3
Aged 35 to 39	9,586	100.0	17.7	18.0	34.4	19.0	6.8	3.2	0.9
Aged 40 to 44	8,155	100.0	14.7	14.9	35.2	20.7	8.8	4.9	0.8
Women ever married									
Aged 18 to 44	36,847	100.0	19.6	22.0	33.8	16.0	5.7	2.5	0.4
Aged 35 to 39	8,587	100.0	11.9	18.4	37.4	20.7	7.3	3.5	0.8
Aged 40 to 44	7,543	100.0	10.2	14.7	37.3	22.1	9.5	5.2	0.9
Women never married									
Aged 18 to 44	15,739	100.0	81.0	10.5	5.0	2.0	0.8	0.6	0.1
Aged 35 to 39	999	100.0	67.9	15.1	8.4	3.7	2.7	1.1	1.1
Aged 40 to 44	612	100.0	70.5	16.4	8.8	2.3	0.6	1.4	0.1
White women									
All marital statuses									
Aged 18 to 44	43,870	100.0	39.2	17.8	25.4	11.8	3.9	1.6	0.3
Aged 35 to 39	8,071	100.0	18.5	17.2	35.4	19.3	6.3	2.6	0.7
Aged 40 to 44	6,983	100.0	14.8	14.9	35.5	21.2	8.4	4.4	0.8
Women ever married									
Aged 18 to 44	31,909	100.0	20.3	22.1	34.0	15.8	5.2	2.1	0.4
Aged 35 to 39	7,384	100.0	12.4	18.2	38.2	20.9	6.8	2.8	0.7
Aged 40 to 44	6,529	100.0	10.0	15.2	37.6	22.7	9.0	4.7	0.9
Women never married									
Aged 18 to 44	11,960	100.0	89.4	6.5	2.6	1.0	0.4	0.2	–
Aged 35 to 39	687	100.0	84.5	6.4	5.2	2.3	1.2	0.4	–
Aged 40 to 44	454	100.0	82.6	11.1	5.1	0.4	–	0.7	0.1

(continued next page)

Almanac of Consumer Markets

Childbearing Patterns

MARITAL STATUS AND FERTILITY
35–44

(continued from previous page)

(number of children ever born to women aged 18 to 44 and those aged 35 to 44, by race and marital status, number of women in thousands)

	all women	total	none	one	two	three	four	five and six	seven or more
Black women									
All marital statuses									
Aged 18 to 44	6,835	100.0	30.3	23.9	23.1	12.0	6.0	4.1	0.7
Aged 35 to 39	1,174	100.0	12.8	22.9	25.8	18.0	10.8	7.3	2.4
Aged 40 to 44	881	100.0	15.8	16.0	30.4	16.7	11.4	9.1	0.6
Women ever married									
Aged 18 to 44	3,611	100.0	13.6	22	31.3	17.4	9.2	5.7	0.8
Aged 35 to 39	881	100.0	7.6	19.0	28.8	21.6	12.2	8.8	2.0
Aged 40 to 44	736	100.0	12.5	12.7	32.5	18.3	13.2	10.1	0.7
Women never married									
Aged 18 to 44	3,225	100.0	48.9	26.1	14.0	5.9	2.4	2.2	0.5
Aged 35 to 39	292	100.0	28.6	34.7	16.6	7.2	6.5	2.7	3.6
Aged 40 to 44	145	100.0	32.6	33.1	19.6	8.5	2.4	3.8	–
Hispanic women									
All marital statuses									
Aged 18 to 44	4,326	100.0	33.6	17.0	22.7	15.6	5.6	4.4	1.0
Aged 35 to 39	715	100.0	17.3	10.5	23.7	28.5	9.8	7.7	2.5
Aged 40 to 44	579	100.0	10.0	12.3	29.1	20.6	9.3	14.6	4.2
Women ever married									
Aged 18 to 44	3,012	100.0	17.2	19.4	28.9	20.3	7.0	5.8	1.5
Aged 35 to 39	616	100.0	11.7	10.3	24.9	31.3	10.5	8.4	2.9
Aged 40 to 44	513	100.0	5.5	10.2	29.9	23.2	10.5	15.9	4.7
Women never married									
Aged 18 to 44	1,314	100.0	71.3	11.5	8.6	4.9	2.4	1.3	–
Aged 35 to 39	98	100.0	52.9	11.9	15.9	11.0	5.3	3.0	–
Aged 40 to 44	66	100.0	B	B	B	B	B	B	B

Source: Fertility of American Women: June 1988, Bureau of the Census, Current Population Reports, Series P-20, No. 436

Note: The symbol "B" means that the base number of women was too small to calculate a reliable percent distribution. Hispanic women are of any race.

158   Almanac of Consumer Markets

Summary of Educational Attainment

EDUCATIONAL ATTAINMENT
35–44

MOST HIGHLY EDUCATED

People aged 35 to 44 are the most highly educated group of Americans. Nearly half of them completed one to three years of college and 27 percent finished four or more years.

(years of school completed by persons aged 25 and over, by selected characteristics, numbers in thousands)

	number	4 years of high school or more	1 or more years of college	4 or more years of college
All persons	149,144	75.6%	37.0%	19.9%
Age groups:				
25 to 34	42,635	86.5	45.4	23.9
35 to 44	**33,632**	**85.9**	**46.8**	**26.5**
45 to 54	23,018	77.6	35.6	19.5
55 to 64	21,883	67.8	28.0	14.9
65 to 74	17,232	56.9	21.9	10.6
75 years and older	10,743	42.0	18.0	8.9
Sex:				
Male	70,677	76.0	40.6	23.6
Female	78,476	75.3	33.6	16.5
Race:				
White	129,170	77.0	37.8	20.5
Black	15,580	63.4	26.4	10.7
Asian and other	4,394	78.4	50.9	33.4
Hispanic origin:				
Hispanic	9,449	50.9	21.9	8.6
Non-Hispanic	139,695	77.3	38.0	20.6
Region:				
Northeast	32,030	76.5	36.8	22.2
Midwest	36,322	77.4	33.7	17.6
South	50,848	70.8	34.1	18.3
West	29,943	80.6	45.9	22.8
Metropolitan residence:				
Metropolitan area	115,614	77.6	40.0	22.1
Nonmetropolitan area	33,529	68.7	26.5	12.6

Source: Educational Attainment in the United States: March 1987 and March 1986, Bureau of the Census, Current Population Reports, Series P-20, No. 428

Age and Education

EDUCATIONAL ATTAINMENT
35–44

TO BE CONTINUED

Younger members (aged 35 to 39) of this age group are slightly more likely than older members (aged 40 to 44) to have completed four or more years of college—27 percent versus 26 percent. The share of men and women with one to three years of college also decreases with age among 35-to-44-year-olds.

(years of school completed by persons aged 35 to 44, by sex and single year of age, numbers in thousands)

	number	total	not high school graduate	high school graduate	1 to 3 years of college	4 or more years of college	median years
Males aged 35 to 39	9,163	100.0%	12.3%	34.0%	22.2%	31.5%	13.5
Age 35	1,895	100.0	10.7	39.2	21.8	28.3	13.0
Age 36	1,763	100.0	13.0	35.0	21.3	30.7	13.3
Age 37	1,797	100.0	12.4	31.9	23.3	32.5	13.8
Age 38	1,828	100.0	11.3	33.8	23.4	31.5	13.6
Age 39	1,881	100.0	14.1	30.2	21.1	34.7	13.8
Males aged 40 to 44	7,365	100.0	15.9	34.7	18.9	30.5	13.0
Age 40	1,786	100.0	15.1	31.5	21.7	31.7	13.4
Age 41	1,376	100.0	15.6	34.6	18.4	31.4	13.0
Age 42	1,473	100.0	18.0	36.6	18.1	27.5	12.9
Age 43	1,365	100.0	14.4	37.6	16.8	31.3	12.9
Age 44	1,364	100.0	16.8	34.3	18.8	30.1	13.0
Females aged 35 to 39	9,423	100.0	13.6	43.0	21.1	22.4	12.8
Age 35	1,927	100.0	11.3	44.3	20.9	23.4	12.9
Age 36	1,898	100.0	12.5	43.6	20.5	23.3	12.9
Age 37	1,920	100.0	15.3	39.9	23.5	21.3	12.9
Age 38	1,786	100.0	15.8	40.6	20.9	22.7	12.8
Age 39	1,894	100.0	13.0	46.3	19.4	21.2	12.8
Females aged 40 to 44	7,680	100.0	15.2	44.5	18.6	21.8	12.8
Age 40	1,839	100.0	12.9	41.8	21.2	24.3	12.9
Age 41	1,509	100.0	16.0	42.5	17.4	24.1	12.8
Age 42	1,427	100.0	15.8	43.0	19.3	21.8	12.8
Age 43	1,476	100.0	15.8	49.1	18.0	17.3	12.7
Age 44	1,428	100.0	16.1	46.7	16.5	20.7	12.7

Source: Educational Attainment in the United States: March 1987 and 1986, Bureau of the Census, Current Population Reports, Series P-20, No. 428

Note: Numbers may not add to total due to rounding.

Sex, Race, and Ethnicity

EDUCATIONAL ATTAINMENT
35–44

PERPETUAL STUDENTS

People in this age group are more likely than those in any other age group to have completed one to three years of college (47 percent) or four or more years of college (27 percent). Twenty-seven percent of whites and 14 percent of blacks aged 35 to 44 are in the most highly educated group.

(years of school completed by persons aged 25 and older and those aged 35 to 44, by sex, race, and Hispanic origin, numbers in thousands)

	number	total	not high school graduate	high school graduate	1 to 3 years of college	4 or more years of college
All persons aged 25 and older	149,144	100.0%	24.4%	38.7%	17.1%	19.9%
White	129,170	100.0	23.0	39.2	17.2	20.5
Black	15,580	100.0	36.6	37.1	15.7	10.7
Hispanic origin	9,449	100.0	49.1	29.0	13.3	8.6
All persons aged 35 to 44	33,632	100.0	14.1	39.1	20.3	26.5
White	28,960	100.0	12.9	39.1	20.8	27.3
Black	3,552	100.0	23.9	43.7	18.5	14.0
Hispanic origin	2,437	100.0	42.6	32.6	15.2	9.5
Males aged 25 and older	70,677	100.0	24.0	35.4	17.1	23.6
White	61,678	100.0	22.7	35.6	17.2	24.5
Black	6,919	100.0	37.0	36.5	15.5	11.0
Hispanic origin	4,614	100.0	48.2	28.0	14.2	9.7
Males aged 35 to 44	16,528	100.0	13.9	34.3	20.7	31.0
White	14,389	100.0	12.8	34.1	21.1	32.0
Black	1,601	100.0	24.4	41.3	18.5	15.8
Hispanic origin	1,202	100.0	41.0	29.7	18.3	11.0
Females aged 25 and older	78,467	100.0	24.7	41.6	17.1	16.5
White	67,492	100.0	23.3	42.6	17.3	16.9
Black	8,661	100.0	36.2	37.5	15.8	10.4
Hispanic origin	4,835	100.0	50.0	30.0	12.5	7.5
Females aged 35 to 44	17,103	100.0	14.3	43.6	20.0	22.1
White	14,571	100.0	13.0	43.9	20.4	22.7
Black	1,952	100.0	23.3	45.6	18.6	12.5
Hispanic origin	1,235	100.0	43.9	35.5	12.2	8.3

Source: Educational Attainment in the United States: March 1987 and March 1986, Bureau of the Census, Current Population Reports, Series P-20, No. 428
Note: Hispanics are of any race. Numbers may not add to total due to rounding.

Householders

EDUCATIONAL ATTAINMENT
35–44

EDUCATED HOUSEHOLDERS

Male householders aged 35 to 54 are more likely to have finished four or more years of college than their counterparts in any other age group. The proportion of female householders with four or more years of college is highest (24 percent) among 25-to-34-year-olds, followed by these 35-to-54-year-olds at 20 percent.

(years of school completed by householders aged 35 to 54, by sex, race, and Hispanic origin, numbers in thousands)

	number	total	not high school graduate	high school graduate	1 to 3 years of college	4 or more years of college	median years
Male householders	24,091	100.0%	16.4%	35.1%	18.8%	29.7%	13.0
White	21,295	100.0	15.4	35.2	19.1	30.3	13.0
Black	2,014	100.0	28.1	38.5	17.0	16.3	12.6
Hispanic origin	1,476	100.0	45.5	27.7	15.0	11.7	12.2
Female householders	7,824	100.0	21.6	39.0	19.1	20.3	12.7
White	5,897	100.0	18.7	38.2	20.0	23.0	12.8
Black	1,698	100.0	30.7	43.0	16.2	10.1	12.4
Hispanic origin	631	100.0	51.5	28.4	11.4	8.9	11.7

Source: Educational Attainment in the United States: March 1987 and March 1986, *Bureau of the Census, Current Population Reports, Series P-20, No. 428*

Note: The Census Bureau grouped householders aged 45 to 54 with those aged 35 to 44 for this tabulation. Hispanics are of any race. Numbers may not add to total due to rounding.

Labor Force Status

LABOR FORCE
35–44

HIGH EMPLOYMENT, LOW UNEMPLOYMENT

Women aged 35 to 44 are even more likely to be in the labor force than 25-to-34-year-old women. Men in both age groups show a 95 percent labor force participation rate, with unemployment lower among 35-to-44-year-olds than among those ten years younger.

(labor force status of all persons aged 16 and older, aged 18 to 64, and those aged 35 to 44, by sex and race, numbers in thousands)

	total population	total in labor force	percent of population in labor force	number employed	number unemployed	percent of labor force unemployed	not in labor force
Males aged 16 and older	86,899	66,207	76.2%	62,107	4,101	6.2%	20,692
White	75,189	57,779	76.8	54,647	3,132	5.4	17,410
Black	9,128	6,486	71.1	5,661	826	12.7	2,642
Males aged 18 to 64	71,443	62,563	87.6	58,864	3,699	5.9	8,880
White	61,583	54,522	88.5	51,705	2,818	5.2	7,061
Black	7,615	6,179	81.1	5,427	750	12.1	1,437
Males aged 35 to 44	16,475	15,587	94.6	14,898	689	4.4	888
White	14,338	13,674	95.4	13,138	536	3.9	664
Black	1,587	1,406	88.6	1,283	122	8.7	181
Females aged 16 and older	95,853	53,658	56.0%	50,334	3,324	6.2%	42,195
White	81,769	45,510	55.7	43,142	2,369	5.2	36,258
Black	11,224	6,507	58.0	5,648	858	13.2	4,717
Females aged 18 to 64	75,700	50,799	67.1	47,801	3,000	5.9	24,901
White	63,964	42,999	67.2	40,878	2,120	4.9	20,965
Black	9,262	6,227	67.2	5,438	791	12.7	3,035
Females aged 35 to 44	17,279	12,873	74.5	12,281	592	4.6	4,406
White	14,698	10,907	74.2	10,459	448	4.1	3,791
Black	1,976	1,537	77.8	1,412	125	8.1	439

Source: Annual averages from Employment and Earnings, 1987, Bureau of Labor Statistics

Note: The population here includes all civilian, noninstitutionalized people aged 16 and older.

Extent of Employment

LABOR FORCE
35–44

FULL-TIME WORKERS

Ninety-six percent of 35-to-44-year-old working men and 74 percent of the women have full-time jobs, the best working record of any age group. Of these, fully 85 percent of the men and 79 percent of the women—and almost half of part-time employees—work at least 50 weeks a year.

(work experience in 1987 of workers aged 16 and older and aged 35 to 44, by sex, numbers in thousands)

	\multicolumn{4}{c}{worked at full-time jobs}	\multicolumn{4}{c}{worked at part-time jobs}	non-workers
	total	50-52 weeks	27-49 weeks	1-26 weeks	total	50-52 weeks	27-49 weeks	1-26 weeks	total
Males									
Aged 16 and older	59,740	47,106	7,489	5,143	9,280	3,175	2,165	3,940	18,582
Aged 35 to 44	15,177	12,876	1,677	624	659	269	191	200	1,000
Females									
Aged 16 and older	40,398	29,882	5,788	4,727	18,538	7,774	4,301	6,463	37,580
Aged 35 to 44	10,267	8,119	1,392	755	3,520	1,775	760	985	3,819

Source: The 1988 Current Population Survey, Bureau of Labor Statistics

Note: Numbers may not add to total due to rounding. The categories in this table are not mutually exclusive. Workers may, for example, be counted as both a full-time and a part-time worker if they held jobs of both kinds during the year. For this reason, the total number of workers will be higher and the number of nonworkers lower than in the previous table that uses annual averages of the number of workers in each category. Civilians only.

Kinds of Jobs

LABOR FORCE
35–44

MANAGERS AND PROFESSIONALS

Thirty-two percent of working 35-to-44-year-old men and 31 percent of the women hold managerial and professional jobs. No other age group has such a high proportion of workers in that category—or such low representation among service and farming, forestry and fishing jobs.

(occupations of employed persons aged 16 and older and those aged 35 to 44, by sex, numbers in thousands)

	aged 16+	aged 35-44	males aged 35-44	females aged 35-44	percent aged 16+	percent aged 35-44
All employed persons	112,440	27,179	14,898	12,281	100.0%	100.0%
Managerial and professional	**27,742**	**8,547**	**4,765**	**3,782**	**24.7**	**31.4**
Executive, administrative and managerial	13,316	4,016	2,552	1,464	11.8	14.8
Officials & administrators, public admin.	549	195	119	76	0.5	0.7
Other executive, admin., & managerial	9,190	2,832	1,911	921	8.2	10.4
Management-related occupations	3,577	989	522	467	3.2	3.6
Professional specialty occupations	14,426	4,531	2,213	2,318	12.8	16.7
Engineers	1,731	455	434	21	1.5	1.7
Math & computer scientists	685	224	152	72	0.6	0.8
Natural scientists	388	111	84	27	0.3	0.4
Health diagnosing occupations	793	266	217	49	0.7	1.0
Health assessment & treating	2,148	624	95	529	1.9	2.3
Teachers, college & university	661	204	120	84	0.6	0.8
Teachers, except college & university	3,587	1,328	361	967	3.2	4.9
Lawyers & judges	707	241	197	44	0.6	0.9
Other professional specialty occupations	3,727	1,078	554	524	3.3	4.0
Technical, sales, administrative support	**35,082**	**8,078**	**2,914**	**5,164**	**31.2**	**29.7**
Technicians & related support occupations	3,346	862	424	438	3.0	3.2
Health technologists & technicians	1,142	308	39	269	1.0	1.1
Engineering & science technicians	1,100	272	213	59	1.0	1.0
Techs., except health, engineering, science	1,104	283	173	110	1.0	1.0
Sales occupations	13,480	2,949	1,690	1,259	12.0	10.9
Supervisors & proprietors	3,572	968	668	300	3.2	3.6
Sales reps., finance & business service	2,330	632	370	262	2.1	2.3

(continued next page)

Kinds of Jobs

LABOR FORCE 35–44

(continued from previous page)

(occupations of employed persons aged 16 and older, and those aged 35 to 44, by sex, numbers in thousands)

	aged 16+	aged 35-44	males aged 35-44	females aged 35-44	percent aged 16+	percent aged 35-44
Sales reps., commodities except retail	1,544	429	360	69	1.4%	1.6%
Sales, retail and personal	5,973	909	287	622	5.3	3.3
Sales-related occupations	60	11	5	6	0.1	0.0
Administrative support including clerical	18,256	4,266	799	3,467	16.2	15.7
Supervisors	723	227	107	120	0.6	0.8
Computer equipment operators	914	197	66	131	0.8	0.7
Secretaries, stenographers, & typists	5,004	1,204	15	1,189	4.5	4.4
Financial records processing	2,469	591	48	543	2.2	2.2
Mail & message distributing	961	253	171	82	0.9	0.9
Other admin. support including clerical	8,185	1,795	394	1,401	7.3	6.6
Service occupations	15,054	2,885	1,041	1,844	13.4	10.6
Private household	934	141	3	138	0.8	0.5
Protective services	1,907	507	454	53	1.7	1.9
Service, except private hhld. & protective	12,213	2,237	584	1,653	10.9	8.2
Food service	5,204	699	177	522	4.6	2.6
Health service	1,873	416	35	381	1.7	1.5
Cleaning & building service	2,886	589	299	290	2.6	2.2
Personal service	2,249	533	74	459	2.0	2.0
Precision production, craft, repair	13,568	3,339	3,019	320	12.1	12.3
Mechanics & repairers	4,445	1,125	1,078	47	0.4	4.1
Construction trades	5,011	1,144	1,119	25	4.5	4.2
Other production, craft, repair	4,112	1,070	822	248	3.7	3.9
Operators, fabricators, laborers	17,486	3,747	2,688	1,059	15.6	13.8
Machine operators, assemblers, inspectors	7,994	1,859	1,073	786	7.1	6.8
Transportation, material moving	4,712	1,171	1,062	109	4.2	4.3
Handlers, equip. cleaners, helpers, laborers	4,779	717	553	164	4.3	2.6
Farming, forestry, fishing	3,507	583	471	112	3.1	2.1
Farm operators & managers	1,317	252	210	42	1.2	0.9
Farm workers & related occupations	2,013	289	222	67	1.8	1.1
Forestry and fishing occupations	177	42	38	4	0.2	0.2

Source: Unpublished annual data for 1987, Bureau of Labor Statistics

Note: Numbers may not add to total due to rounding. Civilian, noninstitutionalized employees only.

Workers in the 1990s

LABOR FORCE
35–44

WOMEN WORKERS ON THE RISE

During the 1990s the labor force participation of women aged 35 to 44 will increase more than that of any other age or gender group. Men aged 35 to 44, on the other hand, will show a slight decline in their labor force participation, a downward trend expected for all men except those who are under age 25.

(labor force and labor force participation rates* for persons aged 16 and older and those aged 35 to 44, by sex, race, and ethnicity, in 1990 and 2000, numbers in thousands)

	1990 number	1990 participation rate	2000 number	2000 participation rate	1990–2000 percent change
Both sexes, aged 16 and older	124,457	66.2%	138,775	67.8%	11.5%
White	106,648	66.5	116,701	68.2	9.4
Black	13,788	64.6	16,334	66.0	18.5
Hispanic	9,718	65.9	14,086	67.1	44.9
Asian and other	4,021	64.8	5,740	65.8	42.8
Males, aged 16 and older	67,909	75.8	73,136	74.7	7.7
Males, aged 35 to 44	17,290	94.4	20,133	93.9	16.4
White	15,040	95.0	17,100	94.5	13.7
Black	1,664	90.3	2,225	90.7	33.7
Hispanic	1,358	94.0	2,234	93.2	64.5
Asian and other	586	91.0	808	90.5	37.9
Females, aged 16 and older	56,548	57.4	65,639	61.5	16.1
Females, aged 35 to 44	14,641	76.9	18,438	84.2	25.9
White	12,330	76.8	15,264	84.6	23.8
Black	1,783	78.7	2,409	82.8	35.1
Hispanic	922	64.0	1,549	71.6	68.0
Asian and other	528	73.6	765	81.5	44.9

*Labor force participation rates are the ratio of people in the labor force to the total population of a given sex, age and race or ethnicity.

Source: Unpublished data from the Bureau of Labor Statistics

Note: The labor force here includes civilians who are working or looking for work. Hispanics are of any race.

Household Income

INCOME
35–44

LARGEST HOUSEHOLDS

Although they are only 21 percent of all households, households headed by Americans aged 35 to 44 account for 26 percent of household income. Their average household size of 3.33 persons per household is the largest of any age group, a factor that helps reduce the income per household member to $11,900.

(household income and income per household member, for all households and for households by age of householder, numbers for 1988 in thousands, income is for 1987)

	households number	households percent	persons in household number	persons in household percent	persons per household	total household income $ billions	total household income percent	per household member
All households	91,066	100.0%	240,722	100.0%	2.64	$2,927.2	100.0%	$12,160
Age of householder								
under 25	5,228	5.7	12,117	5.0	2.32	102.0	3.5	8,415
25 to 34	20,583	22.6	58,724	24.4	2.85	621.6	21.2	10,586
35 to 44	19,323	21.2	64,351	26.7	3.33	763.8	26.1	11,870
45 to 54	13,630	15.0	41,379	17.2	3.04	597.0	20.4	14,426
55 to 64	12,846	14.1	30,151	12.5	2.35	447.3	15.3	14,835
65 and older	19,456	21.4	33,999	14.1	1.75	395.6	13.5	11,635

Source: The 1988 Current Population Survey, Bureau of the Census

Individual Income

INCOME
35–44

CLIMBING THE INCOME LADDER

With a median income of over $26,800, men aged 35 to 44 are more likely than all income-producing men to have high incomes. Thirty-two percent of 35-to-44-year-old men have incomes between $35,000 and $50,000 and another 13 percent have incomes of $50,000 or more. On the other hand, 71 percent of 35-to-44-year-old income-generating women bring in less than $20,000.

(income distribution and median income for males and females aged 15 and older and aged 35 to 44, numbers for 1988 in thousands, income is for 1987)

	males aged 15 and older		males aged 35 to 44	
	number	percent	number	percent
All males	90,284	–	17,077	–
All males with income	85,623	100.0%	16,817	100.0%
Less than $5,000	13,025	15.2	1,022	6.1
$5,000 to $9,999	12,066	14.1	1,302	7.7
$10,000 to $14,999	11,708	13.7	1,488	8.8
$15,000 to $19,999	9,887	11.5	1,760	10.5
$20,000 to $24,999	8,714	10.2	2,009	11.9
$25,000 to $29,999	7,266	8.5	1,989	11.8
$30,000 to $34,999	6,124	7.2	1,856	11.0
$35,000 to $49,999	9,941	11.6	3,141	18.7
$50,000 to $74,999	4,669	5.5	1,518	9.0
$75,000 and over	2,225	2.6	732	4.4
Median income, all with income		$17,752		$26,828
Median income, year-round, full-time workers		$26,722		$30,655

	females aged 15 and older		females aged 35 to 44	
	number	percent	number	percent
All females	98,168	–	17,606	–
All females with income	89,279	100.0%	16,423	100.0%
Less than $5,000	30,715	34.4	4,364	26.6
$5,000 to $9,999	19,782	22.2	2,787	17.0
$10,000 to $14,999	13,313	14.9	2,423	14.8
$15,000 to $19,999	9,470	10.6	2,072	12.6
$20,000 to $24,999	6,321	7.1	1,673	10.2
$25,000 to $29,999	3,768	4.2	1,131	6.9
$30,000 to $34,999	2,331	2.6	755	4.6
$35,000 to $49,999	2,602	2.9	900	5.5
$50,000 to $74,999	708	0.8	246	1.5
$75,000 and over	268	0.3	71	0.4
Median income, all with income		$8,101		$11,969
Median income, year-round, full-time workers		$17,504		$19,897

Source: Money Income and Poverty Status in the United States: 1987, Bureau of the Census, Current Population Reports, Series P-20, No. 161
Note: Numbers may not add to total due to rounding.

Income and Age

INCOME
35–44

HEADED TOWARD THE TOP

Half of all households headed by a 35-to-44-year-old bring in $35,000 or more, and 26 percent can claim at least $50,000. Household incomes of the remaining households headed by people in this age group are divided fairly evenly between under $20,000 (24 percent) and $20,000 to $35,000 (26 percent).

(household income by age of householder, numbers for 1988 in thousands, income is for 1987)

	total	under 25	25 to 34	35 to 44	45 to 54	55 to 64	65 to 74	75 +
All households	91,066	5,228	20,583	19,323	13,630	12,846	11,410	8,045
All households	100.0%	100.0%	100.0%	100.0%	100.0%	100.0%	100.0%	100.0%
Less than $10,000	18.4	30.3	13.6	10.3	10.4	17.4	27.1	44.6
$10,000 to $14,999	10.6	15.8	9.6	6.6	6.6	9.5	17.3	18.5
$15,000 to $19,999	10.0	14.1	11.1	7.4	6.8	9.7	13.8	11.8
$20,000 to $24,999	9.2	11.5	11.1	8.3	7.2	9.1	10.1	7.5
$25,000 to $29,999	8.4	9.0	10.6	8.5	7.6	8.0	8.3	4.3
$30,000 to $34,999	7.7	6.8	9.7	9.0	7.8	7.2	6.0	3.2
$35,000 to $39,999	6.8	4.5	8.6	9.0	7.2	6.3	4.2	2.4
$40,000 to $44,999	5.8	2.3	6.7	7.9	7.4	6.0	3.0	1.7
$45,000 to $49,999	4.6	1.3	5.1	6.6	5.9	4.7	2.4	1.5
$50,000 to $59,999	6.7	2.1	6.7	9.6	10.1	7.5	2.7	1.9
$60,000 to $74,999	5.5	1.5	4.2	7.9	9.9	6.3	2.1	1.2
$75,000 and over	6.3	0.9	3.0	8.9	13.1	8.3	3.0	1.4
Median household income	$25,986	$16,204	$26,923	$34,926	$37,250	$27,538	$16,906	$11,261

Source: The 1988 Current Population Survey, Bureau of the Census

Note: Numbers may not add to total due to rounding.

Income of Married Couples

INCOME
35–44

HIGH-INCOME HOUSEHOLDS

Only married couples aged 45 to 54 have a higher median income ($45,200) than those in this age group. Married couples aged 35 to 44 who do not have children under age 18 living in the home have a median income of nearly $45,000 and 41 percent of them have incomes of at least $50,000.

(household income of married-couple householder families with and without children under 18 at home, householders aged 35 to 44, numbers for 1988 in thousands, income is for 1987)

	married-couple householder aged 35 to 44		
	total	with children under 18 at home	without children under 18 at home
All households	12,448	10,121	2,327
All households	100.0%	100.0%	100.0%
Less than $10,000	3.5	3.6	3.4
$10,000 to $14,999	3.6	3.8	3.0
$15,000 to $19,999	5.6	5.8	4.5
$20,000 to $24,999	6.7	6.9	5.8
$25,000 to $29,999	7.8	8.0	6.8
$30,000 to $34,999	9.5	10.0	7.2
$35,000 to $39,999	10.3	10.7	8.7
$40,000 to $44,999	9.6	9.4	10.3
$45,000 to $49,999	8.2	8.0	9.1
$50,000 to $59,999	12.4	12.3	13.1
$60,000 to $74,999	10.8	10.4	12.8
$75,000 and over	11.9	11.2	15.2
Median household income	$41,275	$40,372	$44,977

Source: The 1988 Current Population Survey, Bureau of the Census

Note: Numbers may not add to total due to rounding.

Income of Other Family Households

INCOME
35–44

HIGHER-INCOME MEN

Thirty-four percent of families headed by unmarried 35-to-44-year-old men have incomes under $20,000 and 38 percent of them bring in over $35,000. On the other hand, 56 percent of the families headed by women in this category have incomes under $20,000, while only 17 percent of them bring in $35,000 or more.

(household income of unmarried female- and male-householder families with and without children under 18 at home, householders aged 35 to 44, numbers for 1988, in thousands, income is for 1987)

	female householder aged 35 to 44			male householder aged 35 to 44		
	total	with children under 18 at home	without children under 18 at home	total	with children under 18 at home	without children under 18 at home
All households	2,765	2,281	484	639	416	223
All households	100.0%	100.0%	100.0%	100.0%	100.0%	100.0%
Less than $10,000	29.8	32.9	15.1	13.3	13.7	12.6
$10,000 to $14,999	13.9	14.0	13.2	10.8	10.1	12.1
$15,000 to $19,999	11.8	11.8	11.4	9.9	11.3	7.2
$20,000 to $24,999	11.6	11.6	11.6	8.3	7.5	9.9
$25,000 to $29,999	8.9	8.4	11.2	10.5	10.3	11.2
$30,000 to $34,999	7.0	6.4	10.1	9.2	9.6	8.5
$35,000 to $39,999	5.7	5.3	7.4	8.0	7.5	9.0
$40,000 to $44,999	2.9	2.8	3.5	8.8	10.1	6.3
$45,000 to $49,999	2.4	2.3	3.1	4.4	4.6	4.5
$50,000 to $59,999	3.1	2.0	8.3	6.6	6.5	7.2
$60,000 to $74,999	1.3	1.1	2.7	5.6	4.6	7.2
$75,000 and over	1.6	1.3	2.7	4.7	4.3	4.9
Median household income	$17,262	$16,006	$24,145	$28,487	$28,083	$29,019

Source: The 1988 Current Population Survey, Bureau of the Census

Note: Numbers may not add to total due to rounding.

Income of Nonfamily Households

INCOME
35–44

BREADWINNERS

Among nonfamilies, the highest median incomes are claimed by 35-to-44-year-old men and women, whether they live alone or with others. Female householders in this age group who live with others do better financially than those who live alone.

(household income of nonfamily households by household type, householders aged 35 to 44, numbers for 1988 in thousands, income is for 1987)

	total number	living alone			living with others		
		total	male householder	female householder	total	male householder	female householder
All nonfamily households	3,471	2,837	1,776	1,061	635	431	204
All nonfamily households	100.0%	100.0%	100.0%	100.0%	100.0%	100.0%	100.0%
Less than $10,000	18.7	21.8	20.3	24.3	5.0	4.9	5.9
$10,000 to $14,999	10.7	11.6	11.1	12.4	6.6	7.2	5.4
$15,000 to $19,999	9.9	10.4	9.1	12.6	7.7	8.4	6.4
$20,000 to $24,999	11.1	12.1	11.7	12.6	6.6	6.3	7.4
$25,000 to $29,999	10.7	11.6	10.6	13.3	6.5	7.0	5.9
$30,000 to $34,999	8.8	8.8	8.9	8.7	8.8	7.7	11.3
$35,000 to $39,999	7.1	7.0	7.5	6.3	7.1	9.0	2.9
$40,000 to $44,999	5.8	4.6	5.9	2.5	11.3	8.1	18.1
$45,000 to $49,999	4.3	3.8	4.3	2.9	6.8	7.9	4.4
$50,000 to $59,999	5.4	4.2	5.2	2.4	10.9	12.3	7.8
$60,000 to $74,999	2.8	1.5	1.8	0.9	8.7	9.0	7.8
$75,000 and over	4.6	2.6	3.5	1.0	13.7	11.8	17.2
Median household income	$24,586	$21,967	$23,500	$20,007	$40,825	$39,791	$42,020

Source: The 1988 Current Population Survey, Bureau of the Census

Note: Nonfamilies are either people living alone or living with an individual (or individuals) unrelated to the householder. Numbers may not add to total due to rounding.

Income and Race, Families

INCOME
35–44

INCOME GAP

At $38,000, the median income of white family households headed by 35-to-44-year-olds is more than $15,000 higher than that of black family households. But 36 percent of white married couples and 26 percent of black married couples have household incomes of $50,000 or more while another 53 percent of white couples and 55 percent of black couples have incomes in the $20,000 to $50,000 range.

(household income of family households by race and household type for householders aged 35 to 44, numbers for 1988 in thousands, income is for 1987)

white family households

	total	married couple	male householder	female householder
All households	13,551	11,093	518	1,940
Total	100.0%	100.0%	100.0%	100.0%
Less than $10,000	7.1	3.3	12.0	27.4
$10,000 to $19,999	11.4	8.7	22.2	24.1
$20,000 to $29,999	15.9	14.4	19.9	23.6
$30,000 to $39,999	18.9	19.8	18.9	14.1
$40,000 to $49,999	16.1	18.3	12.0	5.1
$50,000 to $59,999	11.0	12.6	6.8	3.2
$60,000 to $74,999	9.4	11.0	5.0	1.4
$75,000 and over	10.2	12.1	3.3	1.2
Median household income	$38,058	$41,826	$27,498	$19,224

black family households

	total	married couple	male householder	female householder
All households	1,764	925	92	747
Total	100.0%	100.0%	100.0%	100.0%
Less than $10,000	21.8	5.4	30.4	41.0
$10,000 to $19,999	23.0	13.8	29.3	33.6
$20,000 to $29,999	16.0	18.3	17.4	12.9
$30,000 to $39,999	15.0	20.9	9.8	8.6
$40,000 to $49,999	9.8	15.4	5.4	3.5
$50,000 to $59,999	6.4	11.2	6.5	0.4
$60,000 to $74,999	4.5	8.4	–	0.1
$75,000 and over	3.5	6.5	1.1	–
Median household income	$22,718	$35,578	$17,221	$12,155

Source: Money Income of Households, Families, and Persons in the United States: 1987, *Bureau of the Census, Current Population Reports, Series P-60, No. 162*
Note: Numbers may not add to total due to rounding.

Income and Race, Nonfamilies

INCOME
35–44

PEAK INCOMES

Incomes of nonfamily householders are highest among those aged 35 to 44. The difference in median incomes of white and black householders is also highest in this age group—$9,300. But 35 percent of white and 17 percent of black householders have incomes of $30,000 or more.

(householder income of nonfamily householders by race and household type for householders aged 35 to 44, numbers for 1988 in thousands, income is for 1987)

	white householder total	white male householder	white female householder	black householder total	black male householder	black female householder
All households	2,875	1,827	1,048	502	313	189
Total	100.0%	100.0%	100.0%	100.0%	100.0%	100.0%
Less than $10,000	19.3	17.4	22.6	35.5	37.4	31.7
$10,000 to $19,999	21.2	20.1	23.2	26.7	22.0	34.9
$20,000 to $24,999	12.6	11.9	13.6	11.6	13.7	7.9
$25,000 to $29,999	12.4	12.1	12.9	9.6	7.3	13.8
$30,000 to $34,999	9.8	9.8	9.9	5.4	4.5	6.3
$35,000 to $49,999	15.7	17.8	12.1	8.6	10.9	4.2
$50,000 and over	9.0	11.1	5.5	2.8	4.5	–
Median householder income	$23,593	$25,252	$21,270	$14,281	$14,380	$14,158

Source: Money Income of Households, Families, and Persons in the United States: 1987, *Bureau of the Census, Current Population Reports, Series P-60, No. 162*

Note: Numbers may not add to total due to rounding. Householder income is the total money income of the householder only.

Income of Hispanic Households

INCOME 35–44

SOMEWHERE IN BETWEEN

At $24,000, the median income of Hispanic families is $13,900 below the median for white families and $1,500 above that of black families headed by 35-to-44-year-olds. But almost half of the Hispanic families and 37 percent of the nonfamilies in this age group have household incomes of $25,000 or more.

(household income of Hispanic households by household type, for householders aged 35 to 44, numbers for 1988 in thousands, income is for 1987)

	total	family households		
		married couple	male householder	female householder
All households	1,193	845	61	287
Total	100.0%	100.0%	100.0%	100.0%
Less than $15,000	31.2	19.8	31.1	64.8
$15,000 to $24,999	20.5	21.4	27.9	15.7
$25,000 and over	48.4	58.8	39.3	19.5
Median household income	$24,195	$30,120	–	$9,638

		nonfamily households			
		male householder		female householder	
	total	living alone	living with others	living alone	living with others
All households	171	83	24	55	9
Total	100.0%	100.0%	100.0%	100.0%	100.0%
Less than $15,000	42.1	48.2	16.7	45.5	22.2
$15,000 to $24,999	21.1	22.9	33.3	16.4	–
$25,000 and over	36.8	28.9	50.0	36.4	77.8
Median household income	$19,037	$15,444	–	–	–

Source: The 1988 Current Population Survey, Bureau of the Census

Note: Numbers may not add to total due to rounding. Hispanics are of any race. Median income is unreliable and is therefore not given when the category contains fewer than 75,000 households.

Income of Dual-Earner Couples

INCOME 35–44

ON THE JOB

There is a larger share of dual-earners among married couples aged 35 to 44—68 percent—than among married couples in any other age group. Their median household income is $44,600 and 70 percent have an income of $35,000 or more.

(household income for all dual-earner married couples and for those with married-couple householders aged 35 to 44, numbers for 1988 in thousands, income is for 1987)

	householder all ages			householder aged 35 to 44		
	total	with children under 18 at home	without children under 18 at home	total	with children under 18 at home	without children under 18 at home
All households	26,227	14,989	11,238	8,423	6,588	1,835
All households	100.0%	100.0%	100.0%	100.0%	100.0%	100.0%
Less than $15,000	5.7	6.0	5.4	3.9	4.0	3.5
$15,000 to $19,999	5.1	5.4	4.7	3.7	3.9	3.2
$20,000 to $24,999	7.3	7.8	6.6	6.0	6.2	5.4
$25,000 to $29,999	8.3	9.0	7.5	7.0	7.3	6.0
$30,000 to $34,999	9.4	10.2	8.3	9.1	9.8	6.6
$35,000 to $39,999	10.3	11.2	9.0	10.8	11.5	8.2
$40,000 to $44,999	9.6	9.8	9.3	10.3	10.0	11.0
$45,000 to $49,999	8.1	8.2	7.9	9.3	9.0	10.3
$50,000 to $59,999	13.0	12.5	13.6	14.6	14.6	14.7
$60,000 to $74,999	11.2	10.2	12.5	12.5	12.1	14.1
$75,000 and over	12.1	9.6	15.3	12.9	11.7	17.1
Median household income	$41,904	$40,044	$44,508	$44,588	$43,617	$47,884

Source: The 1988 Current Population Survey, Bureau of the Census

Note: Numbers may not add to total due to rounding.

Income and Education

INCOME 35–44

TWENTY PERCENT AT THE TOP

Of 35-to-44-year-old householders with four or more years of college, only 10 percent have household incomes under $20,000, while an impressive 20 percent bring in $75,000 or more.

(household income of householders aged 35 to 44, by years of school completed by householder, numbers for 1988 in thousands, income is for 1987)

	total	not high school graduate	high school graduate	1 to 3 years of college	4 or more years of college
All households	19,323	2,588	6,653	4,193	5,890
All households	100.0%	100.0%	100.0%	100.0%	100.0%
Less than $10,000	10.3	29.5	11.0	8.1	2.7
$10,000 to $19,999	14.0	26.8	16.6	12.0	6.9
$20,000 to $29,999	16.8	15.9	20.5	17.7	12.3
$30,000 to $39,999	18.0	13.9	20.6	19.4	15.8
$40,000 to $49,999	14.5	6.4	14.5	17.2	16.2
$50,000 to $59,999	9.6	4.4	8.1	11.3	12.5
$60,000 to $74,999	7.9	2.2	5.2	7.5	13.6
$75,000 and over	8.9	0.8	3.5	7.0	19.9

Source: The 1988 Current Population Survey, Bureau of the Census.

Note: Numbers may not add to total due to rounding.

Future Income

INCOME
35–44

GROWTH AT THE TOP

In five years there will be more households headed by 35-to-44-year-olds in every income category. The number of those bringing in $60,000 or more will climb a full 26 percent between 1990 and 1995.

(projections of the number of households with householders aged 35 to 44, by household income, 1990 and 1995, numbers in thousands, income is in 1985 dollars)

	1990 number	1990 percent	1995 number	1995 percent	percent change 1990-1995
All households	21,245	100.0%	23,916	100.0%	12.6%
Less than $10,000	2,409	11.3	2,607	10.9	8.2
$10,000 to $19,999	3,344	15.7	3,561	14.9	6.5
$20,000 to $29,999	3,947	18.6	4,305	18.0	9.0
$30,000 to $39,999	4,011	18.9	4,334	18.1	8.0
$40,000 to $49,999	2,813	13.2	3,350	14.0	19.1
$50,000 to $59,999	1,876	8.8	2,186	9.1	16.5
$60,000 to $74,999	1,431	6.7	1,798	7.5	25.6
$75,000 and over	1,410	6.6	1,773	7.4	25.7
Median household income	$32,300		$33,428		

Source: American Demographics, *May to August, 1986,* based on the national econometric model of Wharton Economic Forecasting Association and on household projections from the Bureau of the Census

Note: Numbers may not add to total due to rounding.

Annual Expenditures

EXPENDITURES 35–44

AVERAGE SPENDERS

Households headed by a 35-to-44-year-old have a spending pattern very much like the national average. They do, however, devote a slightly larger share of their spending dollar to food, housing, and apparel than the average household and they spend about $600 over the average for entertainment and $900 more for insurance and pensions.

(average annual expenditure and percent distribution of expenditures for all households and for householders aged 35 to 44, number of households in thousands)

	all households		householder aged 35 to 44	
	average annual expenditure	*percent of all expenditures*	*average annual expenditure*	*percent of all expenditures*
Number of households	93,741		18,138	
Total expenditure	$22,710	100.0%	$29,587	100.0%
Food	3,363	14.8	4,410	14.9
Food at home	2,313	10.2	3,056	10.3
Food away from home	1,049	4.6	1,354	4.6
Alcoholic beverages	273	1.2	300	1.0
Housing	6,888	30.3	9,108	30.8
Shelter	3,986	17.6	5,444	18.4
Owned dwellings	2,305	10.1	3,569	12.1
Mortgage interest and charges	1,428	6.3	2,580	8.7
Property taxes	417	1.8	457	1.5
Maintenance, repairs, insurance, and other expenses	460	2.0	532	1.8
Rented dwellings	1,269	5.6	1,300	4.4
Other lodging	412	1.8	576	1.9
Fuels, utilities, and public services	1,646	7.2	1,937	6.5
Natural gas	248	1.1	276	0.9
Electricity	674	3.0	830	2.8
Fuel oil and other fuels	107	0.5	104	0.4
Telephone	471	2.1	546	1.8
Water and other public services	145	0.6	180	0.6
Household operations	353	1.6	481	1.6
Domestic services	288	1.3	397	1.3
Other household expenses	65	0.3	84	0.3
Household furnishings, equipment	903	4.0	1,246	4.2
Household textiles	83	0.4	122	0.4
Furniture	303	1.3	432	1.5
Floor coverings	51	0.2	91	0.3
Major appliances	155	0.7	167	0.6

(continued next page)

Annual Expenditures

EXPENDITURES 35–44

(continued from previous page)

(average annual expenditure and percent distribution of expenditures for all households and for householders aged 35 to 44, number of households in thousands)

	all households		householder aged 35 to 44	
	average annual expenditure	percent of all expenditures	average annual expenditure	percent of all expenditures
Small appliances, miscellaneous housewares	55	0.2	70	0.2
Miscellaneous household equipment	256	1.1	364	1.2
Apparel	1,149	5.1	1,588	5.4
Men and boys	283	1.2	418	1.4
Men, 16 and over	228	1.0	289	1.0
Boys, 2 to 15	55	0.2	129	0.4
Women and girls	462	2.0	638	2.2
Women, 16 and over	396	1.7	477	1.6
Girls, 2 to 15	66	0.3	161	0.5
Children under 2	45	0.2	48	0.2
Footwear	123	0.5	178	0.6
Other apparel products and services	237	1.0	306	1.0
Transportation	4,815	21.2	6,152	20.8
Cars and trucks, new (net outlay)	1,414	6.2	1,876	6.3
Cars and trucks, used (net outlay)	897	3.9	1,108	3.7
Other vehicles	29	0.1	36	0.1
Vehicle finance charges	270	1.2	377	1.3
Gasoline and motor oil	916	4.0	1,146	3.9
Maintenance and repairs	458	2.0	555	1.9
Vehicle insurance	420	1.8	516	1.7
Public transportation	248	1.1	302	1.0
Vehicle rental, licenses, other charges	163	0.7	238	0.8
Health care	1,062	4.7	1,005	3.4
Health insurance	371	1.6	313	1.1
Medical services	502	2.2	546	1.8
Medicines and medical supplies	189	0.8	146	0.5
Entertainment	1,087	4.8	1,657	5.6
Fees and admissions	308	1.4	451	1.5
Television, radios, sound equipment	373	1.6	529	1.8
Other equipment and services	406	1.8	678	2.3
Personal care	207	0.9	243	0.8
Reading	140	0.6	178	0.6
Education	298	1.3	393	1.3
Tobacco and smoking supplies	230	1.0	271	0.9
Miscellaneous	323	1.4	381	1.3
Contributions and support payments	746	3.3	833	2.8
Personal insurance and pensions	2,129	9.4	3,067	10.4
Life insurance and other personal insurance	293	1.3	369	1.2
Retirement, pensions, Social Security	1,836	8.1	2,697	9.1

Source: The 1986 Consumer Expenditure Survey, Bureau of Labor Statistics

Expenditures by Income

EXPENDITURES
35–44

VARIABLE SPENDING PATTERNS

The share of the household budget devoted to food declines as household income increases. That pattern does not hold for all expense categories—the highest-income households spend a bigger portion of their spending dollar on insurance and pensions (13 percent) than the lowest-income households (4 percent) and households bringing in $10,000 to $15,000 spend proportionally more on housing (33 percent) than their counterparts with higher or lower incomes.

(annual average expenditure of household with householders aged 35 to 44, by household income, number of households in thousands)

	all households	under $10,000	$10-14,999	$15-19,999	$20-29,999	$30-39,999	$40,000+
Number of households	16,542	2,363	1,332	1,449	3,293	2,933	5,174
Total expenditure	$29,195	$16,137	$17,258	$19,545	$23,573	$28,725	$44,776
Food	4,308	3,178	3,273	3,256	3,854	4,259	5,701
Food at home	2,988	2,469	2,474	2,418	2,767	2,957	3,675
Food away from home	1,320	709	798	838	1,087	1,302	2,026
Alcoholic beverages	317	178	191	246	288	318	451
Housing	8,899	5,512	5,620	5,940	6,862	8,457	13,667
Shelter	5,319	3,288	3,357	3,543	3,916	4,986	8,332
Owned dwellings	3,480	1,602	1,212	1,389	2,162	3,254	6,474
Rented dwellings	1,308	1,452	1,937	1,963	1,471	1,255	824
Other lodging	531	236	208	191	282	477	1,034
Fuels, utilities, public services	1,927	1,557	1,439	1,590	1,814	1,981	2,356
Household operations	463	211	236	178	338	385	839
Household furnishings, equipment	1,191	455	588	629	795	1,104	2,140
Apparel and services	1,582	890	973	1,065	1,216	1,515	2,469
Transportation	5,982	3,267	3,330	4,028	5,072	5,996	9,024
Vehicles	2,845	1,391	1,367	1,911	2,252	2,844	4,532
Gasoline and motor oil	1,232	825	924	994	1,233	1,309	1,518
Other vehicle expenses	1,621	866	903	965	1,373	1,657	2,471
Public transportation	285	186	136	159	215	187	503
Health care	966	637	668	889	863	990	1,267
Entertainment	1,605	765	880	933	1,182	1,563	2,656
Personal care	232	125	152	153	200	230	346

(continued next page)

Expenditures by Income

EXPENDITURES 35–44

(continued from previous page)

(annual average expenditure of household with householders aged 35 to 44, by household income, number of households in thousands)

	all households	under $10,000	$10-14,999	$15-19,999	$20-29,999	$30-39,999	$40,000+
Reading	179	93	98	120	154	171	275
Education	372	179	146	234	244	327	665
Tobacco and smoking supplies	276	293	297	297	278	287	249
Miscellaneous	396	202	209	379	354	364	581
Cash contributions	870	246	350	399	623	749	1,647
Personal insurance and pensions	3,211	574	1,073	1,607	2,383	3,499	5,778
Life and other insurance	374	172	190	207	337	407	565
Retirement, pensions, Social Security	2,837	402	883	1,400	2,046	3,092	5,213

Source: The 1986 Consumer Expenditure Survey, Bureau of Labor Statistics

Note: All households include complete income reporters only. Total expenditure exceeds total income in some income categories due to a number of factors including the underreporting of income, borrowing, and the use of savings.

Weekly Shopping

EXPENDITURES
35–44

ABOVE AVERAGE SPENDERS

Households headed by 35-to-44-year-olds spend over 30 percent more than the average household on cereals and cereal products, beef, dairy products other than milk and cream, food away from home, and nonalcoholic beverages. Their weekly shopping tabs are higher than average for all frequently purchased items.

(average weekly expenditures for all households and for householders aged 35 to 44)

	all households	index all households	householders aged 35 to 44	index householders aged 35 to 44
Food, total	$59.60	100	$77.43	130
Food at home, total	37.73	100	48.10	127
Cereals and cereal products	1.78	100	2.38	134
Bakery products	3.51	100	4.52	129
Beef	3.63	100	4.86	134
Pork	2.23	100	2.86	128
Other meats	1.52	100	1.97	130
Poultry	1.64	100	1.99	121
Fish and seafood	1.22	100	1.43	117
Eggs	0.57	100	0.68	119
Fresh milk and cream	2.35	100	2.93	125
Other dairy products	2.47	100	3.32	134
Fresh fruits	1.96	100	2.23	114
Fresh vegetables	1.77	100	2.09	118
Processed fruits	1.38	100	1.76	128
Processed vegetables	1.03	100	1.23	119
Sugar and other sweets	1.42	100	1.85	130
Fats and oils	0.99	100	1.24	125
Miscellaneous foods	4.53	100	5.88	130
Nonalcoholic beverages	3.71	100	4.87	131
Food away from home	21.87	100	29.33	134
Nonfood items				
Alcoholic beverages	4.84	100	5.12	106
Tobacco products and smoking supplies	3.60	100	4.51	125
Pet food	1.09	100	1.38	127
Personal care products and services	5.01	100	6.43	128
Non-prescription drugs and supplies	2.31	100	2.32	100
Housekeeping supplies	6.07	100	7.90	130

Source: The 1986 Consumer Expenditure Survey, Bureau of Labor Statistics

Note: An index of 100 represents the average. An index of 132 means that the average weekly expenditure of the subgroup is 32 percent above the average for all households. An index of 68 indicates spending that is 32 percent below average. Numbers may not add to total due to rounding.

Future Expenditures

EXPENDITURES
35-44

SPENDING UP BY $121 BILLION

Households headed by 35-to-44-year-olds will spend an estimated 121 billion dollars more in 2000 than in 1990. This spending increase is due to the 19 percent rise in the number of households in this age group during the 1990s.

(projected aggregate expenditures in 1990 and 2000 for all households and for households by age of householder, in billions of dollars)

1990 aggregate annual expenditures in billions

	all households	under 25	25-34	35-44	45-54	55-64	65-74	75+
Number of households (in thousands)	94,227	4,663	21,183	21,245	14,429	12,311	11,672	8,724
Total expenditures (in billions of dollars)	$2,203.1	$64.2	$476.6	$628.6	$441.2	$292.8	$197.2	$102.5
Food	330.8	9.4	70.3	93.7	64.1	43.9	32.3	17.2
Food at home	225.1	5.9	44.8	64.9	41.8	30.9	23.0	13.7
Food away from home	101.5	3.6	21.2	28.8	22.2	13.0	9.3	3.5
Alcoholic beverages	25.4	1.6	7.5	6.4	4.7	3.0	1.8	0.6
Housing	667.6	19.2	158.3	193.5	121.9	80.8	58.3	35.6
Shelter	385.6	12.4	97.2	115.7	71.7	42.4	28.8	17.5
Owned dwellings	229.7	1.8	50.3	75.8	46.9	28.2	17.9	8.7
Rented dwellings	115.2	9.5	41.6	27.6	13.1	8.4	7.2	7.6
Other lodging	40.8	1.0	5.2	12.2	11.6	5.8	3.7	1.2
Fuels, utilities, and public services	160.0	3.7	32.0	41.2	29.6	23.2	18.6	11.8
Household operations	34.2	0.7	9.6	10.2	3.8	3.7	2.9	3.3
Household furnishings, equipment	87.8	2.4	19.5	26.5	16.8	11.6	8.0	3.0
Apparel and services	111.0	4.1	24.6	33.7	22.8	13.8	8.3	3.6
Transportation	464.9	15.6	107.0	130.7	98.7	61.1	37.7	14.2
Health care	103.7	1.6	14.5	21.4	16.9	16.0	17.9	15.4
Entertainment	106.0	3.1	23.3	35.2	20.6	13.0	8.0	2.6
Personal care	20.1	0.6	3.7	5.2	3.8	3.1	2.3	1.3
Reading	13.6	0.3	2.6	3.8	2.6	1.9	1.6	0.8
Education	27.6	2.7	3.9	8.3	8.8	2.9	0.8	0.1
Tobacco and smoking supplies	22.0	0.8	4.9	5.8	4.5	3.3	2.0	0.7
Miscellaneous	31.5	0.6	6.5	8.1	5.9	4.5	3.6	2.3
Contributions and support payments	74.2	0.7	7.3	17.7	17.4	12.9	12.5	5.7
Personal insurance and pensions	208.9	3.9	46.4	65.2	48.5	32.6	10.0	2.3

(continued next page)

Future Expenditures

EXPENDITURES
35–44

(continued from previous page)

(projected aggregate expenditures in 2000 for all households and for households by age of householder, in billions of dollars)

	\multicolumn{8}{c}{2000 aggregate annual expenditures in billions}
	all households	under 25	25-34	35-44	45-54	55-64	65-74	75+
Number of households (in thousands)	105,933	4,442	18,004	25,339	21,603	13,903	11,516	11,126
Total expenditures (in billions of dollars)	$2,532.4	$61.1	$405.1	$749.7	$660.6	$330.6	$194.6	$130.7
Food	379.7	9.0	59.7	111.7	95.9	49.5	31.9	22.0
Food at home	258.9	5.6	38.1	77.4	62.6	34.9	22.7	17.5
Food away from home	117.2	3.4	18.0	34.3	33.2	14.7	9.1	4.5
Alcoholic beverages	28.3	1.5	6.4	7.6	7.0	3.4	1.7	0.7
Housing	760.3	18.3	134.5	230.8	182.5	91.3	57.5	45.3
Shelter	438.2	11.8	82.6	137.9	107.3	47.9	28.4	22.3
Owned dwellings	265.8	1.7	42.8	90.4	70.3	31.9	17.6	11.1
Rented dwellings	123.4	9.1	35.4	32.9	19.7	9.5	7.2	9.7
Other lodging	49.1	0.9	4.4	14.6	17.4	6.5	3.7	1.5
Fuels, utilities, and public services	183.6	3.5	27.2	49.1	44.3	26.2	18.3	15.0
Household operations	38.0	0.7	8.2	12.2	5.7	4.1	2.9	4.2
Household furnishings, equipment	100.5	2.3	16.6	31.6	25.2	13.1	7.9	3.8
Apparel and services	127.6	3.9	20.9	40.2	34.2	15.6	8.2	4.6
Transportation	533.7	14.8	90.9	155.9	147.7	69.0	37.2	18.1
Health care	120.0	1.5	12.4	25.5	25.3	18.1	17.7	19.6
Entertainment	121.7	3.0	19.8	42.0	30.9	14.7	7.9	3.3
Personal care	23.1	0.5	3.2	6.2	5.7	3.5	2.3	1.7
Reading	15.7	0.3	2.2	4.5	3.9	2.2	1.6	1.0
Education	33.2	2.6	3.3	10.0	13.1	3.3	0.8	0.2
Tobacco and smoking supplies	25.2	0.8	4.2	6.9	6.8	3.7	2.0	0.9
Miscellaneous	36.2	0.6	5.5	9.7	8.9	5.0	3.5	2.9
Contributions and support payments	88.2	0.6	6.2	21.1	26.0	14.5	12.3	7.3
Personal insurance and pensions	243.2	3.7	39.4	77.7	72.7	36.8	9.9	2.9

Source: *The 1986 Consumer Expenditure Survey, Bureau of Labor Statistics* and *Projections of the Number of Households and Families:1986 to 2000, Bureau of the Census, Series P-25, No. 986*

Note: Aggregate expenditures are the sum of the total expenditures of all households in the nation or of all households in an age group. Projections are based on the average annual expenditures in 1986 and have not been adjusted for inflation. Projections show how total annual expenditures would change as the number of households in the age group changes during the 1990s. All other factors such as price and expenditure pattern are held constant and are not accounted for in these projections.

Composition of Wealth

WEALTH
35-44

ASSET BUILDERS

Households headed by members of this age group account for 26 percent of all household income and 16 percent of household wealth. They are more likely to hold every type of asset except homes, CDs, and money market funds and more likely to have mortgages and other debts than are households in general.

(percentage of households with assets and debts and the mean value of owners' holdings in 1986 dollars, for all households and householders aged 35 to 44, numbers in thousands)

	percent owning		mean holdings of owners	
	all households	householder aged 35 to 44	all households	householder aged 35 to 44
Number of households	83,042	18,412	83,042	18,412
Assets				
Home	65.7%	63.7%	$80,650	$90,654
Other real estate	22.4	24.6	118,892	111,198
Public stock	19.3	20.9	81,367	20,048
Bonds	20.2	24.5	28,116	6,232
Checking and saving accounts	89.2	93.2	7,445	5,456
IRA's and Keoghs	27.3	33.2	18,752	10,925
CD's and money market	27.9	22.2	31,575	18,455
Business assets (net)	12.4	16.9	210,310	137,728
Automobiles	85.9	93.3	7,964	8,843
Employer accounts	14.8	18.0	26,704	20,153
Other*	45.7	55.7	22,282	11,002
Debts				
Mortgage, principle residence	38.40%	54.10%	$34,564	$39,431
Other debts	64.6	91.0	15,881	19,083

*Cash value of life insurance, trusts, and notes owned by individuals.

Source: The 1986 Survey of Consumer Finances, Federal Reserve Board

Note: Wealth here accounts for all major household assets and liabilities except for non-auto consumer durables, collectibles such as artwork, and the present value of expected future benefits from pensions or social security. These households are less likely to own homes but more likely to have mortgage debt than are all households because the all-household measures include those who own a home but have no outstanding mortgage.

Almanac of Consumer Markets

Household Savings

WEALTH
35-44

PUTTING IT AWAY

In the three year period, 1983 to 1986, households headed by someone aged 35 to 44 had an increase in their net worth of $23,301. This savings is 13 percent of the total household income they received from 1983 to 1985 and represents about 17 percent of all household savings accumulated during those years.

(average household savings 1983 to 1986 in current dollars, share of total savings and percentage of 1983 to 1985 total household income that is savings for households by age of householder, marital status, race and Hispanic origin, homeownership status, and household income)

	average savings for 3 year period	share of total savings	median 3-year savings as a percentage of 1983-1985 median income
All households	$24,402	100.0%	9.7%
Age of householder			
under age 35	17,912	18.7	7.1
35 to 44	**23,301**	**16.8**	**12.6**
45 to 54	46,606	22.4	16.1
55 to 64	39,392	20.9	9.8
65 and older	33,867	21.3	5.9
Marital status			
Married	40,392	91.8	13.8
Singe male	9,242	3.2	3.1
Single female	6,405	5.0	2.8
Race			
White	34,913	97.8	11.4
Black/Hispanic	3,679	2.2	2.4
Homeownership status			
Homeowner	39,426	88.2	16.1
Renter	10,107	11.8	4.0
Household income			
Less than $10,000	871	0.5	0.0
$10,000 to $20,000	6,633	5.9	4.8
$20,000 to $50,000	18,835	27.2	15.8
$50,000 to $100,000	70,545	27.3	22.8
$100,000 and over	455,294	39.2	44.2

Source: The 1986 Survey of Consumer Finances, Federal Reserve Board

Note: Household savings is the difference in household net worth between 1986 and 1983, expressed in 1986 dollars. Net worth (wealth) is defined as gross assets minus gross debts. Net worth here accounts for all major household assets and liabilities except for non-auto consumer durables, collectibles such as artwork, and the present value of expected future benefits from pensions or social security.

Owners and Renters

WEALTH
35–44

IT TAKES TWO

Just over two-thirds of householders aged 35 to 44 live in their own home and married couples head 77 percent of those home-owning households. Among 35-to-44-year-olds, white householders are most likely to be homeowners (71 percent) followed by Hispanics (50 percent) and blacks (42 percent).

(owner- and renter-occupied households by race of householder and household type, for householders aged 35 to 44, numbers in thousands, ownership status as of March 1988)

	total	white	black	Hispanic origin
All households	19,323	16,426	2,266	1,364
Owner households	12,963	11,673	957	680
Family households				
Married-couple	9,972	9,138	578	518
Male householder	388	330	44	24
Female householder	1,225	983	214	79
Nonfamily households				
Male householder	878	773	76	34
Female householder	500	449	45	25
Renter households	6,359	4,753	1,310	684
Family households				
Married-couple	2,476	1,956	347	327
Male householder	251	188	48	37
Female householder	1,540	958	534	208
Nonfamily households				
Male householder	1,328	1,054	237	73
Female householder	765	599	143	39

Source: Household and Family Characteristics: March 1988, *Bureau of the Census, Current Population Reports, Series P-20, No. 424*

Note: Hispanics are of any race. Numbers may not add to total due to rounding.

Health Status

HEALTH
35-44

FEELIN' GOOD

Seventy-three percent of men and 68 percent of women aged 35 to 44 rate their health as excellent or very good. The proportion of people with poor health is 24 times higher among those with household incomes under $10,000 than in the over $35,000 group.

(self-assessed health status of persons aged 35 to 44, by sex, race and household income, number of persons in thousands)

	all persons	all health statuses	excellent	very good	good	fair	poor
Both sexes, all races	32,548	100.0%	40.5%	29.7%	21.8%	6.1%	1.8%
Male	15,858	100.0	43.1	29.8	19.6	5.6	2.0
Female	16,689	100.0	38.1	29.6	24.0	6.6	1.7
White	27,950	100.0	42.2	30.6	20.3	5.4	1.5
Black	3,410	100.0	27.5	22.2	33.6	12.0	4.8
Asian and other	1,188	100.0	38.3	30.4	24.5	6.1	0.6
Household income							
Less than $10,000	2,424	100.0%	21.2%	21.9%	29.0%	20.6%	7.3%
$10,000 to $19,999	4,662	100.0	30.5	25.9	29.7	9.8	4.0
$20,000 to $34,999	8,919	100.0	38.1	32.9	22.6	5.3	1.1
$35,000 and over	12,475	100.0	50.5	30.6	16.1	2.6	0.3

Source: The 1986 National Health Interview Survey, National Center for Health Statistics

Note: All persons includes those of unknown health status, all health statuses includes only those with known health status. Household income includes only those persons with known household income. Numbers may not add to total due to rounding.

Height

HEALTH
35–44

EYE-TO-EYE

The average man or woman aged 35 to 44 is the same height as the average American man or woman. A typical 35-to-44-year-old man stands 5'9" tall and the average woman in this age group is 5'4" tall.

(cumulative percentage of height of males and females aged 35 to 44 and their average height, by race)

height, males	cumulative percentage	height, females	cumulative percentage
Less than 60 inches	0.3%	Less than 55 inches	–
Less than 61 inches	0.3	Less than 56 inches	0.1%
Less than 62 inches	0.9	Less than 57 inches	0.3
Less than 63 inches	2.1	Less than 58 inches	1.0
Less than 64 inches	3.7	Less than 59 inches	1.9
Less than 65 inches	6.4	Less than 60 inches	4.6
Less than 66 inches	12.4	Less than 61 inches	7.8
Less than 67 inches	17.6	Less than 62 inches	18.2
Less than 68 inches	26.4	Less than 63 inches	33.1
Less than 69 inches	42.5	Less than 64 inches	49.9
Less than 70 inches	57.0	Less than 65 inches	63.9
Less than 71 inches	70.7	Less than 66 inches	78.1
Less than 72 inches	81.1	Less than 67 inches	87.9
Less than 73 inches	90.0	Less than 68 inches	93.4
Less than 74 inches	95.1	Less than 69 inches	97.2
Less than 75 inches	97.8	Less than 70 inches	99.2
Less than 76 inches	99.2	Less than 71 inches	99.4
All height categories	100.0%	All height categories	100.0%
Average height, all races	**69.4 inches**	**Average height, all races**	**64.1 inches**
White	69.6	White	64.1
Black	69.5	Black	63.3

Source: Anthropometric Reference Data and Prevalence of Overweight: United States, 1976-80, National Center for Health Statistics, National Health Survey Series 11, No. 238.

Note: Height is without shoes.

Weight

HEALTH
35–44

POUNDS AND PEOPLE

Twenty-nine percent of men and 27 percent of women aged 35 to 44 weigh more than the weight to height (overweight) standard of the National Center for Health Statistics. The average 35-to-44-year-old woman weighs 148 pounds and the average man in this age group weighs 178 pounds.

(cumulative percentage of weight of males and females aged 35 to 44, and their average weight and percent overweight, by race)

weight, males	cumulative percentage	weight, females	cumulative percentage
Less than 100 pounds	–	Less than 90 pounds	0.1%
Less than 110 pounds	0.7%	Less than 100 pounds	1.7
Less than 120 pounds	1.3	Less than 110 pounds	6.1
Less than 130 pounds	4.3	Less than 120 pounds	17.8
Less than 140 pounds	8.1	Less than 130 pounds	32.3
Less than 150 pounds	15.5	Less than 140 pounds	50.4
Less than 160 pounds	26.7	Less than 150 pounds	63.6
Less than 170 pounds	41.2	Less than 160 pounds	73.0
Less than 180 pounds	54.9	Less than 170 pounds	80.2
Less than 190 pounds	68.4	Less than 180 pounds	84.5
Less than 200 pounds	79.2	Less than 190 pounds	88.8
Less than 210 pounds	85.8	Less than 200 pounds	91.9
Less than 220 pounds	91.0	Less than 220 pounds	95.2
Less than 230 pounds	94.9	Less than 240 pounds	97.5
Less than 240 pounds	97.3	Less than 260 pounds	99.0
Less than 250 pounds	98.8	Less than 280 pounds	99.7
All weight categories	100.0%	All weight categories	100.0%
Average weight, all races	**178.4 pounds**	**Average weight, all races**	**147.8 pounds**
White	179.4	White	145.6
Black	181.9	Black	165.9
Percent overweight, all races	**28.9%**	**Percent overweight, all races**	**27.0%**
White	28.2	White	24.8
Black	40.9	Black	40.8
Percent severely overweight, all races	**8.9%**	**Percent severely overweight, all races**	**12.1%**
White	8.3	White	10.3
Black	17.1	Black	26.3

Source: Anthropometric Reference Data and Prevalence of Overweight: United States, 1976-80, *National Center for Health Statistics, National Health Survey Series 11, No. 238.*

Notes: Weight includes clothing weight, estimated as ranging from 0.20 to 0.62 pounds. Overweight is defined in terms of a body mass index which is determined by dividing weight in kilograms by height in meters squared. Overweight people have a body mass index equal to or greater than that at the 85th percentile of men and women aged 20 to 29. Severe overweight means a body mass index equal to or greater than at the 95th percentile of men and women aged 20 to 29.

Acute Conditions

HEALTH
35–44

BUGGING US ALL

Like other adults, men and women aged 35 to 44 are more likely to suffer from flus than from any other acute condition. Men in this age group are also likely to report having colds and open wounds and cuts while women add colds and sprains and strains to the list of their top ailments.

(number of acute conditions reported in a year for all persons and those aged 35 to 44, by sex, numbers in thousands)

	males all ages	males aged 35 to 44	females all ages	females aged 35 to 44
All acute conditions	191,369	18,771	257,177	27,130
Infective and parasitic diseases	23,122	2,053	31,244	3,192
Common childhood diseases	2,565	0	1,876	0
Intestinal virus, unspecified	4,244	372	5,288	803
Viral infections, unspecified	9,621	1,256	14,273	1,240
Other	6,692	424	9,807	1,148
Respiratory conditions	99,216	10,450	129,626	14,126
Common cold	30,445	2,831	32,983	2,955
Other acute upper respiratory infections	8,472	612	13,320	1,052
Influenza	55,256	6,203	75,295	9,577
Acute bronchitis	1,960	199	4,315	380
Pneumonia	1,365	401	1,277	108
Other respiratory conditions	1,718	203	2,435	55
Digestive system conditions	5,860	739	9,112	437
Dental conditions	1,059	101	1,955	0
Indigestion, nausea and vomiting	3,299	329	4,670	249
Other digestive conditions	1,502	309	2,487	188
Injuries	34,588	3,215	29,706	4,367
Fractures and dislocations	4,367	523	3,978	371
Sprains and strains	6,127	548	6,208	1,126
Open wounds and lacerations	11,153	686	5,094	1,001
Contusions and superficial injuries	7,986	685	7,191	1,132
Other current injuries	4,955	773	7,235	737

(continued next page)

Acute Conditions

HEALTH
35–44

(continued from previous page)

(number of acute conditions reported in a year for all persons and those aged 35 to 44, by sex, numbers in thousands)

	males all ages	males aged 35 to 44	females all ages	females aged 35 to 44
Selected other acute conditions	**21,183**	**1,542**	**40,385**	**3,695**
Eye conditions	1,072	0	2,080	188
Acute ear infections	8,689	390	10,116	851
Other ear conditions	1,884	109	2,193	180
Acute urinary conditions	989	191	4,399	380
Disorders of menstruation	–	–	2,251	263
Other disorders of female genital tract	–	–	2,174	276
Delivery and other conditions of pregnancy	–	–	4,466	198
Skin conditions	2,065	191	3,597	237
Acute musculoskeletal conditions	3,038	580	3,972	628
Headache, excluding migraine	1,253	82	2,461	493
Fever, unspecified	2,192	0	2,675	0
All other acute conditions	**7,400**	**773**	**17,104**	**1,313**

Source: The 1986 National Health Interview Survey, National Center for Health Statistics

Note: An acute condition is defined by The National Health Interview Survey as an illness or injury that usually lasts less than three months and was first noticed less than three months before the respondent's interview. The acute condition must also have caused the person to restrict activities for at least a half a day or to have contacted a physician. The data are based only on information given by the respondent and are subject to recall and selective reporting error. Numbers may not add to total due to rounding.

Chronic Conditions

HEALTH
35–44

STILL SUFFERING FROM SINUSES

Sinusitis, high blood pressure, hay fever, hearing impairments, and back deformities are the most frequently reported chronic problems of men aged 35 to 44. Women in this age group say they are most likely to suffer from sinusitis, hay fever, back deformities, migraine headaches, and high blood pressure.

(number of selected chronic conditions reported in a year for all persons and those aged 35 to 44, by sex, numbers in thousands)

	males all ages	males aged 35 to 44	females all ages	females aged 35 to 44
Selected skin and musculoskeletal conditions				
Arthritis	10,751	1,268	20,160	1,317
Gout, including gouty arthritis	1,515	127	713	22
Intervertebral disc disorders	2,522	789	1,645	519
Bone spur or tendonitis, unspecified	781	218	898	140
Disorders of bone or cartilage	449	45	943	104
Trouble with bunions	594	183	2,321	295
Bursitis, unclassified	1,641	244	2,464	530
Sebaceous skin cyst	640	111	881	182
Trouble with acne	2,193	43	2,116	318
Psoriasis	1,069	201	1,262	248
Dermatitis	3,851	436	5,696	931
Trouble with dry, itching skin, unclassified	1,994	321	2,606	517
Trouble with ingrown nails	2,352	377	3,030	348
Trouble with corns and calluses	1,669	392	3,164	548
Impairments				
Visual impairment	4,994	757	3,358	276
Color blindness	2,694	515	272	20
Cataracts	1,534	22	3,497	80
Glaucoma	735	27	967	37
Hearing impairment	11,727	1,589	9,004	811
Tinnitus	3,388	536	2,927	201
Speech impairment	1,924	153	871	77
Absence of extremity(s)	374	49	24	0
Paralysis, entire body, one side of body, or both legs	200	57	152	0
Partial paralysis of body or legs	236	0	99	23
Deformity of back	6,812	1,398	9,676	1,922
Deformity of upper extremities	1,622	407	1,475	189
Deformity of lower extremities	6,454	1,089	5,739	801
Selected digestive conditions				
Ulcer	2,116	438	2,378	369
Hernia of abdominal cavity	2,300	310	2,283	220
Gastritis or duodenitis	1,080	202	1,813	215

(continued next page)

Chronic Conditions

HEALTH 35–44

(continued from previous page)

(number of selected chronic conditions reported in a year for all persons and those aged 35 to 44, by sex, numbers in thousands)

	males all ages	males aged 35 to 44	females all ages	females aged 35 to 44
Frequent indigestion	2,504	565	2,811	483
Enteritis or colitis	574	110	1,820	295
Spastic colon	264	44	1,377	335
Diverticula of intestines	404	51	1,508	124
Frequent constipation	1,002	56	3,537	336
Selected conditions of the genitourinary, nervous, endocrine, metabolic, and blood system				
Goiter or other disorders of the thyroid	420	28	2,789	370
Diabetes	2,949	190	3,635	116
Anemias	570	0	2,617	423
Epilepsy	656	87	863	92
Migraine headache	2,068	324	6,448	1,775
Neuralgia or neuritis, unspecified	215	29	364	47
Kidney trouble	1,305	244	2,662	206
Bladder disorders	516	58	3,253	361
Diseases of prostate	1,281	71	–	–
Inflammatory female genital diseases	–	–	427	109
Noninflammatory female genital diseases	–	–	1,095	185
Menstrual disorders	–	–	2,097	539
Selected circulatory conditions				
Ischemic heart disease	4,091	186	2,809	111
Tachycardia or rapid heart	700	74	1,226	136
Heart murmurs	1,310	232	2,583	282
Other heart rhythm disorders	499	0	800	44
Other heart diseases	1,482	74	2,265	155
High blood pressure (hypertension)	12,512	2,065	16,457	1,426
Cerebrovascular disease	1,156	25	1,646	80
Hardening of the arteries	1,428	0	1,225	24
Varicose veins	1,042	120	5,814	797
Hemorrhoids	4,568	1,100	5,341	1,104
Selected respiratory conditions				
Chronic bronchitis	4,707	660	6,671	830
Asthma	4,670	543	5,019	759
Hay fever or allergic rhinitis without asthma	10,136	1,747	11,566	1,998
Chronic sinusitis	14,636	3,027	19,749	4,291
Deviated nasal septum	825	207	465	132
Chronic disease of tonsils or adenoids	1,071	42	2,068	78
Emphysema	1,201	27	796	26

Source: The 1986 National Health Interview Survey, National Center for Health Statistics

Note: Chronic conditions are defined by the National Health Interview Survey as conditions that either a) were first noticed three months or more before the date of the interview or b) belong to a group of conditions (such as heart disease or diabetes) that are considered chronic regardless of when they began. Totals for all chronic conditions are not shown because the National Health Interview Survey does not measure the total number of chronic conditions for each person. The data are based only on information given by the respondent and are subject to recall and selective reporting error.

Activity Restrictions

HEALTH
35–44

HIGHER FEMALE ABSENTEEISM

Compared with the population in general, 35-to-44-year-olds have fewer work-loss and bed-rest days due to illness or injury. Working women in this age group miss six whole or half days of work a year and men who work have four work-loss days. Workers from higher income households tend to have fewer absences due to illness and injury than those from households with lower incomes.

(number of days of activity restriction reported in a year and per person due to acute and chronic conditions, by type of restriction and sex, race, and household income, for all persons and those aged 35 to 44, numbers in thousands)

	number of days per year		number of days per person	
	bed day	work-loss day	bed day	work-loss day
All ages	1,547,980	833,396	6.5	5.4
Male	613,113	401,503	5.4	4.8
Female	934,867	431,892	7.7	6.0
White	1,298,039	716,187	6.5	5.4
Black	220,102	99,332	7.7	5.4
Household income				
Less than $10,000	384,962	90,268	11.5	6.1
$10,000 to $19,999	346,115	162,604	7.7	6.1
$20,000 to $34,999	326,166	254,563	5.2	5.7
$35,000 and over	275,957	232,139	4.3	4.6
All aged 35 to 44	**166,025**	**129,998**	**5.1**	**4.9**
Male	75,317	62,074	4.7	4.3
Female	90,708	67,924	5.4	5.7
White	135,002	111,421	4.8	4.9
Black	27,281	15,878	8.0	6.2
Household income				
Less than $10,000	37,349	8,057	15.4	6.2
$10,000 to $19,999	30,932	26,229	6.6	7.3
$20,000 to $34,999	42,697	43,288	4.8	5.8
$35,000 and over	35,355	38,541	2.8	3.6

Source: The 1986 National Health Interview Survey, National Center for Health Statistics

Note: Numbers may not add to total due to rounding. A bed day is one during which a person stayed in bed more than half a day because of illness or injury. All hospital days for inpatients are considered bed days even if the patient was not in bed more than half a day. A work-loss day is one on which a currently employed person aged 18 or older missed more than half a day of work. The data are based only on information given by the respondent and is subject to recall and selective reporting error.

Cause of Death

HEALTH
35–44

THE BIG TWO

For all people aged 35 and older, the two leading causes of death are cancer and heart disease. Twenty-one percent of deaths among 35-to-44-year-olds are caused by cancer and 18 percent are from heart diseases. The 10 leading causes of death account for 78 percent of all deaths in this age group.

(ten leading causes of death among persons aged 35 to 44)

	number of deaths persons aged 35 to 44	number of deaths all ages	percent accounted for by persons aged 35 to 44
All causes	70,393	2,105,361	3.3%
Malignant neoplasms (cancer)	14,991	469,376	3.2
Heart diseases	12,415	765,490	1.6
Accidents and adverse effects	10,295	95,277	10.8
Suicide	5,013	30,904	16.2
Homicide and legal intervention	3,783	21,731	17.4
Chronic liver disease and cirrhosis	3,188	26,159	12.2
Cerebrovascular diseases	2,351	149,643	1.6
Diabetes mellitus	1,174	37,184	3.2
Pneumonia and influenza	1,200	69,812	1.7
Chronic obstructive pulmonary diseases and allied conditions	542	76,559	0.7
All other causes	15,441	363,226	4.3

Source: Advance Report of Final Mortality Statistics, 1986, *National Center for Health Statistics, Vol. 37, No. 6*

Chapter 6

CONSUMERS AGED 45 TO 54

This is the growth group of the 1990s. Here are some reasons for watching them.

They have the highest incomes, they are the biggest spenders, and there will be many more of them.

- The number of 45-to-54-year-olds will increase 47 percent between 1990 and 2000 when they will be 14 percent of the entire U.S. population.

- They will head 20 percent of all households in 2000.

- Households in this age group are most likely to include a married couple—66 percent of them do. However, only a third of those married-couple households contain children under the age of 18.

- Nonfamily households with a householder aged 45 to 54 will increase 70 percent during the 1990s.

- Ninety-one percent of men and 69 percent of women aged 45 to 54 are now in the labor force. By 2000, three-quarters of the women in this age group are expected to be labor force participants.

- Compared with households headed by members of the other age groups, these have the highest median household income—over $37,000.

- Married couples in this age group have a median household income of $45,200. Dual-earner married couples are at the top of the income chart with a median income of $50,300.

- They account for 21 percent of all household wealth.

- Households in this age group spend more on food, transportation, and insurance and pensions than households in any other age group.

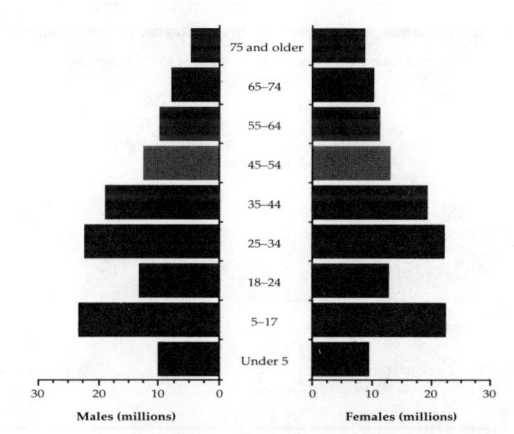

1990

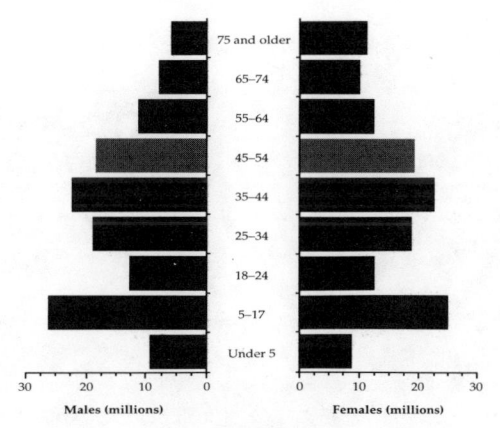

2000

Almanac of Consumer Markets

Share of Total Population

POPULATION
45–54

MORE BIG EARNERS

By 2000, 45-to-54-year-olds' share of the population pie will grow dramatically, boosting them from 10 percent of all Americans in 1990 to a full 14 percent by 2000. The number of people in this age group will grow by 47 percent during the 1990s.

(total population and the number of persons aged 45 to 54, in thousands, by sex, 1960 to 1980, and projections for 1990 to 2000)

	1960 number	1960 percent of total	1970 number	1970 percent of total	1980 number	1980 percent of total	1990 number	1990 percent of total	1995 number	1995 percent of total	2000 number	2000 percent of total
All ages	180,671	100.0%	205,052	100.0%	227,757	100.0%	252,293	100.0%	264,077	100.0%	274,479	100.0%
All aged 45 to 54	20,578	11.4	23,316	11.4	22,754	10.0	25,551	10.1	31,689	12.0	37,672	13.7
Males	10,142	5.6	11,253	5.5	10,996	4.8	12,423	4.9	15,471	5.9	18,472	6.7
Females	10,436	5.8	12,063	5.9	11,758	5.2	13,128	5.2	16,220	6.1	19,201	7.0

Source: Annual Projections of the Population by Age, Sex, and Race, for the United States: 1983 to 2080, *Bureau of the Census, Current Population Reports, Series 17 and the Bureau of the Census*

Note: Total population includes Armed Forces overseas; 1960 to 1980 are based on censuses; projections are based on the Census Bureau's Series 17 projections that incorporate illegal immigration and higher levels of emigration than other Census Bureau projections. Series 17 is consistent with current estimates of illegal aliens living in the United States. Numbers may not add to total due to rounding.

Sex, Race, and Ethnicity

POPULATION
45–54

CHANGING PROFILE

Although the number of 45-to-54-year-olds as a whole will surge up 47 percent during the 1990s, the number of blacks, Hispanics, and Asians will be climbing even faster. Blacks will increase from 10 to 11 percent of the age group, Hispanics from 7 to 8 percent, Asians from 3 to 4 percent—and the number of whites will slide from 80 to 77 percent.

(projections of the total population and persons aged 45 to 54, in thousands, by sex, race, and Hispanic origin, 1990 to 2000)

	1990	1995	2000	percent change 1990–2000
All ages	**252,293**	**264,077**	**274,479**	**8.8%**
White	191,594	195,347	197,634	3.2
Black	30,915	33,237	35,440	14.6
Hispanic	21,854	25,991	30,295	38.6
Asians and other races	7,930	9,502	11,110	40.1
All aged 45 to 54	**25,551**	**31,689**	**37,672**	**47.4**
White	20,446	25,097	29,145	42.5
Black	2,579	3,216	4,080	58.2
Hispanic	1,718	2,258	2,983	73.6
Asians and other races	808	1,118	1,464	81.3
All males aged 45 to 54	**12,423**	**15,471**	**18,472**	**48.7**
White	10,056	12,394	14,440	43.6
Black	1,149	1,447	1,863	62.1
Hispanic	828	1,100	1,482	79.0
Asians and other races	390	529	687	76.2
All females aged 45 to 54	**13,128**	**16,220**	**19,201**	**46.3**
White	10,390	12,702	14,704	41.5
Black	1,431	1,768	2,217	54.9
Hispanic	890	1,158	1,502	68.8
Asians and other races	417	592	778	86.6

Source: Projections of the Population of the United States by Age, Sex, and Race: 1983 to 2080, *Bureau of the Census, Current Population Reports, Series P-25, No. 952, Series 17*

Note: Series 17 projections incorporate illegal immigration and higher levels of emigration than other Census Bureau projections and are consistent with current estimates of illegal aliens living in the United States. Total population includes Armed Forces living overseas. In this table Hispanics have been separated out of the racial groups; categories do not overlap. Numbers may not add to total due to rounding.

State Populations

POPULATION
45–54

BABY BOOM SPELLS GROWTH

The aging of the baby boom will be reflected by major increases in the number of 45-to-54-year-olds in every state in the Union, with the biggest jumps occurring in Alaska, Arizona, Colorado Nevada, New Hampshire, and New Mexico.

(resident population and the number of persons aged 45 to 54, in thousands, in Census Bureau divisions and states in 1980 and projections for 1990 to 2010)

Note: Inconsistencies between the data in this table and the preceding two tables are due to different assumptions about immigration and emigration on which the projections are based, and the inclusion of Armed Forces overseas in the total population. This table is based on the resident population only.

	census 1980	1990	projections 2000	2010	percent change 1990–2000	percent change 2000–2010
All ages	226,546	249,891	267,747	282,055	7.1%	5.3%
All aged 45 to 54	22,800	25,480	37,216	43,200	46.1	16.1
New England	**1,271**	**1,355**	**1,950**	**2,313**	**43.9**	**18.6**
Connecticut	339	366	504	586	37.7	16.3
Maine	112	122	182	210	49.2	15.4
Massachusetts	585	598	843	999	41.0	18.5
New Hampshire	90	116	194	244	67.2	25.8
Rhode Island	98	99	145	175	46.5	20.7
Vermont	48	55	82	96	49.1	17.1
Middle Atlantic	**4,031**	**4,045**	**5,332**	**6,040**	**31.8**	**13.3**
New Jersey	827	882	1,209	1,443	37.1	19.4
New York	1,909	1,941	2,479	2,782	27.7	12.2
Pennsylvania	1,296	1,222	1,644	1,815	34.5	10.4
East North Central	**4,222**	**4,260**	**5,761**	**6,338**	**35.2**	**10.0**
Illinois	1,161	1,186	1,570	1,729	32.4	10.1
Indiana	550	566	758	838	33.9	10.6
Michigan	931	933	1,288	1,423	38.0	10.5
Ohio	1,127	1,103	1,479	1,614	34.1	9.1
Wisconsin	453	473	666	735	40.8	10.4

(continued on next page)

State Populations

(continued from previous page)

(resident population and the number of persons aged 45 to 54, in thousands, in Census Bureau divisions and states in 1980 and projections for 1990 to 2010)

	census 1980	projections 1990	projections 2000	projections 2010	percent change 1990–2000	percent change 2000–2010
All ages	226,546	249,891	267,747	282,055	7.1%	5.3%
All aged 45 to 54	22,800	25,480	37,216	43,200	46.1	16.1
West North Central	**1,665**	**1,749**	**2,458**	**2,722**	**40.5**	**10.7**
Iowa	282	270	356	363	31.9	2.0
Kansas	232	242	345	379	42.6	9.9
Minnesota	380	429	630	708	46.9	12.4
Missouri	497	534	742	855	39.0	15.2
Nebraska	151	151	205	220	35.8	7.3
North Dakota	59	59	87	92	47.5	5.7
South Dakota	65	64	94	105	46.9	11.7
South Atlantic	**3,735**	**4,566**	**6,945**	**8,533**	**52.1**	**22.9**
Delaware	63	68	97	123	42.6	26.8
District of Columbia	63	64	86	105	34.4	22.1
Florida	989	1,324	2,091	2,624	57.9	25.5
Georgia	528	684	1,093	1,395	59.8	27.6
Maryland	447	518	754	917	45.6	21.6
North Carolina	601	700	1,044	1,274	49.1	22.0
South Carolina	299	353	537	648	52.1	20.7
Virginia	546	665	986	1,187	48.3	20.4
West Virginia	198	189	257	259	36.0	0.8
East South Central	**1,440**	**1,591**	**2,266**	**2,621**	**42.4**	**15.7**
Alabama	389	421	600	711	42.5	18.5
Kentucky	354	381	529	574	38.8	8.5
Mississippi	232	257	372	451	44.7	21.2
Tennessee	465	531	765	885	44.1	15.7
West South Central	**2,272**	**2,726**	**4,173**	**4,902**	**53.1**	**17.5**
Arkansas	217	249	349	400	40.2	14.6
Louisiana	394	427	605	668	41.7	10.4
Oklahoma	299	337	477	531	41.5	11.3
Texas	1,361	1,712	2,743	3,303	60.2	20.4

(continued on next page)

State Populations

POPULATION 45–54

(continued from previous page)

(resident population and the number of persons aged 45 to 54, in thousands, in Census Bureau divisions and states in 1980 and projections for 1990 to 2010)

	census 1980	1990	projections 2000	2010	percent change 1990–2000	percent change 2000–2010
All ages	226,546	249,891	267,747	282,055	7.1%	5.3%
All aged 45 to 54	22,800	25,480	37,216	43,200	46.1	16.1
Mountain	**1,040**	**1,335**	**2,207**	**2,588**	**65.3**	**17.3**
Arizona	252	354	605	758	70.9	25.3
Colorado	271	345	570	641	65.2	12.5
Idaho	81	99	150	157	51.5	4.7
Montana	73	81	117	121	44.4	3.4
Nevada	86	119	209	256	75.6	22.5
New Mexico	122	155	262	326	69.0	24.4
Utah	113	136	221	257	62.5	16.3
Wyoming	42	46	73	74	58.7	1.4
Pacific	**3,125**	**3,851**	**6,124**	**7,143**	**59.0**	**16.6**
Alaska	34	55	91	105	65.5	15.4
California	2,360	2,926	4,625	5,534	58.1	19.7
Hawaii	94	110	175	210	59.1	20.0
Oregon	243	279	453	462	62.4	2.0
Washington	392	480	781	831	62.7	6.4

Source: Projections of the Population of States by Age, Sex and Race: 1988 to 2010, *Bureau of the Census, Current Population Reports, Series P-25, No. 1017*

Note: Numbers may not add to total due to rounding.

State-by-State Changes

POPULATION
45–54

INCREASING EVERYWHERE

The nation can look forward to many more people in the big-earning, big-spending 45-to-54-year age group, with growth rates between 1990 and 2000 ranging from Nevada's high of 76 percent to New York's 28 percent.

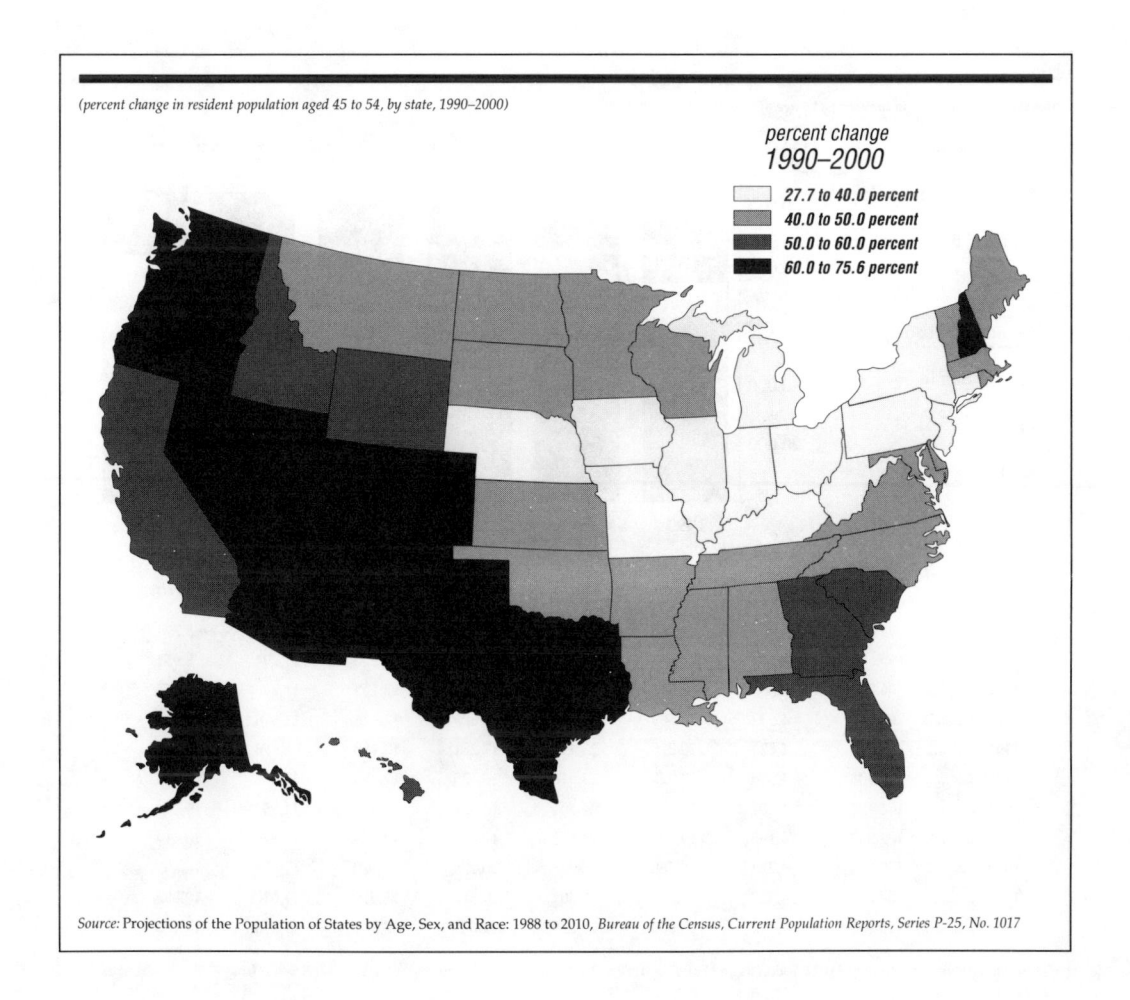

(percent change in resident population aged 45 to 54, by state, 1990–2000)

percent change
1990–2000

- 27.7 to 40.0 percent
- 40.0 to 50.0 percent
- 50.0 to 60.0 percent
- 60.0 to 75.6 percent

Source: Projections of the Population of States by Age, Sex, and Race: 1988 to 2010, *Bureau of the Census, Current Population Reports, Series P-25, No. 1017*

Number of Households

HOUSEHOLDS
45–54

AGING BABY BOOMERS

By 2000, aging baby boomers will contribute to a 50 percent jump in the number of 45-to-54-year-old householders, for a gain over the decade of 717,000 new households per year. Although family households will be growing by 45 percent, nonfamily households will leap up a full 70 percent.

(number of households, in thousands, by age of householder, 1990–2000)

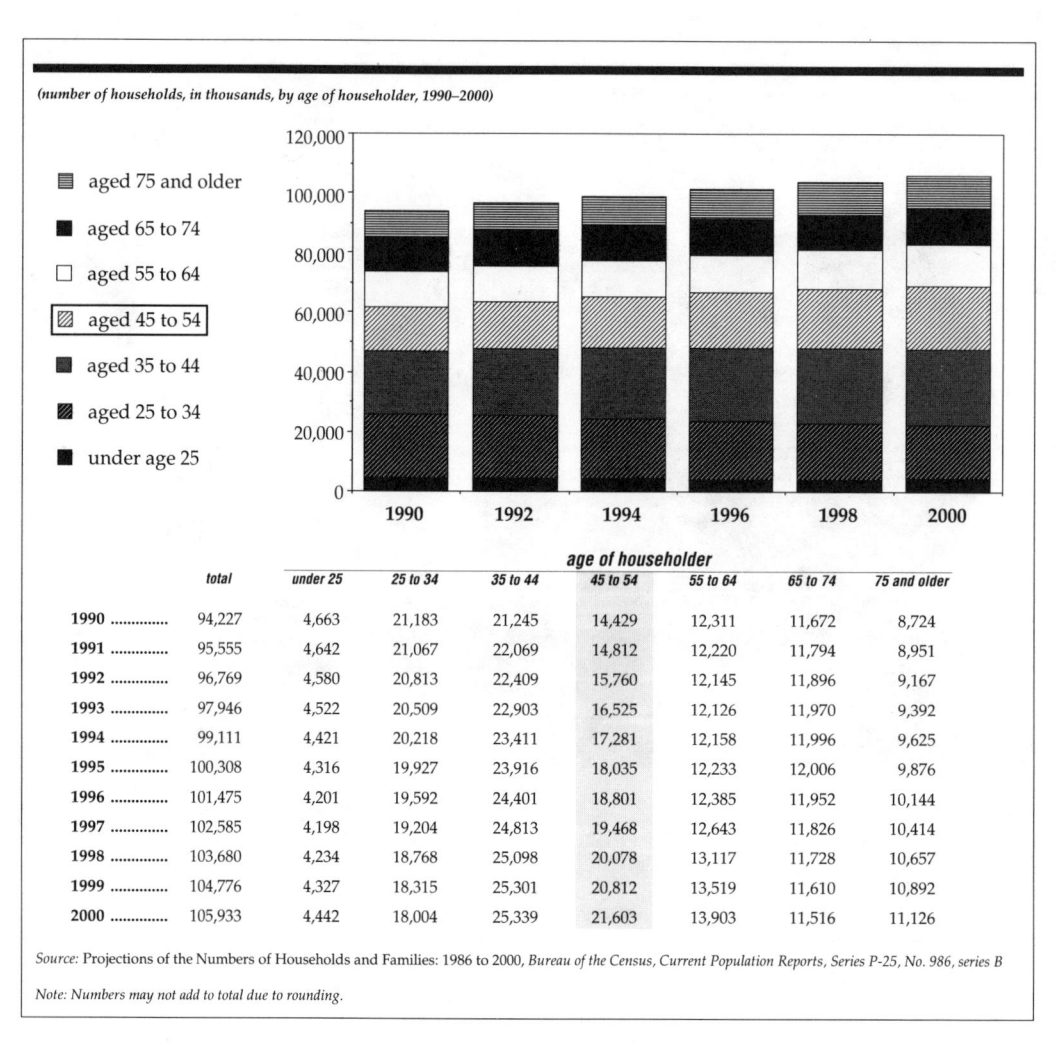

Legend:
- aged 75 and older
- aged 65 to 74
- aged 55 to 64
- aged 45 to 54
- aged 35 to 44
- aged 25 to 34
- under age 25

	total	under 25	25 to 34	35 to 44	45 to 54	55 to 64	65 to 74	75 and older
1990	94,227	4,663	21,183	21,245	14,429	12,311	11,672	8,724
1991	95,555	4,642	21,067	22,069	14,812	12,220	11,794	8,951
1992	96,769	4,580	20,813	22,409	15,760	12,145	11,896	9,167
1993	97,946	4,522	20,509	22,903	16,525	12,126	11,970	9,392
1994	99,111	4,421	20,218	23,411	17,281	12,158	11,996	9,625
1995	100,308	4,316	19,927	23,916	18,035	12,233	12,006	9,876
1996	101,475	4,201	19,592	24,401	18,801	12,385	11,952	10,144
1997	102,585	4,198	19,204	24,813	19,468	12,643	11,826	10,414
1998	103,680	4,234	18,768	25,098	20,078	13,117	11,728	10,657
1999	104,776	4,327	18,315	25,301	20,812	13,519	11,610	10,892
2000	105,933	4,442	18,004	25,339	21,603	13,903	11,516	11,126

Source: Projections of the Numbers of Households and Families: 1986 to 2000, *Bureau of the Census, Current Population Reports, Series P-25, No. 986, series B*

Note: Numbers may not add to total due to rounding.

Types of Households

HOUSEHOLDS
45–54

TIME AND MONEY

Four out of five householders aged 45 to 54 are family heads and two-thirds are married couples. By this age, many of their children have left home, which leaves them with more discretionary income to spend on luxuries and leisure activities.

(household types for all households and for householders aged 45 to 54, numbers in thousands)

	all households total	all households percent of households in category	householder aged 45 to 54 total	householder aged 45 to 54 percent of households in category
All households	91,066	100.0%	13,630	100.0%
Family households	65,133	71.5	11,138	81.7
Married couple	51,809	56.9	9,069	66.5
With children under age 18 at home	24,600	27.0	3,980	29.2
Without children under age 18 at home	27,209	29.9	5,089	37.3
Female householder	10,608	11.6	1,629	12.0
With children under age 18 at home	6,273	6.9	593	4.4
Without children under age 18 at home	4,335	4.8	1,036	7.6
Male householder	2,715	3.0	440	3.2
With children under age 18 at home	1,047	1.1	176	1.3
Without children under age 18 at home	1,669	1.8	264	1.9
Nonfamily households	25,993	28.5	2,492	18.3
Living alone	21,889	24.0	2,131	15.6
Female householder	13,101	14.4	1,094	8.0
Male householder	8,788	9.7	1,037	7.6
Living with others	4,044	4.4	361	2.6
Female householder	1,523	1.7	138	1.0
Male householder	2,521	2.8	223	1.6

Source: The 1988 Current Population Survey, Bureau of the Census

Note: Numbers may not add to total due to rounding.

Future Household Types

HOUSEHOLDS
45–54

A DWINDLING SHARE

Although the number of family households headed by 45-to-54-year-olds will grow by 45 percent during the 1990s, the proportion of family households will continue to decline. In 1980, families were 85 percent of all households in this age group—they will be 80 percent of all households in 2000.

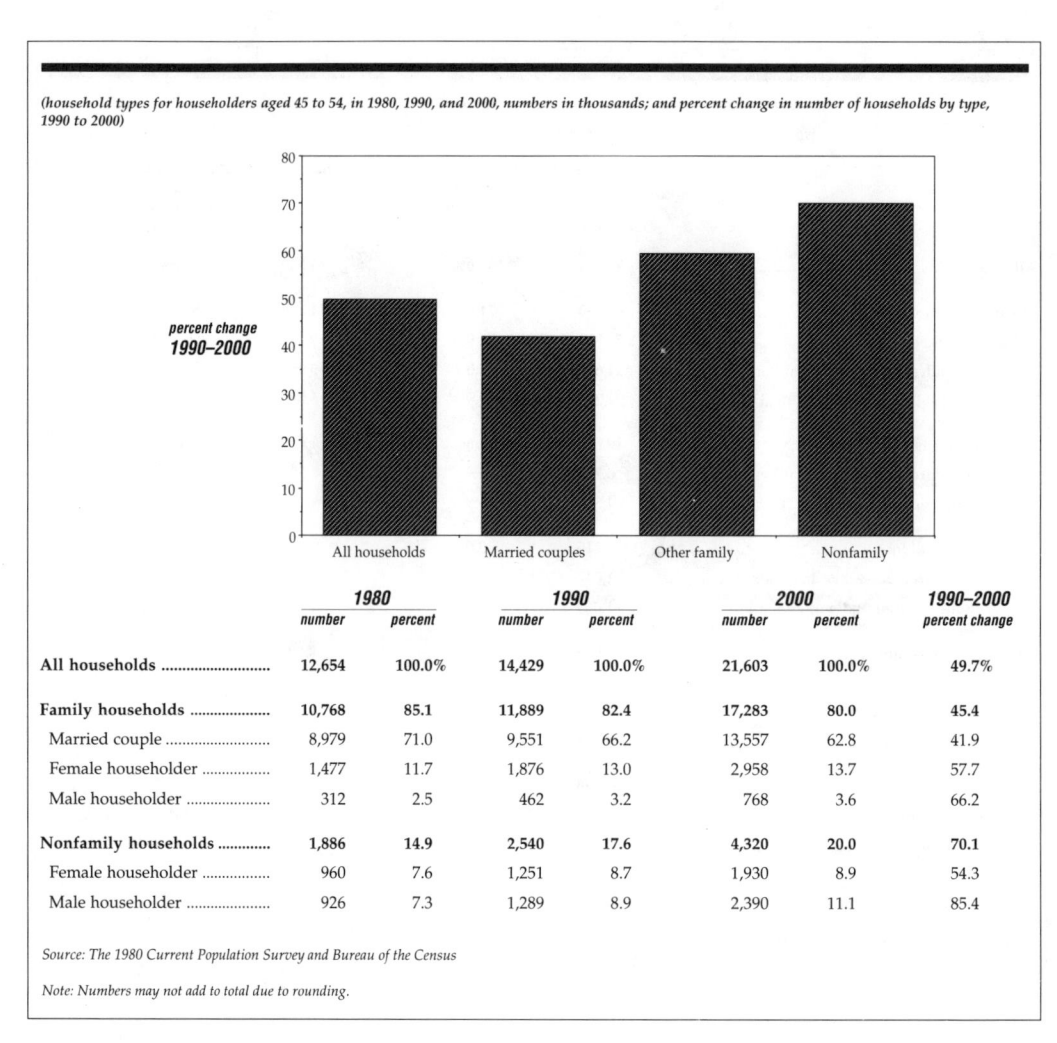

(household types for householders aged 45 to 54, in 1980, 1990, and 2000, numbers in thousands; and percent change in number of households by type, 1990 to 2000)

percent change 1990–2000

	1980 number	1980 percent	1990 number	1990 percent	2000 number	2000 percent	1990–2000 percent change
All households	12,654	100.0%	14,429	100.0%	21,603	100.0%	49.7%
Family households	10,768	85.1	11,889	82.4	17,283	80.0	45.4
Married couple	8,979	71.0	9,551	66.2	13,557	62.8	41.9
Female householder	1,477	11.7	1,876	13.0	2,958	13.7	57.7
Male householder	312	2.5	462	3.2	768	3.6	66.2
Nonfamily households	1,886	14.9	2,540	17.6	4,320	20.0	70.1
Female householder	960	7.6	1,251	8.7	1,930	8.9	54.3
Male householder	926	7.3	1,289	8.9	2,390	11.1	85.4

Source: The 1980 Current Population Survey and Bureau of the Census

Note: Numbers may not add to total due to rounding.

Marital Status

MARITAL STATUS
45–54

MOST-MARRIED AGE GROUP

No other age group tops 45-to-54-year-olds when it comes to marriage—76 percent of them are married and living with their spouses. Another 11 percent are divorced, 4 percent are widowed, and about 5 percent are still single. The figures vary by race: 79 percent of whites, 70 percent of Hispanics, and 54 percent of blacks are married and living with their spouses.

(marital status of persons aged 15 and older and those aged 45 to 54, by sex, race and Hispanic origin, numbers in thousands)

	all	total	single never married	married spouse present	married spouse absent	divorced	widowed
Males all ages							
All races/ethnicities	89,368	100.0%	30.0%	58.5%	2.9%	6.3%	2.4%
White	77,212	100.0	28.2	60.9	2.5	6.2	2.3
Black	9,472	100.0	42.9	40.4	6.0	7.5	3.3
Hispanic origin	6,517	100.0	36.4	49.9	6.2	5.8	1.6
Aged 45 to 54							
All races/ethnicities	11,151	100.0	5.9	80.5	3.6	8.8	1.2
White	9,721	100.0	5.5	82.0	3.0	8.5	1.0
Black	1,078	100.0	10.3	65.0	8.7	13.2	2.8
Hispanic origin	693	100.0	7.4	74.9	5.8	10.5	1.4
Females all ages							
All races/ethnicities	97,320	100.0	23.0	53.7	3.6	8.3	11.4
White	83,003	100.0	21.0	56.6	2.7	8.0	11.6
Black	11,447	100.0	36.5	32.7	9.2	10.4	11.2
Hispanic origin	6,588	100.0	26.6	51.2	7.7	8.3	6.2
Females aged 45 to 54							
All races/ethnicities	11,866	100.0	4.4	72.4	4.2	13.1	5.8
White	10,121	100.0	3.9	76.0	3.0	12.1	5.0
Black	1,359	100.0	8.5	45.3	13.6	21.0	11.6
Hispanic origin	758	100.0	6.6	65.2	8.4	13.6	6.3

Source: Marital Status and Living Arrangements: March 1987, *Bureau of the Census, Current Population Reports, Series P-20, No. 423*

Note: Hispanics may be of any race. Numbers may not add to total due to rounding.

Number of Marriages and Divorces

MARITAL STATUS
45–54

EVENTFUL NUMBERS

Fewer than 1 percent of first marriages involve men or women aged 45 to 54. These middle-aged men, however, account for 11 percent of all divorces and 14 percent of all remarriages, while the women lag slightly behind with 8 percent of divorces and 10 percent of remarriages.

(number of marriages and divorces for all Americans and for those aged 45 to 54)

	all persons male	all persons female	persons aged 45 to 54 male	persons aged 45 to 54 female	percent involving persons aged 45 to 54 male	percent involving persons aged 45 to 54 female
All marriages	1,858,783	1,858,783	99,702	68,827	5.4%	3.7%
First marriages	1,185,904	1,196,119	9,162	5,609	0.8	0.5
Remarriages	635,086	623,867	89,215	62,281	14.0	9.8
Previously divorced	499,735	485,848	70,945	43,004	14.2	8.6
Divorces	577,713	577,713	63,234	44,671	10.9	7.7

Source: Advance Report of Final Marriage Statistics, 1985 and Advance Report of Final Divorce Statistics, 1985, *National Center for Health Statistics*

Note: Numbers will not add to total because all divorces include those not stating their age and all marriages include those not stating whether they were previously married.

Summary of Educational Attainment

EDUCATIONAL ATTAINMENT
45–54

AVERAGE EDUCATION

The educational attainment of 45-to-54-year-olds is about the same as that of Americans in general. One in every five persons in this age group has completed four or more years of college.

(years of school completed by persons aged 25 and over, by selected characteristics, numbers in thousands)

	number	4 years of high school or more	1 or more years of college	4 or more years of college
All persons	149,144	75.6%	37.0%	19.9%
Age groups:				
25 to 34	42,635	86.5	45.4	23.9
35 to 44	33,632	85.9	46.8	26.5
45 to 54	**23,018**	**77.6**	**35.6**	**19.5**
55 to 64	21,883	67.8	28.0	14.9
65 to 74	17,232	56.9	21.9	10.6
75 years and older	10,743	42.0	18.0	8.9
Sex:				
Male	70,677	76.0	40.6	23.6
Female	78,476	75.3	33.6	16.5
Race:				
White	129,170	77.0	37.8	20.5
Black	15,580	63.4	26.4	10.7
Asian and other	4,394	78.4	50.9	33.4
Hispanic origin:				
Hispanic	9,449	50.9	21.9	8.6
Non-Hispanic	139,695	77.3	38.0	20.6
Region:				
Northeast	32,030	76.5	36.8	22.2
Midwest	36,322	77.4	33.7	17.6
South	50,848	70.8	34.1	18.3
West	29,943	80.6	45.9	22.8
Metropolitan residence:				
Metropolitan area	115,614	77.6	40.0	22.1
Nonmetropolitan area	33,529	68.7	26.5	12.6

Source: Educational Attainment in the United States: March 1987 and March 1986, Bureau of the Census, Current Population Reports, Series P-20, No. 428

Age and Education

EDUCATIONAL ATTAINMENT
45–54

A LIFETIME FOR LEARNING

There are sizeable differences in educational attainment within this age group. While 18 percent of men and women aged 50 to 54 have completed four or more years of college, 21 percent of those aged 45 to 49 are that highly educated.

(years of school completed by persons aged 45 to 54, by sex and single year of age, numbers in thousands)

	number	total	not high school graduate	high school graduate	1 to 3 years of college	4 or more years of college	median years
Males aged 45 to 49	5,909	100.0%	20.0%	36.6%	17.4%	26.1%	12.8
Age 45	1,228	100.0	20.4	36.3	17.6	25.7	12.8
Age 46	1,202	100.0	18.2	37.4	17.6	26.7	12.8
Age 47	1,251	100.0	20.2	36.5	15.9	27.7	12.8
Age 48	1,178	100.0	17.5	36.8	19.3	26.3	12.9
Age 49	1,051	100.0	23.8	35.9	16.4	23.7	12.7
Males aged 50 to 54	5,242	100.0	25.8	37.1	13.8	23.4	12.7
Age 50	1,116	100.0	23.5	37.8	12.3	26.6	12.7
Age 51	1,077	100.0	25.3	34.4	15.2	24.9	12.7
Age 52	1,071	100.0	26.0	39.4	13.3	21.3	12.6
Age 53	954	100.0	26.1	37.7	14.8	21.5	12.6
Age 54	1,025	100.0	28.3	35.9	13.8	22.0	12.6
Females aged 45 to 49	6,255	100.0	20.3	45.8	17.8	16.2	12.6
Age 45	1,381	100.0	19.8	45.8	17.7	16.8	12.7
Age 46	1,310	100.0	18.8	44.7	20.3	16.2	12.7
Age 47	1,236	100.0	20.1	44.0	19.8	16.1	12.7
Age 48	1,156	100.0	21.8	45.8	16.0	16.2	12.6
Age 49	1,173	100.0	21.3	48.8	14.5	15.5	12.6
Females aged 50 to 54	5,611	100.0	24.2	48.3	14.7	12.8	12.5
Age 50	1,185	100.0	22.4	49.5	14.8	13.2	12.6
Age 51	1,122	100.0	22.7	49.5	15.5	12.4	12.6
Age 52	1,173	100.0	27.1	44.6	14.1	14.2	12.5
Age 53	1,043	100.0	23.6	51.8	13.1	11.2	12.5
Age 54	1,089	100.0	25.0	46.4	15.9	12.8	12.5

Source: Educational Attainment in the United States: March 1987 and 1986, Bureau of the Census, Current Population Reports, Series P-20, No. 428

Note: Numbers may not add to total due to rounding.

Sex, Race, and Ethnicity

EDUCATIONAL ATTAINMENT
45–54

ADVANTAGED MEN

Although not as highly educated as younger people, 16 percent of those aged 45 to 54 completed one to three years of college and nearly 20 percent completed four or more years. Among 45-to-54-year-olds, men of all races and ethnicity are more likely than their female counterparts to have finished four years of college.

(years of school completed by persons aged 25 and older and those aged 45 to 54, by sex, race, and Hispanic origin, numbers in thousands)

	number	total	not high school graduate	high school graduate	1 to 3 years of college	4 or more years of college
All persons aged 25 and older	149,144	100.0%	24.4%	38.7%	17.1%	19.9%
White	129,170	100.0	23.0	39.2	17.2	20.5
Black	15,580	100.0	36.6	37.1	15.7	10.7
Hispanic origin	9,449	100.0	49.1	29.0	13.3	8.6
All persons aged 45 to 54	23,018	100.0	22.4	42.1	16.0	19.5
White	19,842	100.0	20.5	43.1	16.4	20.0
Black	2,438	100.0	38.8	37.5	12.6	11.1
Hispanic origin	1,451	100.0	53.4	27.6	10.1	8.8
Males aged 25 and older	70,677	100.0	24.0	35.4	17.1	23.6
White	61,678	100.0	22.7	35.6	17.2	24.5
Black	6,919	100.0	37.0	36.5	15.5	11.0
Hispanic origin	4,614	100.0	48.2	28.0	14.2	9.7
Males aged 45 to 54	11,151	100.0	22.7	36.8	15.7	24.8
White	9,721	100.0	21.1	37.4	15.9	25.6
Black	1,078	100.0	40.0	34.5	13.9	11.9
Hispanic origin	693	100.0	53.8	27.1	8.4	10.7
Females aged 25 and older	78,467	100.0	24.7	41.6	17.1	16.5
White	67,492	100.0	23.3	42.6	17.3	16.9
Black	8,661	100.0	36.2	37.5	15.8	10.4
Hispanic origin	4,835	100.0	50.0	30.0	12.5	7.5
Females aged 45 to 54	11,866	100.0	22.1	47.0	16.3	14.6
White	10,121	100.0	20.0	48.4	16.9	14.7
Black	1,360	100.0	37.9	39.8	11.7	10.4
Hispanic origin	758	100.0	53.0	28.1	11.5	7.1

Source: Educational Attainment in the United States: March 1987 and March 1986, *Bureau of the Census, Current Population Reports, Series P-20, No. 428*

Note: Hispanics are of any race. Numbers may not add to total due to rounding.

Householders

EDUCATIONAL ATTAINMENT
45–54

EDUCATED MEN

Male householders aged 35 to 54 are more likely to have finished four or more years of college than those in any other age group. The proportion of female householders with four or more years of college is highest (24 percent) among 25-to-34-year-olds, followed by these 35-to-54-year-olds at 20 percent.

(years of school completed by householders aged 35 to 54, by sex, race, and Hispanic origin, numbers in thousands)

	number	total	not high school graduate	high school graduate	1 to 3 years of college	4 or more years of college	median years
Male householders	24,091	100.0%	16.4%	35.1%	18.8%	29.7%	13.0
White	21,295	100.0	15.4	35.2	19.1	30.3	13.0
Black	2,014	100.0	28.1	38.5	17.0	16.3	12.6
Hispanic origin	1,476	100.0	45.5	27.7	15.0	11.7	12.2
Female householders	7,824	100.0	21.6	39.0	19.1	20.3	12.7
White	5,897	100.0	18.7	38.2	20.0	23.0	12.8
Black	1,698	100.0	30.7	43.0	16.2	10.1	12.4
Hispanic origin	631	100.0	51.5	28.4	11.4	8.9	11.7

Source: Educational Attainment in the United States: March 1987 and March 1986, *Bureau of the Census, Current Population Reports, Series P-20, No. 428*

Note: The Census Bureau grouped householders aged 45-to-54 with those aged 35-to-44 for this tabulation. Hispanics are of any race. Numbers may not add to total due to rounding.

Labor Force Status

LABOR FORCE
45–54

TOPPING AND MATCHING THE PRIMES

Ninety-one percent of 45-to-54-year-old men are in the labor force, compared with 88 percent of all male prime-aged workers—those who are 18 to 64. Sixty-seven percent of women in this age group are in the labor force; a percentage which exactly matches that for all prime-aged working women.

(labor force status of all persons aged 16 and older, aged 18 to 64, and those aged 45 to 54, by sex and race, numbers in thousands)

	total population	total in labor force	percent of population in labor force	number employed	number unemployed	percent of labor force unemployed	not in labor force
Males aged 16 and older	86,899	66,207	76.2%	62,107	4,101	6.2%	20,692
White	75,189	57,779	76.8	54,647	3,132	5.4	17,410
Black	9,128	6,486	71.1	5,661	826	12.7	2,642
Males aged 18 to 64	71,443	62,563	87.6	58,864	3,699	5.9	8,880
White	61,583	54,522	88.5	51,705	2,818	5.2	7,061
Black	7,615	6,179	81.1	5,427	750	12.1	1,437
Males aged 45 to 54	11,215	10,176	90.7	9,750	426	4.2	1,039
White	9,771	8,945	91.6	8,596	350	3.9	826
Black	1,092	915	83.7	853	61	6.7	178
Females aged 16 and older	95,853	53,658	56.0	50,334	3,324	6.2%	42,195
White	81,769	45,510	55.7	43,142	2,369	5.2	36,258
Black	11,224	6,507	58.0	5,648	858	13.2	4,717
Females aged 18 to 64	75,700	50,799	67.1	47,801	3,000	5.9	24,901
White	63,964	42,999	67.2	40,878	2,120	4.9	20,965
Black	9,262	6,227	67.2	5,438	791	12.7	3,035
Females aged 45 to 54	11,968	8,034	67.1	7,737	298	3.7	3,934
White	10,194	6,847	67.2	6,620	227	3.3	3,347
Black	1,368	924	67.5	860	63	6.9	444

Source: Annual averages from Employment and Earnings, 1987, Bureau of Labor Statistics

Note: The population here includes all civilian, noninstitutionalized people aged 16 and older.

Extent of Employment

LABOR FORCE
45–54

WORKING FULL-TIME

Among working 45-to-54-year-olds, 96 percent of men and 75 percent of women are full-time employees, and the vast majority of them are on the job year-round. More than half of the women aged 45 to 54 who work part-time are also on the job at least 50 weeks a year.

(work experience in 1987 of workers aged 16 and older and aged 45 to 54, by sex, numbers in thousands)

	\multicolumn{4}{c}{worked at full-time jobs}	\multicolumn{4}{c}{worked at part-time jobs}	non-workers
	total	50-52 weeks	27-49 weeks	1-26 weeks	total	50-52 weeks	27-49 weeks	1-26 weeks	total
Males									
Aged 16 and older	59,740	47,106	7,489	5,143	9,280	3,175	2,165	3,940	18,582
Aged 45 to 54	10,123	8,784	953	386	425	187	116	123	927
Females									
Aged 16 and older	40,398	29,882	5,788	4,727	18,538	7,774	4,301	6,463	37,580
Aged 45 to 54	6,611	5,376	779	456	2,234	1,179	538	517	3,430

Source: The 1988 Current Population Survey, Bureau of Labor Statistics

Note: Numbers may not add to total due to rounding. The categories in this table are not mutually exclusive. Workers may, for example, be counted as both a full-time and a part-time worker if they held jobs of both kinds during the year. For this reason, the total number of workers will be higher and the number of nonworkers lower than in the previous table that uses annual averages of the number of workers in each category. Civilians only.

Kinds of Jobs

LABOR FORCE
45–54

HIGHLY PROFESSIONAL

Nearly 30 percent of working 45-to-54-year-olds are in managerial and professional occupations, compared with 25 percent of all employees. Thirty-one percent of working men aged 45-to-54 and 27 percent of the women have managerial or professional jobs.

(occupations of employed persons aged 16 and older and those aged 45 to 54, by sex, numbers in thousands)

	aged 16+	aged 45-54	males aged 45-54	females aged 45-54	percent aged 16+	percent aged 45-54
All employed persons	112,440	17,487	9,750	7,737	100.0%	100.0%
Managerial and professional	27,742	5,111	3,037	2,074	24.7	29.2
Executive, administrative, and managerial	13,316	2,609	1,735	874	11.8	14.9
Officials & administrators, public admin.	549	142	93	49	0.5	0.8
Other exececutive, admin., & managerial	9,190	1,881	1,304	577	8.2	10.8
Management-related occupations	3,577	587	339	248	3.2	3.4
Professional specialty occupations	14,426	2,502	1,302	1,200	12.8	14.3
Engineers	1,731	329	316	13	1.5	1.9
Math & computer scientists	685	101	72	29	0.6	0.6
Natural scientists	388	67	58	9	0.4	4.0
Health diagnosing occupations	793	150	136	14	0.7	0.9
Health assessment & treating	2,148	327	32	295	1.9	1.9
Teachers, college & university	661	149	100	49	0.6	0.9
Teachers, except college & university	3,587	703	194	509	3.2	4
Lawyers & judges	707	97	87	10	0.6	0.6
Other professional specialty occupations	3,727	580	309	271	3.3	3.3
Technical, sales, administrative support	35,082	5,106	1,818	3,288	31.2	29.2
Technicians & related support occupations	3,346	433	238	195	3.0	2.5
Health technologists & technicians	1,142	153	18	135	1.0	0.9
Engineering & science technicians	1,100	156	134	22	1.0	0.9
Techs., except health, engineering, science	1,104	123	85	38	1.0	0.7
Sales occupations	13,480	1,909	1,100	809	12.1	10.9
Supervisors & proprietors	3,572	666	474	192	3.2	3.8
Sales reps., finance & business service	2,330	400	244	156	2.1	2.3

(continued next page)

Kinds of Jobs

LABOR FORCE 45–54

(continued from previous page)
(occupations of employed persons aged 16 and older and those aged 45 to 54, by sex, numbers in thousands)

	aged 16+	aged 45-54	males aged 45-54	females aged 45-54	percent aged 16+	percent aged 45-54
Sales reps., commodities except retail	1,544	247	217	30	1.4%	1.4%
Sales, retail and personal	5,973	586	164	422	5.3	3.4
Sales-related occupations	60	10	2	8	0.1	0.1
Administrative support including clerical	**18,256**	**2,764**	**480**	**2,284**	**16.2**	**15.8**
Supervisors	723	156	72	84	0.6	0.9
Computer equipment operators	914	98	28	70	0.8	0.6
Secretaries, stenographers, & typists	5,004	861	12	849	4.5	4.9
Financial records processing	2,469	409	28	381	2.2	2.3
Mail & message distributing	961	136	94	42	0.9	0.8
Other admin. support including clerical	8,185	1,104	246	858	7.3	6.3
Service occupations	**15,054**	**1,940**	**669**	**1,271**	**13.4**	**11.1**
Private household	934	125	3	122	0.8	0.7
Protective services	1,907	275	243	32	1.7	1.6
Service, except private hhld. & protective	12,213	1,540	422	1,118	10.9	8.8
Food service	5,204	492	102	390	4.6	2.8
Health service	1,873	302	19	283	1.7	1.7
Cleaning & building service	2,886	465	245	220	2.6	2.7
Personal service	2,249	282	57	225	2.0	1.6
Precision production, craft, repair	**13,568**	**2,262**	**2,062**	**200**	**12.1**	**12.9**
Mechanics & repairers	4,445	775	751	24	0.4	4.4
Construction trades	5,011	706	696	10	4.5	4.0
Other production, craft, repair	4,112	780	613	167	3.7	4.5
Operators, fabricators, laborers	**17,486**	**2,581**	**1,779**	**802**	**15.6**	**14.8**
Machine operators, assemblers, inspectors	7,994	1,309	692	617	7.1	7.5
Transportation, material moving	4,712	831	759	72	4.2	4.8
Handlers, equip. cleaners, helpers, laborers	4,779	441	328	113	4.3	2.5
Farming, forestry, fishing	**3,507**	**488**	**387**	**101**	**3.1**	**2.8**
Farm operators & managers	1,317	252	201	51	1.2	1.4
Farm workers & related occupations	2,013	206	157	49	1.8	1.2
Forestry and fishing occupations	177	30	29	1	0.2	0.2

Source: *Unpublished annual data for 1987, Bureau of Labor Statistics*

Note: *Numbers may not add to total due to rounding. Civilian, noninstitutionalized employees only.*

Workers in the 1990s

LABOR FORCE
45–54

MORE FEMALE WORKERS

By 2000, 75 percent of women aged 45 to 54 will be in the labor force—60 percent of them were workers in 1980. Continuing the trend of recent decades, men aged 45 to 54 will be less likely to work in 2000 than in 1990.

(labor force and labor force participation rates* for persons aged 16 and older and those aged 45 to 54, by sex, race, and ethnicity, in 1990 and 2000, numbers in thousands)

	1990 number	1990 participation rate	2000 number	2000 participation rate	1990–2000 percent change
Aged 16 and older	124,457	66.2%	138,775	67.8%	11.5%
White	106,648	66.5	116,701	68.2	9.4
Black	13,788	64.6	16,334	66.0	18.5
Hispanic	9,718	65.9	14,086	67.1	44.9
Asian and other	4,021	64.8	5,740	65.8	42.8
Males aged 16 and older	67,909	75.8	73,136	74.7	7.7
Males, aged 45 to 54	11,136	90.7	16,332	90.1	46.7
White	9,798	91.6	14,193	91.0	44.9
Black	984	83.7	1,526	83.8	55.1
Hispanic	732	89.1	1,297	88.2	77.2
Asian and other	354	88.1	613	87.4	73.2
Females aged 16 and older	56,548	57.4	65,639	61.5	16.1
Females, aged 45 to 54	8,985	69.0	14,220	75.4	58.3
White	7,664	69.0	11,964	75.6	56.1
Black	1,019	69.0	1,677	75.1	64.6
Hispanic	535	60.3	1,000	66.7	86.9
Asian and other	302	68.2	579	73.5	91.7

*Labor force participation rates are the ratio of people in the labor force to the total population of a given sex, age and race or ethnicity.

Source: Unpublished data from the Bureau of Labor Statistics

Note: The labor force here includes civilians who are working or looking for work. Hispanics are of any race.

Household Income

INCOME
45–54

THE HAVES

Although they head only 15 percent of all households, 45-to-54-year-olds account for over 20 percent of household income, which works out to $14,400 per household member, an amount topped only by 55-to-64-year-olds.

(household income and income per household member, for all households and for households by age of householder, numbers for 1988 in thousands, income is for 1987)

	households		persons in household			total household income		
	number	percent	number	percent	persons per household	$ billions	percent	per household member
All households	91,066	100.0%	240,722	100.0%	2.64	$2,927.2	100.0%	$12,160
Age of householder								
under 25	5,228	5.7	12,117	5.0	2.32	102.0	3.5	8,415
25 to 34	20,583	22.6	58,724	24.4	2.85	621.6	21.2	10,586
35 to 44	19,323	21.2	64,351	26.7	3.33	763.8	26.1	11,870
45 to 54	13,630	15.0	41,379	17.2	3.04	597.0	20.4	14,426
55 to 64	12,846	14.1	30,151	12.5	2.35	447.3	15.3	14,835
65 and older	19,456	21.4	33,999	14.1	1.75	395.6	13.5	11,635

Source: The 1988 Current Population Survey, Bureau of the Census

Individual Income

INCOME
45–54

UP AND AWAY

Fifty-eight percent of income-producing men and 17 percent of the women aged 45 to 54 bring in over $25,000—incomes that can be claimed by only 35 percent and 11 percent, respectively, of all income-generating men and women.

(income distribution and median income for males and females aged 15 and older and aged 45 to 54, numbers for 1988 in thousands, income is for 1987)

	males aged 15 and older number	males aged 15 and older percent	males aged 45 to 54 number	males aged 45 to 54 percent
All males	90,284	–	11,520	–
All males with income	85,623	100.0%	11,342	100.0%
Less than $5,000	13,025	15.2	802	7.1
$5,000 to $9,999	12,066	14.1	761	6.7
$10,000 to $14,999	11,708	13.7	1,061	9.4
$15,000 to $19,999	9,887	11.5	997	8.8
$20,000 to $24,999	8,714	10.2	1,165	10.3
$25,000 to $29,999	7,266	8.5	1,144	10.1
$30,000 to $34,999	6,124	7.2	1,136	10.0
$35,000 to $49,999	9,941	11.6	2,278	20.1
$50,000 to $74,999	4,669	5.5	1,317	11.6
$75,000 and over	2,225	2.6	679	6.0
Median income, all with income		$17,752		$28,685
Median income, year-round, full-time workers		$26,722		$32,821

	females aged 15 and older number	females aged 15 and older percent	females aged 45 to 54 number	females aged 45 to 54 percent
All females	98,168	–	12,275	–
All females with income	89,279	100.0%	11,151	100.0%
Less than $5,000	30,715	34.4	3,198	28.7
$5,000 to $9,999	19,782	22.2	1,883	16.9
$10,000 to $14,999	13,313	14.9	1,695	15.2
$15,000 to $19,999	9,470	10.6	1,413	12.7
$20,000 to $24,999	6,321	7.1	1,086	9.7
$25,000 to $29,999	3,768	4.2	686	6.2
$30,000 to $34,999	2,331	2.6	459	4.1
$35,000 to $49,999	2,602	2.9	529	4.7
$50,000 to $74,999	708	0.8	144	1.3
$75,000 and over	268	0.3	59	0.5
Median income, all with income		$8,101		$11,219
Median income, year-round, full-time workers		$17,504		$19,087

Source: Money Income and Poverty Status in the United States: 1987, *Bureau of the Census, Current Population Reports,* Series P-20, No. 161
Note: Numbers may not add to total due to rounding.

Income and Age

INCOME
45–54

HIGH-INCOME HOUSEHOLDS

No other age group can top the proportion of 45-to-54-year-olds that bring in at least $50,000 in household income—one-third of them do. Another 21 percent of households headed by people aged 45 to 54 have incomes between $35,000 and $50,000.

(household income by age of householder, numbers for 1988 in thousands, income is for 1987)

	total	under 25	25 to 34	35 to 44	45 to 54	55 to 64	65 to 74	75+
All households	91,066	5,228	20,583	19,323	13,630	12,846	11,410	8,045
All households	100.0%	100.0%	100.0%	100.0%	100.0%	100.0%	100.0%	100.0%
Less than $10,000	18.4	30.3	13.6	10.3	10.4	17.4	27.1	44.6
$10,000 to $14,999	10.6	15.8	9.6	6.6	6.6	9.5	17.3	18.5
$15,000 to $19,999	10.0	14.1	11.1	7.4	6.8	9.7	13.8	11.8
$20,000 to $24,999	9.2	11.5	11.1	8.3	7.2	9.1	10.1	7.5
$25,000 to $29,999	8.4	9.0	10.6	8.5	7.6	8.0	8.3	4.3
$30,000 to $34,999	7.7	6.8	9.7	9.0	7.8	7.2	6.0	3.2
$35,000 to $39,999	6.8	4.5	8.6	9.0	7.2	6.3	4.2	2.4
$40,000 to $44,999	5.8	2.3	6.7	7.9	7.4	6.0	3.0	1.7
$45,000 to $49,999	4.6	1.3	5.1	6.6	5.9	4.7	2.4	1.5
$50,000 to $59,999	6.7	2.1	6.7	9.6	10.1	7.5	2.7	1.9
$60,000 to $74,999	5.5	1.5	4.2	7.9	9.9	6.3	2.1	1.2
$75,000 and over	6.3	0.9	3.0	8.9	13.1	8.3	3.0	1.4
Median household income	$25,986	$16,204	$26,923	$34,926	$37,250	$27,538	$16,906	$11,261

Source: The 1988 Current Population Survey, Bureau of the Census

Note: Numbers may not add to total due to rounding.

Income of Married Couples

INCOME
45–54

PEAKING OUT

Nearly 44 percent of married couples in this age group have incomes of $50,000 or more compared with 27 percent of all married couples. Household income for all types of families peaks among householders aged 45 to 54 except for female householders without children at home.

(household income of married-couple householder families with and without children under 18 at home, householders aged 45 to 54, numbers for 1988 in thousands, income is for 1987)

	\multicolumn{3}{c}{married-couple householder aged 45 to 54}		
	total	with children under 18 at home	without children under 18 at home
All households	9,069	3,980	5,089
All households	100.0%	100.0%	100.0%
Less than $10,000	4.4	4.3	4.5
$10,000 to $14,999	3.7	4.3	3.3
$15,000 to $19,999	4.4	4.3	4.5
$20,000 to $24,999	6.0	5.8	6.1
$25,000 to $29,999	6.7	6.5	6.8
$30,000 to $34,999	7.8	7.1	8.4
$35,000 to $39,999	8.0	9.0	7.2
$40,000 to $44,999	8.4	8.8	8.0
$45,000 to $49,999	7.3	7.0	7.6
$50,000 to $59,999	12.7	13.2	12.3
$60,000 to $74,999	13.1	12.9	13.2
$75,000 and over	17.6	16.8	18.1
Median household income	$45,242	$44,785	$45,894

Source: The 1988 Current Population Survey, Bureau of the Census

Note: Numbers may not add to total due to rounding.

Income of Other Family Households

INCOME
45–54

PEAK INCOMES

Household income for all family types—except women without children—peaks among householders aged 45 to 54. Forty-seven percent of households headed by unmarried men in this age group and 26 percent of those headed by women have incomes of at least $35,000.

(household income of unmarried female- and male-householder families with and without children under 18 at home, householders aged 45 to 54, numbers for 1988, in thousands, income is for 1987)

	female householder aged 45 to 54			male householder aged 45 to 54		
	total	with children under 18 at home	without children under 18 at home	total	with children under 18 at home	without children under 18 at home
All households	1,629	593	1,036	440	176	264
All households	100.0%	100.0%	100.0%	100.0%	100.0%	100.0%
Less than $10,000	21.9	34.7	14.6	8.2	5.7	9.5
$10,000 to $14,999	12.3	11.3	12.9	7.7	11.4	5.3
$15,000 to $19,999	12.8	15.5	11.3	6.1	5.7	6.4
$20,000 to $24,999	9.5	9.3	9.7	9.8	10.8	9.1
$25,000 to $29,999	9.3	8.6	9.7	7.3	4.0	9.5
$30,000 to $34,999	8.2	5.4	9.8	13.6	14.8	12.9
$35,000 to $39,999	6.3	4.7	7.0	6.8	5.1	8.0
$40,000 to $44,999	5.2	2.7	6.6	9.8	6.8	12.1
$45,000 to $49,999	4.1	2.7	4.9	3.2	4.5	2.3
$50,000 to $59,999	4.6	2.5	5.7	12.3	14.8	10.6
$60,000 to $74,999	3.1	0.8	4.4	7.3	7.4	7.2
$75,000 and over	2.7	1.5	3.3	8.0	9.1	7.2
Median household income	$21,443	$16,506	$26,145	$33,806	$33,908	$33,738

Source: The 1988 Current Population Survey, Bureau of the Census

Note: Numbers may not add to total due to rounding.

Income of Nonfamily Households

INCOME
45–54

COMPARATIVE DISADVANTAGE

Although 45-to-54-year-old family householders have the highest median household income of all families, their nonfamily counterparts can't make the same claim (nonfamilies headed by 35-to-44-years-olds have the highest median incomes). Median incomes for nonfamily households in this age group, however, are consistently higher than those of nonfamilies in general.

(household income of nonfamily households by household type, householders aged 45 to 54, numbers for 1988 in thousands, income is for 1987)

	total number	living alone total	living alone male householder	living alone female householder	living with others total	living with others male householder	living with others female householder
All nonfamily households	2,492	2,131	1,037	1,094	361	223	138
All nonfamily households	100.0%	100.0%	100.0%	100.0%	100.0%	100.0%	100.0%
Less than $10,000	25.4	27.8	24.9	30.6	11.4	9.0	14.5
$10,000 to $14,999	13.0	13.6	13.0	14.2	9.7	9.0	11.6
$15,000 to $19,999	11.4	11.9	9.5	14.2	8.6	9.9	6.5
$20,000 to $24,999	9.8	10.1	9.3	10.8	8.6	9.0	8.0
$25,000 to $29,999	9.6	9.9	9.8	10.0	8.0	5.8	11.6
$30,000 to $34,999	6.3	6.1	5.2	6.9	8.3	8.1	8.0
$35,000 to $39,999	5.2	5.1	4.8	5.3	5.8	7.2	3.6
$40,000 to $44,999	5.0	4.7	6.5	3.1	6.4	6.7	5.8
$45,000 to $49,999	2.2	2.0	2.7	1.5	3.3	0.0	8.7
$50,000 to $59,999	3.7	3.0	4.8	1.2	7.8	5.8	10.9
$60,000 to $74,999	3.5	2.9	4.5	1.3	7.2	7.2	6.5
$75,000 and over	4.8	3.0	4.9	1.2	15.2	22.0	4.3
Median household income	$20,001	$18,293	$21,036	$16,926	$30,796	$34,554	$29,169

Source: The 1988 Current Population Survey, Bureau of the Census

Note: Nonfamilies are either people living alone or living with an individual (or individuals) unrelated to the householder. Numbers may not add to total due to rounding.

Income and Race, Families

INCOME
45–54

PEAK INCOME GAP

The difference between white and black median family income is highest in this age group—$17,100. But the incomes of families headed by 45-to-54-year-olds are also higher than those in the other age groups. Forty-four percent of white married couples and 26 percent of black married couples aged 45 to 54 have incomes of $50,000 or more.

(household income of family households by race and household type for householders aged 45 to 54, numbers for 1988 in thousands, income is for 1987)

	white family households			
	total	married couple	male householder	female householder
All households	9,516	8,096	336	1,083
Total	100.0%	100.0%	100.0%	100.0%
Less than $10,000	5.5	4.0	6.0	17.2
$10,000 to $19,999	10.0	8.0	12.8	24.7
$20,000 to $29,999	13.2	12.0	17.3	20.8
$30,000 to $39,999	16.1	15.7	23.2	17.2
$40,000 to $49,999	15.2	16.0	14.6	9.5
$50,000 to $59,999	11.9	12.9	10.7	5.4
$60,000 to $74,999	11.9	13.3	7.1	2.8
$75,000 and over	16.0	18.2	8.9	2.4
Median household income	$42,970	$46,159	$34,618	$24,214

	black family households			
	total	married couple	male householder	female householder
All households	1,188	649	75	464
Total	100.0%	100.0%	100.0%	100.0%
Less than $10,000	20.2	9.7	17.3	35.3
$10,000 to $19,999	17.3	10.9	24.0	25.2
$20,000 to $29,999	17.9	19.7	16.0	15.5
$30,000 to $39,999	14.6	17.7	14.7	9.7
$40,000 to $49,999	12.8	15.7	14.7	8.4
$50,000 to $59,999	6.6	10.3	10.7	0.9
$60,000 to $74,999	5.4	8.3	–	2.2
$75,000 and over	5.1	7.7	–	2.4
Median household income	$25,844	$35,665	$22,146	$16,223

Source: Money Income of Households, Families, and Persons in the United States: 1987, Bureau of the Census, Current Population Reports, Series P-60, No. 162

Note: Numbers may not add to total due to rounding. Median income is unreliable and is therefore not given when the category contains fewer than 75,000 households.

Income and Race, Nonfamilies

INCOME
45–54

RELATIVE ADVANTAGE

Thirty percent of white nonfamily householders aged 45 to 54 have incomes of $30,000 or more and 11 percent of these householders have incomes of $50,000 or more. For black nonfamily householders, the proportion with incomes of $30,000 or more is 13 percent. As in the other age groups, white male householders have the highest median income, followed by white female householders.

(householder income of nonfamily householders by race and household type for householders aged 45 to 54, numbers for 1988 in thousands, income is for 1987)

	white householder			black householder		
	total	male householder	female householder	total	male householder	female householder
All households	2,061	1,032	1,029	387	205	182
Total	100.0%	100.0%	100.0%	100.0%	100.0%	100.0%
Less than $10,000	24.9	21.4	28.5	43.7	43.4	44.0
$10,000 to $19,999	25.5	23.0	28.1	25.8	23.4	28.6
$20,000 to $24,999	9.8	8.7	11.1	9.3	8.3	10.4
$25,000 to $29,999	9.8	9.3	10.4	8.5	8.8	8.2
$30,000 to $34,999	6.5	4.8	8.2	3.6	6.8	–
$35,000 to $49,999	12.5	14.6	10.3	6.7	7.3	5.5
$50,000 and over	10.9	18.3	3.5	2.3	2.0	2.7
Median householder income	$19,814	$23,092	$17,375	$12,299	$12,704	$11,837

Source: Money Income of Households, Families, and Persons in the United States: 1987, *Bureau of the Census, Current Population Reports, Series P-60, No. 162*

Note: Numbers may not add to total due to rounding. Householder income is the total money income of the householder only.

Income of Hispanic Households

INCOME 45–54

FAMILY INCOME PEAK

Median income peaks with this age group for Hispanic family households. Fifty-nine percent of married couples, 64 percent of male householder families, and 27 percent of female householder families have incomes of $25,000 or more.

(household income of Hispanic households, by household type, for householders aged 45 to 54, numbers for 1988 in thousands, income is for 1987)

		family households		
	total	married couple	male householder	female householder
All households	712	515	39	158
Total	100.0%	100.0%	100.0%	100.0%
Less than $15,000	24.7	20.4	15.4	41.1
$15,000 to $24,999	22.9	20.4	20.5	31.6
$25,000 and over	52.4	59.2	64.1	27.2
Median household income	$26,247	$29,728	–	$16,938

		nonfamily households			
		male householder		female householder	
	total	living alone	living with others	living alone	living with others
All households	113	57	18	36	2
Total	100.0%	100.0%	100.0%	100.0%	100.0%
Less than $15,000	61.1	64.9	27.8	72.2	50.0
$15,000 to $24,999	20.4	17.5	44.4	13.9	–
$25,000 and over	18.6	15.8	27.8	16.7	50.0
Median household income	$10,867	–	–	–	–

Source: The 1988 Current Population Survey, Bureau of the Census

Note: Numbers may not add to total due to rounding. Hispanics are of any race. Median income is unreliable and is therefore not given when the category contains fewer than 75,000 households.

Income of Dual-Earner Couples

INCOME
45–54

TOP OF THE INCOME CHART

A hefty 63 percent of married couples in this age group are dual earners, and their median household income of $50,300 is 11 percent greater than that of all married 45-to-54-year-olds. Over half of them have incomes of $50,000 or more, and 20 percent have at least $75,000.

(household income for all dual-earner married couples and for those with married-couple householders aged 45 to 54, numbers for 1988 in thousands, income is for 1987)

	householder all ages			householder aged 45 to 54		
	total	with children under 18 at home	without children under 18 at home	total	with children under 18 at home	without children under 18 at home
All households	26,227	14,989	11,238	5,744	2,539	3,205
All households	100.0%	100.0%	100.0%	100.0%	100.0%	100.0%
Less than $15,000	5.7	6.0	5.4	4.2	3.9	4.4
$15,000 to $19,999	5.1	5.4	4.7	3.0	3.2	2.9
$20,000 to $24,999	7.3	7.8	6.6	5.2	5.2	5.2
$25,000 to $29,999	8.3	9.0	7.5	5.6	5.7	5.5
$30,000 to $34,999	9.4	10.2	8.3	6.9	6.5	7.2
$35,000 to $39,999	10.3	11.2	9.0	7.6	9.3	6.2
$40,000 to $44,999	9.6	9.8	9.3	8.5	9.4	7.7
$45,000 to $49,999	8.1	8.2	7.9	8.3	8.1	8.5
$50,000 to $59,999	13.0	12.5	13.6	14.6	15.0	14.2
$60,000 to $74,999	11.2	10.2	12.5	16.3	15.8	16.8
$75,000 and over	12.1	9.6	15.3	19.9	17.9	21.4
Median household income	$41,904	$40,044	$44,508	$50,336	$49,188	$51,550

Source: The 1988 Current Population Survey, Bureau of the Census

Note: Numbers may not add to total due to rounding.

Income and Education

INCOME
45–54

MORE COLLEGE EQUALS MORE INCOME

Sixty percent of 45-to-54-year-old householders with four or more years of college have household incomes of $50,000 or more. Just 38 percent of householders with one to three years of college have incomes in that range.

(household income of householders aged 45 to 54 by years of school completed by householder, numbers for 1988 in thousands, income is for 1987)

	total	not high school graduate	high school graduate	1 to 3 years of college	4 or more years of college
All households	13,630	3,048	5,082	2,172	3,329
All households	100.0%	100.0%	100.0%	100.0%	100.0%
Less than $10,000	10.4	24.5	8.7	6.4	2.9
$10,000 to $19,999	13.4	21.5	15.3	10.8	4.6
$20,000 to $29,999	14.8	19.3	17.2	13.5	7.8
$30,000 to $39,999	15.0	13.1	17.7	16.3	11.8
$40,000 to $49,999	13.3	9.0	15.4	14.7	13.1
$50,000 to $59,999	10.1	5.6	9.6	13.4	12.6
$60,000 to $74,999	10.0	3.7	9.6	11.7	15.1
$75,000 and over	13.1	3.3	6.6	13.1	32.1

Source: The 1988 Current Population Survey, Bureau of the Census.

Note: Numbers may not add to total due to rounding.

Future Income

INCOME
45–54

RISE OF THE HIGH ROLLERS

The aging baby boom will boost the number of 45-to-54-year-old householders from 14.4 million in 1990 to over 18 million by 1995, with high-income households increasing the fastest. The number of households with incomes between $50,000 and $75,000 will grow 32 percent over the five year period, and those bringing in at least $75,000 will rise an impressive 34 percent.

(projections of the number of households with householders aged 45 to 54, by household income, 1990 and 1995, numbers in thousands, income is in 1985 dollars)

	1990 number	1990 percent	1995 number	1995 percent	percent change 1990-1995
All households	14,429	100.0%	18,035	100.0%	25.0%
Less than $10,000	1,735	12.0	2,097	11.6	20.9
$10,000 to $19,999	2,310	16.0	2,784	15.4	20.5
$20,000 to $29,999	2,459	17.0	2,995	16.6	21.8
$30,000 to $39,999	2,356	16.3	2,927	16.2	24.3
$40,000 to $49,999	1,831	12.7	2,284	12.7	24.7
$50,000 to $59,999	1,389	9.6	1,816	10.1	30.7
$60,000 to $74,999	1,130	7.8	1,502	8.3	32.9
$75,000 and over	1,219	8.5	1,631	9.0	33.8
Median household income	$33,000		$33,900		

Source: American Demographics, May to August, 1986, based on the national econometric model of Wharton Economic Forecasting Association and on household projections from the Bureau of the Census

Note: Numbers may not add to total due to rounding.

Annual Expenditures

EXPENDITURES
45–54

BIG SPENDERS

Households headed by a 45-to-54-year-old spend more than any other age group—$30,600 on average. They devote a smaller share of their spending dollar to food, housing, health care, and entertainment than the average household but more to transportation, apparel, contributions, and insurance and pensions.

(average annual expenditure and percent distribution of expenditures for all households and for householders aged 45 to 54, number of households in thousands)

	all households		householder aged 45 to 54	
	average annual expenditure	percent of all expenditures	average annual expenditure	percent of all expenditures
Number of households	93,741		12,678	
Total expenditure	$22,710	100.0%	$30,577	100.0%
Food	3,363	14.8	4,439	14.5
Food at home	2,313	10.2	2,900	9.5
Food away from home	1,049	4.6	1,538	5.0
Alcoholic beverages	273	1.2	325	1.1
Housing	6,888	30.3	8,448	27.6
Shelter	3,986	17.6	4,966	16.2
Owned dwellings	2,305	10.1	3,252	10.6
Mortgage interest and charges	1,428	6.3	2,044	6.7
Property taxes	417	1.8	612	2.0
Maintenance, repairs, insurance, and other expenses	460	2.0	597	2.0
Rented dwellings	1,269	5.6	910	3.0
Other lodging	412	1.8	804	2.6
Fuels, utilities, and public services	1,646	7.2	2,050	6.7
Natural gas	248	1.1	304	1.0
Electricity	674	3.0	853	2.8
Fuel oil and othe fuels	107	0.5	113	0.4
Telephone	471	2.1	581	1.9
Water and other public services	145	0.6	200	0.7
Household operations	353	1.6	265	0.9
Domestic services	288	1.3	182	0.6
Other household expenses	65	0.3	83	0.3
Household furnishings, equipment	903	4.0	1,167	3.8
Household textiles	83	0.4	107	0.3
Furniture	303	1.3	353	1.2
Floor coverings	51	0.2	60	0.2
Major appliances	155	0.7	205	0.7

(continued next page)

Annual Expenditures

EXPENDITURES 45–54

(continued from previous page)

(average annual expenditure and percent distribution of expenditures for all households and for householders aged 45 to 54, number of households in thousands)

	all households		householder aged 45 to 54	
	average annual expenditure	percent of all expenditures	average annual expenditure	percent of all expenditures
Small appliances, miscellaneous housewares	55	0.2	81	0.3
Miscellaneous household equipment	256	1.1	361	1.2
Apparel	**1,149**	**5.1**	**1,581**	**5.2**
Men and boys	283	1.2	414	1.4
Men, 16 and over	228	1.0	350	1.1
Boys, 2 to 15	55	0.2	64	0.2
Women and girls	462	2.0	670	2.2
Women, 16 and over	396	1.7	602	2.0
Girls, 2 to 15	66	0.3	68	0.2
Children under 2	45	0.2	34	0.1
Footwear	123	0.5	167	0.5
Other apparel products and services	237	1.0	296	1.0
Transportation	**4,815**	**21.2**	**6,838**	**22.4**
Cars and trucks, new (net outlay)	1,414	6.2	2,061	6.7
Cars and trucks, used (net outlay)	897	3.9	1,310	4.3
Other vehicles	29	0.1	35	0.1
Vehicle finance charges	270	1.2	394	1.3
Gasoline and motor oil	916	4.0	1,219	4.0
Maintenance and repairs	458	2.0	633	2.1
Vehicle insurance	420	1.8	600	2.0
Public transportation	248	1.1	373	1.2
Vehicle rental, licesnes, other charges	163	0.7	214	0.7
Health care	**1,062**	**4.7**	**1,172**	**3.8**
Health insurance	371	1.6	395	1.3
Medical services	502	2.2	545	1.8
Medicines and medical supplies	189	0.8	232	0.8
Entertainment	**1,087**	**4.8**	**1,431**	**4.7**
Fees and admissions	308	1.4	432	1.4
Television, radios, sound equipment	373	1.6	508	1.7
Other equipment and services	406	1.8	491	1.6
Personal care	207	0.9	264	0.9
Reading	140	0.6	179	0.6
Education	298	1.3	607	2.0
Tobacco and smoking supplies	230	1.0	314	1.0
Miscellaneous	323	1.4	412	1.3
Contributions and support payments	746	3.3	1,205	3.9
Personal insurance and pensions	**2,129**	**9.4**	**3,363**	**11.0**
Life insurance and other personal insurance	293	1.3	444	1.5
Retirement, pensions, Social Security	1,836	8.1	2,918	9.5

Source: The 1986 Consumer Expenditure Survey, Bureau of Labor Statistics

Expenditures by Income

EXPENDITURES
45–54

BIG SPENDERS

Households with incomes over $40,000 typically spend $3,450 more on housing than the average household in this age group. Their expenses exceed the average by $2,990 for transportation, by $2,690 for insurance and pensions, by $840 for food away from home, and by at least $800 for apparel and entertainment.

(annual average expenditure of household with householders aged 45 to 54, by household income, number of households in thousands)

	all households	under $10,000	$10-14,999	$15-19,999	$20-29,999	$30-39,999	$40,000+
Number of households	11,184	2,004	876	836	1,854	1,780	3,834
Total expenditure	$30,289	$17,274	$17,214	$21,594	$24,081	$30,172	$45,050
Food	4,380	3,176	3,262	3,469	3,640	4,348	5,837
Food at home	2,934	2,314	2,525	2,555	2,622	3,013	3,549
Food away from home	1,446	863	737	914	1,017	1,335	2,288
Alcoholic beverages	331	163	157	208	273	337	509
Housing	8,281	5,382	5,556	6,073	6,621	8,222	11,734
Shelter	4,783	3,056	3,201	3,534	3,787	4,743	6,822
Owned dwellings	3,233	1,704	1,669	1,898	2,381	3,474	4,984
Rented dwellings	824	1,051	1,243	1,325	1,020	680	471
Other lodging	726	301	290	311	386	590	1,366
Fuels, utilities, public services	2,082	1,650	1,626	1,763	1,850	2,102	2,584
Household operations	273	127	156	157	159	220	483
Household furnishings, equipment	1,143	549	573	619	826	1,157	1,846
Apparel and services	1,607	915	936	1,077	1,212	1,608	2,428
Transportation	6,304	3,322	3,034	4,598	5,393	6,587	9,294
Vehicles	2,823	1,321	774	2,014	2,483	2,835	4,414
Gasoline and motor oil	1,324	872	947	1,138	1,232	1,475	1,661
Other vehicle expenses	1,790	939	942	1,271	1,473	1,945	2,626
Public transportation	367	190	373	176	205	333	593
Health care	1,185	898	1,011	1,248	976	1,196	1,459
Entertainment	1,448	825	763	803	949	1,572	2,255
Personal care	262	161	170	185	200	259	383

(continued next page)

Expenditures by Income

(continued from previous page)

(annual average expenditure of household with householders aged 45 to 54, by household income, number of households in thousands)

	all households	under $10,000	$10-14,999	$15-19,999	$20-29,999	$30-39,999	$40,000+
Reading	179	105	101	127	152	184	257
Education	613	233	136	221	234	473	1,254
Tobacco and smoking supplies	307	253	271	366	330	323	313
Miscellaneous	488	201	237	434	555	412	709
Cash contributions	1,317	733	359	1,029	830	896	2,337
Personal insurance and pensions	3,590	908	1,222	1,755	2,717	3,754	6,280
Life and other insurance	454	348	257	368	349	474	615
Retirement, pensions, Social Security	3,136	560	965	1,387	2,368	3,281	5,665

Source: The 1986 Consumer Expenditure Survey, Bureau of Labor Statistics

Note: All households include complete income reporters only. Total expenditure exceeds total income in some income categories due to a number of factors including the underreporting of income, borrowing, and the use of savings.

Weekly Shopping

EXPENDITURES
45–54

SELECTING EXPENSIVE FOODS

The average weekly expenditure of households headed by a 45-to-54-year-old is 31 percent higher than that of an average American household. Their weekly tab for beef, pork, fish seafood, and eggs is at least 40 percent higher than average.

(average weekly expenditure for all households and for householders aged 45 to 54)

	all households	index all households	householders aged 45 to 54	index householders aged 45 to 54
Food, total	$59.60	100	$78.22	131
Food at home, total	37.73	100	50.75	135
Cereals and cereal products	1.78	100	2.32	130
Bakery products	3.51	100	4.54	129
Beef	3.63	100	5.32	147
Pork	2.23	100	3.16	142
Other meats	1.52	100	2.04	134
Poultry	1.64	100	2.30	140
Fish and seafood	1.22	100	1.80	148
Eggs	0.57	100	0.85	149
Fresh milk and cream	2.35	100	2.95	126
Other dairy products	2.47	100	3.24	131
Fresh fruits	1.96	100	2.45	125
Fresh vegetables	1.77	100	2.32	131
Processed fruits	1.38	100	1.74	126
Processed vegetables	1.03	100	1.44	140
Sugar and other sweets	1.42	100	1.93	136
Fats and oils	0.99	100	1.31	132
Miscellaneous foods	4.53	100	6.04	133
Nonalcoholic beverages	3.71	100	4.98	134
Food away from home	21.87	100	27.47	126
Nonfood items				
Alcoholic beverages	4.84	100	5.78	119
Tobacco products and smoking supplies	3.60	100	5.07	141
Pet food	1.09	100	1.30	119
Personal care products and services	5.01	100	6.35	127
Non-prescription drugs and supplies	2.31	100	2.79	121
Housekeeping supplies	6.07	100	7.48	123

Source: The 1986 Consumer Expenditure Survey, Bureau of Labor Statistics

Note: An index of 100 represents the average. An index of 132 means that the average weekly expenditure of the subgroup is 32 percent above the average for all households. An index of 68 indicates spending that is 32 percent below average. Numbers may not add to total due to rounding.

Future Expenditures

EXPENDITURES
45–54

MARKETERS, TAKE AIM

Households headed by 45-to-54-year-olds will spend a whopping 219 billion dollars more in 2000 than in 1990. Driving this spending boom is a 50 percent growth in the number of households in this age group during the 1990s.

(projected aggregate expenditures in 1990 and 2000 for all households and for households by age of householder, in billions of dollars)

	\multicolumn{8}{c}{1990 aggregate annual expenditures in billions}
	all households	under 25	25-34	35-44	45-54	55-64	65-74	75+
Number of households (in thousands)	94,227	4,663	21,183	21,245	14,429	12,311	11,672	8,724
Total expenditures (in billions of dollars)	$2,203.1	$64.2	$476.6	$628.6	$441.2	$292.8	$197.2	$102.5
Food	330.8	9.4	70.3	93.7	64.1	43.9	32.3	17.2
Food at home	225.1	5.9	44.8	64.9	41.8	30.9	23.0	13.7
Food away from home	101.5	3.6	21.2	28.8	22.2	13.0	9.3	3.5
Alcoholic beverages	25.4	1.6	7.5	6.4	4.7	3.0	1.8	0.6
Housing	667.6	19.2	158.3	193.5	121.9	80.8	58.3	35.6
Shelter	385.6	12.4	97.2	115.7	71.7	42.4	28.8	17.5
Owned dwellings	229.7	1.8	50.3	75.8	46.9	28.2	17.9	8.7
Rented dwellings	115.2	9.5	41.6	27.6	13.1	8.4	7.2	7.6
Other lodging	40.8	1.0	5.2	12.2	11.6	5.8	3.7	1.2
Fuels, utilities, and public services	160.0	3.7	32.0	41.2	29.6	23.2	18.6	11.8
Household operations	34.2	0.7	9.6	10.2	3.8	3.7	2.9	3.3
Household furnishings, equipment	87.8	2.4	19.5	26.5	16.8	11.6	8.0	3.0
Apparel and services	111.0	4.1	24.6	33.7	22.8	13.8	8.3	3.6
Transportation	464.9	15.6	107.0	130.7	98.7	61.1	37.7	14.2
Health care	103.7	1.6	14.5	21.4	16.9	16.0	17.9	15.4
Entertainment	106.0	3.1	23.3	35.2	20.6	13.0	8.0	2.6
Personal care	20.1	0.6	3.7	5.2	3.8	3.1	2.3	1.3
Reading	13.6	0.3	2.6	3.8	2.6	1.9	1.6	0.8
Education	27.6	2.7	3.9	8.3	8.8	2.9	0.8	0.1
Tobacco and smoking supplies	22.0	0.8	4.9	5.8	4.5	3.3	2.0	0.7
Miscellaneous	31.5	0.6	6.5	8.1	5.9	4.5	3.6	2.3
Contributions and support payments	74.2	0.7	7.3	17.7	17.4	12.9	12.5	5.7
Personal insurance and pensions	208.9	3.9	46.4	65.2	48.5	32.6	10.0	2.3

(continued next page)

Almanac of Consumer Markets

Future Expenditures

EXPENDITURES
45–54

(continued from previous page)

(projected aggregate expenditures in 2000 for all households and for households by age of householder, in billions of dollars)

	\multicolumn{8}{c}{2000 aggregate annual expenditures in billions}
	all households	under 25	25-34	35-44	45-54	55-64	65-74	75+
Number of households (in thousands)	105,933	4,442	18,004	25,339	21,603	13,903	11,516	11,126
Total expenditures (in billions of dollars)	$2,532.4	$61.1	$405.1	$749.7	$660.6	$330.6	$194.6	$130.7
Food	379.7	9.0	59.7	111.7	95.9	49.5	31.9	22.0
Food at home	258.9	5.6	38.1	77.4	62.6	34.9	22.7	17.5
Food away from home	117.2	3.4	18.0	34.3	33.2	14.7	9.1	4.5
Alcoholic beverages	28.3	1.5	6.4	7.6	7.0	3.4	1.7	0.7
Housing	760.3	18.3	134.5	230.8	182.5	91.3	57.5	45.3
Shelter	438.2	11.8	82.6	137.9	107.3	47.9	28.4	22.3
Owned dwellings	265.8	1.7	42.8	90.4	70.3	31.9	17.6	11.1
Rented dwellings	123.4	9.1	35.4	32.9	19.7	9.5	7.2	9.7
Other lodging	49.1	0.9	4.4	14.6	17.4	6.5	3.7	1.5
Fuels, utilities, and public services	183.6	3.5	27.2	49.1	44.3	26.2	18.3	15.0
Household operations	38.0	0.7	8.2	12.2	5.7	4.1	2.9	4.2
Household furnishings, equipment	100.5	2.3	16.6	31.6	25.2	13.1	7.9	3.8
Apparel and services	127.6	3.9	20.9	40.2	34.2	15.6	8.2	4.6
Transportation	533.7	14.8	90.9	155.9	147.7	69.0	37.2	18.1
Health care	120.0	1.5	12.4	25.5	25.3	18.1	17.7	19.6
Entertainment	121.7	3.0	19.8	42.0	30.9	14.7	7.9	3.3
Personal care	23.1	0.5	3.2	6.2	5.7	3.5	2.3	1.7
Reading	15.7	0.3	2.2	4.5	3.9	2.2	1.6	1.0
Education	33.2	2.6	3.3	10.0	13.1	3.3	0.8	0.2
Tobacco and smoking supplies	25.2	0.8	4.2	6.9	6.8	3.7	2.0	0.9
Miscellaneous	36.2	0.6	5.5	9.7	8.9	5.0	3.5	2.9
Contributions and support payments	88.2	0.6	6.2	21.1	26.0	14.5	12.3	7.3
Personal insurance and pensions	243.2	3.7	39.4	77.7	72.7	36.8	9.9	2.9

Source: *The 1986 Consumer Expenditure Survey*, Bureau of Labor Statistics and *Projections of the Number of Households and Families:1986 to 2000*, Bureau of the Census, Series P-25, No. 986

Note: Aggregate expenditures are the sum of the total expenditures of all households in the nation or of all households in an age group. Projections are based on the average annual expenditures in 1986 and have not been adjusted for inflation. Projections show how total annual expenditures would change as the number of households in the age group changes during the 1990s. All other factors such as price and expenditure pattern are held constant and are not accounted for in these projections.

Composition of Wealth

WEALTH
45–54

THE INVESTMENT SET

Households headed by 45-to-54-year-olds account for 21 percent of all household wealth. Compared with households in general, larger proportions of households in this age group own every asset type except checking and saving accounts and they are more likely to have acquired debts.

(percentage of households with assets and debts and the mean value of owners' holdings in 1986 dollars, for all households and householders aged 45 to 54, numbers in thousands)

	percent owning – all households	percent owning – householder aged 45 to 54	mean holdings of owners – all households	mean holdings of owners – householder aged 45 to 54
Number of households	83,042	14,293	83,042	14,293
Assets				
Home	65.7%	79.0%	$80,650	$88,990
Other real estate	22.4	24.8	118,892	122,254
Public stock	19.3	21.2	81,367	54,138
Bonds	20.2	23.4	28,116	20,869
Checking and saving accounts	89.2	88.5	7,445	5,970
IRA's and Keoghs	27.3	39.6	18,752	17,718
CD's and money market	27.9	25.5	31,575	29,577
Business assets (net)	12.4	14.0	210,310	254,381
Automobiles	85.9	89.1	7,964	10,011
Employer accounts	14.8	22.3	26,704	36,483
Other*	45.7	51.1	22,282	24,486
Debts				
Mortgage, principle residence	38.40%	52.60%	$34,564	$30,246
Other debts	64.6	83.1	15,881	14,453

*Cash value of life insurance, trusts, and notes owned by individuals.

Source: The 1986 Survey of Consumer Finances, Federal Reserve Board

Note: Wealth here accounts for all major household assets and liabilities except for non-auto consumer durables, collectibles such as artwork, and the present value of expected future benefits from pensions or social security.

Household Savings

WEALTH
45–54

TOP SAVERS

In the three year period, 1983 to 1986, households headed by someone aged 45 to 54 had an increase in their net worth of $46,606. This savings is 16 percent of the household income they received from 1983 to 1985 and represents about 22 percent of all household savings accumulated during those years.

(average household savings 1983 to 1986 in current dollars, share of total savings and percentage of 1983 to 1985 total household income that is savings for households by age of householder, marital status, race and Hispanic origin, homeownership status, and household income)

	average savings for 3 year period	share of total savings	median 3-year savings as a percentage of 1983-1985 median income
All households	$24,402	100.0%	9.7%
Age of householder			
under age 35	17,912	18.7	7.1
35 to 44	23,301	16.8	12.6
45 to 54	46,606	22.4	16.1
55 to 64	39,392	20.9	9.8
65 and older	33,867	21.3	5.9
Marital status			
Married	40,392	91.8	13.8
Singe male	9,242	3.2	3.1
Single female	6,405	5.0	2.8
Race			
White	34,913	97.8	11.4
Black/Hispanic	3,679	2.2	2.4
Homeownership status			
Homeowner	39,426	88.2	16.1
Renter	10,107	11.8	4.0
Household income			
Less than $10,000	871	0.5	0.0
$10,000 to $20,000	6,633	5.9	4.8
$20,000 to $50,000	18,835	27.2	15.8
$50,000 to $100,000	70,545	27.3	22.8
$100,000 and over	455,294	39.2	44.2

Source: The 1986 Survey of Consumer Finances, Federal Reserve Board

Note: Household savings is the difference in household net worth between 1986 and 1983, expressed in 1986 dollars. Net worth (wealth) is defined as gross assets minus gross debts. Net worth here accounts for all major household assets and liabilities except for non-auto consumer durables, collectibles such as artwork, and the present value of expected future benefits from pensions or social security.

Owners and Renters

WEALTH
45–54

AMERICAN DREAM

More than three-quarters (76 percent) of householders in this age group own rather than rent their dwellings. This is not the age group with the highest proportion of owners since homeownership is higher among householders aged 55 to 64 (80 percent) and aged 65 to 74 (78 percent). Seventy-nine percent of white householders aged 45 to 54 are homeowners compared with 54 percent of black and 50 percent of Hispanic householders.

(owner- and renter-occupied households by race of householder and household type, for householders aged 45 to 54, numbers in thousands, ownership status as of March 1988)

	total	white	black	Hispanic origin
All households	13,630	11,577	1,575	825
Owner households	10,363	9,184	857	412
Family households				
Married-couple	7,858	7,135	492	319
Male householder	309	247	43	20
Female householder	950	687	210	44
Nonfamily households				
Male householder	581	516	59	20
Female householder	665	598	54	9
Renter households	3,267	2,392	718	414
Family households				
Married-couple	1,210	961	157	196
Male householder	131	89	32	20
Female householder	680	396	254	114
Nonfamily households				
Male householder	679	516	146	55
Female householder	567	431	128	29

Source: Household and Family Characteristics: March 1988, *Bureau of the Census, Current Population Reports, Series P-20, No. 424*

Note: Hispanics are of any race. Numbers may not add to total due to rounding.

Health Status

STAYING WELL

Sixty-three percent of men and 57 percent of women aged 45 to 54 rate their health as excellent or very good. But 10 percent consider themselves in fair health and 4 percent say their health is poor. The proportion of 45-to-54-year-olds with poor health in the lowest income group is 16 times greater than that proportion in the highest income group.

(self-assessed health status of persons aged 45 to 54, by sex, race and household income, number of persons in thousands)

	all persons	all health statuses	excellent	very good	good	fair	poor
Both sexes, all races	22,665	100.0%	32.1%	27.8%	26.4%	9.8%	4.0%
Male	10,965	100.0	35.8	27.2	24.3	8.8	3.9
Female	11,700	100.0	28.6	28.3	28.3	10.7	4.1
White	19,502	100.0	33.4	28.8	25.6	8.7	3.5
Black	2,413	100.0	19.4	20.7	32.3	19.1	8.5
Asian and other	750	100.0	37.4	24.1	27.1	8.5	2.9
Household income							
Less than $10,000	1,598	100.0%	13.2%	17.0%	23.2%	28.8%	17.7%
$10,000 to $19,999	3,003	100.0	21.0	21.5	31.9	17.3	8.2
$20,000 to $34,999	5,446	100.0	32.1	26.1	29.9	10.3	1.6
$35,000 and over	9,047	100.0	40.7	33.3	21.2	3.6	1.1

Source: The 1986 National Health Interview Survey, National Center for Health Statistics

Note: All persons includes those of unknown health status, all health statuses includes only those with known health status. Household income includes only those persons with known household income. Numbers may not add to total due to rounding.

Height

HEALTH
45–54

ABOUT AVERAGE

More than half of all women aged 35 and older are under 5'4" tall, as are 57 percent of women aged 45 to 54 and three-quarters of those aged 65 to 74. The average height of men aged 45 to 54 is 5'9", the same as the average American man.

(cumulative percentage of height of males and females aged 45 to 54 and their average height, by race)

height, males	cumulative percentage	height, females	cumulative percentage
Less than 60 inches	–	Less than 55 inches	0.1%
Less than 61 inches	0.2%	Less than 56 inches	0.3
Less than 62 inches	0.7	Less than 57 inches	0.3
Less than 63 inches	1.5	Less than 58 inches	1.2
Less than 64 inches	2.6	Less than 59 inches	4.2
Less than 65 inches	5.7	Less than 60 inches	8.9
Less than 66 inches	11.4	Less than 61 inches	16.2
Less than 67 inches	21.2	Less than 62 inches	27.7
Less than 68 inches	33.6	Less than 63 inches	39.8
Less than 69 inches	50.4	Less than 64 inches	57.2
Less than 70 inches	63.4	Less than 65 inches	70.5
Less than 71 inches	76.9	Less than 66 inches	84.6
Less than 72 inches	85.8	Less than 67 inches	91.2
Less than 73 inches	93.4	Less than 68 inches	96.3
Less than 74 inches	98.0	Less than 69 inches	98.2
Less than 75 inches	99.4	Less than 70 inches	99.6
Less than 76 inches	99.7	Less than 71 inches	99.8
All height categories	100.0%	All height categories	100.0%
Average height, all races	**69.0 inches**	**Average height, all races**	**63.5 inches**
White	69.1	White	63.6
Black	68.6	Black	63.7

Source: Anthropometric Reference Data and Prevalence of Overweight: United States, 1976-80, *National Center for Health Statistics, National Health Survey Series 11, No. 238.*

Note: Height is without shoes.

Weight

HEALTH
45–54

30 PERCENT OVERWEIGHT

Over 30 percent of all men and women aged 45 to 54 weigh more than the weight to height (overweight) standard of the National Center for Health Statistics. The average 45-to-54-year-old woman weighs 150 pounds and the average man in this age group weighs 178 pounds.

(cumulative percentage of weight of males and females aged 45 to 54, and their average weight and percent overweight, by race)

weight, males	cumulative percentage	weight, females	cumulative percentage
Less than 100 pounds	–	Less than 90 pounds	0.7%
Less than 110 pounds	–	Less than 100 pounds	2.4
Less than 120 pounds	1.3%	Less than 110 pounds	6.9
Less than 130 pounds	3.2	Less than 120 pounds	17.0
Less than 140 pounds	7.6	Less than 130 pounds	29.0
Less than 150 pounds	17.1	Less than 140 pounds	44.5
Less than 160 pounds	27.2	Less than 150 pounds	56.7
Less than 170 pounds	43.4	Less than 160 pounds	69.3
Less than 180 pounds	57.6	Less than 170 pounds	77.3
Less than 190 pounds	68.7	Less than 180 pounds	84.3
Less than 200 pounds	77.4	Less than 190 pounds	89.1
Less than 210 pounds	85.7	Less than 200 pounds	92.5
Less than 220 pounds	90.7	Less than 220 pounds	96.1
Less than 230 pounds	94.6	Less than 240 pounds	97.8
Less than 240 pounds	96.9	Less than 260 pounds	99.1
Less than 250 pounds	98.4	Less than 280 pounds	99.3
All weight categories	100.0%	All weight categories	100.0%
Average weight, all races	**178.4 pounds**	**Average weight, all races**	**149.9 pounds**
White	178.6	White	148.4
Black	181.7	Black	171.2
Percent overweight, all races	**31.0%**	**Percent overweight, all races**	**32.5%**
White	30.5	White	29.9
Black	41.4	Black	61.2
Percent severely overweight, all races	**10.7%**	**Percent severely overweight, all races**	**12.9%**
White	10.7	White	12.2
Black	12.0	Black	21.9

Source: Anthropometric Reference Data and Prevalence of Overweight: United States, 1976-80, *National Center for Health Statistics, National Health Survey Series 11, No. 238.*

Notes: Weight includes clothing weight, estimated as ranging from 0.20 to 0.62 pounds. Overweight is defined in terms of a body mass index which is determined by dividing weight in kilograms by height in meters squared. Overweight people have a body mass index equal to or greater than that at the 85th percentile of men and women aged 20 to 29. Severe overweight means a body mass index equal to or greater than at the 95th percentile of men and women aged 20 to 29.

Acute Conditions

HEALTH
45–54

THE COMMON FLU

Like other adults, men and women aged 45 to 54 are more likely to suffer from flus than from any other acute condition—at least one-third of all reported acute ailments in this age group are flus. In terms of reported frequency, colds and other respiratory infections follow in second and third place.

(number of acute conditions reported in a year for all persons and those aged 45 to 54, by sex, numbers in thousands)

	males all ages	males aged 45 to 54	females all ages	females aged 45 to 54
All acute conditions	191,369	11,721	257,177	17,345
Infective and parasitic diseases	23,122	1,241	31,244	1,212
Common childhood diseases	2,565	0	1,876	0
Intestinal virus, unspecified	4,244	0	5,288	303
Viral infections, unspecified	9,621	926	14,273	802
Other	6,692	316	9,807	107
Respiratory conditions	99,216	6,613	129,626	8,926
Common cold	30,445	1,702	32,983	1,534
Other acute upper respiratory infections	8,472	514	13,320	1,081
Influenza	55,256	4,194	75,295	5,739
Acute bronchitis	1,960	0	4,315	377
Pneumonia	1,365	0	1,277	195
Other respiratory conditions	1,718	203	2,435	0
Digestive system conditions	5,860	438	9,112	1,022
Dental conditions	1,059	0	1,955	145
Indigestion, nausea and vomiting	3,299	156	4,670	563
Other digestive conditions	1,502	283	2,487	314
Injuries	34,588	1,852	29,706	3,138
Fractures and dislocations	4,367	287	3,978	712
Sprains and strains	6,127	210	6,208	829
Open wounds and lacerations	11,153	489	5,094	525
Contusions and superficial injuries	7,986	207	7,191	540
Other current injuries	4,955	660	7,235	532

(continued next page)

Acute Conditions

HEALTH
45–54

(continued from previous page)

(number of acute conditions reported in a year for all persons and those aged 45 to 54, by sex, numbers in thousands)

	males		females	
	all ages	aged 45 to 54	all ages	aged 45 to 54
Selected other acute conditions	**21,183**	**718**	**40,385**	**1,712**
Eye conditions	1,072	100	2,080	100
Acute ear infections	8,689	0	10,116	187
Other ear conditions	1,884	209	2,193	0
Acute urinary conditions	989	207	4,399	625
Disorders of menstruation	–	–	2,251	87
Other disorders of female genital tract	–	–	2,174	0
Delivery and other conditions of pregnancy	–	–	4,466	0
Skin conditions	2,065	0	3,597	223
Acute musculoskeletal conditions	3,038	201	3,972	313
Headache, excluding migraine	1,253	0	2,461	178
Fever, unspecified	2,192	0	2,675	0
All other acute conditions	**7,400**	**857**	**17,104**	**1,336**

Source: The 1986 National Health Interview Survey, National Center for Health Statistics

Note: An acute condition is defined by The National Health Interview Survey as an illness or injury that usually lasts less than three months and was first noticed less than three months before the respondent's interview. The acute condition must also have caused the person to restrict activities for at least a half a day or to have contacted a physician. The data are based only on information given by the respondent and are subject to recall and selective reporting error. Numbers may not add to total due to rounding.

Chronic Conditions

HEALTH
45–54

ARTHRITIS AND HIGH BLOOD PRESSURE

The number one chronic condition plaguing members of younger age groups is a respiratory problem—either bronchitis or sinusitis. Among 45-to-54-year-olds, however, men are most likely to suffer from high blood pressure and the most frequently reported chronic concern of women is arthritis.

(number of selected chronic conditions reported in a year for all persons and those aged 45 to 54, by sex, numbers in thousands)

	males all ages	males aged 45 to 54	females all ages	females aged 45 to 54
Selected skin and musculoskeletal conditions				
Arthritis	10,751	1,531	20,160	3,416
Gout, including gouty arthritis	1,515	275	713	92
Intervertebral disc disorders	2,522	398	1,645	192
Bone spur or tendonitis, unspecified	781	97	898	68
Disorders of bone or cartilage	449	25	943	79
Trouble with bunions	594	134	2,321	243
Bursitis, unclassified	1,641	262	2,464	291
Sebaceous skin cyst	640	111	881	144
Trouble with acne	2,193	77	2,116	60
Psoriasis	1,069	193	1,262	171
Dermatitis	3,851	275	5,696	538
Trouble with dry, itching skin, unclassified	1,994	204	2,606	170
Trouble with ingrown nails	2,352	239	3,030	455
Trouble with corns and calluses	1,669	99	3,164	602
Impairments				
Visual impairment	4,994	502	3,358	448
Color blindness	2,694	300	272	80
Cataracts	1,534	113	3,497	72
Glaucoma	735	0	967	48
Hearing impairment	11,727	1,634	9,004	767
Tinnitus	3,388	591	2,927	328
Speech impairment	1,924	149	871	0
Absence of extremity(s)	374	56	24	0
Paralysis, entire body, one side of body, or both legs	200	0	152	0
Partial paralysis of body or legs	236	18	99	0
Deformity of back	6,812	1,075	9,676	1,051
Deformity of upper extremities	1,622	276	1,475	252
Deformity of lower extremities	6,454	996	5,739	852
Selected digestive conditions				
Ulcer	2,116	233	2,378	285
Hernia of abdominal cavity	2,300	378	2,283	213
Gastritis or duodenitis	1,080	204	1,813	200

(continued next page)

Chronic Conditions

HEALTH 45–54

(continued from previous page)

(number of selected chronic conditions reported in a year for all persons and those aged 45 to 54, by sex, numbers in thousands)

	males all ages	males aged 45 to 54	females all ages	females aged 45 to 54
Frequent indigestion	2,504	302	2,811	244
Enteritis or colitis	574	23	1,820	79
Spastic colon	264	29	1,377	262
Diverticula of intestines	404	0	1,508	137
Frequent constipation	1,002	116	3,537	520
Selected conditions of the genitourinary, nervous, endocrine, metabolic, and blood system				
Goiter or other disorders of the thyroid	420	102	2,789	481
Diabetes	2,949	526	3,635	522
Anemias	570	87	2,617	308
Epilepsy	656	57	863	39
Migraine headache	2,068	347	6,448	793
Neuralgia or neuritis, unspecified	215	21	364	40
Kidney trouble	1,305	123	2,662	146
Bladder disorders	516	24	3,253	391
Diseases of prostate	1,281	125	–	–
Inflammatory female genital diseases	–	–	427	14
Noninflammatory female genital diseases	–	–	1,095	242
Menstrual disorders	–	–	2,097	212
Selected circulatory conditions				
Ischemic heart disease	4,091	742	2,809	332
Tachycardia or rapid heart	700	185	1,226	163
Heart murmurs	1,310	68	2,583	241
Other heart rhythm disorders	499	63	800	108
Other heart diseases	1,482	234	2,265	207
High blood pressure (hypertension)	12,512	2,184	16,457	2,520
Cerebrovascular disease	1,156	111	1,646	69
Hardening of the arteries	1,428	184	1,225	83
Varicose veins	1,042	181	5,814	1,085
Hemorrhoids	4,568	775	5,341	662
Selected respiratory conditions				
Chronic bronchitis	4,707	295	6,671	541
Asthma	4,670	337	5,019	363
Hay fever or allergic rhinitis without asthma	10,136	1,294	11,566	1,343
Chronic sinusitis	14,636	1,932	19,749	2,393
Deviated nasal septum	825	90	465	47
Chronic disease of tonsils or adenoids	1,071	0	2,068	57
Emphysema	1,201	104	796	70

Source: The 1986 National Health Interview Survey, National Center for Health Statistics

Note: Chronic conditions are defined by the National Health Interview Survey as conditions that either a) were first noticed three months or more before the date of the interview or b) belong to a group of conditions (such as heart disease or diabetes) that are considered chronic regardless of when they began. Totals for all chronic conditions are not shown because the National Health Interview Survey does not measure the total number of chronic conditions for each person. The data are based only on information given by the respondent and are subject to recall and selective reporting error.

Activity Restrictions

HEALTH
45–54

HIGHER INCOMES, FEWER ABSENCES

Workers in the lowest household income category have seven more work-loss days a year than workers in the highest income group. Men aged 45 to 54 have fewer work-loss and bed-rest days a year due to illness and injury than men in general. Women in this age group, however, miss one more work day a year than the typical working woman.

(number of days of activity restriction reported in a year and per person due to acute and chronic conditions, by type of restriction and sex, race, and household income, for all persons and those aged 45 to 54, numbers in thousands)

	number of days per year		number of days per person	
	bed day	work-loss day	bed day	work-loss day
All ages	1,547,980	833,396	6.5	5.4
Male	613,113	401,503	5.4	4.8
Female	934,867	431,892	7.7	6.0
White	1,298,039	716,187	6.5	5.4
Black	220,102	99,332	7.7	5.4
Household income				
Less than $10,000	384,962	90,268	11.5	6.1
$10,000 to $19,999	346,115	162,604	7.7	6.1
$20,000 to $34,999	326,166	254,563	5.2	5.7
$35,000 and over	275,957	232,139	4.3	4.6
All aged 45 to 54	156,470	111,573	6.9	6.4
Male	64,602	53,857	5.9	5.5
Female	91,868	57,716	7.9	7.4
White	121,860	94,646	6.2	6.2
Black	32,175	15,246	13.3	8.9
Household income				
Less than $10,000	36,747	7,692	23.0	11.5
$10,000 to $19,999	34,518	17,498	11.5	8.3
$20,000 to $34,999	30,451	37,381	5.6	8.5
$35,000 and over	31,224	35,912	3.5	4.6

Source: The 1986 National Health Interview Survey, National Center for Health Statistics

Note: Numbers may not add to total due to rounding. A bed day is one during which a person stayed in bed more than half a day because of illness or injury. All hospital days for inpatients are considered bed days even if the patient was not in bed more than half a day. A work-loss day is one on which a currently employed person aged 18 or older missed more than half a day of work. The data are based only on information given by the respondent and are subject to recall and selective reporting error.

Cause of Death

MIDLIFE DISEASES

One-third of all deaths of 45-to-54-year-olds are from cancer and another 29 percent are caused by heart diseases. Together, the ten leading causes of death account for 86 percent of all deaths in this age group. The average remaining lifetime for people aged 45 to 50 is 33 years and 28.6 years for those aged 50 to 55.

(ten leading causes of death among persons aged 45 to 54)

	number of deaths persons aged 45 to 54	number of deaths all ages	percent accounted for by persons aged 45 to 54
All causes	115,161	2,105,361	5.5%
Malignant neoplasms (cancer)	37,800	469,376	8.1
Heart diseases	32,982	765,490	4.3
Accidents and adverse effects	7,005	95,277	7.4
Cerebrovascular diseases	4,648	149,643	3.1
Chronic liver disease and cirrhosis	4,632	26,159	17.7
Suicide	3,736	30,904	12.1
Chronic obstructive pulmonary diseases	2,235	76,559	2.9
Diabetes mellitus	2,158	37,184	5.8
Homicide and legal intervention	1,895	21,731	8.7
Pneumonia and influenza	1,600	69,812	2.3
All other causes	16,470	363,226	4.5

Source: Advance Report of Final Mortality Statistics, 1986, *National Center for Health Statistics, Vol. 37, No. 6*

Chapter 7

CONSUMERS AGED 55 TO 64

This is a growth market for the 1990s and the 21st century. Here are some key factors to watch.

During the 1990s, the number of these mature consumers and the number of households they head will be growing.

- Between 1990 and 2000 the number of people aged 55 to 64 will increase by almost 14 percent.

- Although three-quarters of the 13 million 55-to-64-year-old householders live in families, fewer than 10 percent of them still have children under 18 at home.

- During the 1990s the number of households headed by 55-to-64-year-olds will climb 13 percent. The fastest growing types of households in this age group will be male-headed families (up 19 percent) and male-headed nonfamilies (up 31 percent).

- Only 68 percent of the men in this age group and 43 percent of the women are in the work force.

- Income per household member in this age group is $14,800 and median household income is $27,600.

- Thirty-seven percent of married couples aged 55 to 64 are dual earners and their median household income is $45,200—$9,400 higher than the median for all married couples in this age group.

- An above-average share of this age group's spending dollar goes to health care, contributions, and insurance and pensions.

- Households in this age group will spend 38 billion dollars more in 2000 than in 1990.

- Households headed by 55-to-64-year-olds account for 22 percent of all household wealth.

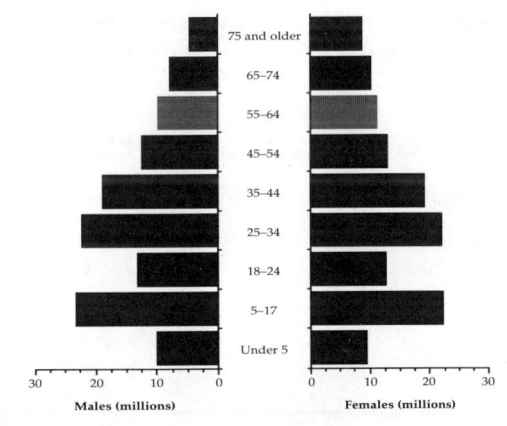

1990

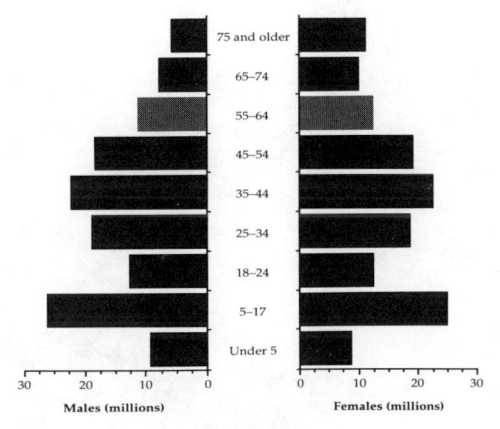

2000

Almanac of Consumer Markets 251

Share of Total Population

POPULATION
55–64

MORE MATURE AMERICANS

Although there will be more 55-to-64-year-olds by 2000, their share of the population will bump up only 1 percentage point. Compared with other age groups, the share of the population held by those aged 55 to 64 has remained fairly stable since 1960.

(total population and the number of persons aged 55 to 64, in thousands, by sex, 1960 to 1980, and projections for 1990 to 2000)

	1960 number	1960 percent of total	1970 number	1970 percent of total	1980 number	1980 percent of total	1990 number	1990 percent of total	1995 number	1995 percent of total	2000 number	2000 percent of total
All ages	180,671	100.0%	205,052	100.0%	227,757	100.0%	252,293	100.0%	264,077	100.0%	274,479	100.0%
All aged 55 to 64	15,625	8.6	18,682	9.1	21,762	9.6	21,145	8.4	21,091	8.0	24,028	8.8
Males	7,559	4.2	8,833	4.3	10,180	4.5	9,906	3.9	9,932	3.8	11,384	4.1
Females	8,067	4.5	9,849	4.8	11,582	5.1	11,239	4.5	11,159	4.2	12,643	4.6

Source: Annual Projections of the Population by Age, Sex, and Race, for the United States: 1983 to 2080, *Bureau of the Census, Current Population Reports, Series 17* and the Bureau of the Census

Note: Total population includes Armed Forces overseas; 1960 to 1980 are based on censuses; projections are based on the Census Bureau's Series 17 projections that incorporate illegal immigration and higher levels of emigration than other Census Bureau projections. Series 17 is consistent with current estimates of illegal aliens living in the United States. Numbers may not add to total due to rounding.

Sex, Race, and Ethnicity

POPULATION
55–64

MORE BLACKS, HISPANICS, ASIANS

As with every other age group, the turn of the century will see the proportion of whites giving way to proportionately more blacks, Hispanics, and Asians. During the 1990s whites will slide from 82 to 80 percent of 55-to-64-year-olds, while blacks will increase from 9 to 10 percent, Hispanics from 6 to 7 percent, and Asians from 3 to 4 percent.

(projections of the total population and persons aged 55 to 64, in thousands, by sex, race, and Hispanic origin, 1990 to 2000)

	1990	1995	2000	percent change 1990–2000
All ages	252,293	264,077	274,479	8.8%
White	191,594	195,347	197,634	3.2
Black	30,915	33,237	35,440	14.6
Hispanic	21,854	25,991	30,295	38.6
Asians and other races	7,930	9,502	11,110	40.1
All aged 55 to 64	21,145	21,091	24,028	13.6
White	17,424	16,968	19,115	9.7
Black	1,962	2,036	2,318	18.1
Hispanic	1,207	1,388	1,699	40.8
Asians and other races	552	700	896	62.3
All males aged 55 to 64	9,906	9,932	11,384	14.9
White	8,271	8,108	9,190	11.1
Black	830	860	983	18.4
Hispanic	566	649	799	41.2
Asians and other races	240	314	412	71.6
All females aged 55 to 64	11,239	11,159	12,643	12.5
White	9,154	8,859	9,923	8.4
Black	1,133	1,178	1,335	17.8
Hispanic	642	740	900	40.2
Asians and other races	310	382	485	56.5

Source: Projections of the Population of the United States by Age, Sex, and Race: 1983 to 2080, *Bureau of the Census, Current Population Reports, Series P-25, No. 952, Series 17*

Note: Series 17 projections incorporate illegal immigration and higher levels of emigration than other Census Bureau projections and are consistent with current estimates of illegal aliens living in the United States. Total population includes Armed Forces living overseas. In this table Hispanics have been separated out of the racial groups; categories do not overlap. Numbers may not add to total due to rounding.

State Populations

POPULATION
55–64

NATIONAL GAINS

Top gainers among the 45 states with more 55-to-64-year-olds by 2000 are Alaska, Arizona, Georgia, Nevada, New Hampshire, and Washington.

(resident population and the number of persons aged 55 to 64, in thousands, in Census Bureau divisions and states in 1980 and projections for 1990 to 2010)

Note: Inconsistencies between the data in this table and the preceding two tables are due to different assumptions about immigration and emigration on which the projections are based and the inclusion of Armed Forces overseas in the total population. This table is based on the resident population only.

	census 1980	1990	projections 2000	2010	percent change 1990–2000	percent change 2000–2010
All ages	226,546	249,891	267,747	282,055	7.1%	5.3%
All aged 55 to 64	21,703	21,363	24,158	35,430	13.1	46.7
New England	**1,265**	**1,161**	**1,245**	**1,797**	**7.2**	**44.3**
Connecticut	336	307	333	460	8.5	38.1
Maine	108	105	114	170	8.6	49.1
Massachusetts	588	524	541	768	3.2	42.0
New Hampshire	85	91	116	187	27.5	61.2
Rhode Island	105	91	94	138	3.3	46.8
Vermont	45	43	50	74	16.3	48.0
Middle Atlantic	**3,963**	**3,605**	**3,652**	**4,863**	**1.3**	**33.2**
New Jersey	798	766	823	1,133	7.4	37.7
New York	1,820	1,685	1,720	2,226	2.1	29.4
Pennsylvania	1,345	1,154	1,109	1,504	-3.9	35.6
East North Central	**3,987**	**3,607**	**3,717**	**5,072**	**3.0**	**36.5**
Illinois	1,103	994	1,026	1,373	3.2	33.8
Indiana	512	471	495	669	5.1	35.2
Michigan	864	776	803	1,116	3.5	39.0
Ohio	1,071	963	964	1,307	0.1	35.6
Wisconsin	436	403	428	607	6.2	41.8

(continued on next page)

State Populations

POPULATION
55–64

(continued from previous page)

(resident population and the number of persons aged 55 to 64, in thousands, in Census Bureau divisions and states in 1980 and projections for 1990 to 2010)

	census 1980	projections 1990	projections 2000	projections 2010	percent change 1990–2000	percent change 2000–2010
All ages	226,546	249,891	267,747	282,055	7.1%	5.3%
All aged 55 to 64	21,703	21,363	24,158	35,430	13.1	46.7
West North Central	**1,609**	**1,503**	**1,600**	**2,267**	**6.5**	**41.7**
Iowa	279	238	235	314	-1.3	33.6
Kansas	226	213	223	320	4.7	43.5
Minnesota	360	345	392	575	13.6	46.7
Missouri	480	462	502	706	8.7	40.6
Nebraska	143	135	136	188	0.7	38.2
North Dakota	57	53	52	77	-1.9	48.1
South Dakota	65	59	59	87	0.0	47.5
South Atlantic	**3,625**	**3,941**	**4,769**	**7,208**	**21.0**	**51.1**
Delaware	59	61	65	94	6.6	44.6
District of Columbia	63	54	58	80	7.4	37.9
Florida	1,120	1,349	1,662	2,536	23.2	52.6
Georgia	463	517	671	1,068	29.8	59.2
Maryland	403	404	479	701	18.6	46.3
North Carolina	551	593	702	1,049	18.4	49.4
South Carolina	279	288	351	534	21.9	52.1
Virginia	489	509	617	919	21.2	48.9
West Virginia	198	166	165	226	-0.6	37.0
East South Central	**1,337**	**1,324**	**1,510**	**2,174**	**14.0**	**44.0**
Alabama	359	359	404	582	12.5	44.1
Kentucky	332	316	348	487	10.1	39.9
Mississippi	217	215	251	367	16.7	46.2
Tennessee	430	434	507	737	16.8	45.4
West South Central	**2,030**	**2,179**	**2,602**	**3,996**	**19.4**	**53.6**
Arkansas	224	215	252	357	17.2	41.7
Louisiana	351	349	385	552	10.3	43.4
Oklahoma	281	278	315	455	13.3	44.4
Texas	1,175	1,337	1,651	2,631	23.5	59.4

(continued on next page)

State Populations

POPULATION 55–64

(continued from previous page)

(resident population and the number of persons aged 55 to 64, in thousands, in Census Bureau divisions and states in 1980 and projections for 1990 to 2010)

	census 1980	1990	projections 2000	2010	percent change 1990–2000	percent change 2000–2010
All ages	226,546	249,891	267,747	282,055	7.1%	5.3%
All aged 55 to 64	21,703	21,363	24,158	35,430	13.1	46.7
Mountain	**954**	**1,047**	**1,344**	**2,179**	**28.4**	**62.1**
Arizona	257	316	419	686	32.6	63.7
Colorado	229	250	316	517	26.4	63.6
Idaho	79	71	90	138	26.8	53.3
Montana	72	65	73	108	12.3	47.9
Nevada	78	91	125	211	37.4	68.8
New Mexico	107	125	157	260	25.6	65.6
Utah	99	101	125	201	23.8	60.8
Wyoming	35	30	37	59	23.3	59.5
Pacific	**2,931**	**2,995**	**3,719**	**5,875**	**24.2**	**58.0**
Alaska	21	32	41	69	28.1	68.3
California	2,194	2,309	2,839	4,461	23.0	57.1
Hawaii	85	96	115	179	19.8	55.7
Oregon	248	208	265	429	27.4	61.9
Washington	283	350	458	739	30.9	61.4

Source: Projections of the Population of States by Age, Sex and Race: 1988 to 2010, *Bureau of the Census, Current Population Reports, Series P-25, No. 1017*

Note: Numbers may not add to total due to rounding.

State-by-State Changes

POPULATION
55–64

BUCKING A TREND

Only Iowa, North Dakota, Pennsylvania, and West Virginia will have fewer 55-to-64-year-olds in 2000 than in 1990.

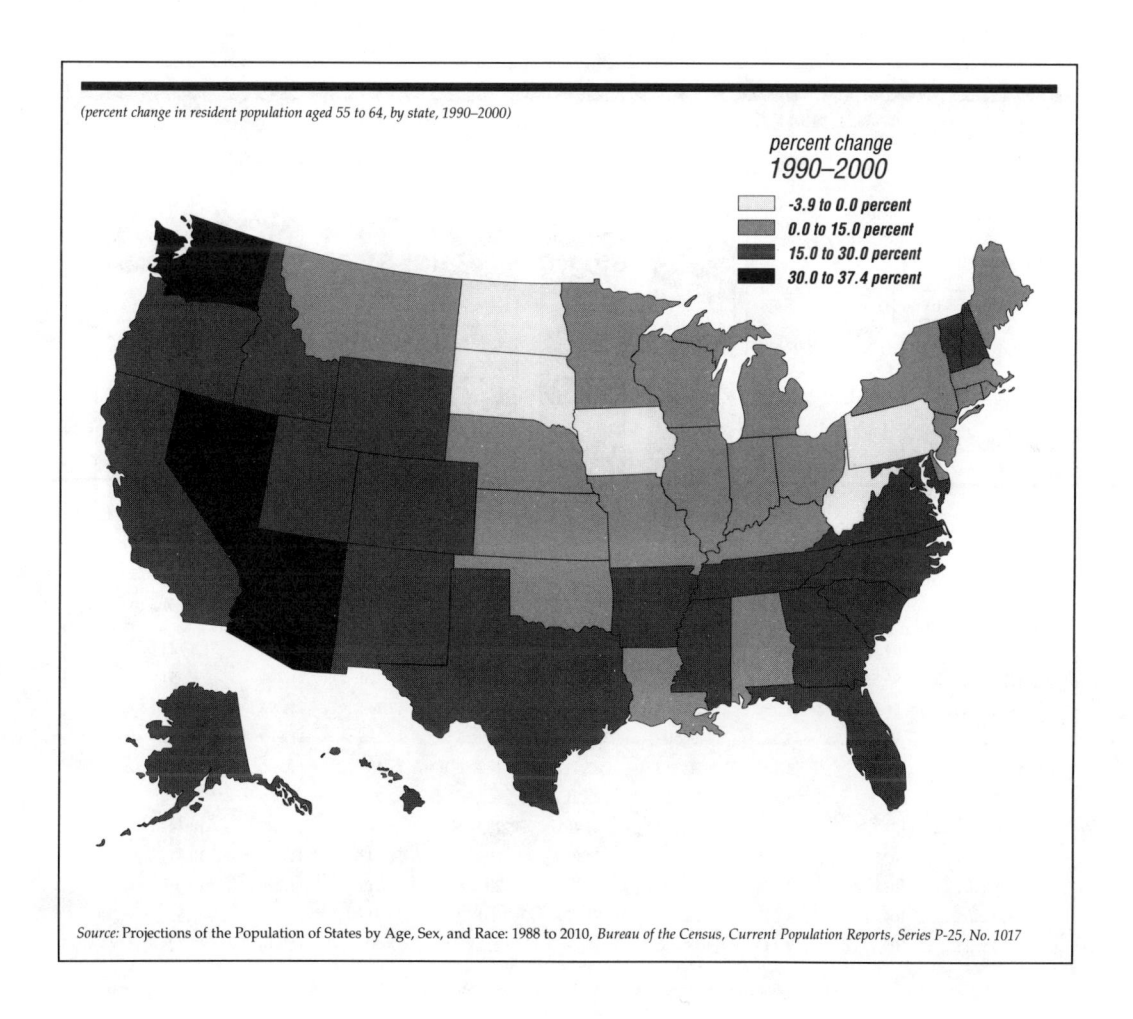

(percent change in resident population aged 55 to 64, by state, 1990–2000)

percent change
1990–2000
- -3.9 to 0.0 percent
- 0.0 to 15.0 percent
- 15.0 to 30.0 percent
- 30.0 to 37.4 percent

Source: Projections of the Population of States by Age, Sex, and Race: 1988 to 2010, *Bureau of the Census, Current Population Reports,* Series P-25, No. 1017

Number of Households

HOUSEHOLDS
55–64

GROWTH AHEAD

The number of 55-to-64-year-old householders will grow 13 percent during the 1990s, with family- and nonfamily-growth more equal than in other age groups.

(number of households, in thousands, by age of householder, 1990–2000)

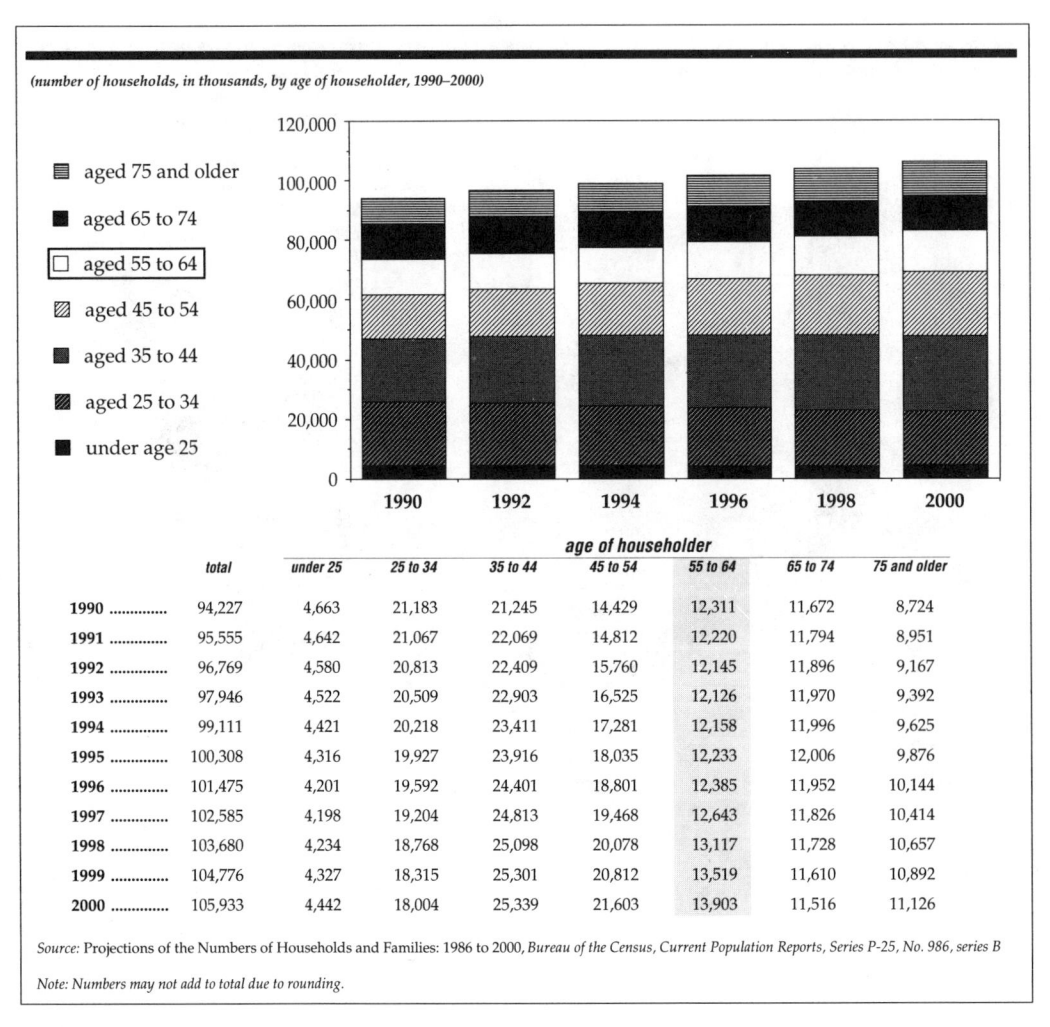

Legend:
- aged 75 and older
- aged 65 to 74
- aged 55 to 64
- aged 45 to 54
- aged 35 to 44
- aged 25 to 34
- under age 25

	total	under 25	25 to 34	35 to 44	45 to 54	55 to 64	65 to 74	75 and older
1990	94,227	4,663	21,183	21,245	14,429	12,311	11,672	8,724
1991	95,555	4,642	21,067	22,069	14,812	12,220	11,794	8,951
1992	96,769	4,580	20,813	22,409	15,760	12,145	11,896	9,167
1993	97,946	4,522	20,509	22,903	16,525	12,126	11,970	9,392
1994	99,111	4,421	20,218	23,411	17,281	12,158	11,996	9,625
1995	100,308	4,316	19,927	23,916	18,035	12,233	12,006	9,876
1996	101,475	4,201	19,592	24,401	18,801	12,385	11,952	10,144
1997	102,585	4,198	19,204	24,813	19,468	12,643	11,826	10,414
1998	103,680	4,234	18,768	25,098	20,078	13,117	11,728	10,657
1999	104,776	4,327	18,315	25,301	20,812	13,519	11,610	10,892
2000	105,933	4,442	18,004	25,339	21,603	13,903	11,516	11,126

Source: Projections of the Numbers of Households and Families: 1986 to 2000, Bureau of the Census, Current Population Reports, Series P-25, No. 986, series B

Note: Numbers may not add to total due to rounding.

Types of Households

HOUSEHOLDS
55–64

75 PERCENT FAMILIES

Although three-quarters of the 13 million 55-to-64-year-old householders live in families, fewer than 10 percent of them still have children under age 18 at home. The remaining quarter of all households in that age group are nonfamilies and the majority of these, 62 percent, are women who live alone.

(household types for all households and for householders aged 55 to 64, numbers in thousands)

	all households		householder aged 55 to 64	
	total	percent of households in category	total	percent of households in category
All households	91,066	100.0%	12,846	100.0%
Family households	**65,133**	**71.5**	**9,707**	**75.6**
Married couple	51,809	56.9	8,216	64.0
With children under age 18 at home	24,600	27.0	777	6.0
Without children under age 18 at home	27,209	29.9	7,439	57.9
Female householder	10,608	11.6	1,155	9.0
With children under age 18 at home	6,273	6.9	98	0.8
Without children under age 18 at home	4,335	4.8	1,057	8.2
Male householder	2,715	3.0	336	2.6
With children under age 18 at home	1,047	1.1	43	0.3
Without children under age 18 at home	1,669	1.8	293	2.3
Nonfamily households	**25,993**	**28.5**	**3,139**	**24.4**
Living alone	21,889	24.0	2,974	23.2
Female householder	13,101	14.4	1,933	15.0
Male householder	8,788	9.7	1,040	8.1
Living with others	4,044	4.4	166	1.3
Female householder	1,523	1.7	61	0.5
Male householder	2,521	2.8	105	0.8

Source: The 1988 Current Population Survey, Bureau of the Census

Note: Numbers may not add to total due to rounding.

Future Household Types

HOUSEHOLDS
55–64

MORE MALE HOUSEHOLDERS

The number of householders aged 55 to 64 will rise during the 1990s, along with householders aged 35 to 54 and 75 and older. A 31 percent gain in the number of men heading nonfamily groups is the most dramatic change anticipated for this age group.

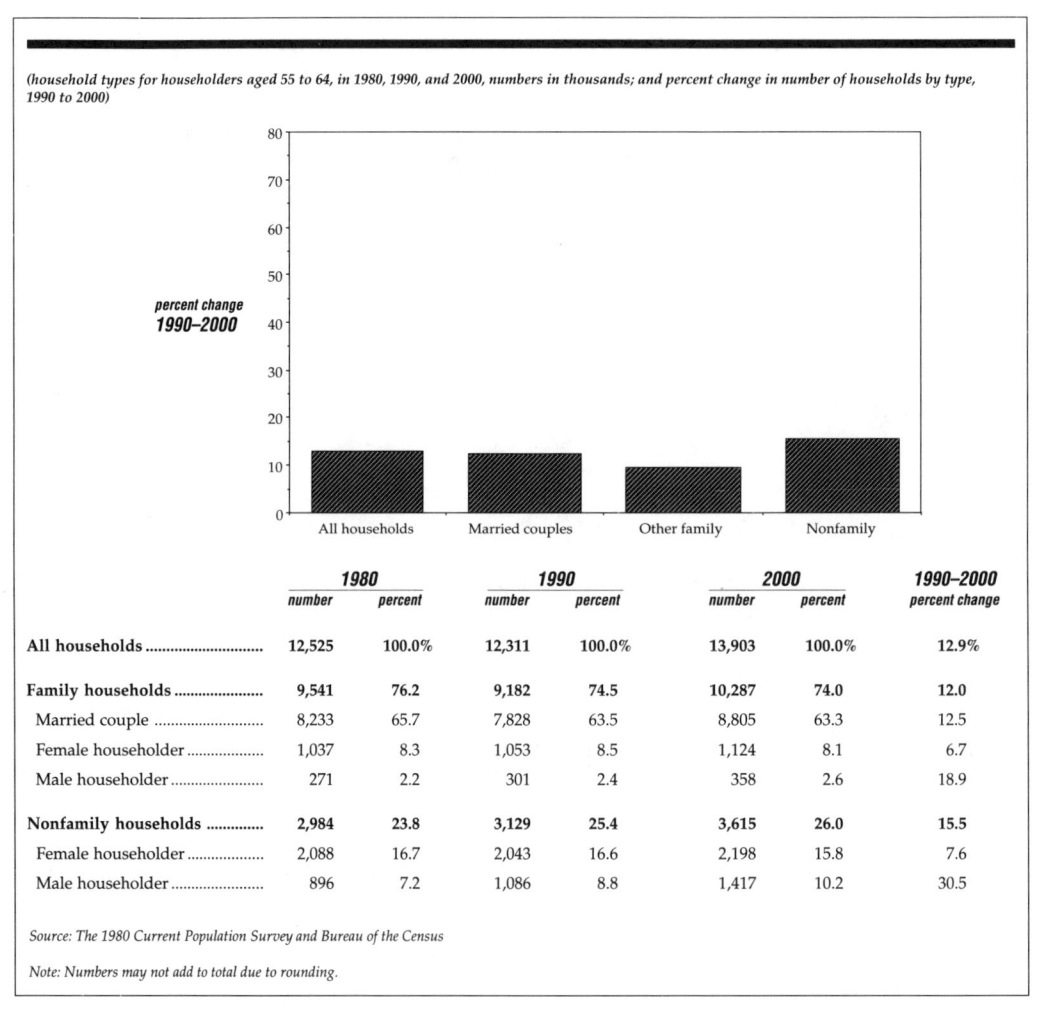

(household types for householders aged 55 to 64, in 1980, 1990, and 2000, numbers in thousands; and percent change in number of households by type, 1990 to 2000)

	1980 number	1980 percent	1990 number	1990 percent	2000 number	2000 percent	1990–2000 percent change
All households	12,525	100.0%	12,311	100.0%	13,903	100.0%	12.9%
Family households	9,541	76.2	9,182	74.5	10,287	74.0	12.0
Married couple	8,233	65.7	7,828	63.5	8,805	63.3	12.5
Female householder	1,037	8.3	1,053	8.5	1,124	8.1	6.7
Male householder	271	2.2	301	2.4	358	2.6	18.9
Nonfamily households	2,984	23.8	3,129	25.4	3,615	26.0	15.5
Female householder	2,088	16.7	2,043	16.6	2,198	15.8	7.6
Male householder	896	7.2	1,086	8.8	1,417	10.2	30.5

Source: The 1980 Current Population Survey and Bureau of the Census

Note: Numbers may not add to total due to rounding.

Marital Status

MARITAL STATUS
55–64

WIDOWHOOD ON THE RISE

Compared with people ten years younger, this age group is slightly less likely to be married or divorced, and a bit more likely to be widowed—74 percent are married and living with their spouses, 8 percent are divorced, and 10 percent are widowed. Widowhood has its greatest impact among women; although 3 percent of men in this age group have lost their spouses, a full 17 percent of all women aged 55 to 64—and 24 percent of black women—are widowed.

(marital status of persons aged 15 and older and those aged 55 to 64, by sex, race and Hispanic origin, numbers in thousands)

	all	total	single never married	married spouse present	married spouse absent	divorced	widowed
Males all ages							
All races/ethnicities	89,368	100.0%	30.0%	58.5%	2.9%	6.3%	2.4%
White	77,212	100.0	28.2	60.9	2.5	6.2	2.3
Black	9,472	100.0	42.9	40.4	6.0	7.5	3.3
Hispanic origin	6,517	100.0	36.4	49.9	6.2	5.8	1.6
Males aged 55 to 64							
All races/ethnicities	10,277	100.0	5.8	81.3	2.7	7.3	2.9
White	9,123	100.0	5.1	83.8	2.0	6.6	2.6
Black	911	100.0	12.0	56.6	10.1	15.4	6.0
Hispanic origin	472	100.0	5.7	74.8	7.2	7.4	4.7
Females all ages							
All races/ethnicities	97,320	100.0	23.0	53.7	3.6	8.3	11.4
White	83,003	100.0	21.0	56.6	2.7	8.0	11.6
Black	11,447	100.0	36.5	32.7	9.2	10.4	11.2
Hispanic origin	6,588	100.0	26.6	51.2	7.7	8.3	6.2
Females aged 55 to 64							
All races/ethnicities	11,606	100.0	4.2	67.1	3.0	9.0	16.7
White	10,184	100.0	3.8	70.0	2.0	8.4	15.8
Black	1,151	100.0	7.7	42.6	10.4	15.1	24.2
Hispanic origin	571	100.0	6.1	57.3	9.8	10.9	15.9

Source: Marital Status and Living Arrangements: March 1987, *Bureau of the Census, Current Population Reports, Series P-20, No. 423*

Note: Hispanics may be of any race. Numbers may not add to total due to rounding.

Number of Marriages and Divorces

MARITAL STATUS
55–64

MARITAL STABILITY

Fewer than 3 percent of people marrying and fewer than 4 percent of those divorcing are aged 55 to 64. Men and women in this age group account for 8 percent and 5 percent, respectively, of remarriages.

(number of marriages and divorces for all Americans and for those aged 55 to 64)

	all persons male	all persons female	persons aged 55 to 64 male	persons aged 55 to 64 female	percent involving persons aged 55 to 64 male	percent involving persons aged 55 to 64 female
All marriages	1,858,783	1,858,783	52,314	31,320	2.8%	1.7%
First marriages	1,185,904	1,196,119	3,858	2,140	0.3	0.2
Remarriages	635,086	623,867	47,713	28,679	7.5	4.5
Previously divorced	499,735	485,848	26,802	11,590	5.4	2.3
Divorces	577,713	577,713	23,873	14,718	4.1	2.5

Source: Advance Report of Final Marriage Statistics, 1985 and Advance Report of Final Divorce Statistics, 1985, *National Center for Health Statistics*

Note: Numbers will not add to total because all divorces include those not stating their age and all marriages include those not stating whether they were previously married.

Summary of Educational Attainment

EDUCATIONAL ATTAINMENT
55–64

DWINDLING BY DEGREE

The share of 55-to-64-year-olds that completed four years of college is below that of Americans in general—15 percent versus 20 percent. Just 13 percent of all people aged 55-to-64 completed one to three years of college.

(years of school completed by persons aged 25 and over, by selected characteristics, numbers in thousands)

	number	4 years of high school or more	1 or more years of college	4 or more years of college
All persons	149,144	75.6%	37.0%	19.9%
Age groups:				
25 to 34	42,635	86.5	45.4	23.9
35 to 44	33,632	85.9	46.8	26.5
45 to 54	23,018	77.6	35.6	19.5
55 to 64	**21,883**	**67.8**	**28.0**	**14.9**
65 to 74	17,232	56.9	21.9	10.6
75 years and older	10,743	42.0	18.0	8.9
Sex:				
Male	70,677	76.0	40.6	23.6
Female	78,476	75.3	33.6	16.5
Race:				
White	129,170	77.0	37.8	20.5
Black	15,580	63.4	26.4	10.7
Asian and other	4,394	78.4	50.9	33.4
Hispanic origin:				
Hispanic	9,449	50.9	21.9	8.6
Non-Hispanic	139,695	77.3	38.0	20.6
Region:				
Northeast	32,030	76.5	36.8	22.2
Midwest	36,322	77.4	33.7	17.6
South	50,848	70.8	34.1	18.3
West	29,943	80.6	45.9	22.8
Metropolitan residence:				
Metropolitan area	115,614	77.6	40.0	22.1
Nonmetropolitan area	33,529	68.7	26.5	12.6

Source: Educational Attainment in the United States: March 1987 and March 1986, *Bureau of the Census, Current Population Reports, Series P-20, No. 428*

Age and Education

EDUCATIONAL ATTAINMENT
55–64

PART OF THE PAST

Men in this age group are almost twice as likely as women to have completed four or more years of college. Twenty percent of men aged 55 to 64 and 11 percent of the women are that highly educated. Younger members of this age group tend to be more highly educated than their older counterparts.

(years of school completed by persons aged 55 to 64, by sex and single year of age, numbers in thousands)

	number	total	not high school graduate	high school graduate	1 to 3 years of college	4 or more years of college	median years
Males aged 55 to 59	5,276	100.0%	32.4%	35.0%	13.3%	19.3%	12.5
Age 55	1,030	100.0	28.3	35.6	15.2	20.8	12.6
Age 56	1,005	100.0	29.9	35.9	11.8	22.2	12.6
Age 57	1,059	100.0	32.7	33.8	14.4	19.3	12.5
Age 58	1,059	100.0	34.7	36.4	12.4	16.5	12.4
Age 59	1,122	100.0	35.8	33.2	13.0	18.0	12.4
Males aged 60 to 64	5,002	100.0	35.7	32.5	11.8	19.9	12.4
Age 60	1,109	100.0	35.2	33.6	12.1	19.2	12.4
Age 61	937	100.0	36.2	31.1	12.0	20.8	12.4
Age 62	1,062	100.0	37.6	31.6	12.3	18.5	12.4
Age 63	947	100.0	37.7	34.2	9.3	18.8	12.4
Age 64	947	100.0	31.9	31.9	13.3	22.9	12.6
Females aged 55 to 59	5,830	100.0	30.0	44.7	14.0	11.3	12.4
Age 55	1,112	100.0	27.3	48.1	12.9	11.7	12.5
Age 56	1,253	100.0	30.9	44.1	14.0	11.0	12.4
Age 57	1,133	100.0	29.7	44.0	14.0	12.2	12.5
Age 58	1,171	100.0	31.6	42.6	14.0	11.8	12.4
Age 59	1,162	100.0	30.2	44.9	15.0	10.1	12.4
Females aged 60 to 64	5,776	100.0	31.5	45.4	13.2	10.0	12.4
Age 60	1,274	100.0	29.3	47.6	13.1	10.0	12.4
Age 61	1,086	100.0	29.7	48.6	11.9	9.8	12.4
Age 62	1,165	100.0	30.1	45.5	12.8	11.6	12.4
Age 63	1,165	100.0	34.6	42.1	14.8	8.6	12.4
Age 64	1,086	100.0	33.4	43.3	13.4	9.9	12.4

Source: Educational Attainment in the United States: March 1987 and 1986, Bureau of the Census, Current Population Reports, Series P-20, No. 428

Note: Numbers may not add to total due to rounding.

Sex, Race, and Ethnicity

EDUCATIONAL ATTAINMENT
55–64

EDUCATED MEN

Just 15 percent of 55-to-64-year-olds have completed four or more years of college. That proportion is higher for white men—one in five of them completed at least four years of college—but lower for women, blacks and Hispanics.

(years of school completed by persons aged 25 and older and those aged 55 to 64, by sex, race, and Hispanic origin, numbers in thousands)

	number	total	not high school graduate	high school graduate	1 to 3 years of college	4 or more years of college
All persons aged 25 and older	149,144	100.0%	24.4%	38.7%	17.1%	19.9%
White	129,170	100.0	23.0	39.2	17.2	20.5
Black	15,580	100.0	36.6	37.1	15.7	10.7
Hispanic origin	9,449	100.0	49.1	29.0	13.3	8.6
All persons aged 55 to 64	21,883	100.0	32.2	39.8	13.1	14.9
White	19,306	100.0	29.4	41.5	13.5	15.6
Black	2,063	100.0	58.0	25.3	10.1	6.6
Hispanic origin	1,042	100.0	64.6	21.8	7.7	6.0
Males aged 25 and older	70,677	100.0	24.0	35.4	17.1	23.6
White	61,678	100.0	22.7	35.6	17.2	24.5
Black	6,919	100.0	37.0	36.5	15.5	11.0
Hispanic origin	4,614	100.0	48.2	28.0	14.2	9.7
Males aged 55 to 64	10,278	100.0	34.0	33.8	12.6	19.6
White	9,122	100.0	31.0	35.3	12.9	20.7
Black	911	100.0	64.2	19.9	9.7	6.3
Hispanic origin	472	100.0	63.1	22.5	7.4	7.4
Females aged 25 and older	78,467	100.0	24.7	41.6	17.1	16.5
White	67,492	100.0	23.3	42.6	17.3	16.9
Black	8,661	100.0	36.2	37.5	15.8	10.4
Hispanic origin	4,835	100.0	50.0	30.0	12.5	7.5
Females aged 55 to 64	11,606	100.0	30.7	45.1	13.6	10.6
White	10,184	100.0	28.0	47.0	14.0	11.0
Black	1,152	100.0	53.2	29.5	10.4	6.9
Hispanic origin	570	100.0	66.3	21.2	8.1	4.6

Source: Educational Attainment in the United States: March 1987 and March 1986, Bureau of the Census, Current Population Reports, Series P-20, No. 428
Note: Hispanics are of any race. Numbers may not add to total due to rounding.

Householders

EDUCATIONAL ATTAINMENT
55–64

GENDER DIFFERENCES

The number of male householders aged 55 to 64 that completed four or more years of college is nearly double the number of their female counterparts. An additional 13 percent of both the men and the women finished one to three years of college.

(years of school completed by householders aged 55 to 64, by sex, race, and Hispanic origin, numbers in thousands)

	number	total	not high school graduate	high school graduate	1 to 3 years of college	4 or more years of college	median years
Male householders	9,252	100.0%	32.5%	34.3%	13.0%	20.2%	12.5
White	8,361	100.0	30.2	35.6	13.2	21.0	12.6
Black	680	100.0	62.4	20.3	10.4	6.9	10.4
Hispanic origin	390	100.0	58.5	24.4	8.5	8.2	10.1
Female householders	3,615	100.0	34.9	41.4	13.2	10.5	12.4
White	2,921	100.0	30.9	44.5	13.4	11.3	12.4
Black	621	100.0	54.4	26.6	12.1	7.1	11.5
Hispanic origin	200	100.0	74.0	14.5	7.5	5.0	8.3

Source: Educational Attainment in the United States: March 1987 and March 1986, *Bureau of the Census, Current Population Reports, Series P-20, No. 428*
Note: Hispanics are of any race. Numbers may not add to total due to rounding.

Labor Force Status

LABOR FORCE
55–64

STARTING TO RETIRE

By the time they're 55 to 64 years old, both men and women are far less likely to be in the labor force than all prime-aged workers (those 18 to 64), their participation rates dropping to 68 percent for men and only 43 percent for women. Black women who are approaching retirement age are more likely than white women to continue working.

(labor force status of all persons aged 16 and older, aged 18 to 64, and those aged 55 to 64, by sex and race, numbers in thousands)

	total population	total in labor force	percent of population in labor force	number employed	number unemployed	percent of labor force unemployed	not in labor force
Males aged 16 and older	86,899	66,207	76.2%	62,107	4,101	6.2%	20,692
White	75,189	57,779	76.8	54,647	3,132	5.4	17,410
Black	9,128	6,486	71.1	5,661	826	12.7	2,642
Males aged 18 to 64	71,443	62,563	87.6	58,864	3,699	5.9	8,880
White	61,583	54,522	88.5	51,705	2,818	5.2	7,061
Black	7,615	6,179	81.1	5,427	750	12.1	1,437
Males aged 55 to 64	10,267	6,940	67.6	6,682	258	3.7	3,327
White	9,101	6,200	68.1	5,991	209	3.4	2,901
Black	944	586	62.1	547	39	6.6	358
Females aged 16 and older	95,853	53,658	56.0%	50,334	3,324	6.2%	42,195
White	81,769	45,510	55.7	43,142	2,369	5.2	36,258
Black	11,224	6,507	58.0	5,648	858	13.2	4,717
Females aged 18 to 64	75,700	50,799	67.1	47,801	3,000	5.9	24,901
White	63,964	42,999	67.2	40,878	2,120	4.9	20,965
Black	9,262	6,227	67.2	5,438	791	12.7	3,035
Females aged 55 to 64	11,567	4,937	42.7	4,783	155	3.1	6,630
White	10,141	4,297	42.4	4,172	124	2.9	5,844
Black	1,153	512	44.4	489	23	4.5	641

Source: Annual averages from Employment and Earnings, 1987, Bureau of Labor Statistics

Note: The population here includes all civilian, noninstitutionalized people aged 16 and older.

Extent of Employment

LABOR FORCE
55–64

EARLY RETIREMENT

Eighty percent of 55-to-64-year-old workers are employed full-time, with the vast majority of them on the job year-round. Among part-time workers in this age group, 54 percent of the women and 45 percent of the men worked for at least 50 weeks.

(work experience in 1987 of workers aged 16 and older and aged 55 to 64, by sex, numbers in thousands)

	\multicolumn{4}{c}{worked at full-time jobs}	\multicolumn{4}{c}{worked at part-time jobs}	non-workers
	total	50-52 weeks	27-49 weeks	1-26 weeks	total	50-52 weeks	27-49 weeks	1-26 weeks	total
Males									
Aged 16 and older	59,740	47,106	7,489	5,143	9,280	3,175	2,165	3,940	18,582
Aged 55 to 64	6,623	5,398	706	518	801	357	181	262	2,761
Females									
Aged 16 and older	40,398	29,882	5,788	4,727	18,538	7,774	4,301	6,463	37,580
Aged 55 to 64	3,785	2,928	504	353	1,775	962	374	440	5,896

Source: The 1988 Current Population Survey, Bureau of Labor Statistics

Note: Numbers may not add to total due to rounding. The categories in this table are not mutually exclusive. Workers may, for example, be counted as both a full-time and a part-time worker if they held jobs of both kinds during the year. For this reason, the total number of workers will be higher and the number of nonworkers lower than in the previous table that uses annual averages of the number of workers in each category. Civilians only.

Kinds of Jobs

LABOR FORCE
55–64

SALES & MANAGEMENT

The top three occupational categories for employed 55-to-64-year-old women are: technical, sales, and administrative support, 44 percent; managerial and professional, 22 percent; and service occupations, 20 percent. For men, the figures are: managerial and professional, 30 percent; with technical, sales and administrative support tying at 19 percent with precision production, craft and repair.

(occupations of employed persons aged 16 and older, and those aged 55 to 64, by sex, numbers in thousands)

	aged 16+	aged 55-64	males aged 55-64	females aged 55-64	percent aged 16+	percent aged 55-64
All employed persons	112,440	11,465	6,682	4,783	100.0%	100.0%
Managerial and professional	27,742	3,022	1,992	1,030	24.7	26.4
Executive, administrative, and managerial	13,316	1,621	1,153	468	11.8	14.1
Officials & administrators, public admin.	549	87	58	29	0.5	0.8
Other executive, admin., & managerial	9,190	1,181	870	311	8.2	10.3
Management-related occupations	3,577	353	226	127	3.2	3.1
Professional specialty occupations	14,426	1,402	840	562	12.8	12.2
Engineers	1,731	213	209	4	1.5	1.9
Math & computer scientists	685	34	27	7	0.6	0.3
Natural scientists	388	34	30	4	0.3	0.3
Health diagnosing occupations	793	108	102	6	0.7	0.9
Health assessment & treating	2,148	164	21	143	1.9	1.4
Teachers, college & university	661	94	68	26	0.6	0.8
Teachers, except college & university	3,587	300	96	204	3.2	2.6
Lawyers & judges	707	76	69	7	0.6	0.7
Other professional specialty occupations	3,727	378	218	160	3.3	3.3
Technical, sales, administrative support	35,082	3,374	1,271	2,103	31.2	29.4
Technicians & related support occupations	3,346	198	118	80	3.0	1.7
Health technologists & technicians	1,142	72	11	61	1.0	0.6
Engineering & science technicians	1,100	86	78	8	1.0	0.8
Techs. except health, engineering, science	1,104	41	29	12	1.0	0.4
Sales occupations	13,480	1,397	792	605	12.0	12.2
Supervisors & proprietors	3,572	402	286	116	3.2	3.5
Sales reps, finance & business service	2,330	292	199	93	2.1	2.5

(continued next page)

Almanac of Consumer Markets 269

Kinds of Jobs

LABOR FORCE 55–64

(continued from previous page)
(occupations of employed persons aged 16 and older, and those aged 55 to 64, by sex, numbers in thousands)

	aged 16+	aged 55-64	males aged 55-64	females aged 55-64	percent aged 16+	percent aged 55-64
Sales reps., commodities except retail	1,544	155	141	14	1.4%	1.4%
Sales, retail and personal	5,973	537	163	374	5.3	4.7
Sales-related occupations	60	11	4	7	0.1	0.1
Administrative support including clerical	**18,256**	**1,779**	**361**	**1,418**	**16.2**	**15.5**
Supervisors	723	86	37	49	0.6	0.8
Computer equipment operators	914	52	13	39	0.8	0.5
Secretaries, stenographers, & typists	5,004	446	8	438	4.5	3.9
Financial records processing	2,469	334	27	307	2.2	2.9
Mail & message distributing	961	109	83	26	0.9	1.0
Other admin. support including clerical	8,185	752	193	559	7.3	6.6
Service occupations	**15,054**	**1,502**	**566**	**936**	**13.4**	**13.1**
Private household	934	135	5	130	0.8	1.2
Protective services	1,907	180	156	24	1.7	1.6
Service, except private hhld. & protective	12,213	1,188	406	782	10.9	10.4
Food service	5,204	338	72	266	4.6	2.9
Health service	1,873	193	11	182	1.7	1.7
Cleaning & building service	2,886	466	275	191	2.6	4.1
Personal service	2,249	191	48	143	2.0	1.7
Precision production, craft, repair	**13,568**	**1,395**	**1,274**	**121**	**12.1**	**12.2**
Mechanics & repairers	4,445	445	435	10	0.4	3.9
Construction trades	5,011	453	447	6	4.5	4.0
Other production, craft, repair	4,112	497	392	105	3.7	4.3
Operators, fabricators, laborers	**17,486**	**1,685**	**1,176**	**509**	**15.6**	**14.7**
Machine operators, assemblers, inspectors	7,994	855	450	405	7.1	7.5
Transportation, material moving	4,712	524	484	40	4.2	4.6
Handlers, equip. cleaners, helpers, laborers	4,779	306	242	64	4.3	2.7
Farming, forestry, fishing	**3,507**	**486**	**401**	**85**	**3.1**	**4.2**
Farm operators & managers	1,317	294	252	42	1.2	2.6
Farm workers & related occupations	2,013	177	137	40	1.8	1.5
Forestry and fishing occupations	177	14	12	2	0.2	0.1

Source: Unpublished annual data for 1987, Bureau of Labor Statistics

Note: Numbers may not add to total due to rounding. Civilian, noninstitutionalized employees only.

Workers in the 1990s

LABOR FORCE
55–64

WOMEN STILL GAINING

More workers for the 1990s will be coming from this age group and they will be women. The proportion of women aged 55 to 64 in the labor force will increase by 3 percentage points during the 1990s while a smaller proportion of men in this age group will be working in 2000 than in 1990.

(labor force and labor force participation rates* for persons aged 16 and older and those aged 55 to 64, by sex, race, and ethnicity, in 1990 and 2000, numbers in thousands)

	1990 number	1990 participation rate	2000 number	2000 participation rate	1990-2000 percent change
Both sexes, aged 16 and older	124,457	66.2%	138,775	67.8%	11.5%
White	106,648	66.5	116,701	68.2	9.4
Black	13,788	64.6	16,334	66.0	18.5
Hispanic	9,718	65.9	14,086	67.1	44.9
Asian and other	4,021	64.8	5,740	65.8	42.8
Males, aged 16 and older	67,909	75.8	73,136	74.7	7.7
Males, aged 55 to 64	6,518	65.1	7,238	63.2	11.0
White	5,804	66.0	6,391	64.6	10.1
Black	545	56.7	575	49.9	5.5
Hispanic	381	68.0	538	67.9	41.2
Asian and other	169	68.4	272	66.3	60.9
Females, aged 16 and older	56,548	57.4	65,639	61.5	16.1
Females, aged 55 to 64	4,790	42.8	5,732	45.8	19.7
White	4,121	42.5	4,848	45.6	17.6
Black	517	44.2	639	45.7	23.6
Hispanic	227	35.4	334	37.3	47.1
Asian and other	152	47.5	245	49.8	61.2

*Labor force participation rates are the ratio of people in the labor force to the total population of a given sex, age and race or ethnicity.

Source: Unpublished data from the Bureau of Labor Statistics

Note: The labor force here includes civilians who are working or looking for work. Hispanics are of any race.

Household Income

INCOME
55–64

PER CAPITA PEAK

Fifty-five-to-64-year-olds head 14 percent of all households and garner more than 15 percent of total household income, for an average per household member of $14,800, the highest of any age group.

(household income and income per household member, for all households and for households by age of householder, numbers for 1988 in thousands, income is for 1987)

	households		persons in household			total household income		
	number	percent	number	percent	persons per household	$ billions	percent	per household member
All households	91,066	100.0%	240,722	100.0%	2.64	$2,927.2	100.0%	$12,160
Age of householder								
under 25	5,228	5.7	12,117	5.0	2.32	102.0	3.5	8,415
25 to 34	20,583	22.6	58,724	24.4	2.85	621.6	21.2	10,586
35 to 44	19,323	21.2	64,351	26.7	3.33	763.8	26.1	11,870
45 to 54	13,630	15.0	41,379	17.2	3.04	597.0	20.4	14,426
55 to 64	12,846	14.1	30,151	12.5	2.35	447.3	15.3	14,835
65 and older	19,456	21.4	33,999	14.1	1.75	395.6	13.5	11,635

Source: The 1988 Current Population Survey, Bureau of the Census

Individual Income

INCOME 55–64

MEN ON THE HIGH END

Among 55-to-64-year-olds with income, 55 percent of the men bring in at least $20,000 and a full 12 percent top out at over $50,000. The picture for older income-producing women is different—59 percent have incomes under $10,000.

(income distribution and median income for males and females aged 15 and older and aged 55 to 64, numbers for 1988 in thousands, income is for 1987)

	males aged 15 and older number	males aged 15 and older percent	males aged 55 to 64 number	males aged 55 to 64 percent
All males	90,284	–	10,186	–
All males with income	85,623	100.0%	9,985	100.0%
Less than $5,000	13,025	15.2	907	9.1
$5,000 to $9,999	12,066	14.1	1,209	12.1
$10,000 to $14,999	11,708	13.7	1,229	12.3
$15,000 to $19,999	9,887	11.5	1,179	11.8
$20,000 to $24,999	8,714	10.2	1,078	10.8
$25,000 to $29,999	7,266	8.5	898	9.0
$30,000 to $34,999	6,124	7.2	800	8.0
$35,000 to $49,999	9,941	11.6	1,478	14.8
$50,000 to $74,999	4,669	5.5	781	7.8
$75,000 and over	2,225	2.6	426	4.3
Median income, all with income		$17,752		$21,906
Median income, year-round, full-time workers		$26,722		$30,946

	females aged 15 and older number	females aged 15 and older percent	females aged 55 to 64 number	females aged 55 to 64 percent
All females	98,168	–	11,456	–
All females with income	89,279	100.0%	10,469	100.0%
Less than $5,000	30,715	34.4	3,968	37.9
$5,000 to $9,999	19,782	22.2	2,225	21.3
$10,000 to $14,999	13,313	14.9	1,548	14.8
$15,000 to $19,999	9,470	10.6	1,003	9.6
$20,000 to $24,999	6,321	7.1	629	6.0
$25,000 to $29,999	3,768	4.2	418	4.0
$30,000 to $34,999	2,331	2.6	202	1.9
$35,000 to $49,999	2,602	2.9	328	3.1
$50,000 to $74,999	708	0.8	102	1.0
$75,000 and over	268	0.3	46	0.4
Median income, all with income		$8,101		$7,445
Median income, year-round, full-time workers		$17,504		$17,831

Source: Money Income and Poverty Status in the United States: 1987, *Bureau of the Census, Current Population Reports, Series P-20, No. 161*
Note: Numbers may not add to total due to rounding.

Income and Age

INCOME
55–64

TIME AND MONEY

Nearly 40 percent of households headed by 55-to-64-year-olds have household incomes of $35,000 or more, and 22 percent of them bring in at least $50,000.

(household income by age of householder, numbers for 1988 in thousands, income is for 1987)

	total	under 25	25 to 34	35 to 44	45 to 54	55 to 64	65 to 74	75 +
All households	91,066	5,228	20,583	19,323	13,630	12,846	11,410	8,045
All households	100.0%	100.0%	100.0%	100.0%	100.0%	100.0%	100.0%	100.0%
Less than $10,000	18.4	30.3	13.6	10.3	10.4	17.4	27.1	44.6
$10,000 to $14,999	10.6	15.8	9.6	6.6	6.6	9.5	17.3	18.5
$15,000 to $19,999	10.0	14.1	11.1	7.4	6.8	9.7	13.8	11.8
$20,000 to $24,999	9.2	11.5	11.1	8.3	7.2	9.1	10.1	7.5
$25,000 to $29,999	8.4	9.0	10.6	8.5	7.6	8.0	8.3	4.3
$30,000 to $34,999	7.7	6.8	9.7	9.0	7.8	7.2	6.0	3.2
$35,000 to $39,999	6.8	4.5	8.6	9.0	7.2	6.3	4.2	2.4
$40,000 to $44,999	5.8	2.3	6.7	7.9	7.4	6.0	3.0	1.7
$45,000 to $49,999	4.6	1.3	5.1	6.6	5.9	4.7	2.4	1.5
$50,000 to $59,999	6.7	2.1	6.7	9.6	10.1	7.5	2.7	1.9
$60,000 to $74,999	5.5	1.5	4.2	7.9	9.9	6.3	2.1	1.2
$75,000 and over	6.3	0.9	3.0	8.9	13.1	8.3	3.0	1.4
Median household income	$25,986	$16,204	$26,923	$34,926	$37,250	$27,538	$16,906	$11,261

Source: The 1988 Current Population Survey, Bureau of the Census

Note: Numbers may not add to total due to rounding.

Income of Married Couples

INCOME 55–64

HIGH-INCOME MAJORITY

Over half of married couples in this age group have household incomes of $35,000 or more and 30 percent have incomes in excess of $50,000. Unlike their younger counterparts, 55-to-64-year-olds with children under 18 in the home have a higher median household income than those without children at home.

(household income of married-couple householder families with and without children under 18 at home, householders aged 55 to 64, numbers for 1988 in thousands, income is for 1987)

	married-couple householder aged 55 to 64		
	total	with children under 18 at home	without children under 18 at home
All households	8,216	777	7,439
All households	100.0%	100.0%	100.0%
Less than $10,000	7.4	9.8	7.2
$10,000 to $14,999	6.7	9.3	6.5
$15,000 to $19,999	8.5	6.2	8.7
$20,000 to $24,999	9.3	7.1	9.5
$25,000 to $29,999	8.3	8.8	8.3
$30,000 to $34,999	8.7	6.9	8.8
$35,000 to $39,999	7.6	6.4	7.7
$40,000 to $44,999	7.5	6.2	7.6
$45,000 to $49,999	5.9	4.6	6.0
$50,000 to $59,999	10.1	12.7	9.8
$60,000 to $74,999	8.5	11.2	8.2
$75,000 and over	11.6	10.7	11.7
Median household income	$35,804	$37,236	$35,735

Source: The 1988 Current Population Survey, Bureau of the Census

Note: Numbers may not add to total due to rounding.

Income of Other Family Households

INCOME
55–64

ADVANTAGE TO THE MEN

Of households headed by 55-to-64-year-old unmarried women, nearly half have household incomes under $20,000; 28 percent receive between $20,000 and $35,000, and 24 percent have over $35,000. As with all other age groups, male-headed households are much more prosperous than those headed by women.

(household income of unmarried female- and male-householder families with and without children under 18 at home, householders aged 55 to 64, numbers for 1988, in thousands income is for 1987)

	female householder aged 55 to 64			male householder aged 55 to 64		
	total	with children under 18 at home	without children under 18 at home	total	with children under 18 at home	without children under 18 at home
All households	1,155	98	1,057	336	43	293
All households	100.0%	100.0%	100.0%	100.0%	100.0%	100.0%
Less than $10,000	22.5	32.7	21.7	16.1	18.6	16.0
$10,000 to $14,999	14.1	18.4	13.7	8.3	9.3	8.2
$15,000 to $19,999	11.7	8.2	12.0	14.3	16.3	14.0
$20,000 to $24,999	10.5	17.3	9.8	8.3	14.0	7.5
$25,000 to $29,999	9.8	11.2	9.6	8.0	9.3	8.2
$30,000 to $34,999	7.5	3.1	7.9	8.6	9.3	8.9
$35,000 to $39,999	5.5	3.1	5.7	5.7	16.3	4.1
$40,000 to $44,999	3.8	0.0	4.2	5.7	4.7	5.8
$45,000 to $49,999	3.5	0.0	3.9	4.2	4.7	4.1
$50,000 to $59,999	4.6	4.1	4.5	6.8	2.3	7.8
$60,000 to $74,999	3.9	0.0	4.3	6.5	–	7.5
$75,000 and over	2.7	3.1	2.6	6.8	–	7.8
Median household income	$20,440	$14,133	$21,283	$26,827	–	$28,723

Source: The 1988 Current Population Survey, Bureau of the Census

Note: Median income is unreliable and is therefore not given when the category contains fewer than 75,000 households. Numbers may not add to total due to rounding.

Income of Nonfamily Households

INCOME 55–64

MONEY AND COMPANY

Householders aged 55 to 64 who live with unrelated others have a median income that is almost double that of their counterparts who live alone. Among those householders who live with others, 43 percent of the men and 40 percent of the women have incomes of $35,000 or more.

(household income of nonfamily households by household type, householders aged 55 to 64, numbers for 1988 in thousands, income is for 1987)

	total number	living alone total	living alone male householder	living alone female householder	living with others total	living with others male householder	living with others female householder
All nonfamily households	3,139	2,974	1,040	1,933	166	105	61
All nonfamily households	100.0%	100.0%	100.0%	100.0%	100.0%	100.0%	100.0%
Less than $10,000	41.7	43.2	36.8	46.8	12.7	13.3	11.5
$10,000 to $14,999	15.1	15.4	12.5	17.0	9.6	8.6	11.5
$15,000 to $19,999	11.9	11.9	10.2	12.8	11.4	10.5	13.1
$20,000 to $24,999	8.4	8.2	9.7	7.3	12.0	14.3	8.2
$25,000 to $29,999	6.2	6.0	6.5	5.7	10.8	10.5	11.5
$30,000 to $34,999	3.2	3.4	5.5	2.2	1.8	1.0	3.3
$35,000 to $39,999	3.3	3.1	4.4	2.4	7.2	7.6	6.6
$40,000 to $44,999	3.1	2.7	3.9	2.0	9.6	6.7	14.8
$45,000 to $49,999	2.1	2.0	2.7	1.6	3.6	4.8	3.3
$50,000 to $59,999	1.8	1.5	2.5	1.0	7.2	6.7	8.2
$60,000 to $74,999	1.2	1.0	2.1	0.5	4.8	5.7	3.3
$75,000 and over	2.0	1.6	3.1	0.8	8.4	11.4	3.3
Median household income	$12,056	$11,645	$15,165	$10,707	$27,400	$26,977	–

Source: The 1988 Current Population Survey, Bureau of the Census

Note: Nonfamilies are either people living alone or living with an individual (or individuals) unrelated to the householder. Median income is unreliable and is therefore not given when the category contains fewer than 75,000 households. Numbers may not add to total due to rounding.

Income and Race, Families

INCOME
55–64

INCOME GAP

The median income of white families headed by a 55-to-64-year-old is $14,100 higher than that of black families in this age group. But 47 percent of white married couples and 46 percent of black married couples have household incomes between $20,000 and $50,000 while 31 percent of white couples and 18 percent of black couples have incomes of $50,000 or more.

(household income of family households by race and household type for householders aged 55 to 64, numbers for 1988 in thousands, income is for 1987)

white family households

	total	married couple	male householder	female householder
All households	8,660	7,563	272	825
Total	100.0%	100.0%	100.0%	100.0%
Less than $10,000	8.0	6.8	14.7	17.7
$10,000 to $19,999	16.2	15.0	20.6	25.5
$20,000 to $29,999	17.6	17.4	16.9	19.8
$30,000 to $39,999	16.3	16.4	16.5	15.4
$40,000 to $49,999	13.0	13.6	9.2	8.4
$50,000 to $59,999	9.9	10.4	7.7	5.9
$60,000 to $74,999	8.2	8.6	8.1	4.2
$75,000 and over	10.8	11.8	5.9	3.3
Median household income	$34,571	$36,242	$28,734	$23,909

black family households

	total	married couple	male householder	female householder
All households	832	469	52	311
Total	100.0%	100.0%	100.0%	100.0%
Less than $10,000	24.2	14.9	36.5	35.7
$10,000 to $19,999	24.5	21.3	26.9	28.9
$20,000 to $29,999	21.3	20.5	15.4	23.2
$30,000 to $39,999	11.8	15.4	11.5	6.4
$40,000 to $49,999	6.6	9.8	–	3.2
$50,000 to $59,999	4.4	7.0	–	1.3
$60,000 to $74,999	4.1	6.0	3.8	1.3
$75,000 and over	3.1	5.1	3.8	0.3
Median household income	$20,463	$24,983	–	$13,893

Source: Money Income of Households, Families, and Persons in the United States: 1987, Bureau of the Census, Current Population Reports, Series P-60, No. 162

Note: Numbers may not add to total due to rounding. Median income is unreliable and is therefore not given when the category contains fewer than 75,000 households.

Income and Race, Nonfamilies

INCOME **55-64**

DIFFICULT DIFFERENCE

At $13,100, the median income of white nonfamily householders aged 55 to 64 is $5,400 higher than that of black nonfamily householders. But 18 percent of white householders and 6 percent of black householders have incomes of $30,000 or more. As in the other age groups, white male householders have the highest median income, followed by white female householders.

(householder income of nonfamily householders by race and household type for householders aged 55 to 64, numbers for 1988 in thousands, income is for 1987)

	white householder			black householder		
	total	male householder	female householder	total	male householder	female householder
All households	2,609	952	1,657	491	173	318
Total	100.0%	100.0%	100.0%	100.0%	100.0%	100.0%
Less than $10,000	39.4	34.2	42.5	61.9	48.6	68.6
$10,000 to $19,999	27.8	22.3	30.8	25.3	28.9	23.3
$20,000 to $24,999	8.4	9.1	8.0	5.3	7.5	4.1
$25,000 to $29,999	6.7	6.6	6.7	2.0	4.0	0.9
$30,000 to $34,999	3.8	5.3	3.0	1.6	4.6	–
$35,000 to $49,999	8.8	12.8	6.5	3.9	6.4	2.5
$50,000 and over	5.1	9.7	2.5	0.2	–	0.3
Median householder income	$13,053	$17,065	$11,799	$7,618	$10,119	$6,585

Source: Money Income of Households, Families, and Persons in the United States: 1987, Bureau of the Census, Current Population Reports, Series P-60, No. 162

Note: Numbers may not add to total due to rounding. Householder income is the total money income of the householder only.

Income of Hispanic Households

INCOME
55–64

SIMILAR PATTERN

At $20,600, the median household income of families with a Hispanic householder aged 55 to 64 is close to that of black families ($20,500) in the same age group. This is also true for nonfamilies. Sixty percent of male householder families and 46 percent of married-couple families headed by Hispanics aged 55 to 64 have incomes of $25,000 or more.

(household income of Hispanic households, by household type, for householders aged 55 to 64, numbers for 1988 in thousands, income is for 1987)

family households

	total	married couple	male householder	female householder
All households	510	360	37	113
Total	100.0%	100.0%	100.0%	100.0%
Less than $15,000	33.7	27.2	27.0	57.5
$15,000 to $24,999	24.9	26.9	13.5	22.1
$25,000 and over	41.4	45.8	59.5	21.2
Median household income	$20,611	$22,727	–	$13,068

nonfamily households

	total	male householder living alone	male householder living with others	female householder living alone	female householder living with others
All households	177	60	10	106	1
Total	100.0%	100.0%	100.0%	100.0%	100.0%
Less than $15,000	68.4	63.3	40.0	74.5	–
$15,000 to $24,999	20.3	16.7	30.0	20.8	–
$25,000 and over	10.7	18.3	30.0	3.8	100.0
Median household income	$7,763	–	–	$6,364	–

Source: The 1988 Current Population Survey, Bureau of the Census

Note: Numbers may not add to total due to rounding. Hispanics are of any race. Median income is unreliable and is therefore not given when the category contains fewer than 75,000 households.

Income of Dual-Earner Couples

INCOME 55–64

POWER PLAY

Thirty-seven percent of married couples aged 55 to 64 are dual earners, and their median household income of $45,200 is $9,400 higher than that of all married couples in this age group. Twenty-five percent of the dual earners have incomes between $35,000 and $50,000 and a full 44 percent bring in $50,000 or more.

(household income for all dual-earner married couples and for those with married-couple householders aged 55 to 64, numbers for 1988 in thousands, income is for 1987)

	householder all ages			householder aged 55 to 64		
	total	with children under 18 at home	without children under 18 at home	total	with children under 18 at home	without children under 18 at home
All households	26,227	14,989	11,238	3,045	379	2,665
All households	100.0%	100.0%	100.0%	100.0%	100.3%	100.0%
Less than $15,000	5.7	6.0	5.4	6.1	7.9	5.8
$15,000 to $19,999	5.1	5.4	4.7	4.7	3.4	4.9
$20,000 to $24,999	7.3	7.8	6.6	6.5	5.8	6.6
$25,000 to $29,999	8.3	9.0	7.5	6.3	8.4	6.0
$30,000 to $34,999	9.4	10.2	8.3	7.8	8.2	7.8
$35,000 to $39,999	10.3	11.2	9.0	8.9	8.2	9.0
$40,000 to $44,999	9.6	9.8	9.3	9.2	8.2	9.4
$45,000 to $49,999	8.1	8.2	7.9	6.9	6.9	6.9
$50,000 to $59,999	13.0	12.5	13.6	14.7	18.2	14.2
$60,000 to $74,999	11.2	10.2	12.5	11.9	12.7	11.8
$75,000 and over	12.1	9.6	15.3	17.0	12.4	17.7
Median household income	$41,904	$40,044	$44,508	$45,229	$44,517	$45,305

Source: The 1988 Current Population Survey, Bureau of the Census

Note: Numbers may not add to total due to rounding.

Income and Education

INCOME
55–64

FINISHING COUNTS

Of 55-to-64-year-old householders with incomes of $50,000 or more, 30 percent have just a high school education, 17 percent completed one to three years of college, and 42 percent have four or more years of college.

(household income of householders aged 55 to 64, by years of school completed by householder, numbers for 1988 in thousands, income is for 1987)

	total	not high school graduate	high school graduate	1 to 3 years of college	4 or more years of college
All households	12,846	4,317	4,651	1,640	2,239
All households	100.0%	100.0%	100.0%	100.0%	100.0%
Less than $10,000	17.4	29.2	15.0	10.0	5.0
$10,000 to $19,999	19.2	25.4	20.5	15.4	7.6
$20,000 to $29,999	17.1	17.9	19.8	17.2	9.8
$30,000 to $39,999	13.5	11.9	14.9	15.5	12.1
$40,000 to $49,999	10.7	7.8	11.5	13.5	12.9
$50,000 to $59,999	7.5	3.7	8.4	8.4	12.2
$60,000 to $74,999	6.3	2.3	5.1	9.9	13.6
$75,000 and over	8.3	1.7	4.9	10.4	26.8

Source: The 1988 Current Population Survey, Bureau of the Census.

Note: Numbers may not add to total due to rounding.

Future Income

INCOME
55–64

ROOM AT THE TOP

Between 1990 and 1995, the number of lower-income households headed by 55-to-64-year-olds will decline faster than the number of households in this age group. On the other end of the scale, there will be a 7 percent rise in the number of households with incomes over $50,000.

(projections of the number of households with householders aged 55 to 64, by household income, 1990 and 1995, numbers in thousands, income is in 1985 dollars)

	1990 number	1990 percent	1995 number	1995 percent	percent change 1990-1995
All households	12,311	100.0%	12,233	100.0%	-0.6%
Less than $10,000	2,142	17.4	2,047	16.7	-4.4
$10,000 to $19,999	2,604	21.2	2,498	20.4	-4.1
$20,000 to $29,999	2,311	18.8	2,240	18.3	-3.1
$30,000 to $39,999	1,782	14.5	1,815	14.8	1.9
$40,000 to $49,999	1,190	9.7	1,188	9.7	-0.2
$50,000 to $59,999	846	6.9	899	7.4	6.3
$60,000 to $74,999	629	5.1	684	5.6	8.7
$75,000 and over	807	6.6	864	7.1	7.0
Median household income	$26,100		$27,020		

Source: American Demographics, *May to August, 1986, based on the national econometric model of Wharton Economic Forecasting Association and on household projections from the Bureau of the Census*

Note: Numbers may not add to total due to rounding.

Annual Expenditures

EXPENDITURES
55–64

PREPARING TO RETIRE

An above-average share of this age group's spending dollar goes to health care, contributions, and insurance and pensions. They also devote a slightly larger chunk of their expenditures to food, personal care, reading, and tobacco and smoking supplies than the average household.

(average annual expenditure and percent distribution of expenditures for all households and for householders aged 55 to 64, number of households in thousands)

	all households – average annual expenditure	all households – percent of all expenditures	householder aged 55 to 64 – average annual expenditure	householder aged 55 to 64 – percent of all expenditures
Number of households	93,741		13,166	
Total expenditure	**$22,710**	**100.0%**	**$23,782**	**100.0%**
Food	**3,363**	**14.8**	**3,563**	**15.0**
Food at home	2,313	10.2	2,509	10.5
Food away from home	1,049	4.6	1,054	4.4
Alcoholic beverages	**273**	**1.2**	**241**	**1.0**
Housing	**6,888**	**30.3**	**6,564**	**27.6**
Shelter	3,986	17.6	3,442	14.5
Owned dwellings	2,305	10.1	2,293	9.6
Mortgage interest and charges	1,428	6.3	1,060	4.5
Property taxes	417	1.8	629	2.6
Maintenance, repairs, insurance, and other expenses	460	2.0	604	2.5
Rented dwellings	1,269	5.6	680	2.9
Other lodging	412	1.8	469	2.0
Fuels, utilities, and public services	1,646	7.2	1,883	7.9
Natural gas	248	1.1	311	1.3
Electricity	674	3.0	766	3.2
Fuel oil and other fuels	107	0.5	143	0.6
Telephone	471	2.1	483	2.0
Water and other public services	145	0.6	179	0.8
Household operations	353	1.6	298	1.3
Domestic services	288	1.3	223	0.9
Other household expenses	65	0.3	75	0.3
Household furnishings, equipment	903	4.0	941	4.0
Household textiles	83	0.4	98	0.4
Furniture	303	1.3	270	1.1
Floor coverings	51	0.2	60	0.3
Major appliances	155	0.7	194	0.8

(continued next page)

Annual Expenditures

EXPENDITURES
55–64

(continued from previous page)

(average annual expenditure and percent distribution of expenditures for all households and for householders aged 55 to 64, number of households in thousands)

	all households		householder aged 55 to 64	
	average annual expenditure	percent of all expenditures	average annual expenditure	percent of all expenditures
Small appliances, miscellaneous housewares	55	0.2	69	0.3
Miscellaneous household equipment	256	1.1	250	1.1
Apparel	**1,149**	**5.1**	**1,125**	**4.7**
Men and boys	283	1.2	268	1.1
Men, 16 and over	228	1.0	238	1.0
Boys, 2 to 15	55	0.2	30	0.1
Women and girls	462	2.0	477	2.0
Women, 16 and over	396	1.7	447	1.9
Girls, 2 to 15	66	0.3	30	0.1
Children under 2	45	0.2	36	0.2
Footwear	123	0.5	118	0.5
Other apparel products and services	237	1.0	226	1.0
Transportation	**4,815**	**21.2**	**4,961**	**20.9**
Cars and trucks, new (net outlay)	1,414	6.2	1,465	6.2
Cars and trucks, used (net outlay)	897	3.9	795	3.3
Other vehicles	29	0.1	9	0.0
Vehicle finance charges	270	1.2	260	1.1
Gasoline and motor oil	916	4.0	1,019	4.3
Maintenance and repairs	458	2.0	511	2.1
Vehicle insurance	420	1.8	491	2.1
Public transportation	248	1.1	250	1.1
Vehicle rental, licenses, other charges	163	0.7	160	0.7
Health care	**1,062**	**4.7**	**1,303**	**5.5**
Health insurance	371	1.6	446	1.9
Medical services	502	2.2	598	2.5
Medicines and medical supplies	189	0.8	260	1.1
Entertainment	**1,087**	**4.8**	**1,060**	**4.5**
Fees and admissions	308	1.4	305	1.3
Television, radios, sound equipment	373	1.6	341	1.4
Other equipment and services	406	1.8	414	1.7
Personal care	**207**	**0.9**	**252**	**1.1**
Reading	**140**	**0.6**	**156**	**0.7**
Education	**298**	**1.3**	**235**	**1.0**
Tobacco and smoking supplies	**230**	**1.0**	**265**	**1.1**
Miscellaneous	**323**	**1.4**	**362**	**1.5**
Contributions and support payments	**746**	**3.3**	**1,046**	**4.4**
Personal insurance and pensions	**2,129**	**9.4**	**2,650**	**11.1**
Life insurance and other personal insurance	293	1.3	403	1.7
Retirement, pensions, Social Security	1,836	8.1	2,247	9.4

Source: The 1986 Consumer Expenditure Survey, Bureau of Labor Statistics

Expenditures by Income

EXPENDITURES
55–64

ABOVE AVERAGE SPENDERS

Households bringing in over $40,000 typically spend $21,000 more than the average household in this age group. Their housing expenses are $4,700 above the average and they spend $4,500 more than the average household on transportation.

(annual average expenditure of households with householders aged 55 to 64, by household income, number of households in thousands)

	all households	under $10,000	$10-14,999	$15-19,999	$20-29,999	$30-39,999	$40,000+
Number of households	11,397	3,158	1,462	1,150	1,749	1,305	2,573
Total expenditure	$24,089	$13,315	$16,257	$16,816	$22,371	$26,310	$45,062
Food	3,567	2,357	2,740	3,135	3,515	4,041	5,510
Food at home	2,473	1,836	2,057	2,321	2,479	2,757	3,411
Food away from home	1,094	522	683	815	1,036	1,283	2,099
Alcoholic beverages	247	123	153	145	240	294	480
Housing	6,410	4,383	4,529	4,821	5,772	6,372	11,131
Shelter	3,359	2,275	2,266	2,471	2,936	3,265	6,043
Owned dwellings	2,116	1,236	1,339	1,300	1,694	2,256	4,220
Rented dwellings	714	843	675	874	865	557	484
Other lodging	528	196	252	295	377	451	1,338
Fuels, utilities, public services	1,867	1,494	1,626	1,648	1,827	1,935	2,554
Household operations	277	178	129	142	220	173	636
Household furnishings, equipment	907	436	509	559	790	1,000	1,899
Apparel and services	1,131	548	704	714	994	1,188	2,341
Transportation	5,060	2,619	3,757	3,352	4,559	5,762	9,545
Vehicles	2,319	1,016	1,705	1,078	1,774	2,574	5,065
Gasoline and motor oil	1,083	700	920	924	1,149	1,342	1,539
Other vehicle expenses	1,379	722	987	1,179	1,373	1,568	2,406
Public transportation	279	181	144	172	261	278	535
Health care	1,319	942	1,164	1,326	1,253	1,284	1,929
Entertainment	1,052	446	580	557	1,214	1,129	2,134
Personal care	245	132	167	210	234	287	427

(continued next page)

Expenditures by Income

EXPENDITURES 55–64

(continued from previous page)

(annual average expenditure of households with householders aged 55 to 64, by household income, number of households in thousands)

	all households	under $10,000	$10-14,999	$15-19,999	$20-29,999	$30-39,999	$40,000+
Reading	159	90	111	132	153	205	265
Education	223	86	73	96	233	299	487
Tobacco and smoking supplies	260	227	225	248	288	248	314
Miscellaneous	381	241	334	239	271	452	683
Cash contributions	1,169	346	512	547	1,230	981	2,887
Personal insurance and pensions	2,866	774	1,209	1,293	2,414	3,767	6,929
Life and other insurance	399	291	265	188	319	490	711
Retirement, pensions, Social Security	2,467	483	945	1,105	2,095	3,278	6,219

Source: The 1986 Consumer Expenditure Survey, Bureau of Labor Statistics

Note: All households include complete income reporters only. Total expenditure exceeds total income in some income categories due to a number of factors including the underreporting of income, borrowing, and the use of savings.

Almanac of Consumer Markets

Weekly Shopping

EXPENDITURES
55–64

FISH AND FRUITS

These households spend 50 percent more than the average household on non-prescription drugs and supplies. Households headed by 55-to-64-year-olds are also above-average spenders on fish and seafood and fresh fruits.

(average weekly expenditure for all households and for householders aged 55 to 64)

	all households	index all households	householders aged 55 to 64	index householders aged 55 to 64
Food, total	$59.60	100	$60.28	101
Food at home, total	37.73	100	40.23	107
Cereals and cereal products	1.78	100	1.67	94
Bakery products	3.51	100	3.78	108
Beef	3.63	100	4.04	111
Pork	2.23	100	2.57	115
Other meats	1.52	100	1.63	107
Poultry	1.64	100	1.72	105
Fish and seafood	1.22	100	1.55	127
Eggs	0.57	100	0.59	104
Fresh milk and cream	2.35	100	2.27	97
Other dairy products	2.47	100	2.60	105
Fresh fruits	1.96	100	2.41	123
Fresh vegetables	1.77	100	2.10	119
Processed fruits	1.38	100	1.49	108
Processed vegetables	1.03	100	1.12	109
Sugar and other sweets	1.42	100	1.58	111
Fats and oils	0.99	100	1.14	115
Miscellaneous foods	4.53	100	4.15	92
Nonalcoholic beverages	3.71	100	3.84	104
Food away from home	21.87	100	20.05	92
Nonfood items				
Alcoholic beverages	4.84	100	4.41	91
Tobacco products and smoking supplies	3.60	100	3.85	107
Pet food	1.09	100	0.99	91
Personal care products and services	5.01	100	5.59	112
Non-prescription drugs and supplies	2.31	100	3.47	150
Housekeeping supplies	6.07	100	6.32	104

Source: The 1986 Consumer Expenditure Survey, Bureau of Labor Statistics

Note: An index of 100 represents the average. An index of 132 means that the average weekly expenditure of the subgroup is 32 percent above the average for all households. An index of 68 indicates spending that is 32 percent below average. Numbers may not add to total due to rounding.

Future Expenditures

EXPENDITURES
55–64

MARKET GROWS BY $38 BILLION

These pre-retirement households will spend an estimated 38 billion dollars more in 2000 than in 1990. This increased spending is due to the 13 percent rise in the number of households headed by 55-to-64-year-olds during the decade.

(projected aggregate expenditures in 1990 and 2000 for all households and for households by age of householder, in billions of dollars)

	all households	under 25	25-34	35-44	45-54	55-64	65-74	75+
Number of households (in thousands)	94,227	4,663	21,183	21,245	14,429	12,311	11,672	8,724
Total expenditures (in billions of dollars)	$2,203.1	$64.2	$476.6	$628.6	$441.2	$292.8	$197.2	$102.5
Food	330.8	9.4	70.3	93.7	64.1	43.9	32.3	17.2
Food at home	225.1	5.9	44.8	64.9	41.8	30.9	23.0	13.7
Food away from home	101.5	3.6	21.2	28.8	22.2	13.0	9.3	3.5
Alcoholic beverages	25.4	1.6	7.5	6.4	4.7	3.0	1.8	0.6
Housing	667.6	19.2	158.3	193.5	121.9	80.8	58.3	35.6
Shelter	385.6	12.4	97.2	115.7	71.7	42.4	28.8	17.5
Owned dwellings	229.7	1.8	50.3	75.8	46.9	28.2	17.9	8.7
Rented dwellings	115.2	9.5	41.6	27.6	13.1	8.4	7.2	7.6
Other lodging	40.8	1.0	5.2	12.2	11.6	5.8	3.7	1.2
Fuels, utilities, and public services	160.0	3.7	32.0	41.2	29.6	23.2	18.6	11.8
Household operations	34.2	0.7	9.6	10.2	3.8	3.7	2.9	3.3
Household furnishings, equipment	87.8	2.4	19.5	26.5	16.8	11.6	8.0	3.0
Apparel and services	111.0	4.1	24.6	33.7	22.8	13.8	8.3	3.6
Transportation	464.9	15.6	107.0	130.7	98.7	61.1	37.7	14.2
Health care	103.7	1.6	14.5	21.4	16.9	16.0	17.9	15.4
Entertainment	106.0	3.1	23.3	35.2	20.6	13.0	8.0	2.6
Personal care	20.1	0.6	3.7	5.2	3.8	3.1	2.3	1.3
Reading	13.6	0.3	2.6	3.8	2.6	1.9	1.6	0.8
Education	27.6	2.7	3.9	8.3	8.8	2.9	0.8	0.1
Tobacco and smoking supplies	22.0	0.8	4.9	5.8	4.5	3.3	2.0	0.7
Miscellaneous	31.5	0.6	6.5	8.1	5.9	4.5	3.6	2.3
Contributions and support payments	74.2	0.7	7.3	17.7	17.4	12.9	12.5	5.7
Personal insurance and pensions	208.9	3.9	46.4	65.2	48.5	32.6	10.0	2.3

(continued next page)

Future Expenditures

EXPENDITURES 55–64

(continued from previous page)

(projected aggregate expenditures in 2000 for all households and for households by age of householder, in billions of dollars)

	\multicolumn{7}{c}{2000 aggregate annual expenditures in billions}
	all households	under 25	25-34	35-44	45-54	55-64	65-74	75+
Number of households (in thousands)	105,933	4,442	18,004	25,339	21,603	13,903	11,516	11,126
Total expenditures (in billions of dollars)	$2,532.4	$61.1	$405.1	$749.7	$660.6	$330.6	$194.6	$130.7
Food	379.7	9.0	59.7	111.7	95.9	49.5	31.9	22.0
Food at home	258.9	5.6	38.1	77.4	62.6	34.9	22.7	17.5
Food away from home	117.2	3.4	18.0	34.3	33.2	14.7	9.1	4.5
Alcoholic beverages	28.3	1.5	6.4	7.6	7.0	3.4	1.7	0.7
Housing	760.3	18.3	134.5	230.8	182.5	91.3	57.5	45.3
Shelter	438.2	11.8	82.6	137.9	107.3	47.9	28.4	22.3
Owned dwellings	265.8	1.7	42.8	90.4	70.3	31.9	17.6	11.1
Rented dwellings	123.4	9.1	35.4	32.9	19.7	9.5	7.2	9.7
Other lodging	49.1	0.9	4.4	14.6	17.4	6.5	3.7	1.5
Fuels, utilities, and public services	183.6	3.5	27.2	49.1	44.3	26.2	18.3	15.0
Household operations	38.0	0.7	8.2	12.2	5.7	4.1	2.9	4.2
Household furnishings, equipment	100.5	2.3	16.6	31.6	25.2	13.1	7.9	3.8
Apparel and services	127.6	3.9	20.9	40.2	34.2	15.6	8.2	4.6
Transportation	533.7	14.8	90.9	155.9	147.7	69.0	37.2	18.1
Health care	120.0	1.5	12.4	25.5	25.3	18.1	17.7	19.6
Entertainment	121.7	3.0	19.8	42.0	30.9	14.7	7.9	3.3
Personal care	23.1	0.5	3.2	6.2	5.7	3.5	2.3	1.7
Reading	15.7	0.3	2.2	4.5	3.9	2.2	1.6	1.0
Education	33.2	2.6	3.3	10.0	13.1	3.3	0.8	0.2
Tobacco and smoking supplies	25.2	0.8	4.2	6.9	6.8	3.7	2.0	0.9
Miscellaneous	36.2	0.6	5.5	9.7	8.9	5.0	3.5	2.9
Contributions and support payments	88.2	0.6	6.2	21.1	26.0	14.5	12.3	7.3
Personal insurance and pensions	243.2	3.7	39.4	77.7	72.7	36.8	9.9	2.9

Source: *The 1986 Consumer Expenditure Survey*, Bureau of Labor Statistics and *Projections of the Number of Households and Families:1986 to 2000*, Bureau of the Census, Series P-25, No. 986

Note: Aggregate expenditures are the sum of the total expenditures of all households in the nation or of all households in an age group. Projections are based on the average annual expenditures in 1986 and have not been adjusted for inflation. Projections show how total annual expenditures would change as the number of households in the age group changes during the 1990s. All other factors such as price and expenditure pattern are held constant and are not accounted for in these projections.

Composition of Wealth

WEALTH
55–64

IT ALL ADDS UP

Households headed by 55-to-64-year-olds account for 15 percent of all household income but 22 percent of all household wealth. Three-quarters of households in this age group have equity in their home and they are more likely to hold every type of asset except checking, saving, and employer accounts.

(percentage of households with assets and debts and the mean value of owners' holdings in 1986 dollars, for all households and householders aged 55 to 64, numbers in thousands)

	percent owning		mean holdings of owners	
	all households	householder aged 55 to 64	all households	householder aged 55 to 64
Number of households	83,042	12,688	83,042	12,688
Assets				
Home	65.7%	74.9%	$80,650	$86,860
Other real estate	22.4	28.6	118,892	114,671
Public stock	19.3	23.0	81,367	85,310
Bonds	20.2	21.3	28,116	32,687
Checking and saving accounts	89.2	87.2	7,445	9,781
IRA's and Keoghs	27.3	41.4	18,752	23,015
CD's and money market	27.9	36.2	31,575	29,078
Business assets (net)	12.4	16.2	210,310	267,417
Automobiles	85.9	90.0	7,964	8,191
Employer accounts	14.8	12.5	26,704	57,285
Other*	45.7	48.1	22,282	29,685
Debts				
Mortgage, principle residence	38.40%	32.40%	$34,564	$25,005
Other debts	64.6	80.5	15,881	11,572

*Cash value of life insurance, trusts, and notes owned by individuals.

Source: The 1986 Survey of Consumer Finances, Federal Reserve Board

Note: Wealth here accounts for all major household assets and liabilities except for non-auto consumer durables, collectibles such as artwork, and the present value of expected future benefits from pensions or social security.

Household Savings

WEALTH
55–64

EYEING A RAINY DAY

In the three year period, 1983 to 1986, households headed by someone aged 55 to 64 had an increase in their net worth of $39,392. This savings is 10 percent of the total household income they received from 1983 to 1985 and represents about 21 percent of all household savings accumulated during those years.

(average household savings 1983 to 1986 in current dollars, share of total savings and percentage of 1983 to 1985 total household income that is savings for households by age of householder, marital status, race and Hispanic origin, homeownership status, and household income)

	average savings for 3 year period	share of total savings	median 3-year savings as a percentage of 1983-1985 median income
All households	$24,402	100.0%	9.7%
Age of householder			
under age 35	17,912	18.7	7.1
35 to 44	23,301	16.8	12.6
45 to 54	46,606	22.4	16.1
55 to 64	39,392	20.9	9.8
65 and older	33,867	21.3	5.9
Marital status			
Married	40,392	91.8	13.8
Singe male	9,242	3.2	3.1
Single female	6,405	5.0	2.8
Race			
White	34,913	97.8	11.4
Black/Hispanic	3,679	2.2	2.4
Homeownership status			
Homeowner	39,426	88.2	16.1
Renter	10,107	11.8	4.0
Household income			
Less than $10,000	871	0.5	0.0
$10,000 to $20,000	6,633	5.9	4.8
$20,000 to $50,000	18,835	27.2	15.8
$50,000 to $100,000	70,545	27.3	22.8
$100,000 and over	455,294	39.2	44.2

Source: The 1986 Survey of Consumer Finances, Federal Reserve Board

Note: Household savings is the difference in household net worth between 1986 and 1983, expressed in 1986 dollars. Net worth (wealth) is defined as gross assets minus gross debts. Net worth here accounts for all major household assets and liabilities except for non-auto consumer durables, collectibles such as artwork, and the present value of expected future benefits from pensions or social security.

Owners and Renters

WEALTH
55-64

LIVING THE DREAM

Homeownership peaks among householders aged 55 to 64—fully 80 percent of them live in their own home. As in the other age groups, white householders (82 percent) are more likely to be homeowners than are black (61 percent) or Hispanic (58 percent) householders.

(owner- and renter-occupied households by race of householder and household type, for householders aged 55 to 64, numbers in thousands, ownership status as of March 1988)

	total	white	black	Hispanic origin
All households	12,846	11,270	1,323	687
Owner households	10,228	9,244	805	400
Family households				
Married-couple	7,311	6,799	367	263
Male householder	253	213	29	20
Female householder	826	622	191	60
Nonfamily households				
Male householder	581	511	66	22
Female householder	1,257	1,098	152	36
Renter households	2,618	2,026	518	287
Family households				
Married-couple	905	765	101	97
Male householder	83	58	24	17
Female householder	329	203	120	53
Nonfamily households				
Male householder	564	441	107	48
Female householder	737	559	166	71

Source: Household and Family Characteristics: March 1988, *Bureau of the Census, Current Population Reports, Series P-20, No. 424*

Note: Hispanics are of any race. Numbers may not add to total due to rounding.

Health Status

HEALTH 55–64

A GOOD MAJORITY

Forty-seven percent of men and 44 percent of women aged 55 to 64 rate their health as excellent or very good. But 15 percent consider themselves in fair health and 8 percent say their health is poor. The proportion of 55-to-64-year-olds with poor health in the lowest income group is nearly 10 times greater than that proportion in the highest income group.

(self-assessed health status of persons aged 55 to 64, by sex, race and household income, number of persons in thousands)

	all persons	all health statuses	excellent	very good	good	fair	poor
Both sexes, all races	22,033	100.0%	20.9%	24.4%	32.1%	14.7%	7.9%
Male	10,345	100.0	22.6	24.0	31.0	14.1	8.2
Female	11,688	100.0	19.4	24.6	33.1	15.2	7.7
White	19,487	100.0	21.7	25.2	32.4	13.5	7.3
Black	2,079	100.0	12.1	17.2	28.5	26.9	15.2
Asian and other	466	100.0	28.8	19.2	36.1	11.8	4.1
Household income							
Less than $10,000	2,808	100.0%	8.7%	12.3%	28.0%	27.4%	23.7%
$10,000 to $19,999	4,341	100.0	14.4	22.1	33.6	19.5	10.4
$20,000 to $34,999	5,741	100.0	22.9	27.0	33.9	11.7	4.6
$35,000 and over	5,490	100.0	31.8	28.7	29.8	7.3	2.4

Source: The 1986 National Health Interview Survey, National Center for Health Statistics

Note: All persons includes those of unknown health status, all health statuses includes only those with known health status. Household income includes only those persons with known household income. Numbers may not add to total due to rounding.

Height

GROWING SHORTER

More than half of all women aged 35 and older are under 5'4" tall, as are 64 percent of women aged 55 to 64 and three-quarters of those aged 65 to 74. The average height of men aged 55 to 64 is 5'8"—one inch shorter than the average American man.

(cumulative percentage of height of males and females aged 55 to 64 and their average height, by race)

height, males	cumulative percentage	height, females	cumulative percentage
Less than 60 inches	0.3%	Less than 55 inches	0.3%
Less than 61 inches	0.7	Less than 56 inches	0.5
Less than 62 inches	0.9	Less than 57 inches	1.1
Less than 63 inches	2.8	Less than 58 inches	3.0
Less than 64 inches	5.3	Less than 59 inches	6.4
Less than 65 inches	9.3	Less than 60 inches	11.4
Less than 66 inches	17.5	Less than 61 inches	19.7
Less than 67 inches	29.1	Less than 62 inches	31.7
Less than 68 inches	43.5	Less than 63 inches	45.9
Less than 69 inches	58.2	Less than 64 inches	63.9
Less than 70 inches	71.5	Less than 65 inches	77.4
Less than 71 inches	83.1	Less than 66 inches	88.9
Less than 72 inches	91.0	Less than 67 inches	94.6
Less than 73 inches	96.3	Less than 68 inches	97.7
Less than 74 inches	97.7	Less than 69 inches	99.4
Less than 75 inches	98.9	Less than 70 inches	99.8
Less than 76 inches	99.8	Less than 71 inches	99.8
All height categories	100.0%	All height categories	100.0%
Average height, all races	**68.4 inches**	**Average height, all races**	**63.0 inches**
White	68.4	White	63.0
Black	68.6	Black	63.4

Source: Anthropometric Reference Data and Prevalence of Overweight: United States, 1976-80, *National Center for Health Statistics, National Health Survey Series 11, No. 238.*

Note: Height is without shoes.

Weight

HEALTH
55–64

LIGHTER MEN

Thirty-seven percent of women and 28 percent of men aged 55 to 64 weigh more than the weight to height (overweight) standard of the National Center for Health Statistics. The average 55-to-65-year-old woman weighs 150 pounds and the average man in this age group weighs 174 pounds—four pounds less than the average weight of men aged 45 to 54.

(cumulative percentage of weight of males and females aged 55 to 64, and their average weight and percent overweight, by race)

weight, males	cumulative percentage	weight, females	cumulative percentage
Less than 100 pounds	0.1%	Less than 90 pounds	0.5%
Less than 110 pounds	0.7	Less than 100 pounds	2.1
Less than 120 pounds	1.4	Less than 110 pounds	6.9
Less than 130 pounds	4.1	Less than 120 pounds	15.7
Less than 140 pounds	9.5	Less than 130 pounds	29.0
Less than 150 pounds	19.5	Less than 140 pounds	43.4
Less than 160 pounds	32.3	Less than 150 pounds	56.9
Less than 170 pounds	47.9	Less than 160 pounds	67.8
Less than 180 pounds	62.5	Less than 170 pounds	77.4
Less than 190 pounds	75.8	Less than 180 pounds	83.8
Less than 200 pounds	85.2	Less than 190 pounds	88.7
Less than 210 pounds	90.6	Less than 200 pounds	92.5
Less than 220 pounds	93.4	Less than 220 pounds	96.7
Less than 230 pounds	96.3	Less than 240 pounds	98.2
Less than 240 pounds	98.1	Less than 260 pounds	99.4
Less than 250 pounds	98.4	Less than 280 pounds	99.7
All weight categories	100.0%	All weight categories	100.0%
Average weight, all races	**173.7 pounds**	**Average weight, all races**	**149.6 pounds**
White	174.0	White	148.1
Black	173.3	Black	167.2
Percent overweight, all races	**28.1%**	**Percent overweight, all races**	**37.0%**
White	28.6	White	34.8
Black	26.0	Black	59.4
Percent severely overweight, all races	**9.2%**	**Percent severely overweight, all races**	**14.2%**
White	8.7	White	13.5
Black	12.8	Black	23.3

Source: Anthropometric Reference Data and Prevalence of Overweight: United States, 1976-80, *National Center for Health Statistics, National Health Survey Series 11, No. 238.*

Notes: Weight includes clothing weight, estimated as ranging from 0.20 to 0.62 pounds. Overweight is defined in terms of a body mass index which is determined by dividing weight in kilograms by height in meters squared. Overweight people have a body mass index equal to or greater than that at the 85th percentile of men and women aged 20 to 29. Severe overweight means a body mass index equal to or greater than at the 95th percentile of men and women aged 20 to 29.

Acute Conditions

HEALTH
55–64

SPRAINS AND STRAINS

Flus, colds, and sprains and strains are the most frequently reported ailments of men aged 55 to 64. Women in this age group say they suffer from flus, colds and other respiratory infections. Fourth on the women's list of common problems is sprains and strains.

(number of acute conditions reported in a year for all persons and those aged 55 to 64, by sex, numbers in thousands)

	males all ages	males aged 55 to 64	females all ages	females aged 55 to 64
All acute conditions	191,369	10,236	257,177	16,593
Infective and parasitic diseases	23,122	303	31,244	1,477
Common childhood diseases	2,565	0	1,876	0
Intestinal virus, unspecified	4,244	105	5,288	291
Viral infections, unspecified	9,621	97	14,273	777
Other	6,692	101	9,807	408
Respiratory conditions	99,216	5,864	129,626	8,391
Common cold	30,445	1,827	32,983	1,336
Other acute upper respiratory infections	8,472	187	13,320	920
Influenza	55,256	3,469	75,295	5,700
Acute bronchitis	1,960	224	4,315	184
Pneumonia	1,365	0	1,277	164
Other respiratory conditions	1,718	156	2,435	88
Digestive system conditions	5,860	285	9,112	274
Dental conditions	1,059	0	1,955	0
Indigestion, nausea and vomiting	3,299	102	4,670	156
Other digestive conditions	1,502	183	2,487	118
Injuries	34,588	2,338	29,706	1,803
Fractures and dislocations	4,367	300	3,978	407
Sprains and strains	6,127	746	6,208	673
Open wounds and lacerations	11,153	638	5,094	115
Contusions and superficial injuries	7,986	448	7,191	184
Other current injuries	4,955	206	7,235	424

(continued next page)

Acute Conditions

HEALTH 55–64

(continued from previous page)

(number of acute conditions reported in a year for all persons and those aged 55 to 64, by sex, numbers in thousands)

	males all ages	males aged 55 to 64	females all ages	females aged 55 to 64
Selected other acute conditions	21,183	835	40,385	2,399
Eye conditions	1,072	0	2,080	467
Acute ear infections	8,689	169	10,116	98
Other ear conditions	1,884	0	2,193	99
Acute urinary conditions	989	189	4,399	297
Disorders of menstruation	–	–	2,251	–
Other disorders of female genital tract	–	–	2,174	0
Delivery and other conditions of pregnancy	–	–	4,466	–
Skin conditions	2,065	0	3,597	482
Acute musculoskeletal conditions	3,038	386	3,972	663
Headache, excluding migraine	1,253	90	2,461	292
Fever, unspecified	2,192	0	2,675	0
All other acute conditions	7,400	612	17,104	2,249

Source: The 1986 National Health Interview Survey, National Center for Health Statistics

Note: An acute condition is defined by The National Health Interview Survey as an illness or injury that usually lasts less than three months and was first noticed less than three months before the respondent's interview. The acute condition must also have caused the person to restrict activities for at least a half a day or to have contacted a physician. The data are based only on information given by the respondent and are subject to recall and selective reporting error. Numbers may not add to total due to rounding.

Chronic Conditions

HEALTH
55–64

ARTHRITIS AND HIGH BLOOD PRESSURE

Arthritis is the number one chronic condition reported by men and women aged 55 to 64 and high blood pressure is their second chronic health concern. Women in this age group are also likely to suffer from sinusitis, hearing impairments, and hay fever. Additional common ailments of the men are hearing impairments, sinusitis, and back deformities.

(number of selected chronic conditions reported in a year for all persons and those aged 55 to 64, by sex, numbers in thousands)

	males all ages	males aged 55 to 64	females all ages	females aged 55 to 64
Selected skin and musculoskeletal conditions				
Arthritis	10,751	3,129	20,160	4,646
Gout, including gouty arthritis	1,515	459	713	247
Intervertebral disc disorders	2,522	585	1,645	413
Bone spur or tendonitis, unspecified	781	217	898	358
Disorders of bone or cartilage	449	44	943	162
Trouble with bunions	594	119	2,321	460
Bursitis, unclassified	1,641	488	2,464	602
Sebaceous skin cyst	640	71	881	210
Trouble with acne	2,193	0	2,116	49
Psoriasis	1,069	89	1,262	164
Dermatitis	3,851	282	5,696	489
Trouble with dry, itching skin, unclassified	1,994	248	2,606	315
Trouble with ingrown nails	2,352	432	3,030	346
Trouble with corns and calluses	1,669	396	3,164	422
Impairments				
Visual impairment	4,994	688	3,358	433
Color blindness	2,694	306	272	42
Cataracts	1,534	245	3,497	512
Glaucoma	735	239	967	173
Hearing impairment	11,727	2,201	9,004	1,487
Tinnitus	3,388	731	2,927	549
Speech impairment	1,924	177	871	43
Absence of extremity(s)	374	107	24	0
Paralysis, entire body, one side of body, or both legs	200	63	152	68
Partial paralysis of body or legs	236	45	99	45
Deformity of back	6,812	1,090	9,676	932
Deformity of upper extremities	1,622	244	1,475	262
Deformity of lower extremities	6,454	775	5,739	591
Selected digestive conditions				
Ulcer	2,116	353	2,378	390
Hernia of abdominal cavity	2,300	481	2,283	577
Gastritis or duodenitis	1,080	207	1,813	324

(continued next page)

Chronic Conditions

HEALTH 55–64

(continued from previous page)

(number of selected chronic conditions reported in a year for all persons and those aged 55 to 64, by sex, numbers in thousands)

	males all ages	males aged 55 to 64	females all ages	females aged 55 to 64
Frequent indigestion	2,504	411	2,811	440
Enteritis or colitis	574	109	1,820	286
Spastic colon	264	21	1,377	166
Diverticula of intestines	404	110	1,508	326
Frequent constipation	1,002	82	3,537	270
Selected conditions of the genitourinary, nervous, endocrine, metabolic, and blood system				
Goiter or other disorders of the thyroid	420	128	2,789	589
Diabetes	2,949	933	3,635	867
Anemias	570	43	2,617	137
Epilepsy	656	66	863	117
Migraine headache	2,068	186	6,448	709
Neuralgia or neuritis, unspecified	215	51	364	97
Kidney trouble	1,305	215	2,662	556
Bladder disorders	516	46	3,253	530
Diseases of prostate	1,281	383	–	–
Inflammatory female genital diseases	–	–	427	0
Noninflammatory female genital diseases	–	–	1,095	64
Menstrual disorders	–	–	2,097	0
Selected circulatory conditions				
Ischemic heart disease	4,091	1,057	2,809	509
Tachycardia or rapid heart	700	73	1,226	103
Heart murmurs	1,310	40	2,583	258
Other heart rhythm disorders	499	92	800	227
Other heart diseases	1,482	333	2,265	309
High blood pressure (hypertension)	12,512	2,866	16,457	3,632
Cerebrovascular disease	1,156	255	1,646	376
Hardening of the arteries	1,428	545	1,225	157
Varicose veins	1,042	217	5,814	1,032
Hemorrhoids	4,568	899	5,341	934
Selected respiratory conditions				
Chronic bronchitis	4,707	530	6,671	682
Asthma	4,670	437	5,019	484
Hay fever or allergic rhinitis without asthma	10,136	588	11,566	1,056
Chronic sinusitis	14,636	1,579	19,749	2,456
Deviated nasal septum	825	193	465	23
Chronic disease of tonsils or adenoids	1,071	23	2,068	21
Emphysema	1,201	432	796	216

Source: The 1986 National Health Interview Survey, National Center for Health Statistics

Note: Chronic conditions are defined by the National Health Interview Survey as conditions that either a) were first noticed three months or more before the date of the interview or b) belong to a group of conditions (such as heart disease or diabetes) that are considered chronic regardless of when they began. Totals for all chronic conditions are not shown because the National Health Interview Survey does not measure the total number of chronic conditions for each person. The data are based only on information given by the respondent and are subject to recall and selective reporting error.

Activity Restrictions

HEALTH
55–64

INCOME AND WELL-BEING

Men and women aged 55 to 64 with household incomes of $35,000 or more have at least seven fewer bed days a year due to illness and injury than those from households with incomes under $20,000. Fewer work-loss days are also reported by 55-to-64-year-olds in higher income categories.

(number of days of activity restriction reported in a year and per person due to acute and chronic conditions, by type of restriction and sex, race, and household income, for all persons and those aged 55 to 64, numbers in thousands)

	number of days per year		number of days per person	
	bed day	work-loss day	bed day	work-loss day
All ages	1,547,980	833,396	6.5	5.4
Male	613,113	401,503	5.4	4.8
Female	934,867	431,892	7.7	6.0
White	1,298,039	716,187	6.5	5.4
Black	220,102	99,332	7.7	5.4
Household income				
Less than $10,000	384,962	90,268	11.5	6.1
$10,000 to $19,999	346,115	162,604	7.7	6.1
$20,000 to $34,999	326,166	254,563	5.2	5.7
$35,000 and over	275,957	232,139	4.3	4.6
All aged 55 to 64	215,240	80,120	9.8	6.7
Male	82,117	44,850	7.9	6.6
Female	133,122	35,270	11.4	6.9
White	185,897	71,850	9.5	6.8
Black	26,837	6,546	12.9	6.3
Household income				
Less than $10,000	62,127	7,424	22.1	8.8
$10,000 to $19,999	53,038	21,474	12.2	10.9
$20,000 to $34,999	43,434	22,280	7.6	6.6
$35,000 and over	27,536	20,766	5.0	5.4

Source: The 1986 National Health Interview Survey, National Center for Health Statistics

Note: Numbers may not add to total due to rounding. A bed day is one during which a person stayed in bed more than half a day because of illness or injury. All hospital days for inpatients are considered bed days even if the patient was not in bed more than half a day. A work-loss day is one on which a currently employed person aged 18 or older missed more than half a day of work. The data are based only on information given by the respondent and are subject to recall and selective reporting error.

Cause of Death

HEALTH
55–64

CANCER AND HEART DISEASES

Thirty-five percent of all deaths of 55-to-64-year-olds are from cancer and another 34 percent are caused by heart diseases. Together, the ten leading causes of death account for 88 percent of all deaths in this age group. The average remaining lifetime for people aged 55 to 60 is 24.4 years and 20.5 years for those aged 60 to 65.

(ten leading causes of death among persons aged 55 to 64)

	number of deaths persons aged 55 to 64	number of deaths all ages	percent accounted for by persons aged 55 to 64
All causes	279,029	2,105,361	13.3%
Malignant neoplasms (cancer)	98,805	469,376	21.1
Heart diseases	94,312	765,490	12.3
Cerebrovascular diseases	11,780	149,643	7.9
Chronic obstructive pulmonary diseases and allied conditions	10,485	76,559	13.7
Accidents and adverse effects	7,728	95,277	8.1
Chronic liver disease and cirrhosis	7,163	26,159	27.4
Diabetes mellitus	5,780	37,184	15.5
Pneumonia and influenza	4,144	69,812	5.9
Suicide	3,782	30,904	12.2
Nephritis, nephrotic syndrome, and nephrosis (kidney disorders)	2,115	21,767	9.7
All other causes	32,935	363,190	9.1

Source: Advance Report of Final Mortality Statistics, 1986, *National Center for Health Statistics, Vol. 37, No. 6*

Chapter 8

CONSUMERS AGED 65 TO 74

The number of these active retirees will drop slightly during the 1990s but they will be setting trends of the future.

The number of 65-to-74-year-olds will shrink during the 1990s along with the number of households they head.

- Between 1990 and 2000, the number of people aged 65 to 74 will decline about 1 percent, dropping them from 7.2 percent of the American population to 6.5 percent.

- The number of households headed by members of this age group will dwindle by about 1 percent during the 1990s.

- Families are the rule among 65-to-74-year-olds—60 percent of the households they head are families and over half of them are married couples.

- The three million women who live alone account for almost 75 percent of nonfamily households in this age group.

- Although most of their peers are retired, 16 percent of men and 7 percent of women are still in the work force when they are aged 65 and older. Their labor force participation is expected to decline during the 1990s.

- The median household income of households headed by 65-to-74-year-olds is $16,900. Married couples have a median income of $22,900 and dual-earner married couples come out on top with a median income of $37,200.

- Households headed by a 65-to-74-year-old devote a larger chunk of their spending dollar to food, health care, personal care, and contributions than the average household.

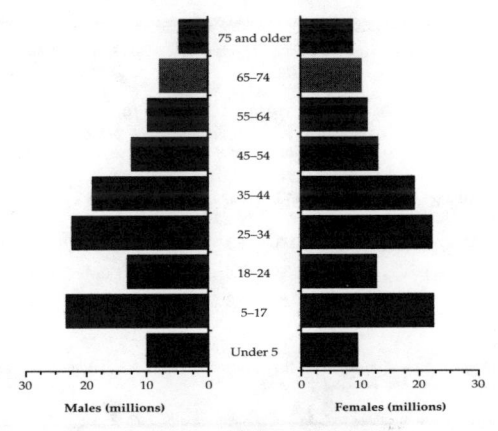

1990

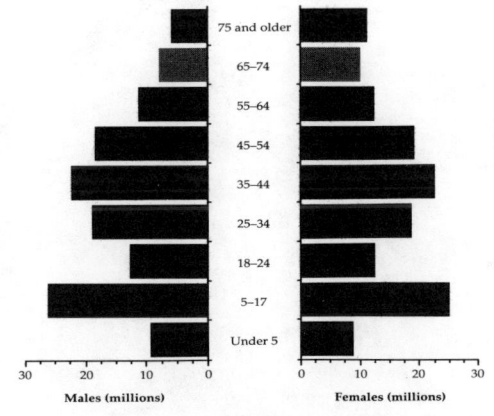

2000

Share of Total Population

POPULATION
65–74

FEWER RETIREES

The number of 65-to-74-year-olds will decline, though not sharply, during the 1990s, dropping them from 7.2 percent of the population in 1990 to 6.5 percent by 2000.

(total population and the number of persons aged 65 to 74, in thousands, by sex, 1960 to 1980, and projections for 1990 to 2000)

	1960 number	1960 percent of total	1970 number	1970 percent of total	1980 number	1980 percent of total	1990 number	1990 percent of total	1995 number	1995 percent of total	2000 number	2000 percent of total
All ages	180,671	100.0%	205,052	100.0%	227,757	100.0%	252,293	100.0%	264,077	100.0%	274,479	100.0%
All aged 65 to 74	11,053	6.1	12,493	6.1	15,653	6.9	18,117	7.2	18,634	7.1	17,860	6.5
Males	5,133	2.8	5,461	2.7	6,791	3.0	7,894	3.1	8,130	3.1	7,840	2.9
Females	5,920	3.3	7,032	3.4	8,862	3.9	10,223	4.1	10,503	4.0	10,020	3.7

Source: Annual Projections of the Population by Age, Sex, and Race, for the United States: 1983 to 2080, *Bureau of the Census, Current Population Reports, Series 17 and the Bureau of the Census*

Note: Total population includes Armed Forces overseas; 1960 to 1980 are based on censuses; projections are based on the Census Bureau's Series 17 projections that incorporate illegal immigration and higher levels of emigration than other Census Bureau projections. Series 17 is consistent with current estimates of illegal aliens living in the United States. Numbers may not add to total due to rounding.

Sex, Race, and Ethnicity

POPULATION
65–74

MORE NONWHITES AND HISPANICS

The number of whites will decrease during the 1990s, falling from 86 to 82 percent of 65-to-74-year-olds. Hispanics and Asians, on the other hand, will increase in number by more than 50 percent during the decade, bringing blacks from 8 to 9 percent of the age group, Hispanics from 4 to 6 percent, and Asians from 2 to 3 percent.

(projections of the total population and persons aged 65 to 74, in thousands, by sex, race, and Hispanic origin, 1990 to 2000)

	1990	1995	2000	percent change 1990–2000
All ages	252,293	264,077	274,479	8.8%
White	191,594	195,347	197,634	3.2
Black	30,915	33,237	35,440	14.6
Hispanic	21,854	25,991	30,295	38.6
Asians and other races	7,930	9,502	11,110	40.1
All aged 65 to 74	18,117	18,634	17,860	-1.4
White	15,578	15,694	14,636	-6.0
Black	1,451	1,543	1,565	7.9
Hispanic	713	910	1,070	50.2
Asians and other races	374	487	589	57.5
All males aged 65 to 74	7,894	8,130	7,840	-0.7
White	6,834	6,923	6,524	-4.5
Black	586	605	602	2.7
Hispanic	315	404	474	50.5
Asians and other races	159	198	240	50.9
All females aged 65 to 74	10,223	10,503	10,020	-2.0
White	8,743	8,771	8,110	-7.2
Black	867	937	962	11.0
Hispanic	398	505	596	49.7
Asians and other races	214	290	352	64.5

Source: Projections of the Population of the United States by Age, Sex, and Race: 1983 to 2080, Bureau of the Census, Current Population Reports, Series P-25, No. 952, Series 17

Note: Series 17 projections incorporate illegal immigration and higher levels of emigration than other Census Bureau projections and are consistent with current estimates of illegal aliens living in the United States. Total population includes Armed Forces living overseas. In this table Hispanics have been separated out of the racial groups; categories do not overlap. Numbers may not add to total due to rounding.

State Populations

POPULATION
65–74

GROWTH IN TWENTY STATES

Although the number of 65-to-74-year-olds will dwindle during the 1990s, 20 states will see growth, most notably Alaska, Arizona, Hawaii, Texas, Georgia, and New Mexico. Those states will each have at least 12 percent more people aged 65 to 74 in 2000 than in 1990.

(resident population and the number of persons aged 65 to 74, in thousands, in Census Bureau divisions and states in 1980 and projections for 1990 to 2010)

Note: Inconsistencies between the data in this table and the preceding two tables are due to different assumptions about immigration and emigration on which the projections are based and the inclusion of Armed Forces overseas in the total population. This table is based on the resident population only.

	census 1980	projections 1990	2000	2010	percent change 1990–2000	percent change 2000–2010
All ages	226,546	249,891	267,747	282,055	7.1%	5.3%
All aged 65 to 74	15,580	18,373	18,243	21,039	-0.7	15.3
New England	**895**	**1,027**	**943**	**1,033**	**-8.2**	**9.5**
Connecticut	219	266	245	270	-7.9	10.2
Maine	82	92	87	96	-5.4	10.3
Massachusetts	423	472	423	449	-10.4	6.1
New Hampshire	61	75	79	99	5.3	25.3
Rhode Island	75	86	75	80	-12.8	6.7
Vermont	34	37	35	41	-5.4	17.1
Middle Atlantic	**2,767**	**3,095**	**2,838**	**2,955**	**-8.3**	**4.1**
New Jersey	531	643	626	688	-2.6	9.9
New York	1,293	1,381	1,297	1,363	-6.1	5.1
Pennsylvania	944	1,072	915	904	-14.6	-1.2
East North Central	**2,705**	**3,057**	**2,770**	**2,919**	**-9.4**	**5.4**
Illinois	762	832	752	797	-9.6	6.0
Indiana	351	398	368	394	-7.5	7.1
Michigan	556	650	583	617	-10.3	5.8
Ohio	707	821	739	756	-10.0	2.3
Wisconsin	331	354	328	356	-7.3	8.5

(continued on next page)

State Populations

POPULATION 65–74

(continued from previous page)

(resident population and the number of persons aged 65 to 74, in thousands, in Census Bureau divisions and states in 1980 and projections for 1990 to 2010)

	census 1980	projections 1990	2000	2010	percent change 1990–2000	percent change 2000–2010
All ages	226,546	249,891	267,747	282,055	7.1%	5.3%
All aged 65 to 74	15,580	18,373	18,243	21,039	-0.7	15.3
West North Central	**1,251**	**1,322**	**1,245**	**1,352**	**-5.8**	**8.6**
Iowa	215	219	188	189	-14.2	0.5
Kansas	173	187	178	191	-4.8	7.3
Minnesota	270	297	287	330	-3.4	15.0
Missouri	381	401	390	433	-2.7	11.0
Nebraska	114	118	111	115	-5.9	3.6
North Dakota	47	47	42	42	-10.6	0.0
South Dakota	51	54	49	50	-9.3	2.0
South Atlantic	**2,763**	**3,552**	**3,822**	**4,626**	**7.6**	**21.0**
Delaware	36	51	52	57	2.0	9.6
District of Columbia	46	47	44	48	-6.4	9.1
Florida	1,059	1,422	1,590	1,904	11.8	19.7
Georgia	331	405	459	601	13.3	30.9
Maryland	247	323	329	398	1.9	21.0
North Carolina	388	494	538	647	8.9	20.3
South Carolina	189	247	255	315	3.2	23.5
Virginia	318	411	429	527	4.4	22.8
West Virginia	147	151	128	130	-15.2	1.6
East South Central	**1,031**	**1,126**	**1,139**	**1,323**	**1.2**	**16.2**
Alabama	278	304	312	359	2.6	15.1
Kentucky	249	269	259	292	-3.7	12.7
Mississippi	180	186	190	225	2.2	18.4
Tennessee	323	367	377	448	2.7	18.8
West South Central	**1,520**	**1,753**	**1,884**	**2,286**	**7.5**	**21.3**
Arkansas	192	202	199	235	-1.5	18.1
Louisiana	255	285	282	320	-1.1	13.5
Oklahoma	225	235	234	272	-0.4	16.2
Texas	847	1,030	1,169	1,458	13.5	24.7

(continued on next page)

State Populations

POPULATION
65–74

(continued from previous page)

(resident population and the number of persons aged 65 to 74, in thousands, in Census Bureau divisions and states in 1980 and projections for 1990 to 2010)

	census 1980	1990	projections 2000	2010	percent change 1990–2000	percent change 2000–2010
All ages	226,546	249,891	267,747	282,055	7.1%	5.3%
All aged 65 to 74	15,580	18,373	18,243	21,039	-0.7	15.3
Mountain	**672**	**902**	**977**	**1,247**	**8.3**	**27.6**
Arizona	202	305	357	458	17.0	28.3
Colorado	149	192	209	266	8.9	27.3
Idaho	58	66	60	78	-9.1	30.0
Montana	52	58	51	59	-12.1	15.7
Nevada	46	74	81	109	9.5	34.6
New Mexico	75	100	112	142	12.0	26.8
Utah	68	83	86	108	3.6	25.6
Wyoming	23	23	21	27	-8.7	28.6
Pacific	**1,976**	**2,538**	**2,625**	**3,298**	**3.4**	**25.6**
Alaska	8	16	19	26	18.8	36.8
California	1,471	1,918	2,033	2,531	6.0	24.5
Hawaii	49	81	93	113	14.8	21.5
Oregon	184	206	179	231	-13.1	29.1
Washington	263	318	301	395	-5.3	31.2

Source: Projections of the Population of States by Age, Sex and Race: 1988 to 2010, *Bureau of the Census, Current Population Reports, Series P-25, No. 1017*

Note: Numbers may not add to total due to rounding.

State-by-State Changes

POPULATION
65–74

THE BIG FOUR

Four states—California, Florida, New York, and Texas—will be home to one-third of all Americans aged 65 to 74 by 2000.

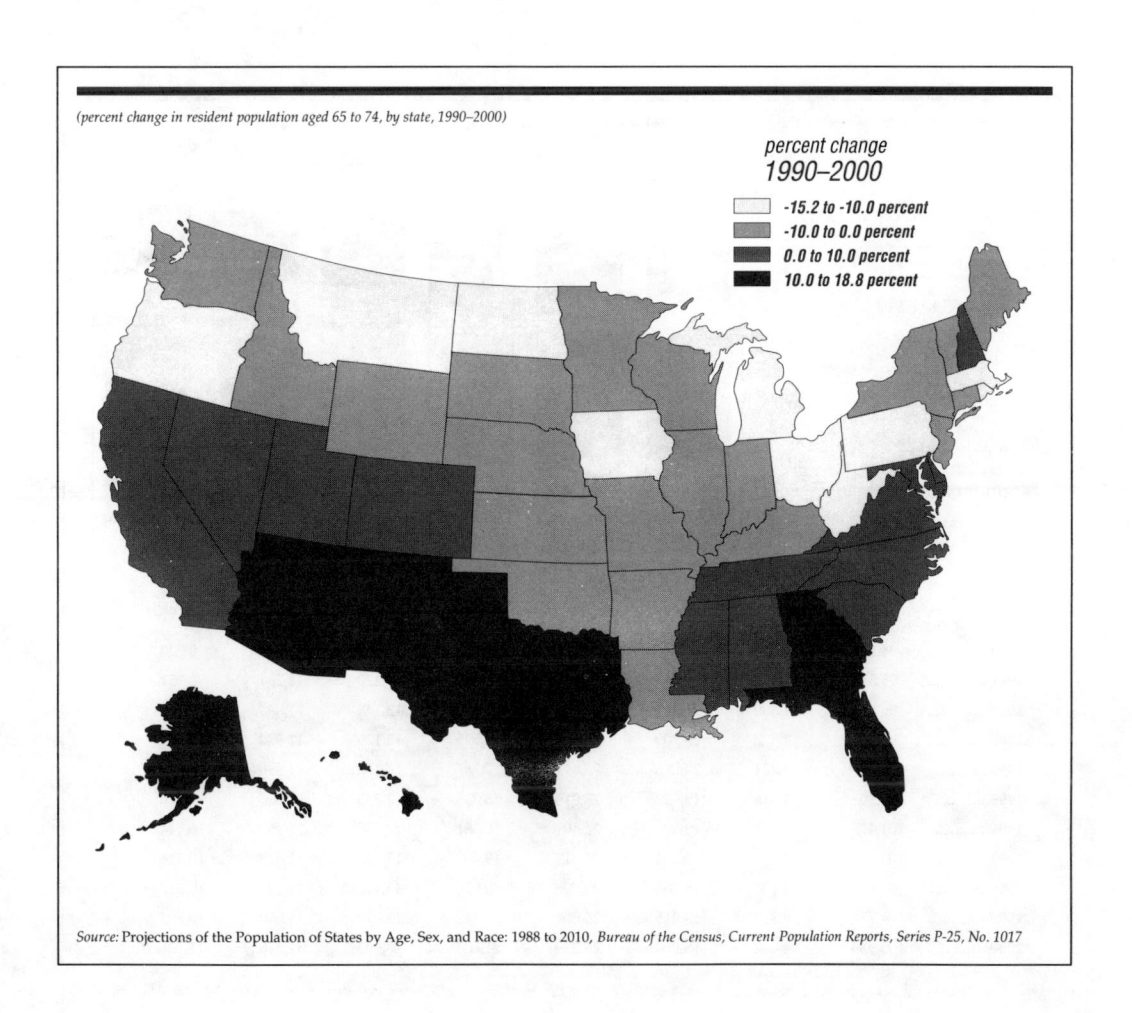

(percent change in resident population aged 65 to 74, by state, 1990–2000)

percent change
1990–2000

- -15.2 to -10.0 percent
- -10.0 to 0.0 percent
- 0.0 to 10.0 percent
- 10.0 to 18.8 percent

Source: Projections of the Population of States by Age, Sex, and Race: 1988 to 2010, *Bureau of the Census, Current Population Reports, Series P-25, No. 1017*

Number of Households

HOUSEHOLDS
65–74

AGING DEPRESSION CHILDREN

The number of householders aged 65 to 74 will decline during the 1990s as the relatively small generation born during the late 1920s and early 1930s moves into this age group. There will be 156,000 fewer households headed by 65-to-74-year-olds in 2000 than in 1990.

(number of households, in thousands, by age of householder, 1990–2000)

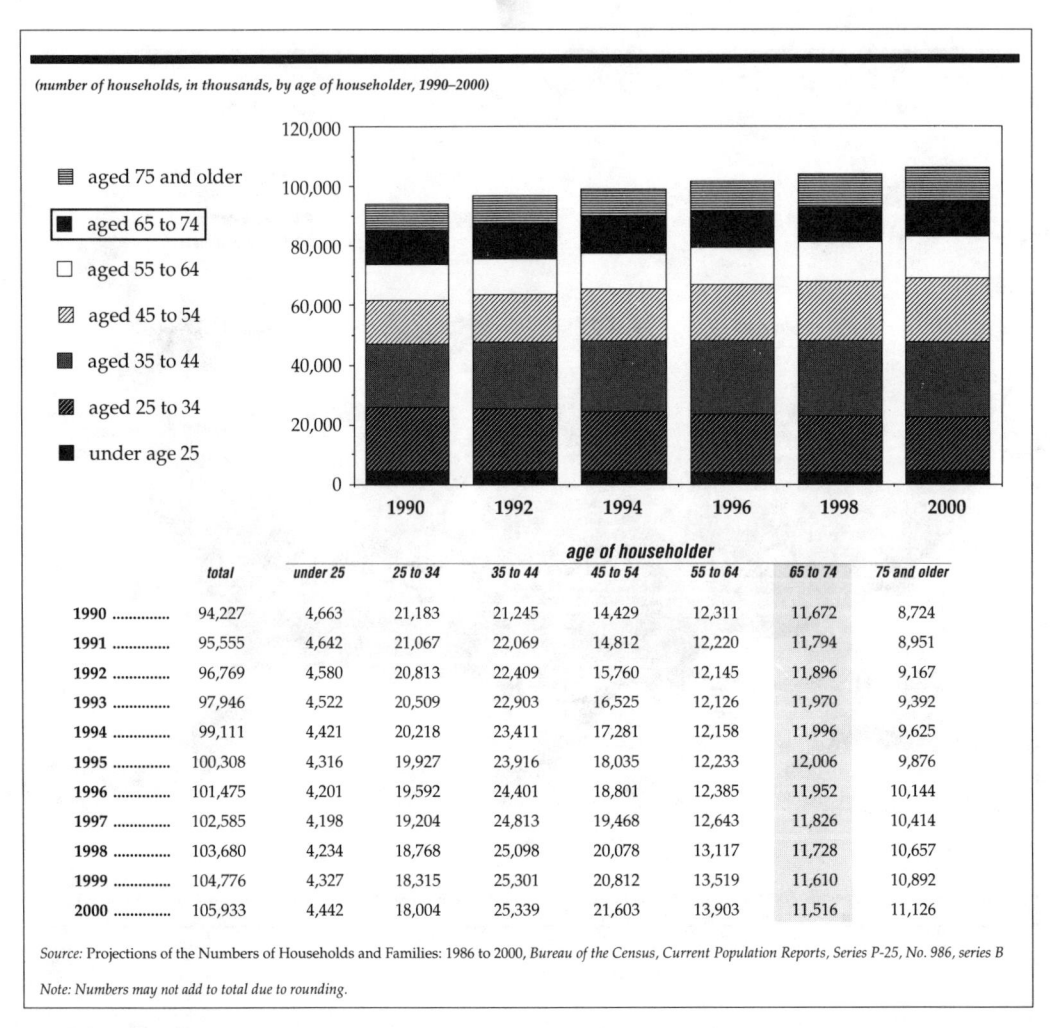

- aged 75 and older
- aged 65 to 74
- aged 55 to 64
- aged 45 to 54
- aged 35 to 44
- aged 25 to 34
- under age 25

	total	under 25	25 to 34	35 to 44	45 to 54	55 to 64	65 to 74	75 and older
1990	94,227	4,663	21,183	21,245	14,429	12,311	11,672	8,724
1991	95,555	4,642	21,067	22,069	14,812	12,220	11,794	8,951
1992	96,769	4,580	20,813	22,409	15,760	12,145	11,896	9,167
1993	97,946	4,522	20,509	22,903	16,525	12,126	11,970	9,392
1994	99,111	4,421	20,218	23,411	17,281	12,158	11,996	9,625
1995	100,308	4,316	19,927	23,916	18,035	12,233	12,006	9,876
1996	101,475	4,201	19,592	24,401	18,801	12,385	11,952	10,144
1997	102,585	4,198	19,204	24,813	19,468	12,643	11,826	10,414
1998	103,680	4,234	18,768	25,098	20,078	13,117	11,728	10,657
1999	104,776	4,327	18,315	25,301	20,812	13,519	11,610	10,892
2000	105,933	4,442	18,004	25,339	21,603	13,903	11,516	11,126

Source: Projections of the Numbers of Households and Families: 1986 to 2000, Bureau of the Census, Current Population Reports, Series P-25, No. 986, series B

Note: Numbers may not add to total due to rounding.

Types of Households

HOUSEHOLDS
65–74

FAMILIES STILL THE RULE

Families are still the rule among 65-to-74-year-olds—62 percent of them live in families. The more than three million women who live alone account for almost 75 percent of nonfamily households in this age group.

(household types for all households and for householders aged 65 to 74, numbers in thousands)

	all households total	percent of households in category	householder aged 65 to 74 total	percent of households in category
All households	91,066	100.0%	11,411	100.0%
Family households	65,133	71.5	7,021	61.5
Married couple	51,809	56.9	5,988	52.5
With children under age 18 at home	24,600	27.0	114	1.0
Without children under age 18 at home	27,209	29.9	5,874	51.5
Female householder	10,608	11.6	806	7.1
With children under age 18 at home	6,273	6.9	17	0.1
Without children under age 18 at home	4,335	4.8	789	6.9
Male householder	2,715	3.0	226	2.0
With children under age 18 at home	1,047	1.1	8	0.1
Without children under age 18 at home	1,669	1.8	218	1.9
Nonfamily households	25,993	28.5	4,390	38.5
Living alone	21,889	24.0	4,243	37.2
Female householder	13,101	14.4	3,229	28.3
Male householder	8,788	9.7	1,014	8.9
Living with others	4,044	4.4	147	1.3
Female householder	1,523	1.7	76	0.7
Male householder	2,521	2.8	72	0.6

Source: The 1988 Current Population Survey, Bureau of the Census

Note: Numbers may not add to total due to rounding.

Future Household Types

HOUSEHOLDS
65–74

STABLE HOUSEHOLDS

Although there will be fewer 65-to-74-year-old householders in 2000 than in 1990, there will be a 9 percent gain in the number of elderly men who head nonfamily groups. These are the children of the Great Depression entering the 1990s and their household structure is relatively stable compared with younger age groups.

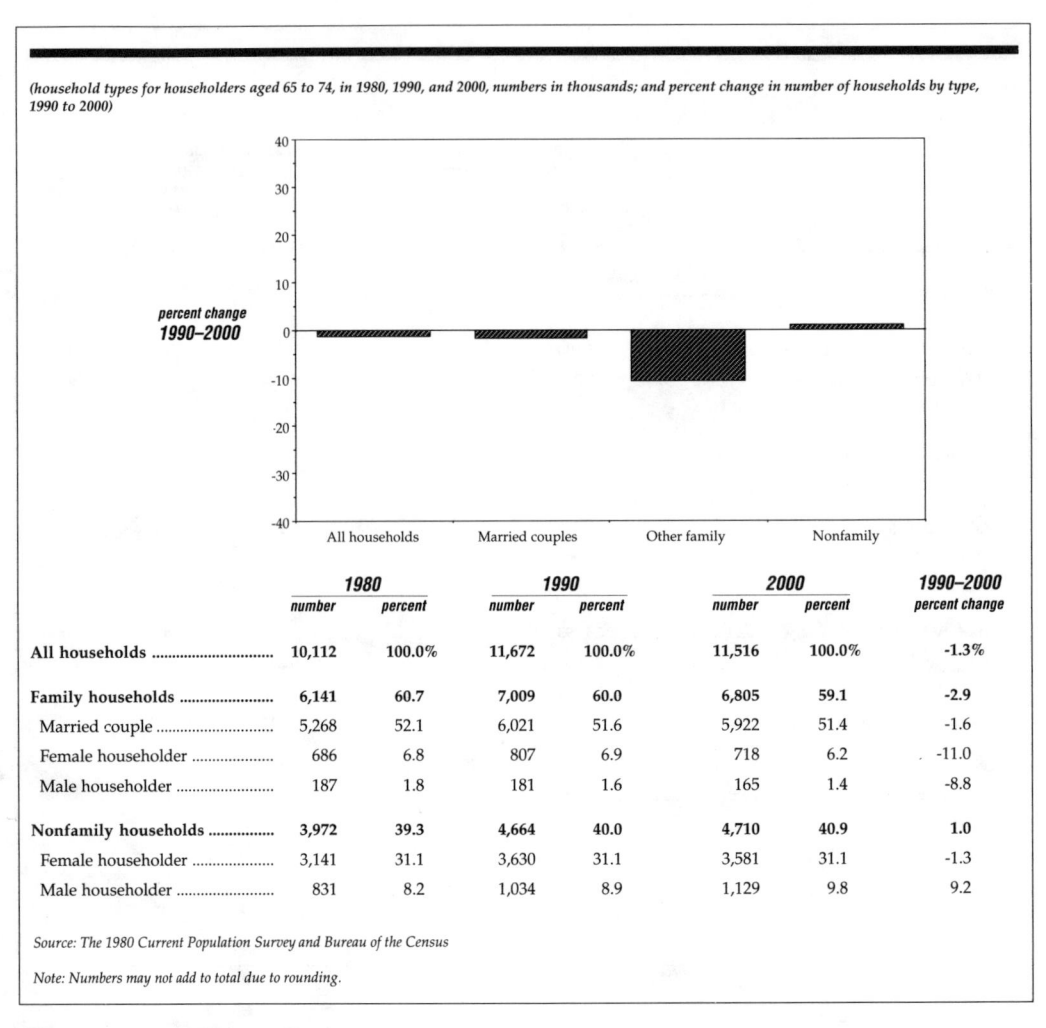

(household types for householders aged 65 to 74, in 1980, 1990, and 2000, numbers in thousands; and percent change in number of households by type, 1990 to 2000)

	1980 number	1980 percent	1990 number	1990 percent	2000 number	2000 percent	1990–2000 percent change
All households	10,112	100.0%	11,672	100.0%	11,516	100.0%	-1.3%
Family households	6,141	60.7	7,009	60.0	6,805	59.1	-2.9
Married couple	5,268	52.1	6,021	51.6	5,922	51.4	-1.6
Female householder	686	6.8	807	6.9	718	6.2	-11.0
Male householder	187	1.8	181	1.6	165	1.4	-8.8
Nonfamily households	3,972	39.3	4,664	40.0	4,710	40.9	1.0
Female householder	3,141	31.1	3,630	31.1	3,581	31.1	-1.3
Male householder	831	8.2	1,034	8.9	1,129	9.8	9.2

Source: The 1980 Current Population Survey and Bureau of the Census

Note: Numbers may not add to total due to rounding.

Marital Status

MARITAL STATUS
65–74

TWO-THIRDS MARRIED

Although 64 percent of people in this age group are married and living with their spouses, the figures vary dramatically by sex: 80 percent of the men have wives, while only 51 percent of the women still have husbands. Only 5 percent of 65-to-74-year-olds are divorced or never-married, while 25 percent are widowed.

(marital status of persons aged 15 and older and those aged 65 to 74, by sex, race and Hispanic origin, numbers in thousands)

	all	total	single never married	married spouse present	married spouse absent	divorced	widowed
Males all ages							
All races/ethnicities	89,368	100.0%	30.0%	58.5%	2.9%	6.3%	2.4%
White	77,212	100.0	28.2	60.9	2.5	6.2	2.3
Black	9,472	100.0	42.9	40.4	6.0	7.5	3.3
Hispanic origin	6,517	100.0	36.4	49.9	6.2	5.8	1.6
Males aged 65 to 74							
All races/ethnicities	7,608	100.0	4.7	79.7	1.8	4.8	9.0
White	6,855	100.0	4.8	81.1	1.3	4.7	8.1
Black	615	100.0	3.6	65.9	5.5	5.7	19.3
Hispanic origin	246	100.0	3.7	74.0	4.1	6.9	11.8
Females all ages							
All races/ethnicities	97,320	100.0	23.0	53.7	3.6	8.3	11.4
White	83,003	100.0	21.0	56.6	2.7	8.0	11.6
Black	11,447	100.0	36.5	32.7	9.2	10.4	11.2
Hispanic origin	6,588	100.0	26.6	51.2	7.7	8.3	6.2
Females aged 65 to 74							
All races/ethnicities	9,624	100.0	4.8	51.0	2.0	5.5	36.7
White	8,581	100.0	4.6	52.6	1.5	5.1	36.2
Black	852	100.0	6.8	34.0	7.0	10.0	42.0
Hispanic origin	328	100.0	8.8	40.2	4.6	11.3	35.1

Source: Marital Status and Living Arrangements: March 1987, *Bureau of the Census, Current Population Reports*, Series P-20, No. 423

Note: Hispanics may be of any race. Numbers may not add to total due to rounding.

Number of Marriages and Divorces

MARITAL STATUS
65–74

STILL GOING DOWN THE AISLE

Elderly men and women are involved in 5 percent and 3 percent, respectively, of all remarriages. They account for fewer than 2 percent of divorces.

(number of marriages and divorces for all Americans and for those aged 65 and older)

	all persons male	all persons female	persons aged 65 and older male	persons aged 65 and older female	percent involving persons aged 65 and older male	percent involving persons aged 65 and older female
All marriages	1,858,783	1,858,783	35,339	18,969	1.9%	1.0%
First marriages	1,185,904	1,196,119	1,515	734	0.1	0.1
Remarriages	635,086	623,867	33,263	17,863	5.2	2.8
Previously divorced	499,735	485,848	8,135	2,687	1.6	0.5
Divorces	577,713	577,713	8,633	4,833	1.5	0.8

Source: Advance Report of Final Marriage Statistics, 1985 and Advance Report of Final Divorce Statistics, 1985, *National Center for Health Statistics*

Note: Numbers will not add to total because all divorces include those not stating their age and all marriages include those not stating whether they were previously married. Persons aged 65 to 74 and 75 and older are grouped together by the National Center for Health Statistics for this analysis.

Summary of Educational Attainment

EDUCATIONAL ATTAINMENT
65–74

MOSTLY HIGH SCHOOL GRADUATES

More than half of 65-to-74-year-olds are high school graduates and another 22 percent have completed at least one year of college. Eleven percent of these veterans of the Depression and World War II managed to complete four years of college.

(years of school completed by persons aged 25 and over, by selected characteristics, numbers in thousands)

	number	4 years of high school or more	1 or more years of college	4 or more years of college
All persons	149,144	75.6%	37.0%	19.9%
Age groups:				
25 to 34	42,635	86.5	45.4	23.9
35 to 44	33,632	85.9	46.8	26.5
45 to 54	23,018	77.6	35.6	19.5
55 to 64	21,883	67.8	28.0	14.9
65 to 74	17,232	56.9	21.9	10.6
75 years and older	10,743	42.0	18.0	8.9
Sex:				
Male	70,677	76.0%	40.6%	23.6%
Female	78,476	75.3	33.6	16.5
Race:				
White	129,170	77.0%	37.8%	20.5%
Black	15,580	63.4	26.4	10.7
Asian and other	4,394	78.4	50.9	33.4
Hispanic origin:				
Hispanic	9,449	50.9%	21.9%	8.6%
Non-Hispanic	139,695	77.3	38.0	20.6
Region:				
Northeast	32,030	76.5%	36.8%	22.2%
Midwest	36,322	77.4	33.7	17.6
South	50,848	70.8	34.1	18.3
West	29,943	80.6	45.9	22.8
Metropolitan residence:				
Metropolitan area	115,614	77.6%	40.0%	22.1%
Nonmetropolitan area	33,529	68.7	26.5	12.6

Source: Educational Attainment in the United States: March 1987 and March 1986, Bureau of the Census, Current Population Reports, Series P-20, No. 428

Age and Education

EDUCATIONAL ATTAINMENT
65–74

STUDENTS OF THE DEPRESSION

Fully 43 percent of the men and women in this age groups never finished high school. But there are big differences in educational attainment among 65-to-74-year-olds. For example, men and women aged 65 are much more likely to have graduated from high school than the oldest members of this age group.

(years of school completed by persons aged 65 to 74, by sex and single year of age, numbers in thousands)

	number	total	not high school graduate	high school graduate	1 to 3 years of college	4 or more years of college	median years
Males aged 65 to 69	4,386	100.0%	40.1%	33.8%	11.2%	14.9%	12.3
Age 65	1,053	100.0	37.5	33.3	14.2	15.0	12.4
Age 66	946	100.0	40.7	33.9	11.6	13.8	12.3
Age 67	885	100.0	37.5	34.4	12.7	15.4	12.4
Age 68	774	100.0	44.3	32.6	7.5	15.4	12.2
Age 69	728	100.0	41.5	34.9	8.7	14.7	12.2
Males aged 70 to 74	3,222	100.0	47.7	28.4	12.2	11.7	12.1
Age 70	730	100.0	44.0	33.3	12.7	10.0	12.2
Age 71	714	100.0	45.1	28.4	15.3	11.1	12.2
Age 72	656	100.0	51.5	25.6	11.7	11.1	11.7
Age 73	527	100.0	46.9	27.1	11.8	14.2	12.1
Age 74	594	100.0	51.7	26.3	8.9	13.0	11.6
Females aged 65 to 69	5,304	100.0	39.5	40.8	11.3	8.5	12.3
Age 65	1,192	100.0	35.9	44.4	11.7	7.9	12.3
Age 66	1,125	100.0	35.7	43.4	12.3	8.6	12.3
Age 67	1,032	100.0	43.5	35.3	10.9	10.4	12.2
Age 68	999	100.0	41.2	41.1	11.8	5.7	12.2
Age 69	957	100.0	41.9	38.9	9.5	9.7	12.2
Females aged 70 to 74	4,320	100.0	47.1	34.2	10.7	8.0	12.1
Age 70	985	100.0	47.3	35.1	9.7	7.8	12.1
Age 71	837	100.0	44.6	38.2	11.2	6.1	12.1
Age 72	887	100.0	44.4	34.8	12.2	8.2	12.2
Age 73	848	100.0	47.4	33.7	11.2	7.7	12.1
Age 74	764	100.0	52.2	28.5	8.9	10.6	11.3

Source: Educational Attainment in the United States: March 1987 and 1986, Bureau of the Census, Current Population Reports, Series P-20, No. 428

Note: Numbers may not add to total due to rounding.

Sex, Race, and Ethnicity

EDUCATIONAL ATTAINMENT
65–74

OLDER AND WISER

Thirty-seven percent of all Americans aged 25 and older have completed some college compared with 25 percent of men and 19 percent of women aged 65 to 74. But one in seven of the men in this age group finished at least four years of college as did one in twelve of the women.

(years of school completed by persons aged 25 and older and those aged 65 to 74, by sex, race, and Hispanic origin, numbers in thousands)

	number	total	not high school graduate	high school graduate	1 to 3 years of college	4 or more years of college
All persons aged 25 and older	149,144	100.0%	24.4%	38.7%	17.1%	19.9%
White	129,170	100.0	23.0	39.2	17.2	20.5
Black	15,580	100.0	36.6	37.1	15.7	10.7
Hispanic origin	9,449	100.0	49.1	29.0	13.3	8.6
All persons aged 65 to 74	17,232	100.0	43.1	35.0	11.3	10.6
White	15,436	100.0	40.3	36.7	12.0	11.0
Black	1,467	100.0	70.1	19.0	4.7	6.3
Hispanic origin	575	100.0	76.0	16.5	4.0	3.7
Males aged 25 and older	70,677	100.0	24.0	35.4	17.1	23.6
White	61,678	100.0	22.7	35.6	17.2	24.5
Black	6,919	100.0	37.0	36.5	15.5	11.0
Hispanic origin	4,614	100.0	48.2	28.0	14.2	9.7
Males aged 65 to 74	7,608	100.0	43.3	31.5	11.6	13.6
White	6,855	100.0	40.6	32.7	12.4	14.3
Black	615	100.0	73.5	17.4	3.3	5.7
Hispanic origin	246	100.0	72.4	16.3	5.3	5.7
Females aged 25 and older	78,467	100.0	24.7	41.6	17.1	16.5
White	67,492	100.0	23.3	42.6	17.3	16.9
Black	8,661	100.0	36.2	37.5	15.8	10.4
Hispanic origin	4,835	100.0	50.0	30.0	12.5	7.5
Females aged 65 to 74	9,624	100.0	42.9	37.8	11.0	8.3
White	8,582	100.0	40.2	39.9	11.6	8.3
Black	852	100.0	67.4	20.1	5.6	6.8
Hispanic origin	328	100.0	78.4	16.8	2.7	2.4

Source: Educational Attainment in the United States: March 1987 and March 1986, Bureau of the Census, Current Population Reports, Series P-20, No. 428

Note: Hispanics are of any race. Numbers may not add to total due to rounding.

Householders

EDUCATIONAL ATTAINMENT
65–74

EDUCATIONAL SEGMENTS

About half of all male and female householders aged 65 and older did not complete high school. But 13 percent of the men and 8 percent of the women finished four or more years of college and another 11 percent completed one to three years of college.

(years of school completed by householders aged 65 and older, by sex, race, and Hispanic origin, numbers in thousands)

	number	total	not high school graduate	high school graduate	1 to 3 years of college	4 or more years of college	median years
Male householders	10,486	100.0%	48.5%	28.2%	10.6%	12.8%	12.1
White	9,497	100.0	45.6	29.5	11.4	13.5	12.1
Black	840	100.0	80.0	13.2	2.3	4.2	7.8
Hispanic origin	311	100.0	77.2	13.2	5.5	4.2	8.1
Female householders	8,511	100.0	51.7	29.8	10.7	7.8	11.7
White	7,576	100.0	48.9	31.6	11.5	8.0	12.0
Black	858	100.0	73.8	15.2	4.9	6.1	8.7
Hispanic origin	236	100.0	78.8	11.4	5.5	4.2	7.3

Source: Educational Attainment in the United States: March 1987 and March 1986, *Bureau of the Census, Current Population Reports, Series P-20, No. 428*

Note: Hispanics are of any race. Numbers may not add to total due to rounding. Householders aged 65 to 74 and 75 and older are grouped together by the Census Bureau for this analysis.

Labor Force Status

LABOR FORCE 65–74

SOME STILL AT WORK

Although most of their peers are retired, 16 percent of men and 7 percent of women are still in the work force when they are 65 and older. Elderly black women are more likely than their white counterparts to remain in the labor force.

(labor force status of all persons aged 16 and older, aged 18 to 64, and those aged 65 and older, by sex and race, numbers in thousands)

	total population	total in labor force	percent of population in labor force	number employed	number unemployed	percent of labor force unemployed	not in labor force
Males aged 16 and older	86,899	66,207	76.2%	62,107	4,101	6.2%	20,692
White	75,189	57,779	76.8	54,647	3,132	5.4	17,410
Black	9,128	6,486	71.1	5,661	826	12.7	2,642
Males aged 18 to 64	71,443	62,563	87.6	58,864	3,699	5.9	8,880
White	61,583	54,522	88.5	51,705	2,818	5.2	7,061
Black	7,615	6,179	81.1	5,427	750	12.1	1,437
Males aged 65 and older	11,632	1,899	16.3	1,850	49	2.6	9,733
White	10,481	1,733	16.5	1,690	43	2.5	8,748
Black	947	130	13.7	124	6	4.3	818
Females aged 16 and older	95,853	53,658	56.0%	50,334	3,324	6.2%	42,195
White	81,769	45,510	55.7	43,142	2,369	5.2	36,258
Black	11,224	6,507	58.0	5,648	858	13.2	4,717
Females aged 18 to 64	75,700	50,799	67.1	47,801	3,000	5.9	24,901
White	63,964	42,999	67.2	40,878	2,120	4.9	20,965
Black	9,262	6,227	67.2	5,438	791	12.7	3,035
Females aged 65 and older	16,476	1,221	7.4	1,191	30	2.4	15,256
White	14,820	1,073	7.2	1,047	25	2.4	13,747
Black	1,405	121	8.6	117	4	3.4	1,283

Source: Annual averages from Employment and Earnings, 1987, Bureau of Labor Statistics

Note: The population here includes all civilian, noninstitutionalized people aged 16 and older, employed and unemployed persons are in the labor force. Persons aged 65 to 74 and 75 and older are grouped together by the Bureau of Labor Statistics for this analysis.

Extent of Employment

LABOR FORCE
65–74

VIRTUALLY ALL RETIRED

Among men aged 65 and older, those who work are slightly more likely (51 percent) to work full-time than part-time. Sixty-one percent of working women in this age group hold part-time jobs.

(work experience in 1987 of workers aged 16 and older and aged 65 and older, by sex, numbers in thousands)

	worked at full-time jobs				worked at part-time jobs				non-workers
	total	50-52 weeks	27-49 weeks	1-26 weeks	total	50-52 weeks	27-49 weeks	1-26 weeks	total
Males									
Aged 16 and older	59,740	47,106	7,489	5,143	9,280	3,175	2,165	3,940	18,582
Aged 65 and older	1,347	904	160	283	1,300	545	249	507	9,190
Females									
Aged 16 and older	40,398	29,882	5,788	4,727	18,538	7,774	4,301	6,463	37,580
Aged 65 and older	700	458	102	140	1,115	507	258	350	14,876

Source: The 1988 Current Population Survey, Bureau of Labor Statistics

Note: Numbers may not add to total due to rounding. The categories in this table are not mutually exclusive. Workers may, for example, be counted as both a full-time and a part-time worker if they held jobs of both kinds during the year. For this reason, the total number of workers will be higher and the number of nonworkers lower than in the previous table that uses annual averages of the number of workers in each category. Persons aged 65 to 74 and 75 and older are grouped together by the Bureau of Labor Statistics for this analysis. Civilians only.

Kinds of Jobs

LABOR FORCE
65–74

WHERE THE ELDERLY WORK

Twenty-nine percent of elderly workers are in technical, sales, and administrative support work, 24 percent are in managerial and professional positions, and 19 percent—only the youngest workers best them in this area—have service jobs.

(occupations of employed persons aged 16 and older, and those aged 65 and older, by sex, numbers in thousands)

	aged 16+	aged 65+	males aged 65+	females aged 65+	percent aged 16+	percent aged 65+
All employed persons	112,440	3,041	1,850	1,191	100.0%	100.0%
Managerial and professional	27,742	727	508	219	24.7	23.9
Executive, admin. and managerial	13,316	370	272	98	11.8	12.2
Officials & administrators, public admin.	549	19	13	6	0.5	0.6
Other executive, admin., & managerial	9,190	261	190	71	8.2	8.6
Management-related occupations	3,577	89	68	21	3.2	2.9
Professional specialty occupations	14,426	357	236	121	12.8	11.7
Engineers	1,731	29	28	1	1.5	1.0
Math & computer scientists	685	5	3	2	0.6	0.2
Natural scientists	388	8	7	1	0.3	0.3
Health diagnosing occupations	793	48	47	1	0.7	1.6
Health assessment & treating	2,148	23	7	16	1.9	0.8
Teachers, college & university	661	21	15	6	0.6	0.7
Teachers, except college & university	3,587	54	14	40	3.2	1.8
Lawyers & judges	707	36	34	2	0.6	1.2
Other professional specialty occupations	3,727	132	79	53	3.3	4.3
Technical, sales, administrative support	35,082	894	416	478	31.2	29.4
Technicians & related support occupations	3,346	29	16	13	3.0	1.0
Health technologists & technicians	1,142	13	2	11	1.0	0.4
Engineering & science technicians	1,100	8	7	1	1.0	0.3
Techs., except health, engineering, science	1,104	8	6	2	1.0	0.3
Sales occupations	13,480	472	295	177	12.0	15.5
Supervisors & proprietors	3,572	125	92	33	3.2	4.1
Sales reps., finance & business service	2,330	105	82	23	2.1	3.5

(continued next page)

Kinds of Jobs

LABOR FORCE 65–74

(continued from previous page)
(occupations of employed persons aged 16 and older, and those aged 65 and older, by sex, numbers in thousands)

	aged 16+	aged 65+	males aged 65+	females aged 65+	percent aged 16+	percent aged 65+
Sales reps., commodities except retail	1,544	41	39	2	1.4%	1.3%
Sales, retail and personal	5,973	197	79	118	5.3	6.5
Sales-related occupations	60	4	3	1	0.1	0.1
Administrative support including clerical	**18,256**	**393**	**106**	**287**	**16.2**	**12.9**
Supervisors	723	9	6	3	0.6	0.3
Computer equipment operators	914	4	2	2	0.8	0.1
Secretaries, stenographers, & typists	5,004	90	4	86	4.5	3.0
Financial records processing	2,469	92	17	75	2.2	3.0
Mail & message distributing	961	33	26	7	0.9	1.1
Other admin. support including clerical	8,185	167	54	113	7.3	5.5
Service occupations	**15,054**	**570**	**223**	**347**	**13.4**	**18.7**
Private household	934	93	2	91	0.8	3.1
Protective services	1,907	76	70	6	1.7	2.5
Service, except private hhld. & protective	12,213	401	152	249	10.9	13.2
Food service	5,204	105	23	82	4.6	3.5
Health service	1,873	44	4	40	1.7	1.4
Cleaning & building service	2,886	142	91	51	2.6	4.7
Personal service	2,249	110	34	76	2.0	3.6
Precision production, craft, repair	**13,568**	**242**	**210**	**32**	**12.1**	**8.0**
Mechanics & repairers	4,445	75	74	1	0.4	2.5
Construction trades	5,011	77	76	1	4.5	2.5
Other production, craft, repair	4,112	90	60	30	3.7	3.0
Operators, fabricators, laborers	**17,486**	**290**	**209**	**81**	**15.6**	**9.5**
Machine operators, assemblers, inspectors	7,994	111	55	56	7.1	3.7
Transportation, material moving	4,712	101	93	8	4.2	3.3
Handlers, equip. cleaners, helpers, laborers	4,779	78	61	17	4.3	2.6
Farming, forestry, fishing	**3,507**	**318**	**284**	**34**	**3.1**	**10.5**
Farm operators & managers	1,317	213	190	23	1.2	7.0
Farm workers & related occupations	2,013	98	87	11	1.8	3.2
Forestry and fishing occupations	177	7	7	0	0.2	0.2

Source: Unpublished annual data for 1987, Bureau of Labor Statistics

Note: Numbers may not add to total due to rounding. Persons aged 65 to 74 and 75 and older are grouped together by the Bureau of Labor Statistics for this analysis. Civilian, noninstitutionalized employees only.

Workers in the 1990s

LABOR FORCE
65–74

FEWER ELDERLY WORKERS

Labor force participation rates for the elderly will fall during the 1990s, with the women's showing a decline of almost 2 percentage points, and the men's dropping a full 4 percentage points.

(labor force and labor force participation rates* for persons aged 16 and older and those aged 65 to 74, by sex, race, and ethnicity, in 1990 and 2000, numbers in thousands)

	1990 number	1990 participation rate	2000 number	2000 participation rate	1990-2000 percent change
Both sexes, aged 16 and older	124,457	66.2%	138,775	67.8%	11.5%
White	106,648	66.5	116,701	68.2	9.4
Black	13,788	64.6	16,334	66.0	18.5
Hispanic	9,718	65.9	14,086	67.1	44.9
Asian and other	4,021	64.8	5,740	65.8	42.8
Males, aged 16 and older	67,909	75.8	73,136	74.7	7.7
Males, aged 65 to 74	1,468	18.3	1,122	14.0	-23.6
White	1,343	18.7	1,001	14.2	-25.5
Black and other	125	14.9	121	11.8	-3.2
Females, aged 16 and older	56,548	57.4	65,639	61.5	16.1
Females, aged 65 to 74	1,053	10.5	885	9.0	-16.0
White	947	10.6	784	9.3	-17.2
Black and other	106	9.5	101	7.4	-4.7

*Labor force participation rates are the ratio of people in the labor force to the total population of a given sex, age and race or ethnicity.

Source: Unpublished data from the Bureau of Labor Statistics

Note: The labor force here includes civilians who are working or looking for work. Hispanics are of any race.

Household Income

INCOME
65–74

SMALLEST HOUSEHOLDS

Americans aged 65 and older head 21 percent of all households and account for 14 percent of total household income. Their households are the smallest and average income per member is $11,600.

(household income and income per household member, for all households and for households by age of householder, numbers for 1988 in thousands, income is for 1987)

	households		persons in household			total household income		
	number	percent	number	percent	persons per household	$ billions	percent	per household member
All households	91,066	100.0%	240,722	100.0%	2.64	$2,927.2	100.0%	$12,160
Age of householder								
under 25	5,228	5.7	12,117	5.0	2.32	102.0	3.5	8,415
25 to 34	20,583	22.6	58,724	24.4	2.85	621.6	21.2	10,586
35 to 44	19,323	21.2	64,351	26.7	3.33	763.8	26.1	11,870
45 to 54	13,630	15.0	41,379	17.2	3.04	597.0	20.4	14,426
55 to 64	12,846	14.1	30,151	12.5	2.35	447.3	15.3	14,835
65 and older	19,456	21.4	33,999	14.1	1.75	395.6	13.5	11,635

Source: The 1988 Current Population Survey, Bureau of the Census

Note: Householders aged 65 to 74 and 75 and older are grouped together by the Census Bureau for this analysis.

Individual Income

INCOME
65–74

SHRINKING INCOMES

Among income-generating people in this age group, 41 percent of the men and 70 percent of the women have incomes of less than $10,000. On the other end of the scale, 8 percent of men aged 65 and older with incomes and a mere 2 percent of the women bring in $35,000 or more.

(income distribution and median income for males and females aged 15 and older and aged 65 and older, numbers 1988 in thousands, income is for 1987)

	males aged 15 and older		males aged 65 and older	
	number	percent	number	percent
All males	90,248	–	11,837	–
All males with income	85,623	100.0%	11,762	100.0%
Less than $5,000	13,025	15.2	1,349	11.5
$5,000 to $9,999	12,066	14.1	3,466	29.5
$10,000 to $14,999	11,708	13.7	2,596	22.1
$15,000 to $19,999	9,887	11.5	1,554	13.2
$20,000 to $24,999	8,714	10.2	923	7.8
$25,000 to $29,999	7,266	8.5	562	4.8
$30,000 to $34,999	6,124	7.2	365	3.1
$35,000 to $49,999	9,941	11.6	515	4.4
$50,000 to $74,999	4,669	5.5	260	2.2
$75,000 and over	2,225	2.6	172	1.5
Median income, all with income		$17,752		$11,854
Median income, year-round, full-time workers		$26,722		$29,715

	females aged 15 and older		females aged 65 and older	
	number	percent	number	percent
All females	98,168	–	16,691	–
All females with income	89,279	100.0%	16,467	100.0%
Less than $5,000	30,715	34.4	5,423	32.9
$5,000 to $9,999	19,782	22.2	6,079	36.9
$10,000 to $14,999	13,313	14.9	2,330	14.1
$15,000 to $19,999	9,470	10.6	1,154	7.0
$20,000 to $24,999	6,321	7.1	588	3.6
$25,000 to $29,999	3,768	4.2	321	1.9
$30,000 to $34,999	2,331	2.6	207	1.3
$35,000 to $49,999	2,602	2.9	243	1.5
$50,000 to $74,999	708	0.8	78	0.5
$75,000 and over	268	0.3	45	0.3
Median income, all with income		$8,101		$6,734
Median income, year-round, full-time workers		$17,504		$19,178

Source: Money Income and Poverty Status in the United States: 1987, Bureau of the Census, Current Population Reports, Series P-20, No. 161
Note: Numbers may not add to total due to rounding. Persons aged 65 to 74 and 75 and older are grouped together by the Census Bureau for this analysis.

Income and Age

INCOME
65–74

POST-RETIREMENT DROP

About one-quarter of households headed by 65-to-74-year-olds have incomes between $20,000 and $35,000. Another 17 percent bring in $35,000 or more, and only 8 percent have $50,000 or more of income. Compared with households in general, households in this age group are more likely to have incomes under $20,000.

(household income by age of householder, numbers for 1988 in thousands, income is for 1987)

				age of householder				
	total	under 25	25 to 34	35 to 44	45 to 54	55 to 64	65 to 74	75+
All households	91,066	5,228	20,583	19,323	13,630	12,846	11,410	8,045
All households	100.0%	100.0%	100.0%	100.0%	100.0%	100.0%	100.0%	100.0%
Less than $10,000	18.4	30.3	13.6	10.3	10.4	17.4	27.1	44.6
$10,000 to $14,999	10.6	15.8	9.6	6.6	6.6	9.5	17.3	18.5
$15,000 to $19,999	10.0	14.1	11.1	7.4	6.8	9.7	13.8	11.8
$20,000 to $24,999	9.2	11.5	11.1	8.3	7.2	9.1	10.1	7.5
$25,000 to $29,999	8.4	9.0	10.6	8.5	7.6	8.0	8.3	4.3
$30,000 to $34,999	7.7	6.8	9.7	9.0	7.8	7.2	6.0	3.2
$35,000 to $39,999	6.8	4.5	8.6	9.0	7.2	6.3	4.2	2.4
$40,000 to $44,999	5.8	2.3	6.7	7.9	7.4	6.0	3.0	1.7
$45,000 to $49,999	4.6	1.3	5.1	6.6	5.9	4.7	2.4	1.5
$50,000 to $59,999	6.7	2.1	6.7	9.6	10.1	7.5	2.7	1.9
$60,000 to $74,999	5.5	1.5	4.2	7.9	9.9	6.3	2.1	1.2
$75,000 and over	6.3	0.9	3.0	8.9	13.1	8.3	3.0	1.4
Median household income	$25,986	$16,204	$26,923	$34,926	$37,250	$27,538	$16,906	$11,261

Source: The 1988 Current Population Survey, Bureau of the Census

Note: Numbers may not add to total due to rounding.

Income of Married Couples

STARTING TO DROP

One in three 65-to-74-year-old married couples has a household income between $20,000 and $35,000, while one in four brings in over $35,000. Twelve percent have incomes of $50,000 or more. A higher median income is seen among couples who have children under 18 living in the home than among those who don't.

(household income of married-couple householder families with and without children under 18 at home, householders aged 65 to 74, numbers for 1988 in thousands, income is for 1987)

	married-couple householder aged 65 to 74		
	total	with children under 18 at home	without children under 18 at home
All households	5,988	114	5,874
All households	100.0%	100.0%	100.0%
Less than $10,000	9.8	11.4	9.8
$10,000 to $14,999	15.8	15.8	15.8
$15,000 to $19,999	15.6	9.6	15.8
$20,000 to $24,999	14.0	14.0	14.0
$25,000 to $29,999	11.1	16.7	11.0
$30,000 to $34,999	8.4	4.4	8.5
$35,000 to $39,999	6.1	3.5	6.1
$40,000 to $44,999	4.0	5.3	4.0
$45,000 to $49,999	3.4	0.0	3.5
$50,000 to $59,999	4.0	6.1	3.9
$60,000 to $74,999	3.2	4.4	3.1
$75,000 and over	4.6	9.6	4.5
Median household income	$22,931	$24,161	$22,908

Source: The 1988 Current Population Survey, Bureau of the Census

Note: Numbers may not add to total due to rounding.

Income of Other Family Households

INCOME
65–74

DISADVANTAGED AND FEMALE

Over half (55 percent) of female householders in this age group have incomes of less than $20,000, an income bracket shared by one-third of their male counterparts. Only 22 percent of families headed by women aged 65 to 74 and 32 percent of those headed by men bring in $35,000 or more.

(household income of unmarried female- and male-householder families with and without children under 18 at home, householders aged 65 to 74, numbers for 1988, in thousands, income is for 1987)

	female householder aged 65 to 74			male householder aged 65 to 74		
	total	with children under 18 at home	without children under 18 at home	total	with children under 18 at home	without children under 18 at home
All households	806	17	789	226	8	218
All households	100.0%	100.0%	100.0%	100.0%	100.0%	100.0%
Less than $10,000	19.0	35.3	18.6	11.1	–	11.5
$10,000 to $14,999	18.5	52.9	17.7	11.9	25.0	11.5
$15,000 to $19,999	17.0	0.0	17.4	10.6	25.0	10.1
$20,000 to $24,999	8.8	0.0	9.0	11.5	37.5	10.6
$25,000 to $29,999	7.7	0.0	7.9	18.1	0.0	18.3
$30,000 to $34,999	6.9	11.8	7.0	5.8	12.5	5.0
$35,000 to $39,999	4.1	5.9	4.2	5.3	–	5.5
$40,000 to $44,999	5.0	0.0	5.1	8.4	–	8.7
$45,000 to $49,999	4.7	0.0	4.8	2.2	–	2.3
$50,000 to $59,999	3.5	0.0	3.5	7.5	–	7.8
$60,000 to $74,999	2.2	0.0	2.3	5.3	–	5.5
$75,000 and over	2.7	0.0	2.8	3.1	–	3.2
Median household income	$18,915	–	$19,095	$26,886	–	$26,989

Source: The 1988 Current Population Survey, Bureau of the Census

Note: Numbers may not add to total due to rounding. Median income is unreliable and is therefore not given when the category contains fewer than 75,000 households.

Income of Nonfamily Households

INCOME
65-74

FOR LOVE OR MONEY

As with other age groups, 65-to-74-year-old nonfamily householders have a higher median income—68 percent higher in this case—if they live with unrelated others than if they live alone. Of those who live with others, 16 percent bring in $35,000 or more, a household income claimed by only 5 percent of those who live on their own.

(household income of nonfamily households by household type, householders aged 65 to 74, numbers for 1988 in thousands, income is for 1987)

	total number	living alone total	living alone male householder	living alone female householder	living with others total	living with others male householder	living with others female householder
All nonfamily households	4,390	4,243	1,014	3,229	147	76	72
All nonfamily households	100.0%	100.0%	100.%0	100.0%	100.0%	100.0%	100.0%
Less than $10,000	53.0	54.1	45.1	56.9	23.1	19.7	26.4
$10,000 to $14,999	19.4	19.1	20.3	18.8	27.2	25.0	29.2
$15,000 to $19,999	10.8	10.7	11.4	10.4	14.3	21.1	6.9
$20,000 to $24,999	5.0	5.0	6.1	4.6	5.4	3.9	6.9
$25,000 to $29,999	4.2	4.1	6.5	3.3	9.5	9.2	9.7
$30,000 to $34,999	2.5	2.4	3.1	2.4	5.4	3.9	6.9
$35,000 to $39,999	1.5	1.3	2.1	1.1	4.8	7.9	1.4
$40,000 to $44,999	0.9	0.8	1.1	0.7	4.1	2.6	5.6
$45,000 to $49,999	0.7	0.7	0.5	0.7	0.7	1.3	0.0
$50,000 to $59,999	0.7	0.7	1.5	0.4	0.7	0.0	1.4
$60,000 to $74,999	0.5	0.5	1.1	0.3	2.0	0.0	4.2
$75,000 and over	0.8	0.8	1.3	0.6	3.4	5.3	1.4
Median household income	$9,362	$9,154	$11,088	$8,776	$15,424	$16,161	–

Source: The 1988 Current Population Survey, Bureau of the Census

Note: Nonfamilies are either people living alone or living with an individual (or individuals) unrelated to the householder. Median income is unreliable and is therefore not given when the category contains fewer than 75,000 households. Numbers may not add to total due to rounding.

Income and Race, Families

INCOME
65–74

STRETCHING IT

At $21,500, the median household income of white families headed by people aged 65 and older is more than $7,000 higher than that of black families. Forty-three percent of white families and 28 percent of black families have incomes between $20,000 and $50,000 while another 11 percent of white families and fewer than 4 percent of black families report incomes of $50,000 or more.

(household income of family households by race and household type for householders aged 65 and older, numbers for 1988 in thousands, income is for 1987)

white family households

	total	married couple	male householder	female householder
All households	9,421	7,926	317	1,179
Total	100.0%	100.0%	100.0%	100.0%
Less than $10,000	12.2	11.5	14.2	16.0
$10,000 to $19,999	33.6	34.2	22.1	32.7
$20,000 to $29,999	22.8	23.3	25.9	18.4
$30,000 to $39,999	12.9	13.0	11.4	12.3
$40,000 to $49,999	7.5	6.9	8.5	10.8
$50,000 to $59,999	4.1	3.8	8.5	4.4
$60,000 to $74,999	3.0	2.9	5.7	2.9
$75,000 and over	4.0	4.3	3.5	2.5
Median household income	$21,474	$21,442	$25,651	$20,592

black family households

	total	married couple	male householder	female householder
All households	906	566	60	279
Total	100.0%	100.0%	100.0%	100.0%
Less than $10,000	30.5	25.4	30.0	41.2
$10,000 to $19,999	38.5	41.9	25.0	34.8
$20,000 to $29,999	16.6	17.7	21.7	12.9
$30,000 to $39,999	7.3	8.5	1.7	5.7
$40,000 to $49,999	3.8	3.4	13.3	2.5
$50,000 to $59,999	1.7	0.9	3.3	2.9
$60,000 to $74,999	1.1	1.8	–	–
$75,000 and over	0.7	0.4	3.3	0.7
Median household income	$14,107	$14,764	–	$12,078

Source: Money Income of Households, Families, and Persons in the United States: 1987, Bureau of the Census, Current Population Reports, Series P-60, No. 162

Note: Numbers may not add to total due to rounding. Median income is unreliable and is therefore not given when the category contains fewer than 75,000 households. Householders aged 65 to 74 and 75 and older are grouped together by the Census Bureau for this analysis.

Income and Race, Nonfamilies

INCOME
65–74

SMALL GAP, SMALL INCOMES

The income gap between white and black nonfamily householders is lowest in this age group but their median incomes are also the lowest. Only 6 percent of white nonfamily householders aged 65 or older and 1 percent of the black householders have incomes of $30,000 or more.

(householder income of nonfamily householders by race and household type for householders aged 65 and older, numbers for 1988 in thousands, income is for 1987)

	white householder			black householder		
	total	male householder	female householder	total	male householder	female householder
All households	8,014	1,731	6,284	851	272	579
Total	100.0%	100.0%	100.0%	100.0%	100.0%	100.0%
Less than $10,000	57.1	45.8	60.2	84.6	83.5	85.1
$10,000 to $19,999	28.2	32.6	27.0	12.6	13.6	11.9
$20,000 to $24,999	5.3	6.0	5.1	0.9	1.5	0.7
$25,000 to $29,999	3.3	5.3	2.7	0.5	–	0.7
$30,000 to $34,999	2.0	3.1	1.8	1.2	1.1	1.2
$35,000 to $49,999	2.6	3.8	2.3	0.2	–	0.3
$50,000 and over	1.6	3.5	1.1	–	–	–
Median householder income	$8,785	$10,800	$8,346	$4,996	$5,890	$4,792

Source: Money Income of Households, Families, and Persons in the United States: 1987, *Bureau of the Census, Current Population Reports, Series P-60, No. 162*

Note: Numbers may not add to total due to rounding. Householder income is the total money income of the householder only. Householders aged 65 to 74 and 75 and older are grouped together by the Census Bureau for this analysis.

Income of Hispanic Households

INCOME
65–74

MARITAL ADVANTAGE

Married-couple Hispanic households in this age group are most likely to have an income of $25,000 or more—30 percent of them do. Only 4 percent of nonfamily households with a Hispanic householder aged 65 to 74 have incomes in that range.

(household income of Hispanic households, by household type for householders aged 65 to 74, numbers for 1988 in thousands, income is for 1987)

family households

	total	married couple	male householder	female householder
All households	222	160	16	46
Total	100.0%	100.0%	100.0%	100.0%
Less than $15,000	47.3	47.5	68.8	41.3
$15,000 to $24,999	25.2	22.5	25.0	34.8
$25,000 and over	27.5	30.0	6.3	26.1
Median household income	$15,786	$16,559	–	–

nonfamily households

	total	male householder living alone	male householder living with others	female householder living alone	female householder living with others
All households	110	35	1	73	–
Total	100.0%	100.0%	100.0%	100.0%	–
Less than $15,000	82.7	77.1	–	87.7	–
$15,000 to $24,999	13.6	22.9	0.0	8.2	–
$25,000 and over	3.6	–	100.0	4.1	–
Median household income	$6,070	–	–	–	–

Source: The 1988 Current Population Survey, Bureau of the Census

Note: Numbers may not add to total due to rounding. Hispanics are of any race. Median income is unreliable and is therefore not given when the category contains fewer than 75,000 households.

Income of Dual-Earner Couples

INCOME
65–74

STILL AT WORK

Not surprisingly, only 7 percent of these retirement-aged married couples are dual earners. Their median income of $37,200 is 62 percent higher than that of all married couples aged 65 to 74.

(household income for all dual-earner married couples and for those with married-couple householders aged 65 to 74, numbers for 1988 in thousands, income is for 1987)

	householder all ages			householder aged 65 to 74		
	total	with children under 18 at home	without children under 18 at home	total	with children under 18 at home	without children under 18 at home
All households	26,227	14,989	11,238	409	8	402
All households	100.0%	100.0%	100.0%	100.0%	100.0%	100.0%
Less than $15,000	5.7	6.0	5.4	8.0	50.0	7.2
$15,000 to $19,999	5.1	5.4	4.7	6.0	25.0	5.7
$20,000 to $24,999	7.3	7.8	6.6	11.2	12.5	11.2
$25,000 to $29,999	8.3	9.0	7.5	10.1	0.0	10.2
$30,000 to $34,999	9.4	10.2	8.3	10.2	0.0	10.4
$35,000 to $39,999	10.3	11.2	9.0	11.0	3.1	11.2
$40,000 to $44,999	9.6	9.8	9.3	7.0	0.0	7.2
$45,000 to $49,999	8.1	8.2	7.9	5.2	0.0	5.2
$50,000 to $59,999	13.0	12.5	13.6	6.2	12.5	6.2
$60,000 to $74,999	11.2	10.2	12.5	9.0	0.0	9.2
$75,000 and over	12.1	9.6	15.3	16.1	0.0	16.4
Median household income	$41,904	$40,044	$44,508	$37,209	–	$37,390

Source: The 1988 Current Population Survey, Bureau of the Census

Note: Numbers may not add to total due to rounding. Median income is unreliable and is therefore not given when the category contains fewer than 75,000 households.

Income and Education

INCOME
65–74

LITTLE EDUCATION MEANS LOW INCOME

As with nearly all other age groups, the more college education a 65-to-74-year-old householder has, the higher his or her household income is likely to be. Twenty-seven percent of those with four or more years of college have household incomes of $50,000 or more—an income claimed by just 12 percent of those who finished one to three years of college.

(household income of householders aged 65 to 74 by years of school completed by householder, numbers for 1988 in thousands, income is for 1987)

	total	not high school graduate	high school graduate	1 to 3 years of college	4 or more years of college
All households	11,411	4,819	3,909	1,321	1,359
All households	100.0%	100.0%	100.0%	100.0%	100.0%
Less than $10,000	27.1	39.8	22.8	15.3	5.7
$10,000 to $19,999	31.1	34.6	32.5	27.0	18.8
$20,000 to $29,999	18.5	13.6	21.4	23.9	22.0
$30,000 to $39,999	10.1	6.8	11.3	12.6	16.3
$40,000 to $49,999	5.4	2.6	5.8	9.2	10.2
$50,000 to $59,999	2.7	1.2	2.4	4.8	7.1
$60,000 to $74,999	2.1	0.7	1.8	3.8	6.4
$75,000 and over	3.0	0.7	2.1	3.3	13.3

Source: The 1988 Current Population Survey, Bureau of the Census.

Note: Numbers may not add to total due to rounding.

Future Income

INCOME
65–74

FAST MONEY

While the number of households headed by people aged 65 and older grows by 7 percent between 1990 and 1995, the number of these households with incomes of $50,000 or more will climb a full 18 percent. Over that time period, elderly high-income households will increase faster than low-income households.

(projections of the number of households with householders aged 65 and older, by household income, 1990 and 1995, numbers in thousands, income is in 1985 dollars)

	1990 number	1990 percent	1995 number	1995 percent	percent change 1990-1995
All households	20,396	100.0%	21,882	100.0%	7.3%
Less than $10,000	8,106	39.7	8,321	38.0	2.7
$10,000 to $19,999	6,117	30.0	6,536	29.9	6.8
$20,000 to $29,999	3,051	15.0	3,409	15.6	11.7
$30,000 to $39,999	1,373	6.7	1,547	7.1	12.7
$40,000 to $49,999	689	3.4	819	3.7	18.8
$50,000 to $59,999	371	1.8	442	2.0	19.1
$60,000 to $74,999	300	1.5	346	1.6	15.4
$75,000 and over	390	1.9	460	2.1	17.9
Median household income	$13,421		$14,008		

Source: American Demographics, May to August, 1986, based on the national econometric model of Wharton Economic Forecasting Association and on household projections from the Bureau of the Census

Note: Numbers may not add to total due to rounding. Householders aged 65 to 74 and 75 and older are grouped together by American Demographics for this analysis.

Annual Expenditures

EXPENDITURES
65–74

RETIREMENT SPENDING

Households headed by a 65-to-74-year-old devote a larger chunk of their spending dollar to food, health care, personal care, and contributions than the average household. They spend an average of $16,900 each.

(average annual expenditure and percent distribution of expenditures for all households and for householders aged 65 to 74, number of households in thousands)

	all households		householder aged 65 to 74	
	average annual expenditure	percent of all expenditures	average annual expenditure	percent of all expenditures
Number of households	93,741		10,763	
Total expenditure	**$22,710**	**100.0%**	**$16,898**	**100.0%**
Food	**3,363**	**14.8**	**2,767**	**16.4**
Food at home	2,313	10.2	1,974	11.7
Food away from home	1,049	4.6	794	4.7
Alcoholic beverages	**273**	**1.2**	**151**	**0.9**
Housing	**6,888**	**30.3**	**4,995**	**29.6**
Shelter	3,986	17.6	2,469	14.6
Owned dwellings	2,305	10.1	1,530	9.1
Mortgage interest and charges	1,428	6.3	362	2.1
Property taxes	417	1.8	557	3.3
Maintenance, repairs, insurance, and other expenses	460	2.0	610	3.6
Rented dwellings	1,269	5.6	621	3.7
Other lodging	412	1.8	318	1.9
Fuels, utilities, and public services	1,646	7.2	1,593	9.4
Natural gas	248	1.1	267	1.6
Electricity	674	3.0	630	3.7
Fuel oil and other fuels	107	0.5	153	0.9
Telephone	471	2.1	399	2.4
Water and other public services	145	0.6	144	0.9
Household operations	353	1.6	250	1.5
Domestic services	288	1.3	182	1.1
Other household expenses	65	0.3	68	0.4
Household furnishings, equipment	903	4.0	683	4.0
Household textiles	83	0.4	77	0.5
Furniture	303	1.3	232	1.4
Floor coverings	51	0.2	50	0.3
Major appliances	155	0.7	138	0.8

(continued next page)

Annual Expenditures 65–74

(continued from previous page)

(average annual expenditure and percent distribution of expenditures for all households and for householders aged 65 to 74, number of households in thousands)

	all households		householder aged 65 to 74	
	average annual expenditure	percent of all expenditures	average annual expenditure	percent of all expenditures
Small appliances, miscellaneous housewares	55	0.2	40	0.2
Miscellaneous household equipment	256	1.1	147	0.9
Apparel	**1,149**	**5.1**	**710**	**4.2**
Men and boys	283	1.2	143	0.8
Men, 16 and over	228	1.0	127	0.8
Boys, 2 to 15	55	0.2	16	0.1
Women and girls	462	2.0	342	2.0
Women, 16 and over	396	1.7	323	1.9
Girls, 2 to 15	66	0.3	19	0.1
Children under 2	45	0.2	12	0.1
Footwear	123	0.5	82	0.5
Other apparel products and services	237	1.0	132	0.8
Transportation	**4,815**	**21.2**	**3,233**	**19.1**
Cars and trucks, new (net outlay)	1,414	6.2	947	5.6
Cars and trucks, used (net outlay)	897	3.9	442	2.6
Other vehicles	29	0.1	6	0.0
Vehicle finance charges	270	1.2	116	0.7
Gasoline and motor oil	916	4.0	687	4.1
Maintenance and repairs	458	2.0	378	2.2
Vehicle insurance	420	1.8	315	1.9
Public transportation	248	1.1	234	1.4
Vehicle rental, licenses, other charges	163	0.7	109	0.6
Health care	**1,062**	**4.7**	**1,537**	**9.1**
Health insurance	371	1.6	631	3.7
Medical services	502	2.2	594	3.5
Medicines and medical supplies	189	0.8	312	1.8
Entertainment	**1,087**	**4.8**	**686**	**4.1**
Fees and admissions	308	1.4	236	1.4
Television, radios, sound equipment	373	1.6	226	1.3
Other equipment and services	406	1.8	224	1.3
Personal care	**207**	**0.9**	**201**	**1.2**
Reading	**140**	**0.6**	**139**	**0.8**
Education	**298**	**1.3**	**69**	**0.4**
Tobacco and smoking supplies	**230**	**1.0**	**174**	**1.0**
Miscellaneous	**323**	**1.4**	**308**	**1.8**
Contributions and support payments	**746**	**3.3**	**1,070**	**6.3**
Personal insurance and pensions	**2,129**	**9.4**	**857**	**5.1**
Life insurance and other personal insurance	293	1.3	318	1.9
Retirement, pensions, Social Security	1,836	8.1	539	3.2

Source: The 1986 Consumer Expenditure Survey, Bureau of Labor Statistics

Expenditures by Income

EXPENDITURES
65–74

HAVING AND SPENDING

The highest-income households in this age group spend at least twice as much as the average household in this age group spends for housing, apparel, transportation, and reading. Their expenses for food away from home, entertainment, education, contributions, and insurance and pensions are over three times greater than average.

(annual average expenditure of households with householders aged 65 to 74, by household income, number of households in thousands)

	all households	under $10,000	$10-14,999	$15-19,999	$20-29,999	$30-39,999	$40,000+
Number of households	9,751	3,741	1,975	1,306	1,236	759	734
Total expenditure	$17,104	$10,336	$14,226	$16,590	$22,495	$25,156	$42,775
Food	2,835	1,870	2,630	3,034	3,402	4,062	5,717
Food at home	2,003	1,491	1,982	2,085	2,374	2,725	3,148
Food away from home	832	379	648	949	1,028	1,338	2,569
Alcoholic beverages	175	81	127	220	264	212	508
Housing	5,114	3,614	4,455	4,880	6,538	7,014	10,560
Shelter	2,556	1,853	2,113	2,407	3,168	3,358	5,726
Owned dwellings	1,601	1,007	1,263	1,539	2,264	2,376	3,726
Rented dwellings	601	695	655	552	481	387	482
Other lodging	351	151	195	316	421	567	1,518
Fuels, utilities, public services	1,609	1,302	1,568	1,580	1,878	2,071	2,401
Household operations	264	170	190	207	381	435	662
Household furnishings, equipment	685	288	584	686	1,111	1,149	1,772
Apparel and services	740	421	515	703	993	1,263	2,067
Transportation	3,184	1,516	2,713	3,370	4,706	4,698	8,482
Vehicles	1,276	489	1,027	1,386	2,165	1,597	3,935
Gasoline and motor oil	736	446	724	816	984	1,099	1,305
Other vehicle expenses	928	487	839	950	1,249	1,684	2,057
Public transportation	243	93	124	218	306	318	1,184
Health care	1,563	1,118	1,548	1,571	1,949	2,027	2,716
Entertainment	681	261	520	791	969	1,088	2,150
Personal care	199	118	168	219	273	326	399

(continued next page)

Expenditures by Income

EXPENDITURES 65–74

(continued from previous page)
(annual average expenditure of households with householders aged 65 to 74, by household income, number of households in thousands)

	all households	under $10,000	$10-14,999	$15-19,999	$20-29,999	$30-39,999	$40,000+
Reading	143	75	130	138	187	233	363
Education	69	32	43	37	60	105	361
Tobacco and smoking supplies	176	134	189	200	212	209	216
Miscellaneous	274	197	229	263	210	199	992
Cash contributions	1,035	687	596	541	1,336	1,514	3,845
Personal insurance and pensions	918	214	360	622	1,398	2,206	4,399
Life and other insurance	291	154	207	239	527	449	741
Retirement, pensions, Social Security	628	59	154	383	871	1,757	3,659

Source: The 1986 Consumer Expenditure Survey, Bureau of Labor Statistics

Note: All households include complete income reporters only. Total expenditure exceeds total income in some income categories due to a number of factors including the underreporting of income, borrowing, and the use of savings.

Weekly Shopping

EXPENDITURES
65–74

SPENDING LESS ON FOOD

These households spend 18 percent less on food at home and 32 percent less on food away from home than the average household. But they are above-average spenders on non-prescription drugs and supplies, fresh fruits, fresh vegetables, and housekeeping supplies.

(average weekly expenditure for all households and for householders aged 65 to 74)

	all households	index all households	householders aged 65 to 74	index householders aged 65 to 74
Food, total	$59.60	100	$45.97	77
Food at home, total	37.73	100	31.12	82
Cereals and cereal products	1.78	100	1.45	81
Bakery products	3.51	100	2.98	85
Beef	3.63	100	2.66	73
Pork	2.23	100	1.83	82
Other meats	1.52	100	1.29	85
Poultry	1.64	100	1.44	88
Fish and seafood	1.22	100	1.13	93
Eggs	0.57	100	0.54	95
Fresh milk and cream	2.35	100	1.92	82
Other dairy products	2.47	100	1.94	79
Fresh fruits	1.96	100	2.15	110
Fresh vegetables	1.77	100	1.80	102
Processed fruits	1.38	100	1.29	93
Processed vegetables	1.03	100	0.89	86
Sugar and other sweets	1.42	100	1.12	79
Fats and oils	0.99	100	0.90	91
Miscellaneous foods	4.53	100	2.89	64
Nonalcoholic beverages	3.71	100	2.92	79
Food away from home	21.87	100	14.84	68
Nonfood items				
Alcoholic beverages	4.84	100	2.85	59
Tobacco products and smoking supplies	3.60	100	2.58	72
Pet food	1.09	100	0.80	73
Personal care products and services	5.01	100	4.44	89
Non-prescription drugs and supplies	2.31	100	2.77	120
Housekeeping supplies	6.07	100	6.28	103

Source: The 1986 Consumer Expenditure Survey, Bureau of Labor Statistics

Note: An index of 100 represents the average. An index of 132 means that the average weekly expenditure of the subgroup is 32 percent above the average for all households. An index of 68 indicates spending that is 32 percent below average. Numbers may not add to total due to rounding.

Future Expenditures

EXPENDITURES
65–74

A 3 BILLION DOLLAR DROP

As the number of households in this age group declines by 1 percent during the 1990s, their aggregate spending will drop by an estimated three billion dollars.

(projected aggregate expenditures in 1990 and 2000 for all households and for households by age of householder, in billions of dollars)

	all households	under 25	25-34	35-44	45-54	55-64	65-74	75+
Number of households (in thousands)	94,227	4,663	21,183	21,245	14,429	12,311	11,672	8,724
Total expenditures (in billions of dollars)	$2,203.1	$64.2	$476.6	$628.6	$441.2	$292.8	$197.2	$102.5
Food	330.8	9.4	70.3	93.7	64.1	43.9	32.3	17.2
Food at home	225.1	5.9	44.8	64.9	41.8	30.9	23.0	13.7
Food away from home	101.5	3.6	21.2	28.8	22.2	13.0	9.3	3.5
Alcoholic beverages	25.4	1.6	7.5	6.4	4.7	3.0	1.8	0.6
Housing	667.6	19.2	158.3	193.5	121.9	80.8	58.3	35.6
Shelter	385.6	12.4	97.2	115.7	71.7	42.4	28.8	17.5
Owned dwellings	229.7	1.8	50.3	75.8	46.9	28.2	17.9	8.7
Rented dwellings	115.2	9.5	41.6	27.6	13.1	8.4	7.2	7.6
Other lodging	40.8	1.0	5.2	12.2	11.6	5.8	3.7	1.2
Fuels, utilities, and public services	160.0	3.7	32.0	41.2	29.6	23.2	18.6	11.8
Household operations	34.2	0.7	9.6	10.2	3.8	3.7	2.9	3.3
Household furnishings, equipment	87.8	2.4	19.5	26.5	16.8	11.6	8.0	3.0
Apparel and services	111.0	4.1	24.6	33.7	22.8	13.8	8.3	3.6
Transportation	464.9	15.6	107.0	130.7	98.7	61.1	37.7	14.2
Health care	103.7	1.6	14.5	21.4	16.9	16.0	17.9	15.4
Entertainment	106.0	3.1	23.3	35.2	20.6	13.0	8.0	2.6
Personal care	20.1	0.6	3.7	5.2	3.8	3.1	2.3	1.3
Reading	13.6	0.3	2.6	3.8	2.6	1.9	1.6	0.8
Education	27.6	2.7	3.9	8.3	8.8	2.9	0.8	0.1
Tobacco and smoking supplies	22.0	0.8	4.9	5.8	4.5	3.3	2.0	0.7
Miscellaneous	31.5	0.6	6.5	8.1	5.9	4.5	3.6	2.3
Contributions and support payments	74.2	0.7	7.3	17.7	17.4	12.9	12.5	5.7
Personal insurance and pensions	208.9	3.9	46.4	65.2	48.5	32.6	10.0	2.3

(continued next page)

Future Expenditures

EXPENDITURES 65–74

(continued from previous page)

(projected aggregate expenditures in 2000 for all households and for households by age of householder, in billions of dollars)

2000 aggregate annual expenditures in billions

	all households	under 25	25-34	35-44	45-54	55-64	65-74	75+
Number of households (in thousands)	105,933	4,442	18,004	25,339	21,603	13,903	11,516	11,126
Total expenditures (in billions of dollars)	$2,532.4	$61.1	$405.1	$749.7	$660.6	$330.6	$194.6	$130.7
Food	379.7	9.0	59.7	111.7	95.9	49.5	31.9	22.0
Food at home	258.9	5.6	38.1	77.4	62.6	34.9	22.7	17.5
Food away from home	117.2	3.4	18.0	34.3	33.2	14.7	9.1	4.5
Alcoholic beverages	28.3	1.5	6.4	7.6	7.0	3.4	1.7	0.7
Housing	760.3	18.3	134.5	230.8	182.5	91.3	57.5	45.3
Shelter	438.2	11.8	82.6	137.9	107.3	47.9	28.4	22.3
Owned dwellings	265.8	1.7	42.8	90.4	70.3	31.9	17.6	11.1
Rented dwellings	123.4	9.1	35.4	32.9	19.7	9.5	7.2	9.7
Other lodging	49.1	0.9	4.4	14.6	17.4	6.5	3.7	1.5
Fuels, utilities, and public services	183.6	3.5	27.2	49.1	44.3	26.2	18.3	15.0
Household operations	38.0	0.7	8.2	12.2	5.7	4.1	2.9	4.2
Household furnishings, equipment	100.5	2.3	16.6	31.6	25.2	13.1	7.9	3.8
Apparel and services	127.6	3.9	20.9	40.2	34.2	15.6	8.2	4.6
Transportation	533.7	14.8	90.9	155.9	147.7	69.0	37.2	18.1
Health care	120.0	1.5	12.4	25.5	25.3	18.1	17.7	19.6
Entertainment	121.7	3.0	19.8	42.0	30.9	14.7	7.9	3.3
Personal care	23.1	0.5	3.2	6.2	5.7	3.5	2.3	1.7
Reading	15.7	0.3	2.2	4.5	3.9	2.2	1.6	1.0
Education	33.2	2.6	3.3	10.0	13.1	3.3	0.8	0.2
Tobacco and smoking supplies	25.2	0.8	4.2	6.9	6.8	3.7	2.0	0.9
Miscellaneous	36.2	0.6	5.5	9.7	8.9	5.0	3.5	2.9
Contributions and support payments	88.2	0.6	6.2	21.1	26.0	14.5	12.3	7.3
Personal insurance and pensions	243.2	3.7	39.4	77.7	72.7	36.8	9.9	2.9

Source: *The 1986 Consumer Expenditure Survey*, Bureau of Labor Statistics and *Projections of the Number of Households and Families: 1986 to 2000*, Bureau of the Census, Series P-25, No. 986

Note: Aggregate expenditures are the sum of the total expenditures of all households in the nation or of all households in an age group. Projections are based on the average annual expenditures in 1986 and have not been adjusted for inflation. Projections show how total annual expenditures would change as the number of households in the age group changes during the 1990s. All other factors such as price and expenditure pattern are held constant and are not accounted for in these projections.

Composition of Wealth

LARGEST SHARE OF WEALTH

Householders aged 65 and older account for a whopping 35 percent of all household wealth. Except for real estate, they are less likely to hold assets than are householders in general but the average amount of asset holdings peaks among over-65-year-olds (in every asset category but homes and autos).

(percentage of households with assets and debts and the mean value of owners' holdings in 1986 dollars, for all households and householders aged 65 and older, numbers in thousands)

	percent owning		mean holdings of owners	
	all households	householder aged 65 and older	all households	householder aged 65 and older
Number of households	83,042	10,328	83,042	10,328
Assets				
Home	65.7%	75.6%	$80,650	$69,756
Other real estate	22.4	23.1	118,892	177,477
Public stock	19.3	18.4	81,367	250,335
Bonds	20.2	16.8	28,116	94,097
Checking and saving accounts	89.2	87.9	7,445	14,132
IRA's and Keoghs	27.3	11.7	18,752	59,056
CD's and money market	27.9	41.7	31,575	52,536
Business assets (net)	12.4	6.5	210,310	475,481
Automobiles	85.9	70.2	7,964	5,573
Employer accounts	14.8	1.5	26,704	127,911
Other*	45.7	40.7	22,282	38,103
Debts				
Mortgage, principle residence	38.40%	12.7%	$34,564	$22,258
Other debts	64.6	57.6	15,881	14,797

*Cash value of life insurance, trusts, and notes owned by individuals.

Source: The 1986 Survey of Consumer Finances, Federal Reserve Board

Note: Wealth here accounts for all major household assets and liabilities except for non-auto consumer durables, collectibles such as artwork, and the present value of expected future benefits from pensions or social security. Wealth is not given separately for householders over age 75 because the measures are not reliable.

Household Savings

WEALTH 65–74

TIME TO REAP

In the three year period, 1983 to 1986, households headed by someone aged 65 and older had an increase in their net worth of $33,867. This savings is 6 percent of the household income they received from 1983 to 1985 and represents about 21 percent of all household savings accumulated during those years.

(average household savings 1983 to 1986 in current dollars, share of total savings and percentage of 1983 to 1985 total household income that is savings for households by age of householder, marital status, race and Hispanic origin, homeownership status, and household income)

	average savings for 3 year period	share of total savings	median 3-year savings as a percentage of 1983-1985 median income
All households	$24,402	100.0%	9.7%
Age of householder			
under age 35	17,912	18.7	7.1
35 to 44	23,301	16.8	12.6
45 to 54	46,606	22.4	16.1
55 to 64	39,392	20.9	9.8
65 and older	**33,867**	**21.3**	**5.9**
Marital status			
Married	40,392	91.8	13.8
Singe male	9,242	3.2	3.1
Single female	6,405	5.0	2.8
Race			
White	34,913	97.8	11.4
Black/Hispanic	3,679	2.2	2.4
Homeownership status			
Homeowner	39,426	88.2	16.1
Renter	10,107	11.8	4.0
Household income			
Less than $10,000	871	0.5	0.0
$10,000 to $20,000	6,633	5.9	4.8
$20,000 to $50,000	18,835	27.2	15.8
$50,000 to $100,000	70,545	27.3	22.8
$100,000 and over	455,294	39.2	44.2

Source: The 1986 Survey of Consumer Finances, Federal Reserve Board

Note: Household savings is the difference in household net worth between 1986 and 1983, expressed in 1986 dollars. Net worth (wealth) is defined as gross assets minus gross debts. Net worth here accounts for all major household assets and liabilities except for non-auto consumer durables, collectibles such as artwork, and the present value of expected future benefits from pensions or social security. Savings is not given separately for householders over age 75 because the measure is not reliable.

Owners and Renters

WEALTH
65–74

A CLOSE SECOND

Although homeownership peaks among householders aged 55 to 64 (80 percent), fully 78 percent of householders aged 65 to 74 live in their own homes. Almost one in four of those homeowners is a woman living alone or with unrelated others. Married couples account for another 61 percent of homeowners in this age group.

(owner- and renter-occupied households by race of householder and household type, for householders aged 65 to 74, numbers in thousands, ownership status as of March 1988)

	total	white	black	Hispanic origin
All households	11,410	10,187	1,063	332
Owner households	8,928	8,220	603	189
Family households				
Married-couple	5,429	5,067	293	120
Male householder	178	156	20	9
Female householder	610	509	92	17
Nonfamily households				
Male householder	600	547	49	15
Female householder	2,111	1,942	149	28
Renter households	2,483	1,967	460	142
Family households				
Married-couple	560	441	86	40
Male householder	48	34	12	7
Female householder	196	128	67	29
Nonfamily households				
Male householder	490	373	111	22
Female householder	1,189	991	184	46

Source: Household and Family Characteristics: March 1988, *Bureau of the Census, Current Population Reports, Series P-20, No. 424*

Note: Hispanics are of any race. Numbers may not add to total due to rounding.

Health Status

HEALTH 65–74

GOOD AND VERY GOOD

About one-third of all men and women aged 65 to 74 rate their health as good. Another 39 percent consider themselves in excellent or very good health and 28 percent say their health is fair or poor. The proportion of 65-to-74-year-olds with poor health in the lowest income group is 5 times greater than that proportion in the highest income group.

(self-assessed health status of persons aged 65 to 74, by sex, race and household income, number of persons in thousands)

	all persons	all health statuses	excellent	very good	good	fair	poor
Both sexes, all races	16,987	100.0%	17.2%	21.5%	33.8%	19.0%	8.5%
Male	7,490	100.0	18.2	22.2	32.5	18.0	9.1
Female	9,496	100.0	16.4	21.0	34.7	19.8	8.0
White	15,254	100.0	17.5	22.2	34.3	18.2	7.8
Black	1,457	100.0	12.1	15.9	29.4	26.5	16.1
Asian and other	275	100.0	28.8	16.4	26.7	23.5	4.6
Household income							
Less than $10,000	3,628	100.0%	10.5%	16.4%	28.8%	29.2%	15.1%
$10,000 to $19,999	5,008	100.0	15.0	20.7	37.0	19.0	8.4
$20,000 to $34,999	3,589	100.0	23.8	25.2	33.5	12.6	4.9
$35,000 and over	1,877	100.0	29.2	24.9	34.0	9.1	2.8

Source: The 1986 National Health Interview Survey, National Center for Health Statistics

Note: All persons includes those of unknown health status, all health statuses includes only those with known health status. Household income includes only those persons with known household income. Numbers may not add to total due to rounding.

Height

HEALTH
65–74

GROWING OLDER, BUT NOT UP

Between ages 18 and 74 the average American gets two inches shorter. Women aged 65 to 74 have an average height of 5′2″ and 17 percent of them are less than 5′ tall. The average man in this age group is 5′7″ tall—two inches shorter than the national average for men.

(cumulative percentage of height of males and females aged 65 to 74 and their average height, by race)

height, males	cumulative percentage	height, females	cumulative percentage
Less than 60 inches	0.2%	Less than 55 inches	0.4%
Less than 61 inches	1.2	Less than 56 inches	1.0
Less than 62 inches	2.7	Less than 57 inches	2.3
Less than 63 inches	6.0	Less than 58 inches	4.2
Less than 64 inches	10.5	Less than 59 inches	9.3
Less than 65 inches	18.3	Less than 60 inches	17.2
Less than 66 inches	29.4	Less than 61 inches	29.0
Less than 67 inches	41.6	Less than 62 inches	44.3
Less than 68 inches	57.8	Less than 63 inches	59.2
Less than 69 inches	70.0	Less than 64 inches	76.4
Less than 70 inches	82.0	Less than 65 inches	87.0
Less than 71 inches	89.6	Less than 66 inches	94.6
Less than 72 inches	94.5	Less than 67 inches	97.9
Less than 73 inches	97.8	Less than 68 inches	99.2
Less than 74 inches	99.2	Less than 69 inches	99.8
Less than 75 inches	99.9	Less than 70 inches	99.9
Less than 76 inches	100.0	Less than 71 inches	100.0
All height categories	100.0%	All height categories	100.0%
Average height, all races	**67.4 inches**	**Average height, all races**	**62.2 inches**
White	67.6	White	62.3
Black	67.4	Black	62.5

Source: Anthropometric Reference Data and Prevalence of Overweight: United States, 1976-80, *National Center for Health Statistics, National Health Survey Series 11, No. 238.*

Note: Height is without shoes.

Weight

HEALTH 65–74

SHEDDING POUNDS

Thirty-nine percent of women and 25 percent of men aged 65 to 74 weigh more than the weight to height (overweight) standard of the National Center for Health Statistics. The average weight of men drops by 9 pounds and women by 3 pounds between ages 55 and 74.

(cumulative percentage of weight of males and females aged 65 to 74, and their average weight and percent overweight, by race)

weight, males	cumulative percentage	weight, females	cumulative percentage
Less than 100 pounds	0.5%	Less than 90 pounds	0.5%
Less than 110 pounds	1.4	Less than 100 pounds	3.1
Less than 120 pounds	5.0	Less than 110 pounds	8.4
Less than 130 pounds	10.5	Less than 120 pounds	17.3
Less than 140 pounds	18.5	Less than 130 pounds	29.5
Less than 150 pounds	30.3	Less than 140 pounds	45.3
Less than 160 pounds	44.7	Less than 150 pounds	60.4
Less than 170 pounds	57.7	Less than 160 pounds	73.3
Less than 180 pounds	71.9	Less than 170 pounds	81.3
Less than 190 pounds	82.0	Less than 180 pounds	86.9
Less than 200 pounds	89.0	Less than 190 pounds	91.5
Less than 210 pounds	94.2	Less than 200 pounds	94.6
Less than 220 pounds	96.4	Less than 220 pounds	97.4
Less than 230 pounds	98.2	Less than 240 pounds	98.8
Less than 240 pounds	99.2	Less than 260 pounds	99.7
Less than 250 pounds	99.6	Less than 280 pounds	99.8
All weight categories	100.0%	All weight categories	100.0%
Average weight, all races	**164.9 pounds**	**Average weight, all races**	**146.8 pounds**
White	166.2	White	145.9
Black	161.7	Black	159.6
Percent overweight, all races	**25.2%**	**Percent overweight, all races**	**38.5%**
White	25.8	White	36.5
Black	26.4	Black	60.8
Percent severely overweight, all races	**8.4%**	**Percent severely overweight, all races**	**13.3%**
White	8.4	White	12.2
Black	10.4	Black	26.1

Source: Anthropometric Reference Data and Prevalence of Overweight: United States, 1976-80, *National Center for Health Statistics, National Health Survey Series 11, No. 238.*

Notes: Weight includes clothing weight, estimated as ranging from 0.20 to 0.62 pounds. Overweight is defined in terms of a body mass index which is determined by dividing weight in kilograms by height in meters squared. Overweight people have a body mass index equal to or greater than that at the 85th percentile of men and women aged 20 to 29. Severe overweight means a body mass index equal to or greater than at the 95th percentile of men and women aged 20 to 29.

Acute Conditions

HEALTH 65–74

STILL FIGHTING THE FLU

Like other adults, 65-to-74-year-olds are most likely to suffer from flu and the common cold. The third most frequently reported acute condition for men this age is open wounds and cuts while women say that musculoskeletal conditions is third on their list of concerns.

(number of acute conditions reported in a year for all persons and those aged 65 to 74, by sex, numbers in thousands)

	males all ages	males aged 65 to 74	females all ages	females aged 65 to 74
All acute conditions	191,369	7,217	257,177	12,869
Infective and parasitic diseases	**23,122**	**626**	**31,244**	**1,158**
Common childhood diseases	2,565	0	1,876	0
Intestinal virus, unspecified	4,244	319	5,288	199
Viral infections, unspecified	9,621	106	14,273	397
Other	6,692	201	9,807	563
Respiratory conditions	**99,216**	**3,155**	**129,626**	**5,426**
Common cold	30,445	1,156	32,983	1,815
Other acute upper respiratory infections	8,472	95	13,320	492
Influenza	55,256	1,629	75,295	2,523
Acute bronchitis	1,960	173	4,315	504
Pneumonia	1,365	0	1,277	93
Other respiratory conditions	1,718	102	2,435	0
Digestive system conditions	**5,860**	**96**	**9,112**	**345**
Dental conditions	1,059	0	1,955	0
Indigestion, nausea and vomiting	3,299	96	4,670	207
Other digestive conditions	1,502	0	2,487	138
Injuries	**34,588**	**1,279**	**29,706**	**2,024**
Fractures and dislocations	4,367	0	3,978	135
Sprains and strains	6,127	197	6,208	409
Open wounds and lacerations	11,153	497	5,094	188
Contusions and superficial injuries	7,986	418	7,191	375
Other current injuries	4,955	167	7,235	918

(continued next page)

Acute Conditions

HEALTH 65–74

(continued from previous page)

(number of acute conditions reported in a year for all persons and those aged 65 to 74, by sex, numbers in thousands)

	males all ages	males aged 65 to 74	females all ages	females aged 65 to 74
Selected other acute conditions	**21,183**	**1,418**	**40,385**	**1,841**
Eye conditions	1,072	410	2,080	90
Acute ear infections	8,689	392	10,116	0
Other ear conditions	1,884	106	2,193	281
Acute urinary conditions	989	98	4,399	220
Disorders of menstruation	–	–	2,251	0
Other disorders of female genital tract	–	–	2,174	0
Delivery and other conditions of pregnancy	–	–	4,466	0
Skin conditions	2,065	217	3,597	631
Acute musculoskeletal conditions	3,038	99	3,972	550
Headache, excluding migraine	1,253	96	2,461	69
Fever, unspecified	2,192	0	2,675	0
All other acute conditions	**7,400**	**643**	**17,104**	**2,074**

Source: The 1986 National Health Interview Survey, National Center for Health Statistics

Note: An acute condition is defined by The National Health Interview Survey as an illness or injury that usually lasts less than three months and was first noticed less than three months before the respondent's interview. The acute condition must also have caused the person to restrict activities for at least a half a day or to have contacted a physician. The data are based only on information given by the respondent and are subject to recall and selective reporting error. Numbers may not add to total due to rounding.

Chronic Conditions

HEALTH
65–74

ARTHRITIS AND HIGH BLOOD PRESSURE

The top two chronic ailments of men and women aged 65 to 74 are arthritis and high blood pressure. Women this age are also likely to suffer from sinusitis, hearing impairments and back deformities. Additional top concerns of the men are hearing impairments, ischemic heart disease, and sinusitis.

(number of selected chronic conditions reported in a year for all persons and those aged 65 to 74, by sex, numbers in thousands)

	males all ages	males aged 65 to 74	females all ages	females aged 65 to 74
Selected skin and musculoskeletal conditions				
Arthritis	10,751	2,589	20,160	4,941
Gout, including gouty arthritis	1,515	378	713	106
Intervertebral disc disorders	2,522	95	1,645	151
Bone spur or tendonitis, unspecified	781	53	898	152
Disorders of bone or cartilage	449	85	943	248
Trouble with bunions	594	55	2,321	505
Bursitis, unclassified	1,641	155	2,464	577
Sebaceous skin cyst	640	55	881	23
Trouble with acne	2,193	0	2,116	25
Psoriasis	1,069	221	1,262	78
Dermatitis	3,851	182	5,696	389
Trouble with dry, itching skin, unclassified	1,994	189	2,606	281
Trouble with ingrown nails	2,352	168	3,030	504
Trouble with corns and calluses	1,669	214	3,164	460
Impairments				
Visual impairment	4,994	693	3,358	483
Color blindness	2,694	261	272	54
Cataracts	1,534	525	3,497	907
Glaucoma	735	196	967	299
Hearing impairment	11,727	2,527	9,004	1,622
Tinnitus	3,388	771	2,927	643
Speech impairment	1,924	83	871	80
Absence of extremity(s)	374	98	24	0
Paralysis, entire body, one side of body, or both legs	200	0	152	20
Partial paralysis of body or legs	236	81	99	16
Deformity of back	6,812	552	9,676	1,071
Deformity of upper extremities	1,622	50	1,475	184
Deformity of lower extremities	6,454	400	5,739	967
Selected digestive conditions				
Ulcer	2,116	387	2,378	340
Hernia of abdominal cavity	2,300	350	2,283	440
Gastritis or duodenitis	1,080	143	1,813	220

(continued next page)

Almanac of Consumer Markets

Chronic Conditions

HEALTH 65–74

(continued from previous page)

(number of selected chronic conditions reported in a year for all persons and those aged 65 to 74, by sex, numbers in thousands)

	males all ages	males aged 65 to 74	females all ages	females aged 65 to 74
Frequent indigestion	2,504	227	2,811	508
Enteritis or colitis	574	53	1,820	138
Spastic colon	264	0	1,377	133
Diverticula of intestines	404	166	1,508	546
Frequent constipation	1,002	161	3,537	708
Selected conditions of the genitourinary, nervous, endocrine, metabolic, and blood system				
Goiter or other disorders of the thyroid	420	70	2,789	334
Diabetes	2,949	721	3,635	841
Anemias	570	89	2,617	326
Epilepsy	656	0	863	23
Migraine headache	2,068	45	6,448	316
Neuralgia or neuritis, unspecified	215	73	364	92
Kidney trouble	1,305	153	2,662	336
Bladder disorders	516	110	3,253	391
Diseases of prostate	1,281	432	–	–
Inflammatory female genital diseases	–	–	427	0
Noninflammatory female genital diseases	–	–	1,095	0
Menstrual disorders	–	–	2,097	0
Selected circulatory conditions				
Ischemic heart disease	4,091	1,252	2,809	801
Tachycardia or rapid heart	700	152	1,226	373
Heart murmurs	1,310	111	2,583	207
Other heart rhythm disorders	499	241	800	186
Other heart diseases	1,482	408	2,265	453
High blood pressure (hypertension)	12,512	2,617	16,457	3,926
Cerebrovascular disease	1,156	458	1,646	337
Hardening of the arteries	1,428	317	1,225	328
Varicose veins	1,042	325	5,814	970
Hemorrhoids	4,568	619	5,341	572
Selected respiratory conditions				
Chronic bronchitis	4,707	305	6,671	762
Asthma	4,670	264	5,019	526
Hay fever or allergic rhinitis without asthma	10,136	450	11,566	781
Chronic sinusitis	14,636	1,141	19,749	1,723
Deviated nasal septum	825	150	465	84
Chronic disease of tonsils or adenoids	1,071	0	2,068	72
Emphysema	1,201	449	796	308

Source: The 1986 National Health Interview Survey, National Center for Health Statistics

Note: Chronic conditions are defined by the National Health Interview Survey as conditions that either a) were first noticed three months or more before the date of the interview or b) belong to a group of conditions (such as heart disease or diabetes) that are considered chronic regardless of when they began. Totals for all chronic conditions are not shown because the National Health Interview Survey does not measure the total number of chronic conditions for each person. The data are based only on information given by the respondent and are subject to recall and selective reporting error.

Activity Restrictions

HEALTH
65–74

THIRTEEN BED-REST DAYS

People aged 65 to 74 each spend 4 percent of the year or about 13 whole or half days in bed because they are ill or injured. Working men in this age group have ten work-loss days a year and women who work have seven such days.

(number of days of activity restriction reported in a year and per person due to acute and chronic conditions, by type of restriction and sex, race, and household income, all persons and those aged 65 to 74, numbers in thousands)

	number of days per year		number of days per person	
	bed day	work-loss day	bed day	work-loss day
All ages	1,547,980	833,396	6.5	5.4
Male	613,113	401,503	5.4	4.8
Female	934,867	431,892	7.7	6.0
White	1,298,039	716,187	6.5	5.4
Black	220,102	99,332	7.7	5.4
Household income				
Less than $10,000	384,962	90,268	11.5	6.1
$10,000 to $19,999	346,115	162,604	7.7	6.1
$20,000 to $34,999	326,166	254,563	5.2	5.7
$35,000 and over	275,957	232,139	4.3	4.6
All aged 65 to 74	219,992	25,618	13.0	8.5
Male	87,182	17,504	11.6	9.7
Female	132,810	8,114	14.0	6.8
White	184,479	24,060	12.1	8.8
Black	32,636	1,558	22.4	6.4
Household income				
Less than $10,000	65,709	3,918	18.1	9.4
$10,000 to $19,999	57,522	8,315	11.5	10.9
$20,000 to $34,999	40,860	3,709	11.4	5.0
$35,000 and over	16,882	4,907	9.0	8.2

Source: The 1986 National Health Interview Survey, National Center for Health Statistics

Note: Numbers may not add to total due to rounding. A bed day is one during which a person stayed in bed more than half a day because of illness or injury. All hospital days for inpatients are considered bed days even if the patient was not in bed more than half a day. A work-loss day is one on which a currently employed person aged 18 or older missed more than half a day of work. The data are based only on information given by the respondent and are subject to recall and selective reporting error.

Cause of Death

HEALTH
65–74

DISEASES OF LONGER LIVES

Sixty-seven percent of all deaths among 65-to-74-year-olds are caused by heart diseases and cancer. Together, the ten leading causes of death account for 88 percent of all deaths in this age group. The average remaining lifetime for people aged 65 to 70 is 16.9 years and 13.6 years for those aged 70 to 75.

(ten leading causes of death among persons aged 65 to 74)

	number of deaths persons aged 65 to 74	number of deaths all ages	percent accounted for by persons aged 65 to 74
All causes	**485,539**	**2,105,361**	**23.1%**
Heart diseases	180,772	765,490	23.6
Malignant neoplasms (cancer)	146,803	469,376	31.3
Cerebrovascular diseases	28,444	149,643	19.0
Chronic obstructive pulmonary diseases and allied conditions	25,866	76,559	33.8
Diabetes mellitus	10,269	37,184	27.6
Pneumonia and influenza	10,154	69,812	14.5
Accidents and adverse effects	8,499	95,277	8.9
Chronic liver diseases and cirrhosis	6,455	26,159	24.7
Nephritis, nephrotic syndrome, and nephrosis (kidney disorder)	4,649	21,767	21.4
Septicemia (infections of the blood stream)	3,915	18,795	20.8
All other causes	59,713	375,299	15.9

Source: Advance Report of Final Mortality Statistics, 1986, *National Center for Health Statistics, Vol. 37, No. 6*

Chapter 9

CONSUMERS AGED 75 AND OLDER

Although consumers aged 75 and older are beginning to slow down, they are the second-fastest growing market.

The number of elderly Americans will be on the rise during the 1990s along with the number of households they head.

- Between 1990 and 2000 the number of Americans aged 75 and older will jump up 27 percent.

- Between 1990 and 2000 the number of households headed by people aged 75 and older will increase by 240,200 each year, for an overall growth of 28 percent.

- Of the nation's eight million households headed by someone aged 75 and older, only 33 percent are married couples and a full 57 percent are nonfamilies. Nearly all—97 percent—nonfamily elderly householders live alone, and 80 percent of those who live alone are women.

- Only 9 percent of elderly Americans completed four or more years of college and most of them (58 percent) did not finish high school.

- Fully three-quarters of households headed by someone aged 75 and older have household incomes of less than $20,000.

- Elderly married couples have the lowest median household income of all married couples—$17,100—with only one in twelve bringing in $50,000 or more.

- Food, housing, and personal care take a bigger chunk from the budgets of elderly households than from households in general. Compared with the other age groups, a large share of their spending dollar—15 percent—goes to health care.

- The elderly market will be an estimated 28 billion dollars larger in 2000 than in 1990.

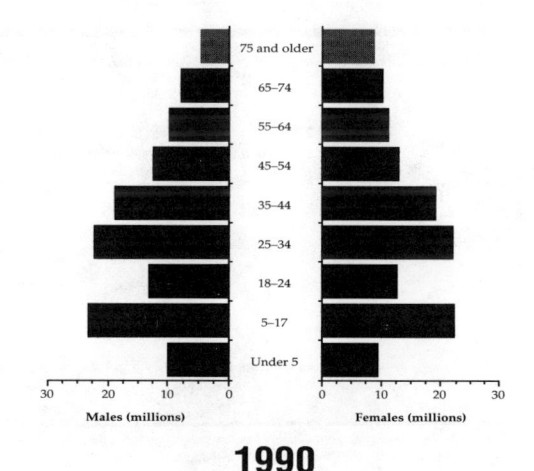

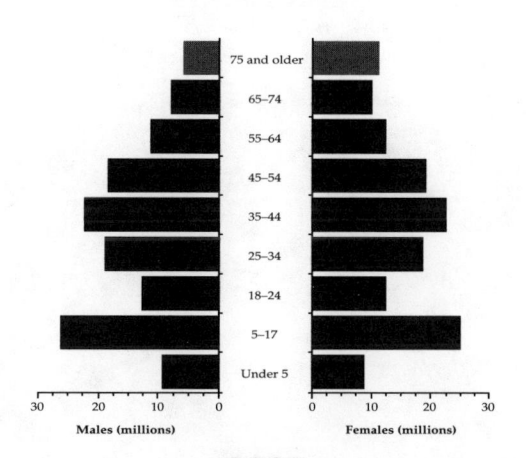

1990

2000

Share of Total Population

POPULATION
75 and older

SECOND-FASTEST GROWING GROUP

The 75 and older age group is second only to those aged 45 to 54 in rate of growth during the 1990s. By the end of the decade the number of these oldest Americans will have surged up 28 percent and they will be 6 percent of the total population.

(total population and the number of persons aged 75 and older, in thousands, by sex, 1960 to 1980, and projections for 1990 to 2000)

	1960 number	1960 percent of total	1970 number	1970 percent of total	1980 number	1980 percent of total	1990 number	1990 percent of total	1995 number	1995 percent of total	2000 number	2000 percent of total
All ages	180,671	100.0%	205,052	100.0%	227,757	100.0%	252,293	100.0%	264,077	100.0%	274,479	100.0%
All aged 75+	5,622	3.1	7,614	3.7	10,051	4.4	13,627	5.4	15,367	5.8	17,261	6.3
Males	2,409	1.3	2,953	1.4	3,575	1.6	4,763	1.9	5,352	2.0	5,996	2.2
Females	3,212	1.8	4,661	2.3	6,476	2.8	8,865	3.5	10,015	3.8	11,266	4.1

Source: Annual Projections of the Population by Age, Sex, and Race, for the United States: 1983 to 2080, *Bureau of the Census, Current Population Reports, Series 17 and the Bureau of the Census*

Note: Total population includes Armed Forces overseas; 1960 to 1980 are based on censuses; projections are based on the Census Bureau's Series 17 projections that incorporate illegal immigration and higher levels of emigration than other Census Bureau projections. Series 17 is consistent with current estimates of illegal aliens living in the United States. Numbers may not add to total due to rounding.

Sex, Race, and Ethnicity

POPULATION
75 and older

DIVERSITY IN THE 1990s

From those under age 5 all the way up to the 75 and older group, there will be declines in the proportion of whites and gains among nonwhites and Hispanics. Between 1990 and 2000, whites will slip from 88 to 86 percent of those aged 75 and older, blacks will remain constant at 8 percent, and Hispanics and Asians will each creep up 1 percentage point, to 4 and 2 percent, respectively, of the elderly.

(projections of the total population and persons aged 75 and older, in thousands, by sex, race, and Hispanic origin, 1990 to 2000)

	1990	1995	2000	percent change 1990–2000
All ages	**252,293**	**264,077**	**274,479**	**8.8%**
White	191,594	195,347	197,634	3.2
Black	30,915	33,237	35,440	14.6
Hispanic	21,854	25,991	30,295	38.6
Asians and other races	7,930	9,502	11,110	40.1
All aged 75 and older	**13,627**	**15,367**	**17,261**	**26.7**
White	11,936	13,371	14,861	24.5
Black	1,079	1,204	1,350	25.1
Hispanic	425	533	691	62.6
Asians and other races	187	259	359	92.0
All males aged 75 and older	**4,763**	**5,352**	**5,996**	**25.9**
White	4,153	4,658	5,178	24.7
Black	370	396	429	15.9
Hispanic	161	199	257	59.6
Asians and other races	79	99	132	67.1
All females aged 75 and older	**8,865**	**10,015**	**11,266**	**27.1**
White	7,783	8,713	9,684	24.4
Black	710	808	920	29.6
Hispanic	263	334	434	65.0
Asians and other races	109	160	228	109.2

Source: Projections of the Population of the United States by Age, Sex, and Race: 1983 to 2080, Bureau of the Census, Current Population Reports, Series P-25, No. 952, Series 17

Note: Series 17 projections incorporate illegal immigration and higher levels of emigration than other Census Bureau projections and are consistent with current estimates of illegal aliens living in the United States. Total population includes Armed Forces living overseas. In this table Hispanics have been separated out of the racial groups; categories do not overlap. Numbers may not add to total due to rounding.

State Populations

POPULATION
75 and older

ELDERLY ON THE RISE

Elderly Americans will be on the rise in every state in the Union during the 1990s, with the biggest gains forecasted for the South Atlantic, Mountain, and Pacific states. By 2000, California, Florida, and New York will be home to 27 percent of all people aged 75 and older.

(resident population and the number of persons aged 75 and older, in thousands, in Census Bureau divisions and states in 1980 and projections for 1990 to 2010)

Note: Inconsistencies between the data in this table and the preceding two tables are due to different assumptions about immigration and emigration on which the projections are based and the inclusion of Armed Forces overseas in the total population. This table is based on the resident population only.

	census 1980	projections 1990	2000	2010	percent change 1990–2000	percent change 2000–2010
All ages	226,546	249,891	267,747	282,055	7.1%	5.3%
All aged 75 and older	9,969	13,187	16,639	18,323	26.2	10.1
New England	**624**	**774**	**940**	**977**	**21.4**	**3.9**
Connecticut	145	190	240	252	26.3	5.0
Maine	59	73	85	89	16.4	4.7
Massachusetts	304	362	432	443	19.3	2.5
New Hampshire	41	56	70	79	25.0	12.9
Rhode Island	51	64	77	77	20.3	0.0
Vermont	24	30	35	36	16.7	2.9
Middle Atlantic	**1,784**	**2,191**	**2,628**	**2,709**	**19.9**	**3.1**
New Jersey	329	427	549	595	28.6	8.4
New York	869	1,009	1,175	1,227	16.5	4.4
Pennsylvania	587	755	904	887	19.7	-1.9
East North Central	**1,788**	**2,228**	**2,630**	**2,680**	**18.0**	**1.9**
Illinois	501	612	707	715	15.5	1.1
Indiana	234	294	349	361	18.7	3.4
Michigan	356	451	544	554	20.6	1.8
Ohio	462	580	702	717	21.0	2.1
Wisconsin	235	291	328	334	12.7	1.8

(continued on next page)

State Populations

POPULATION 75 and older

(continued from previous page)

(resident population and the number of persons aged 75 and older, in thousands, in Census Bureau divisions and states in 1980 and projections for 1990 to 2010)

	census 1980	1990	projections 2000	2010	percent change 1990–2000	percent change 2000–2010
All ages	226,546	249,891	267,747	282,055	7.1%	5.3%
All aged 75 and older	9,969	13,187	16,639	18,323	26.2	10.1
West North Central	**948**	**1,130**	**1,268**	**1,309**	**12.2**	**3.2**
Iowa	173	197	209	200	6.1	-4.3
Kansas	132	159	181	190	13.8	5.0
Minnesota	210	252	292	307	15.9	5.1
Missouri	267	326	374	396	14.7	5.9
Nebraska	92	106	116	119	9.4	2.6
North Dakota	33	41	44	43	7.3	-2.3
South Dakota	40	47	53	53	12.8	0.0
South Atlantic	**1,604**	**2,406**	**3,363**	**3,960**	**39.8**	**17.8**
Delaware	23	32	46	53	43.8	15.2
District of Columbia	27	32	39	41	21.9	5.1
Florida	628	1,007	1,479	1,774	46.9	19.9
Georgia	186	272	369	451	35.7	22.2
Maryland	149	204	279	317	36.8	13.6
North Carolina	215	327	453	540	38.5	19.2
South Carolina	97	150	211	245	40.7	16.1
Virginia	186	266	361	418	35.7	15.8
West Virginia	90	116	127	121	9.5	-4.7
East South Central	**626**	**836**	**1,009**	**1,111**	**20.7**	**10.1**
Alabama	162	223	272	302	22.0	11.0
Kentucky	161	201	235	248	16.9	5.5
Mississippi	110	145	171	189	17.9	10.5
Tennessee	194	268	333	372	24.3	11.7
West South Central	**945**	**1,273**	**1,594**	**1,844**	**25.2**	**15.7**
Arkansas	119	159	187	200	17.6	7.0
Louisiana	150	195	236	257	21.0	8.9
Oklahoma	152	191	215	232	12.6	7.9
Texas	524	728	956	1,155	31.3	20.8

(continued on next page)

State Populations

POPULATION
75 and older

(continued from previous page)

(resident population and the number of persons aged 75 and older, in thousands, in Census Bureau divisions and states in 1980 and projections for 1990 to 2010)

	census 1980	projections 1990	2000	2010	percent change 1990–2000	percent change 2000–2010
All ages	226,546	249,891	267,747	282,055	7.1%	5.3%
All aged 75 and older	9,969	13,187	16,639	18,323	26.2	10.1
Mountain	**389**	**601**	**838**	**988**	**39.4**	**17.9**
Arizona	105	191	298	373	56.0	25.2
Colorado	98	133	179	210	34.6	17.3
Idaho	35	51	61	62	19.6	1.6
Montana	33	44	51	50	15.9	-2.0
Nevada	20	40	59	72	47.5	22.0
New Mexico	41	66	91	111	37.9	22.0
Utah	41	61	79	90	29.5	13.9
Wyoming	14	19	20	20	5.3	0.0
Pacific	**1,261**	**1,749**	**2,370**	**2,744**	**35.5**	**15.8**
Alaska	4	6	11	14	83.3	27.3
California	943	1,296	1,789	2,111	38.0	18.0
Hawaii	28	47	84	111	78.7	32.1
Oregon	118	165	193	192	17.0	-0.5
Washington	167	235	295	315	25.5	6.8

Source: Projections of the Population of States by Age, Sex and Race: 1988 to 2010, *Bureau of the Census, Current Population Reports, Series P-25, No. 1017*

Note: Numbers may not add to total due to rounding.

State-by-State Changes

POPULATION
75 and older

BIG—AND SMALL—GAINERS

Between 1990 and 2000, the top five gainers in the number of people aged 75 and older will be Florida (up 47 percent), Nevada (48 percent), Arizona (56 percent), Hawaii (79 percent), and—the winner—Alaska, at 83 percent. At the bottom of the gainer list is Wyoming at 5 percent.

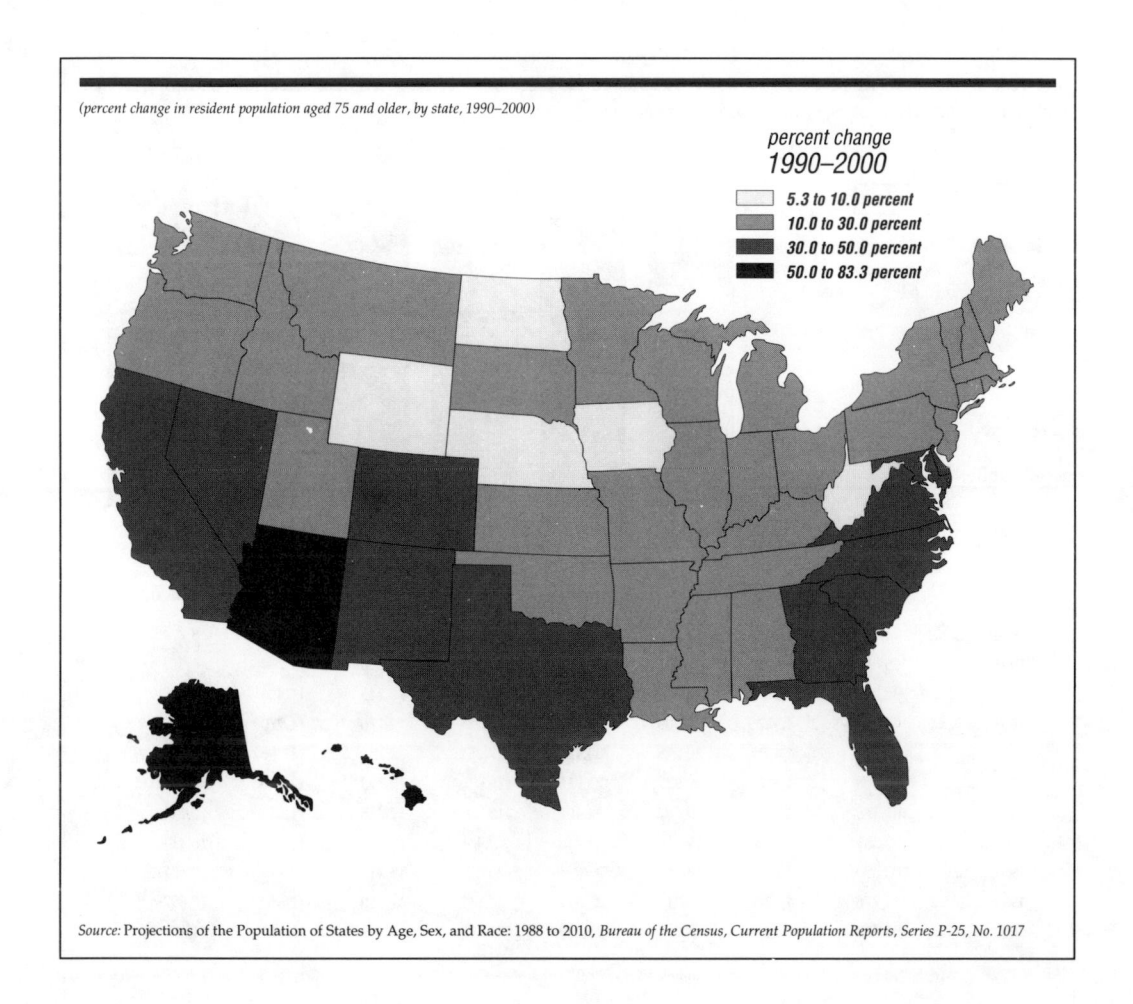

(percent change in resident population aged 75 and older, by state, 1990–2000)

percent change
1990–2000

- 5.3 to 10.0 percent
- 10.0 to 30.0 percent
- 30.0 to 50.0 percent
- 50.0 to 83.3 percent

Source: Projections of the Population of States by Age, Sex, and Race: 1988 to 2010, *Bureau of the Census, Current Population Reports, Series P-25, No. 1017*

Number of Households

HOUSEHOLDS
75 and older

MORE ELDERLY HOUSEHOLDS

Between 1990 and 2000 the number of households headed by people aged 75 and older will increase by 240,200 each year, for an overall growth of 28 percent. The number of nonfamily households will be up 31 percent, while family households will trail with a gain of 24 percent.

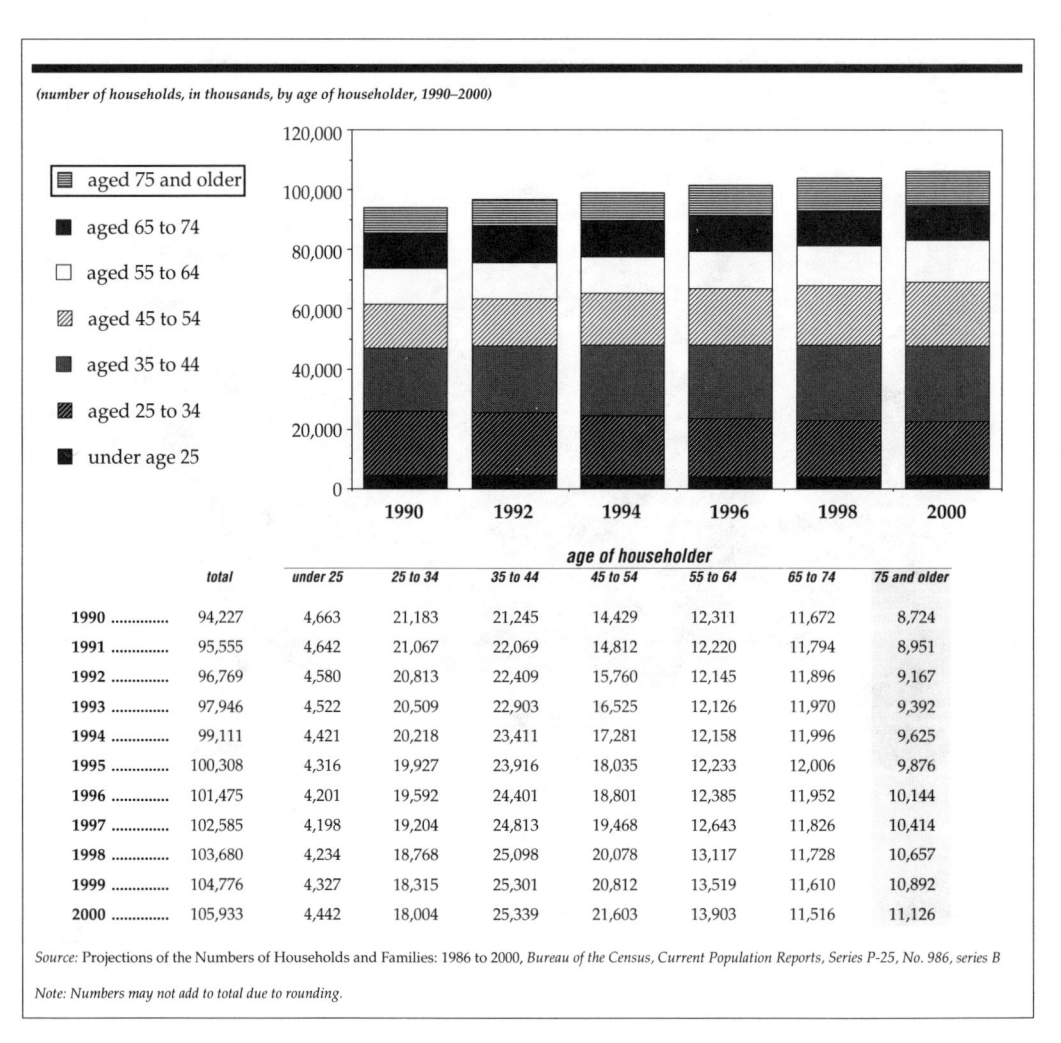

(number of households, in thousands, by age of householder, 1990–2000)

	total	under 25	25 to 34	35 to 44	45 to 54	55 to 64	65 to 74	75 and older
1990	94,227	4,663	21,183	21,245	14,429	12,311	11,672	8,724
1991	95,555	4,642	21,067	22,069	14,812	12,220	11,794	8,951
1992	96,769	4,580	20,813	22,409	15,760	12,145	11,896	9,167
1993	97,946	4,522	20,509	22,903	16,525	12,126	11,970	9,392
1994	99,111	4,421	20,218	23,411	17,281	12,158	11,996	9,625
1995	100,308	4,316	19,927	23,916	18,035	12,233	12,006	9,876
1996	101,475	4,201	19,592	24,401	18,801	12,385	11,952	10,144
1997	102,585	4,198	19,204	24,813	19,468	12,643	11,826	10,414
1998	103,680	4,234	18,768	25,098	20,078	13,117	11,728	10,657
1999	104,776	4,327	18,315	25,301	20,812	13,519	11,610	10,892
2000	105,933	4,442	18,004	25,339	21,603	13,903	11,516	11,126

Source: Projections of the Numbers of Households and Families: 1986 to 2000, *Bureau of the Census, Current Population Reports, Series P-25, No. 986, series B*

Note: Numbers may not add to total due to rounding.

Almanac of Consumer Markets

Types of Households

HOUSEHOLDS
75 and older

A MAJORITY LIVE ALONE

Of the nation's eight million households headed by people aged 75 and older, only 33 percent are married couples and a full 57 percent are nonfamilies. Nearly all—97 percent—nonfamily elderly householders live alone, and 80 percent of those who live alone are women.

(household types for all households and for householders aged 75 and older, numbers in thousands)

	all households total	all households percent of households in category	householder aged 75 and older total	householder aged 75 and older percent of households in category
All households	91,066	100.0%	8,046	100.0%
Family households	65,133	71.5	3,482	43.3
Married couple	51,809	56.9	2,643	32.9
With children under age 18 at home	24,600	27.0	12	0.1
Without children under age 18 at home	27,209	29.9	2,631	32.7
Female householder	10,608	11.6	673	8.4
With children under age 18 at home	6,273	6.9	6	0.1
Without children under age 18 at home	4,335	4.8	667	8.3
Male householder	2,715	3.0	165	2.1
With children under age 18 at home	1,047	1.1	–	–
Without children under age 18 at home	1,669	1.8	165	2.1
Nonfamily households	25,993	28.5	4,564	56.7
Living alone	21,889	24.0	4,441	55.2
Female householder	13,101	14.4	3,541	44.0
Male householder	8,788	9.7	899	11.2
Living with others	4,044	4.4	123	1.5
Female householder	1,523	1.7	89	1.1
Male householder	2,521	2.8	34	0.4

Source: The 1988 Current Population Survey, Bureau of the Census

Note: Numbers may not add to total due to rounding.

Future Household Types

HOUSEHOLDS
75 and older

BIG GAINS SPELL CHANGE

The 30 percent gain projected for the number of 75-and-older householders will be a major feature of the 1990s. Unlike other age groups, they will show fairly high growth in the number of both family and nonfamily households.

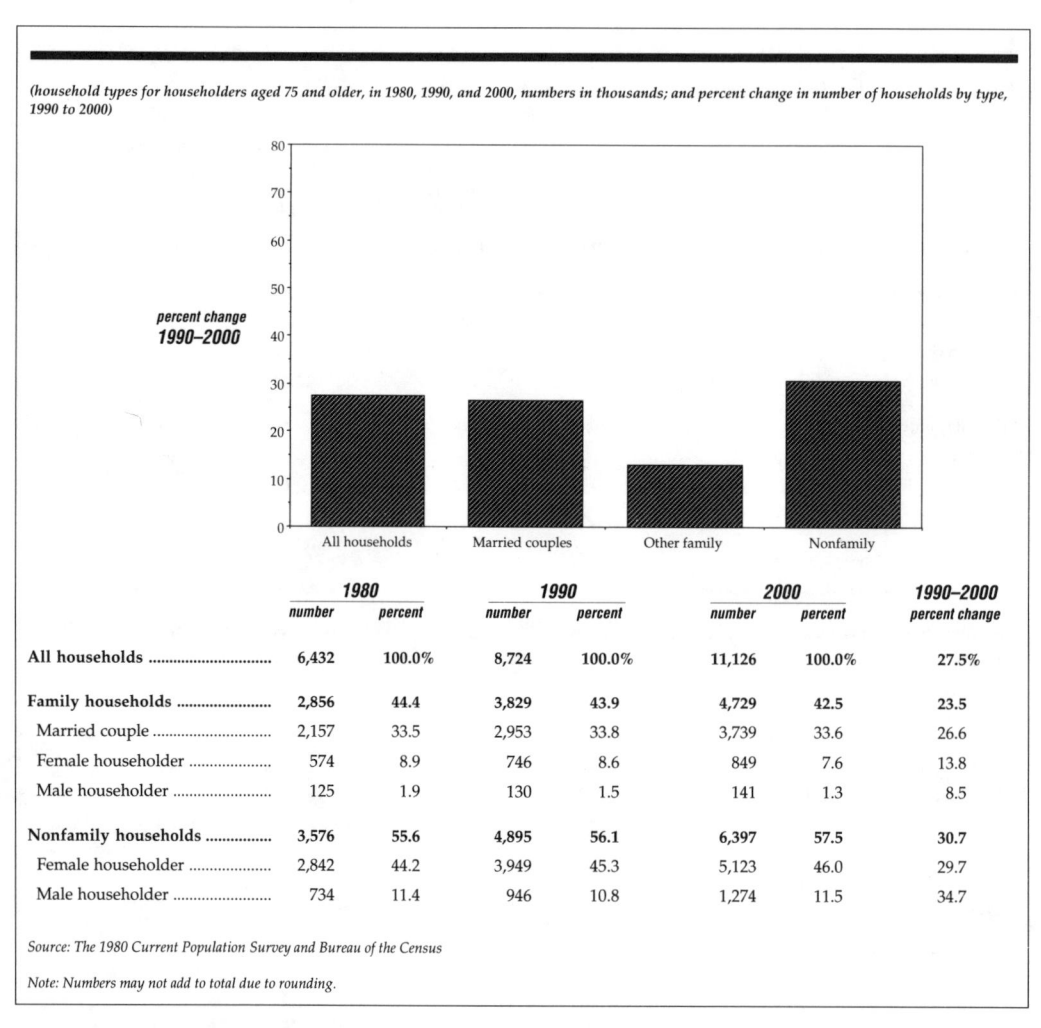

(household types for householders aged 75 and older, in 1980, 1990, and 2000, numbers in thousands; and percent change in number of households by type, 1990 to 2000)

	1980 number	1980 percent	1990 number	1990 percent	2000 number	2000 percent	1990–2000 percent change
All households	6,432	100.0%	8,724	100.0%	11,126	100.0%	27.5%
Family households	2,856	44.4	3,829	43.9	4,729	42.5	23.5
Married couple	2,157	33.5	2,953	33.8	3,739	33.6	26.6
Female householder	574	8.9	746	8.6	849	7.6	13.8
Male householder	125	1.9	130	1.5	141	1.3	8.5
Nonfamily households	3,576	55.6	4,895	56.1	6,397	57.5	30.7
Female householder	2,842	44.2	3,949	45.3	5,123	46.0	29.7
Male householder	734	11.4	946	10.8	1,274	11.5	34.7

Source: The 1980 Current Population Survey and Bureau of the Census

Note: Numbers may not add to total due to rounding.

Marital Status

MARITAL STATUS
75 and older

A MAJORITY WIDOWED

Although 39 percent of the elderly are married and living with their spouses, over half are widowed—24 percent of the men and 67 percent of the women. Whites are more likely than blacks or Hispanics to be currently married, a trend that shows up in every age group except among those under age 25.

(marital status of persons aged 15 and older and those aged 75 and older, by sex, race and Hispanic origin, numbers in thousands)

	all	total	single never married	married spouse present	married spouse absent	divorced	widowed
Males all ages							
All races/ethnicities	89,368	100.0%	30.0%	58.5%	2.9%	6.3%	2.4%
White	77,212	100.0	28.2	60.9	2.5	6.2	2.3
Black	9,472	100.0	42.9	40.4	6.0	7.5	3.3
Hispanic origin	6,517	100.0	36.4	49.9	6.2	5.8	1.6
Males aged 75 and older							
All races/ethnicities	3,970	100.0	4.3	65.9	2.9	3.2	23.6
White	3,574	100.0	4.3	66.4	2.7	3.2	23.3
Black	321	100.0	3.7	60.1	4.7	4.0	27.4
Hispanic origin	142	100.0	4.9	54.9	5.6	7.0	28.2
Females all ages							
All races/ethnicities	97,320	100.0	23.0	53.7	3.6	8.3	11.4
White	83,003	100.0	21.0	56.6	2.7	8.0	11.6
Black	11,447	100.0	36.5	32.7	9.2	10.4	11.2
Hispanic origin	6,588	100.0	26.6	51.2	7.7	8.3	6.2
Females aged 75 and older							
All races/ethnicities	6,773	100.0	6.4	22.4	1.4	2.7	67.0
White	6,163	100.0	6.6	23.1	1.2	2.6	66.5
Black	544	100.0	5.1	15.3	4.4	3.5	71.5
Hispanic origin	189	100.0	6.9	22.2	4.8	5.3	60.8

Source: Marital Status and Living Arrangements: March 1987, *Bureau of the Census, Current Population Reports, Series P-20, No. 423*

Note: Hispanics may be of any race. Numbers may not add to total due to rounding.

Summary of Educational Attainment

EDUCATIONAL ATTAINMENT
75 and older

LIVING AND LEARNING

This is the age group with the lowest share of formally educated members. Only 9 percent of the oldest Americans completed four or more years of college and most of them did not finish high school.

(years of school completed by persons aged 25 and over, by selected characteristics, numbers in thousands)

	number	percentage with 4 years of high school or more	1 or more years of college	4 or more years of college
All persons	149,144	75.6%	37.0%	19.9%
Age groups:				
25 to 34	42,635	86.5	45.4	23.9
35 to 44	33,632	85.9	46.8	26.5
45 to 54	23,018	77.6	35.6	19.5
55 to 64	21,883	67.8	28.0	14.9
65 to 74	17,232	56.9	21.9	10.6
75 years and older	10,743	42.0	18.0	8.9
Sex:				
Male	70,677	76.0	40.6	23.6
Female	78,476	75.3	33.6	16.5
Race:				
White	129,170	77.0	37.8	20.5
Black	15,580	63.4	26.4	10.7
Asian and other	4,394	78.4	50.9	33.4
Hispanic origin:				
Hispanic	9,449	50.9	21.9	8.6
Non-Hispanic	139,695	77.3	38.0	20.6
Region:				
Northeast	32,030	76.5	36.8	22.2
Midwest	36,322	77.4	33.7	17.6
South	50,848	70.8	34.1	18.3
West	29,943	80.6	45.9	22.8
Metropolitan residence:				
Metropolitan area	115,614	77.6	40.0	22.1
Nonmetropolitan area	33,529	68.7	26.5	12.6

Source: Educational Attainment in the United States: March 1987 and March 1986. Bureau of the Census, Current Population Reports, Series P-20, No. 428

Sex, Race, and Ethnicity

EDUCATIONAL ATTAINMENT
75 and older

THE WAY IT WAS

Fifty-six percent of whites and 85 percent of blacks and Hispanics aged 75 and older did not complete high school. But 11 percent of the men and 8 percent of the women finished at least four years of college.

(years of school completed by persons aged 25 and older and those aged 75 and older, by sex, race, and Hispanic origin, numbers in thousands)

	number	total	not high school graduate	high school graduate	1 to 3 years of college	4 or more years of college
All persons aged 25 and older	149,144	100.0%	24.4%	38.7%	17.1%	19.9%
White	129,170	100.0	23.0	39.2	17.2	20.5
Black	15,580	100.0	36.6	37.1	15.7	10.7
Hispanic origin	9,449	100.0	49.1	29.0	13.3	8.6
All persons aged 75 and older	10,743	100.0	58.0	23.9	9.1	8.9
White	9,737	100.0	55.6	25.3	9.7	9.4
Black	865	100.0	84.5	9.6	2.4	3.7
Hispanic origin	331	100.0	84.6	7.9	3.6	3.6
Males aged 25 and older	70,677	100.0	24.0	35.4	17.1	23.6
White	61,678	100.0	22.7	35.6	17.2	24.5
Black	6,919	100.0	37.0	36.5	15.5	11.0
Hispanic origin	4,614	100.0	48.2	28.0	14.2	9.7
Males aged 75 and older	3,970	100.0	60.2	20.3	8.1	11.3
White	3,574	100.0	57.5	21.5	8.8	12.1
Black	321	100.0	91.6	5.6	0.9	1.6
Hispanic origin	142	100.0	91.5	1.4	3.5	3.5
Females aged 25 and older	78,467	100.0	24.7	41.6	17.1	16.5
White	67,492	100.0	23.3	42.6	17.3	16.9
Black	8,661	100.0	36.2	37.5	15.8	10.4
Hispanic origin	4,835	100.0	50.0	30.0	12.5	7.5
Females aged 75 and older	6,773	100.0	56.8	26.0	9.7	7.5
White	6,163	100.0	54.5	27.5	10.3	7.8
Black	544	100.0	80.0	11.9	3.3	4.8
Hispanic origin	189	100.0	80.4	12.2	3.7	3.7

Source: Educational Attainment in the United States: March 1987 and March 1986, Bureau of the Census, Current Population Reports, Series P-20, No. 428
Note: Hispanics are of any race. Numbers may not add to total due to rounding.

Workers in the 1990s

LABOR FORCE
75 and older

FEWER ELDERLY WORKERS

By 2000 only 4 percent of men and 2 percent of women aged 75 and older will be in the labor force. While the number of Asian women and blacks of both sexes in the work force will increase, participation rates for elderly people of all races and ethnicities will decline during the decade.

(labor force and labor force participation rates* for persons aged 16 and older and those aged 75 and older, by sex, race, and ethnicity, in 1990 and 2000, numbers in thousands)

	1990 number	1990 participation rate	2000 number	2000 participation rate	1990-2000 percent change
Both sexes, aged 16 and older	**124,457**	**66.2%**	**138,775**	**67.8%**	**11.5%**
White	106,648	66.5	116,701	68.2	9.4
Black	13,788	64.6	16,334	66.0	18.5
Hispanic	9,718	65.9	14,086	67.1	44.9
Asian and other	4,021	64.8	5,740	65.8	42.8
Males, aged 16 and older	**67,909**	**75.8**	**73,136**	**74.7**	**7.7**
Males, aged 75 and older	**279**	**6.3**	**246**	**4.3**	**-11.8**
White	264	6.6	231	4.5	-12.5
Black	12	3.6	13	3.0	8.3
Hispanic	–	–	–	–	–
Asian and other	3	3.4	2	1.5	-33.3
Females, aged 16 and older	**56,548**	**57.4**	**65,639**	**61.5**	**16.1**
Females, aged 75 and older	**164**	**2.2**	**141**	**1.5**	**-14.0**
White	141	2.1	116	1.4	-17.7
Black	19	3.2	20	2.7	5.3
Hispanic	–	–	–	–	–
Asian and other	4	2.5	5	1.8	25.0

*Labor force participation rates are the ratio of people in the labor force to the total population of a given sex, age and race or ethnicity.

Source: Unpublished data from the Bureau of Labor Statistics

Note: The labor force here includes civilians who are working or looking for work. Hispanics are of any race.

Income and Age

INCOME
75 and older

LOWEST INCOMES

Fully three-quarters of households headed by people aged 75 and older have household incomes of less than $20,000. Only 15 percent of elderly householders bring in between $20,000 and $35,000 and an even smaller 10 percent have incomes of $35,000 or more.

(household income by age of householder, numbers for 1988 in thousands, income is for 1987)

	total	under 25	25 to 34	35 to 44	45 to 54	55 to 64	65 to 74	75 +
All households	91,066	5,228	20,583	19,323	13,630	12,846	11,410	8,045
All households	100.0%	100.0%	100.0%	100.0%	100.0%	100.0%	100.0%	100.0%
Less than $10,000	18.4	30.3	13.6	10.3	10.4	17.4	27.1	44.6
$10,000 to $14,999	10.6	15.8	9.6	6.6	6.6	9.5	17.3	18.5
$15,000 to $19,999	10.0	14.1	11.1	7.4	6.8	9.7	13.8	11.8
$20,000 to $24,999	9.2	11.5	11.1	8.3	7.2	9.1	10.1	7.5
$25,000 to $29,999	8.4	9.0	10.6	8.5	7.6	8.0	8.3	4.3
$30,000 to $34,999	7.7	6.8	9.7	9.0	7.8	7.2	6.0	3.2
$35,000 to $39,999	6.8	4.5	8.6	9.0	7.2	6.3	4.2	2.4
$40,000 to $44,999	5.8	2.3	6.7	7.9	7.4	6.0	3.0	1.7
$45,000 to $49,999	4.6	1.3	5.1	6.6	5.9	4.7	2.4	1.5
$50,000 to $59,999	6.7	2.1	6.7	9.6	10.1	7.5	2.7	1.9
$60,000 to $74,999	5.5	1.5	4.2	7.9	9.9	6.3	2.1	1.2
$75,000 and over	6.3	0.9	3.0	8.9	13.1	8.3	3.0	1.4
Median household income	$25,986	$16,204	$26,923	$34,926	$37,250	$27,538	$16,906	$11,261

Source: The 1988 Current Population Survey, Bureau of the Census

Note: Numbers may not add to total due to rounding.

Income of Married Couples

INCOME
75 and older

SOME AT THE TOP

Elderly married couples have the lowest median household income of all married couples—$17,100—with only one in twelve bringing in $50,000 or more. Sixty percent of couples aged 75 or older have incomes below $20,000, while 23 percent have between $20,000 and $35,000, and 17 percent have over $35,000.

(household income of married-couple householder families with and without children under 18 at home, householders aged 75 and older, numbers for 1988 in thousands, income is for 1987)

	\multicolumn{3}{c}{married-couple householder aged 75 and older}		
	total	with children under 18 at home	without children under 18 at home
All households	2,643	12	2,631
All households	100.0%	100.0%	100.0%
Less than $10,000	18.4	0.0	18.5
$10,000 to $14,999	22.8	50.0	22.7
$15,000 to $19,999	18.7	0.0	18.7
$20,000 to $24,999	11.3	0.0	11.4
$25,000 to $29,999	6.4	0.0	6.4
$30,000 to $34,999	5.4	8.3	5.4
$35,000 to $39,999	4.0	0.0	4.0
$40,000 to $44,999	2.5	0.0	2.5
$45,000 to $49,999	2.5	8.3	2.4
$50,000 to $59,999	3.0	8.3	2.9
$60,000 to $74,999	2.2	0.0	2.2
$75,000 and over	2.9	25.0	2.8
Median household income	$17,139	–	$17,137

Source: The 1988 Current Population Survey, Bureau of the Census

Note: Median income is unreliable and is therefore not given when the category contains fewer than 75,000 households. Numbers may not add to total due to rounding.

Income of Other Family Households

INCOME
75 and older

HOLDING THEIR OWN

Thirty percent of the families headed by elderly men, and 23 percent of those headed by elderly women, have incomes of $35,000 or more. Not surprisingly, 47 percent of the men and 52 percent of the women head families with incomes of less than $20,000.

(household income of unmarried female- and male-householder families with and without children under 18 at home, householders aged 75 and older, numbers for 1988, in thousands, income is for 1987)

	\multicolumn{3}{c}{female householder aged 75 and older}	\multicolumn{3}{c}{male householder aged 75 and older}
	total	with children under 18 at home	without children under 18 at home	total	with children under 18 at home	without children under 18 at home
All households	673	6	667	165	–	165
All households	100.0%	100.0%	100.0%	100.0%	–	100.0%
Less than $10,000	23.6	50.0	23.4	23.0	–	23.0
$10,000 to $14,999	16.0	16.7	16.0	14.5	–	14.5
$15,000 to $19,999	12.8	0.0	12.9	9.1	–	9.1
$20,000 to $24,999	9.5	0.0	9.6	10.9	–	10.9
$25,000 to $29,999	9.2	0.0	9.3	9.1	–	9.1
$30,000 to $34,999	5.5	0.0	5.5	3.6	–	3.6
$35,000 to $39,999	5.3	0.0	5.4	4.2	–	4.2
$40,000 to $44,999	4.5	0.0	4.5	5.5	–	5.5
$45,000 to $49,999	4.3	0.0	4.3	2.4	–	2.4
$50,000 to $59,999	5.2	33.3	4.9	8.5	–	8.5
$60,000 to $74,999	1.8	0.0	1.8	5.5	–	5.5
$75,000 and over	1.8	0.0	1.8	3.6	–	3.6
Median household income	$19,087	–	$19,175	$21,531	–	$21,531

Source: The 1988 Current Population Survey, Bureau of the Census

Note: Median income is unreliable and is therefore not given when the category contains fewer than 75,000 households. Numbers may not add to total due to rounding.

Income of Nonfamily Households

INCOME
75 and older

ROUGH GOING ALONE

Elderly householders who live with unrelated others have a median income that is over $9,000 greater than that of their counterparts who live alone. Of people aged 75 and older who live alone, 67 percent of the women and 57 percent of the men have household incomes under $10,000.

(household income of nonfamily households by household type, householders aged 75 and older, numbers for 1988 in thousands, income is for 1987)

	total number	living alone total	living alone male householder	living alone female householder	living with others total	living with others male householder	living with others female householder
All nonfamily households	4,564	4,441	899	3,541	123	34	89
All nonfamily households	100.0%	100.0%	100.0%	100.0%	100.0%	100.0%	100.0%
Less than $10,000	63.7	64.9	56.6	67.0	21.1	23.5	20.2
$10,000 to $14,999	16.5	16.3	20.1	15.3	25.2	14.7	29.2
$15,000 to $19,999	7.8	7.7	8.3	7.5	13.8	2.9	18.0
$20,000 to $24,999	4.9	4.7	4.8	4.7	12.2	11.8	12.4
$25,000 to $29,999	2.2	2.0	2.8	1.8	8.9	5.9	10.1
$30,000 to $34,999	1.5	1.5	2.3	1.3	2.4	0.0	2.2
$35,000 to $39,999	0.9	0.9	1.2	0.8	3.3	5.9	2.2
$40,000 to $44,999	0.6	0.5	0.7	0.5	1.6	0.0	2.2
$45,000 to $49,999	0.5	0.5	0.7	0.4	1.6	5.9	0.0
$50,000 to $59,999	0.6	0.6	1.9	0.3	2.4	8.8	0.0
$60,000 to $74,999	0.3	0.2	0.1	0.2	3.3	5.9	2.2
$75,000 and over	0.4	0.2	0.3	0.2	4.9	17.6	1.1
Median household income	$7,755	$7,551	$8,870	$7,314	$16,988	–	$15,571

Source: The 1988 Current Population Survey, Bureau of the Census

Note: Nonfamilies are either people living alone or living with an individual (or individuals) unrelated to the householder. Median income is unreliable and is therefore not given when the category contains fewer than 75,000 households. Numbers may not add to total due to rounding.

Income of Hispanic Households

INCOME
75 and older

LOW-INCOME ELDERLY

Sixteen percent of families with Hispanic householders aged 75 and older have an income of $25,000 or more. Seventy-two percent of Hispanic nonfamily households in this age group are elderly women living alone and only 2 percent of them have incomes of $25,000 or more.

(household income of Hispanic households, by household type, for householders aged 75 and older, numbers for 1988 in thousands, income is for 1987)

family households

	total	married couple	male householder	female householder
All households	100	79	5	15
Total	100.0%	100.0%	100.0%	100.0%
Less than $15,000	65.0	69.6	20.0	66.7
$15,000 to $24,999	18.0	16.5	60.0	20.0
$25,000 and over	16.0	15.2	40.0	13.3
Median household income	$11,716	$11,158	–	–

nonfamily households

		male householder		female householder	
	total	living alone	living with others	living alone	living with others
All households	95	25	–	68	2
Total	100.0%	100.0%	–	100.0%	100.0%
Less than $15,000	95.8	100.0	–	94.1	100.0
$15,000 to $24,999	2.1	–	–	2.9	–
$25,000 and over	1.1	–	–	1.5	–
Median household income	$4,652	–	–	–	–

Source: The 1988 Current Population Survey, Bureau of the Census

Note: Numbers may not add to total due to rounding. Hispanics are of any race. Median income is unreliable and is therefore not given when the category contains fewer than 75,000 households.

Income of Dual-Earner Couples

INCOME
75 and older

VERY FEW WORKERS

Very few people aged 75 or older are still in the labor force—only 6 percent of men, and 2 percent of women. A mere 1 percent of elderly married couples are dual-earners.

(household income for all dual-earner married couples and for those with married-couple householders aged 75 and older, numbers for 1988 in thousands, income is for 1987)

	householder, all ages			householder, aged 75 and older		
	total	with children under 18 at home	without children under 18 at home	total	with children under 18 at home	without children under 18 at home
All households	26,227	14,989	11,238	37	–	37
All households	100.0%	100.0%	100.0%	99.9%	–	99.9%
Less than $15,000	5.7	6.0	5.4	8.1	–	8.1
$15,000 to $19,999	5.1	5.4	4.7	18.9	–	18.9
$20,000 to $24,999	7.3	7.8	6.6	5.4	–	5.4
$25,000 to $29,999	8.3	9.0	7.5	2.7	–	2.7
$30,000 to $34,999	9.4	10.2	8.3	10.8	–	10.8
$35,000 to $39,999	10.3	11.2	9.0	2.7	–	2.7
$40,000 to $44,999	9.6	9.8	9.3	8.1	–	8.1
$45,000 to $49,999	8.1	8.2	7.9	5.4	–	5.4
$50,000 to $59,999	13.0	12.5	13.6	-	–	–
$60,000 to $74,999	11.2	10.2	12.5	10.8	–	10.8
$75,000 and over	12.1	9.6	15.3	27.0	–	27.0
Median household income	$41,904	$40,044	$44,508	–	–	–

Source: The 1988 Current Population Survey, Bureau of the Census

Note: Numbers may not add to total due to rounding. Median income is unreliable and is therefore not given when the category contains fewer than 75,000 households.

Almanac of Consumer Markets

Income and Education

INCOME

75 and older

THE EDUCATED ELDERLY

Among the most highly-educated elderly householders, 42 percent have incomes below $20,000, another 42 percent are in the $20,000 to $50,000 range, while the remaining 16 percent bring in $50,000 or more—a high household income claimed by only 6 percent of those who completed only one to three years of college.

(household income of householders aged 75 and older by years of school completed by householder, numbers for 1988 in thousands, income is for 1987)

	total	not high school graduate	high school graduate	1 to 3 years of college	4 or more years of college
All households	8,045	4,443	2,066	700	834
All households	100.0%	100.0%	100.0%	100.0%	100.0%
Less than $10,000	44.7	55.9	37.0	31.1	15.5
$10,000 to $19,999	30.3	28.5	34.8	32.6	27.0
$20,000 to $29,999	11.8	9.0	13.4	15.9	19.4
$30,000 to $39,999	5.6	3.1	6.3	10.3	12.6
$40,000 to $49,999	3.2	1.7	3.3	4.1	9.7
$50,000 to $59,999	1.9	0.9	2.1	3.7	5.5
$60,000 to $74,999	1.2	0.4	1.9	0.9	3.7
$75,000 and over	1.4	0.5	1.3	1.3	6.5

Source: The 1988 Current Population Survey, Bureau of the Census.

Note: Numbers may not add to total due to rounding.

Annual Expenditures

EXPENDITURES
75 and older

COSTLY HEALTH CARE

Food, housing, and personal care take a bigger chunk from the budgets of elderly households than from households in general. Compared with the other age groups, a large share of their spending dollar—15 percent— goes to health care.

(average annual expenditure and percent distribution of expenditures for all households and for householders aged 75 and older, number of households in thousands)

	all households		householder aged 75 and older	
	average annual expenditure	percent of all expenditures	average annual expenditure	percent of all expenditures
Number of households	93,741		8,423	
Total expenditure	$22,710	100.0%	$11,746	100.0%
Food	3,363	14.8	1,975	16.8
Food at home	2,313	10.2	1,571	13.4
Food away from home	1,049	4.6	404	3.4
Alcoholic beverages	273	1.2	67	0.6
Housing	6,888	30.3	4,076	34.7
Shelter	3,986	17.6	2,007	17.1
Owned dwellings	2,305	10.1	995	8.5
Mortgage interest and charges	1,428	6.3	80	0.7
Property taxes	417	1.8	425	3.6
Maintenance, repairs, insurance, and other expenses	460	2.0	490	4.2
Rented dwellings	1,269	5.6	873	7.4
Other lodging	412	1.8	139	1.2
Fuels, utilities, and public services	1,646	7.2	1,349	11.5
Natural gas	248	1.1	240	2.0
Electricity	674	3.0	517	4.4
Fuel oil and other fuels	107	0.5	155	1.3
Telephone	471	2.1	316	2.7
Water and other public services	145	0.6	121	1.0
Household operations	353	1.6	377	3.2
Domestic services	288	1.3	336	2.9
Other household expenses	65	0.3	42	0.4
Household furnishings, equipment	903	4.0	343	2.9
Household textiles	83	0.4	43	0.4
Furniture	303	1.3	78	0.7
Floor coverings	51	0.2	26	0.2
Major appliances	155	0.7	82	0.7

(continued next page)

Annual Expenditures

EXPENDITURES
75 and older

(continued from previous page)

(average annual expenditure and percent distribution of expenditures for all households and for householders aged 75 and older, number of households in thousands)

	all households		householder aged 75 and older	
	average annual expenditure	percent of all expenditures	average annual expenditure	percent of all expenditures
Small appliances, miscellaneous housewares	55	0.2	27	0.2
Miscellaneous household equipment	256	1.1	87	0.7
Apparel	**1,149**	**5.1**	**416**	**3.5**
Men and boys	283	1.2	80	0.7
Men, 16 and over	228	1.0	72	0.6
Boys, 2 to 15	55	0.2	7	0.1
Women and girls	462	2.0	212	1.8
Women, 16 and over	396	1.7	207	1.8
Girls, 2 to 15	66	0.3	4	0.0
Children under 2	45	0.2	6	0.1
Footwear	123	0.5	46	0.4
Other apparel products and services	237	1.0	74	0.6
Transportation	**4,815**	**21.2**	**1,627**	**13.9**
Cars and trucks, new (net outlay)	1,414	6.2	449	3.8
Cars and trucks, used (net outlay)	897	3.9	192	1.6
Other vehicles	29	0.1	9	0.1
Vehicle finance charges	270	1.2	35	0.3
Gasoline and motor oil	916	4.0	369	3.1
Maintenance and repairs	458	2.0	194	1.7
Vehicle insurance	420	1.8	215	1.8
Public transportation	248	1.1	114	1.0
Vehicle rental, licenses, other charges	163	0.7	50	0.4
Health care	**1,062**	**4.7**	**1,761**	**15.0**
Health insurance	371	1.6	653	5.6
Medical services	502	2.2	765	6.5
Medicines and medical supplies	189	0.8	343	2.9
Entertainment	**1,087**	**4.8**	**299**	**2.5**
Fees and admissions	308	1.4	98	0.8
Television, radios, sound equipment	373	1.6	148	1.3
Other equipment and services	406	1.8	53	0.5
Personal care	**207**	**0.9**	**151**	**1.3**
Reading	**140**	**0.6**	**92**	**0.8**
Education	**298**	**1.3**	**15**	**0.1**
Tobacco and smoking supplies	**230**	**1.0**	**82**	**0.7**
Miscellaneous	**323**	**1.4**	**264**	**2.2**
Contributions and support payments	**746**	**3.3**	**658**	**5.6**
Personal insurance and pensions	**2,129**	**9.4**	**262**	**2.2**
Life insurance and other personal insurance	293	1.3	116	1.0
Retirement, pensions, Social Security	1,836	8.1	146	1.2

Source: The 1986 Consumer Expenditure Survey, Bureau of Labor Statistics

Expenditures by Income

EXPENDITURES
75 and older

MAJOR DONORS

Elderly households bringing in at least $40,000 spend an average of three times more and contribute an average of 11 times more than the typical household in this age group.

(annual average expenditure of households with householders aged 75 and older, by household income, number of households in thousands)

	all households	under $10,000	$10-14,999	$15-19,999	$20-29,999	$30-39,999	$40,000+
Number of households	6,943	4,135	1,250	614	495	194	255
Total expenditure	$11,981	$7,907	$12,142	$17,504	$20,468	$22,199	$40,162
Food	1,956	1,514	2,176	2,534	2,691	3,550	4,105
Food at home	1,532	1,244	1,721	1,849	2,072	2,746	2,586
Food away from home	424	270	455	685	619	804	1,519
Alcoholic beverages	75	30	101	98	149	311	324
Housing	4,012	3,176	4,234	5,213	5,377	5,497	9,972
Shelter	1,974	1,585	2,190	2,601	2,584	2,451	4,278
Owned dwellings	953	641	1,129	1,400	1,374	1,353	3,001
Rented dwellings	871	862	909	903	970	800	674
Other lodging	150	82	152	298	240	299	603
Fuels, utilities, public services	1,326	1,142	1,441	1,540	1,620	2,023	2,154
Household operations	369	238	253	565	589	452	2,126
Household furnishings, equipment	343	211	349	507	585	570	1,414
Apparel and services	400	244	361	522	813	935	1,635
Transportation	1,673	766	1,513	3,760	4,068	4,394	5,468
Vehicles	652	155	376	2,206	2,168	2,245	2,150
Gasoline and motor oil	384	246	475	569	644	801	906
Other vehicle expenses	487	274	544	765	908	1,025	1,776
Public transportation	151	90	118	222	347	323	635
Health care	1,680	1,263	1,929	2,430	3,098	2,368	2,210
Entertainment	309	168	320	384	617	1,125	1,151
Personal care	148	100	160	216	253	258	409

(continued next page)

Expenditures by Income

EXPENDITURES: 75 and older

(continued from previous page)

(annual average expenditure of households with householders aged 75 and older, by household income, number of households in thousands)

	all households	under $10,000	$10-14,999	$15-19,999	$20-29,999	$30-39,999	$40,000+
Reading	95	61	115	132	188	142	246
Education	13	11	3	18	18	38	42
Tobacco and smoking supplies	82	60	124	101	106	149	107
Miscellaneous	219	158	234	201	347	240	905
Cash contributions	1,046	267	735	1,667	2,102	1,167	11,596
Personal insurance and pensions	274	90	137	229	641	2,025	1,992
Life and other insurance	113	79	92	117	226	488	250
Retirement, pensions, Social Security	161	10	44	112	415	1,537	1,742

Source: The 1986 Consumer Expenditure Survey, Bureau of Labor Statistics

Note: All households include complete income reporters only. Total expenditure exceeds total income in some income categories due to a number of factors including the underreporting of income, borrowing, and the use of savings.

Weekly Shopping

EXPENDITURES
75 and older

PET FOOD

Households headed by elderly people spend 50 percent more than the average American household on pet food. They are also above-average spenders on non-prescription drugs and supplies.

(average weekly expenditure for all households and for householders aged 75 and over)

	all households	index all households	householders aged 75 and older	index householders aged 75 and older
Food, total	$59.60	100	$34.16	57
Food at home, total	37.73	100	25.39	67
Cereals and cereal products	1.78	100	1.26	71
Bakery products	3.51	100	2.82	80
Beef	3.63	100	2.11	58
Pork	2.23	100	1.56	70
Other meats	1.52	100	0.90	59
Poultry	1.64	100	1.04	63
Fish and seafood	1.22	100	0.73	60
Eggs	0.57	100	0.45	79
Fresh milk and cream	2.35	100	1.60	68
Other dairy products	2.47	100	1.70	69
Fresh fruits	1.96	100	1.85	94
Fresh vegetables	1.77	100	1.41	80
Processed fruits	1.38	100	1.02	74
Processed vegetables	1.03	100	0.69	67
Sugar and other sweets	1.42	100	0.94	66
Fats and oils	0.99	100	0.73	74
Miscellaneous foods	4.53	100	2.28	50
Nonalcoholic beverages	3.71	100	2.31	62
Food away from home	21.87	100	8.78	40
Nonfood items				
Alcoholic beverages	4.84	100	1.10	23
Tobacco products and smoking supplies	3.60	100	1.14	32
Pet food	1.09	100	1.64	150
Personal care products and services	5.01	100	2.58	51
Non-prescription drugs and supplies	2.31	100	2.72	118
Housekeeping supplies	6.07	100	3.68	61

Source: The 1986 Consumer Expenditure Survey, Bureau of Labor Statistics

Note: An index of 100 represents the average. An index of 132 means that the average weekly expenditure of the subgroup is 32 percent above the average for all households. An index of 68 indicates spending that is 32 percent below average. Numbers may not add to total due to rounding.

Future Expenditures

EXPENDITURES
75 and older

GROWING BY $28 BILLION
The elderly market will be an estimated 28 billion dollars larger in 2000 than in 1990. This is due to the increasing numbers of households headed by people aged 75 and older during the decade.

(projected aggregate expenditures in 1990 and 2000 for all households and for households by age of householder, in billions of dollars)

1990 aggregate annual expenditures in billions

	all households	under 25	25-34	35-44	45-54	55-64	65-74	75+
Number of households (in thousands)	94,227	4,663	21,183	21,245	14,429	12,311	11,672	8,724
Total expenditures (in billions of dollars)	$2,203.1	$64.2	$476.6	$628.6	$441.2	$292.8	$197.2	$102.5
Food	330.8	9.4	70.3	93.7	64.1	43.9	32.3	17.2
Food at home	225.1	5.9	44.8	64.9	41.8	30.9	23.0	13.7
Food away from home	101.5	3.6	21.2	28.8	22.2	13.0	9.3	3.5
Alcoholic beverages	25.4	1.6	7.5	6.4	4.7	3.0	1.8	0.6
Housing	667.6	19.2	158.3	193.5	121.9	80.8	58.3	35.6
Shelter	385.6	12.4	97.2	115.7	71.7	42.4	28.8	17.5
Owned dwellings	229.7	1.8	50.3	75.8	46.9	28.2	17.9	8.7
Rented dwellings	115.2	9.5	41.6	27.6	13.1	8.4	7.2	7.6
Other lodging	40.8	1.0	5.2	12.2	11.6	5.8	3.7	1.2
Fuels, utilities, and public services	160.0	3.7	32.0	41.2	29.6	23.2	18.6	11.8
Household operations	34.2	0.7	9.6	10.2	3.8	3.7	2.9	3.3
Household furnishings, equipment	87.8	2.4	19.5	26.5	16.8	11.6	8.0	3.0
Apparel and services	111.0	4.1	24.6	33.7	22.8	13.8	8.3	3.6
Transportation	464.9	15.6	107.0	130.7	98.7	61.1	37.7	14.2
Health care	103.7	1.6	14.5	21.4	16.9	16.0	17.9	15.4
Entertainment	106.0	3.1	23.3	35.2	20.6	13.0	8.0	2.6
Personal care	20.1	0.6	3.7	5.2	3.8	3.1	2.3	1.3
Reading	13.6	0.3	2.6	3.8	2.6	1.9	1.6	0.8
Education	27.6	2.7	3.9	8.3	8.8	2.9	0.8	0.1
Tobacco and smoking supplies	22.0	0.8	4.9	5.8	4.5	3.3	2.0	0.7
Miscellaneous	31.5	0.6	6.5	8.1	5.9	4.5	3.6	2.3
Contributions and support payments	74.2	0.7	7.3	17.7	17.4	12.9	12.5	5.7
Personal insurance and pensions	208.9	3.9	46.4	65.2	48.5	32.6	10.0	2.3

(continued next page)

Future Expenditures

EXPENDITURES
75 and older

(continued from previous page)

(projected aggregate expenditures in 2000 for all households and for households by age of householder, in billions of dollars)

	\multicolumn{8}{c}{2000 aggregate annual expenditures in billions}
	all households	under 25	25-34	35-44	45-54	55-64	65-74	75+
Number of households (in thousands)	105,933	4,442	18,004	25,339	21,603	13,903	11,516	11,126
Total expenditures (in billions of dollars)	$2,532.4	$61.1	$405.1	$749.7	$660.6	$330.6	$194.6	$130.7
Food	379.7	9.0	59.7	111.7	95.9	49.5	31.9	22.0
Food at home	258.9	5.6	38.1	77.4	62.6	34.9	22.7	17.5
Food away from home	117.2	3.4	18.0	34.3	33.2	14.7	9.1	4.5
Alcoholic beverages	28.3	1.5	6.4	7.6	7.0	3.4	1.7	0.7
Housing	760.3	18.3	134.5	230.8	182.5	91.3	57.5	45.3
Shelter	438.2	11.8	82.6	137.9	107.3	47.9	28.4	22.3
Owned dwellings	265.8	1.7	42.8	90.4	70.3	31.9	17.6	11.1
Rented dwellings	123.4	9.1	35.4	32.9	19.7	9.5	7.2	9.7
Other lodging	49.1	0.9	4.4	14.6	17.4	6.5	3.7	1.5
Fuels, utilities, and public services	183.6	3.5	27.2	49.1	44.3	26.2	18.3	15.0
Household operations	38.0	0.7	8.2	12.2	5.7	4.1	2.9	4.2
Household furnishings, equipment	100.5	2.3	16.6	31.6	25.2	13.1	7.9	3.8
Apparel and services	127.6	3.9	20.9	40.2	34.2	15.6	8.2	4.6
Transportation	533.7	14.8	90.9	155.9	147.7	69.0	37.2	18.1
Health care	120.0	1.5	12.4	25.5	25.3	18.1	17.7	19.6
Entertainment	121.7	3.0	19.8	42.0	30.9	14.7	7.9	3.3
Personal care	23.1	0.5	3.2	6.2	5.7	3.5	2.3	1.7
Reading	15.7	0.3	2.2	4.5	3.9	2.2	1.6	1.0
Education	33.2	2.6	3.3	10.0	13.1	3.3	0.8	0.2
Tobacco and smoking supplies	25.2	0.8	4.2	6.9	6.8	3.7	2.0	0.9
Miscellaneous	36.2	0.6	5.5	9.7	8.9	5.0	3.5	2.9
Contributions and support payments	88.2	0.6	6.2	21.1	26.0	14.5	12.3	7.3
Personal insurance and pensions	243.2	3.7	39.4	77.7	72.7	36.8	9.9	2.9

Source: *The 1986 Consumer Expenditure Survey, Bureau of Labor Statistics* and *Projections of the Number of Households and Families:1986 to 2000, Bureau of the Census, Series P-25, No. 986*

Note: Aggregate expenditures are the sum of the total expenditures of all households in the nation or of all households in an age group. Projections are based on the average annual expenditures in 1986 and have not been adjusted for inflation. Projections show how total annual expenditures would change as the number of households in the age group changes during the 1990s. All other factors such as price and expenditure pattern are held constant and are not accounted for in these projections.

Owners and Renters

WEALTH
75 and older

SURVIVING WOMEN

Seventy percent of elderly householders live in their own home. Some 40 percent of these homeowners are married couples and another 38 percent are women who live alone or with unrelated others.

(owner- and renter-occupied households by race of householder and household type, for householders aged 75 and older, numbers in thousands, ownership status as of March 1988)

	total	white	black	Hispanic origin
All households	8,045	7,248	693	194
Owner households	5,666	5,161	449	105
Family households				
Married-couple	2,268	2,092	147	56
Male householder	145	114	27	4
Female householder	513	426	83	9
Nonfamily households				
Male householder	574	516	52	9
Female householder	2,166	2,013	141	26
Renter households	2,379	2,087	244	89
Family households				
Married-couple	375	325	40	23
Male householder	20	12	1	1
Female householder	160	116	38	6
Nonfamily households				
Male householder	359	295	59	15
Female householder	1,464	1,338	106	44

Source: Household and Family Characteristics: March 1988, *Bureau of the Census, Current Population Reports, Series P-20, No. 424*

Note: *Hispanics are of any race. Numbers may not add to total due to rounding.*

Health Status

HEALTH
75 and older

POSITIVE THINKING

Thirty-five percent of elderly men and women rate their health as excellent or very good and another 32 percent say they have good health. Some 22 percent of those aged 75 and older consider themselves in fair health and only 12 percent report poor health.

(self-assessed health status of persons aged 75 and older, by sex, race and household income, number of persons in thousands)

	all persons	all health statuses	excellent	very good	good	fair	poor
Both sexes, all races	10,551	100.0%	15.1%	19.7%	31.5%	21.8%	11.9%
Male	3,866	100.0	14.7	19.9	32.1	22.5	10.9
Female	6,685	100.0	15.4	19.5	31.2	21.4	12.5
White	9,499	100.0	15.5	19.9	32.1	20.9	11.5
Black	841	100.0	9.1	17.9	25.4	30.7	16.9
Asian and other	211	100.0	22.2	18.5	27.4	23.2	8.7
Household income							
Less than $10,000	3,527	100.0%	12.0%	17.0%	32.2%	24.8%	14.2%
$10,000 to $19,999	2,580	100.0	15.5	21.3	31.8	20.9	10.5
$20,000 to $34,999	1,438	100.0	21.8	22.6	28.7	20.6	6.2
$35,000 and over	765	100.0	17.0	21.0	30.5	18.2	13.3

Source: The 1986 National Health Interview Survey, National Center for Health Statistics

Note: All persons includes those of unknown health status, all health statuses includes only those with known health status. Household income includes only those persons with known household income. Numbers may not add to total due to rounding.

Acute Conditions

HEALTH
75 and older

BOTHERED BY BRUISES

After colds and flus, the most common acute condition reported by the elderly is bruises and superficial injuries. Digestive system problems other than those related to dental conditions and indigestion are also mentioned frequently by elderly women.

(number of acute conditions reported in a year for all persons and those aged 75 and older, by sex, numbers in thousands)

	males all ages	males aged 75 and older	females all ages	females aged 75 and older
All acute conditions	191,369	3,051	257,177	9,766
Infective and parasitic diseases	**23,122**	**202**	**31,244**	**433**
Common childhood diseases	2,565	0	1,876	0
Intestinal virus, unspecified	4,244	90	5,288	0
Viral infections, unspecified	9,621	112	14,273	433
Other	6,692	0	9,807	0
Respiratory conditions	**99,216**	**1,265**	**129,626**	**3,420**
Common cold	30,445	645	32,983	881
Other acute upper respiratory infections	8,472	0	13,320	307
Influenza	55,256	413	75,295	1,636
Acute bronchitis	1,960	0	4,315	386
Pneumonia	1,365	107	1,277	211
Other respiratory conditions	1,718	100	2,435	0
Digestive system conditions	**5,860**	**181**	**9,112**	**1,378**
Dental conditions	1,059	0	1,955	131
Indigestion, nausea and vomiting	3,299	86	4,670	332
Other digestive conditions	1,502	95	2,487	915
Injuries	**34,588**	**680**	**29,706**	**1,892**
Fractures and dislocations	4,367	0	3,978	211
Sprains and strains	6,127	45	6,208	294
Open wounds and lacerations	11,153	101	5,094	230
Contusions and superficial injuries	7,986	353	7,191	511
Other current injuries	4,955	181	7,235	646

(continued next page)

Acute Conditions

HEALTH
75 and older

(continued from previous page)

(number of acute conditions reported in a year for all persons and those aged 75 and older, by sex, numbers in thousands)

	males		females	
	all ages	aged 75 and older	all ages	aged 75 and older
Selected other acute conditions	**21,183**	**586**	**40,385**	**1,000**
Eye conditions	1,072	99	2,080	215
Acute ear infections	8,689	0	10,116	0
Other ear conditions	1,884	188	2,193	0
Acute urinary conditions	989	0	4,399	248
Disorders of menstruation	–	–	2,251	–
Other disorders of female genital tract	–	–	2,174	0
Delivery and other conditions of pregnancy	–	–	4,466	–
Skin conditions	2,065	192	3,597	95
Acute musculoskeletal conditions	3,038	107	3,972	344
Headache, excluding migraine	1,253	0	2,461	97
Fever, unspecified	2,192	0	2,675	0
All other acute conditions	**7,400**	**137**	**17,104**	**1,643**

Source: The 1986 National Health Interview Survey, National Center for Health Statistics

Note: An acute condition is defined by The National Health Interview Survey as an illness or injury that usually lasts less than three months and was first noticed less than three months before the respondent's interview. The acute condition must also have caused the person to restrict activities for at least a half a day or to have contacted a physician. The data are based only on information given by the respondent and are subject to recall and selective reporting error. Numbers may not add to total due to rounding.

Chronic Conditions

HEALTH
75 and older

ARTHRITIS AND HEARING PROBLEMS

The top three chronic health problems of elderly men and women are arthritis, high blood pressure, and hearing impairments. Women aged 75 and older are also likely to suffer from cataracts and sinusitis while the men report difficulties with sinusitis and ischemic heart disease.

(number of selected chronic conditions reported in a year for all persons and those aged 75 and older, by sex, numbers in thousands)

	males all ages	males aged 75 and older	females all ages	females aged 75 and older
Selected skin and musculoskeletal conditions				
Arthritis	10,751	1,484	20,160	4,215
Gout, including gouty arthritis	1,515	208	713	210
Intervertebral disc disorders	2,522	98	1,645	74
Bone spur or tendonitis, unspecified	781	38	898	60
Disorders of bone or cartilage	449	21	943	195
Trouble with bunions	594	18	2,321	475
Bursitis, unclassified	1,641	115	2,464	197
Sebaceous skin cyst	640	60	881	17
Trouble with acne	2,193	0	2,116	0
Psoriasis	1,069	52	1,262	219
Dermatitis	3,851	164	5,696	102
Trouble with dry, itching skin, unclassified	1,994	163	2,606	242
Trouble with ingrown nails	2,352	241	3,030	369
Trouble with corns and calluses	1,669	54	3,164	520
Impairments				
Visual impairment	4,994	563	3,358	875
Color blindness	2,694	41	272	0
Cataracts	1,534	540	3,497	1,921
Glaucoma	735	231	967	386
Hearing impairment	11,727	1,687	9,004	2,305
Tinnitus	3,388	396	2,927	536
Speech impairment	1,924	88	871	85
Absence of extremity(s)	374	18	24	24
Paralysis, entire body, one side of body, or both legs	200	17	152	42
Partial paralysis of body or legs	236	41	99	14
Deformity of back	6,812	374	9,676	865
Deformity of upper extremities	1,622	52	1,475	139
Deformity of lower extremities	6,454	413	5,739	832
Selected digestive conditions				
Ulcer	2,116	78	2,378	239
Hernia of abdominal cavity	2,300	270	2,283	625
Gastritis or duodenitis	1,080	45	1,813	181

(continued next page)

Almanac of Consumer Markets

Chronic Conditions

HEALTH
75 and older

(continued from previous page)

(number of selected chronic conditions reported in a year for all persons and those aged 75 and older, by sex, numbers in thousands)

	males all ages	males aged 75 and older	females all ages	females aged 75 and older
Frequent indigestion	2,504	191	2,811	185
Enteritis or colitis	574	27	1,820	460
Spastic colon	264	0	1,377	53
Diverticula of intestines	404	77	1,508	374
Frequent constipation	1,002	156	3,537	729
Selected conditions of the genitourinary, nervous, endocrine, metabolic, and blood system				
Goiter or other disorders of the thyroid	420	41	2,789	266
Diabetes	2,949	407	3,635	739
Anemias	570	48	2,617	152
Epilepsy	656	43	863	46
Migraine headache	2,068	8	6,448	203
Neuralgia or neuritis, unspecified	215	17	364	88
Kidney trouble	1,305	180	2,662	235
Bladder disorders	516	134	3,253	425
Diseases of prostate	1,281	195	–	–
Inflammatory female genital diseases	–	–	427	0
Noninflammatory female genital diseases	–	–	1,095	0
Menstrual disorders	–	–	2,097	0
Selected circulatory conditions				
Ischemic heart disease	4,091	694	2,809	935
Tachycardia or rapid heart	700	60	1,226	185
Heart murmurs	1,310	57	2,583	148
Other heart rhythm disorders	499	95	800	94
Other heart diseases	1,482	243	2,265	857
High blood pressure (hypertension)	12,512	1,124	16,457	3,193
Cerebrovascular disease	1,156	293	1,646	727
Hardening of the arteries	1,428	359	1,225	608
Varicose veins	1,042	124	5,814	635
Hemorrhoids	4,568	236	5,341	439
Selected respiratory conditions				
Chronic bronchitis	4,707	195	6,671	390
Asthma	4,670	108	5,019	276
Hay fever or allergic rhinitis without asthma	10,136	250	11,566	460
Chronic sinusitis	14,636	590	19,749	1,211
Deviated nasal septum	825	0	465	0
Chronic disease of tonsils or adenoids	1,071	0	2,068	21
Emphysema	1,201	169	796	176

Source: The 1986 National Health Interview Survey, National Center for Health Statistics

Note: Chronic conditions are defined by the National Health Interview Survey as conditions that either a) were first noticed three months or more before the date of the interview or b) belong to a group of conditions (such as heart disease or diabetes) that are considered chronic regardless of when they began. Totals for all chronic conditions are not shown because the National Health Interview Survey does not measure the total number of chronic conditions for each person. The data are based only on information given by the respondent and are subject to recall and selective reporting error.

Activity Restrictions

HEALTH
75 and older

MORE ILLNESS AND INJURY

Elderly women spend 22 whole or half days in bed each year because of illness or injury. Men aged 75 and older have about half as many bed days as the women. Workers in this age group actually have fewer work-loss days a year than American workers in general.

(number of days of activity restriction reported in a year and per person due to acute and chronic conditions, by type of restriction and sex, race, and household income, for all persons and those aged 75 and older, numbers in thousands)

	number of days per year		number of days per person	
	bed day	work-loss day	bed day	work-loss day
All ages	**1,547,980**	**833,396**	**6.5**	**5.4**
Male	613,113	401,503	5.4	4.8
Female	934,867	431,892	7.7	6.0
White	1,298,039	716,187	6.5	5.4
Black	220,102	99,332	7.7	5.4
Household income				
Less than $10,000	384,962	90,268	11.5	6.1
$10,000 to $19,999	346,115	162,604	7.7	6.1
$20,000 to $34,999	326,166	254,563	5.2	5.7
$35,000 and over	275,957	232,139	4.3	4.6
All aged 75 and older	**191,207**	**2,883**	**18.1**	**4.6**
Male	44,904	2,217	11.6	5.5
Female	146,303	666	21.9	3.0
White	171,447	2,883	18.0	5.3
Black	16,612	–	19.8	–
Household income				
Less than $10,000	70,012	–	19.9	–
$10,000 to $19,999	44,392	–	17.2	–
$20,000 to $34,999	11,511	–	8.0	–
$35,000 and over	20,106	2,217	26.3	24.6

Source: The 1986 National Health Interview Survey, National Center for Health Statistics

Note: Numbers may not add to total due to rounding. A bed day is one during which a person stayed in bed more than half a day because of illness or injury. All hospital days for inpatients are considered bed days even if the patient was not in bed more than half a day. A work-loss day is one on which a currently employed person aged 18 or older missed more than half a day of work. The data are based only on information given by the respondent and are subject to recall and selective reporting error.

Cause of Death

HEALTH
75 and older

AGING HEARTS

Not surprisingly, deaths among people age 75 and older account for nearly half of all deaths in the nation. Forty-four percent of the deaths in this age group are caused by heart diseases—the leading cause of death for elderly people—and 16 percent are due to cancer.

(ten leading causes of death among persons aged 75 and older)

	number of deaths persons aged 75 and older	number of deaths all ages	percent accounted for by persons aged 75 and older
All causes	1,002,622	2,105,361	47.6%
Heart diseases	438,237	765,490	57.2
Malignant neoplasms (cancer)	161,381	469,376	34.4
Cerebrovascular diseases	100,913	149,643	67.4
Pneumonia and influenza	50,647	69,812	72.5
Chronic obstructive pulmonary diseases and allied conditions	36,783	76,559	48.0
Atherosclerosis	18,790	22,706	82.8
Diabetes mellitus	16,987	37,184	45.7
Accidents and adverse effects	16,635	95,277	17.5
Nephritis, nephrotic syndrome, and nephrosis (kidney disorders)	13,202	21,767	60.7
Septicemia (infections of the blood stream)	10,906	18,795	58.0
All other causes	138,141	378,752	36.5

Source: Advance Report of Final Mortality Statistics, 1986, *National Center for Health Statistics, Vol. 37, No. 6*

Appendix

The tables in this section provide income and expenditure data for all households which are not shown on the corresponding tables for individual age groups.

Income of All Married Couples

(household income of all married-couple householder families with and without children under 18 at home, numbers for 1988 in thousands, income is for 1987)

	all family households	married-couple householders total	with children under 18 at home	without children under 18 at home
All households	65,133	51,809	24,600	27,209
Less than $10,000	7,413	3,364	1,274	2,090
$10,000 to $14,999	5,788	3,963	1,500	2,463
$15,000 to $19,999	6,136	4,564	1,826	2,738
$20,000 to $24,999	6,013	4,721	2,114	2,607
$25,000 to $29,999	5,790	4,695	2,307	2,387
$30,000 to $34,999	5,614	4,781	2,477	2,304
$35,000 to $39,999	5,142	4,508	2,467	2,041
$40,000 to $44,999	4,508	3,997	2,133	1,864
$45,000 to $49,999	3,615	3,247	1,686	1,561
$50,000 to $59,999	5,458	4,941	2,547	2,394
$60,000 to $74,999	4,513	4,177	2,091	2,086
$75,000 and over	5,142	4,852	2,177	2,675

percent distribution	all family households	married-couple householders total	with children under 18 at home	without children under 18 at home
All households	100.0%	100.0%	100.0%	100.0%
Less than $10,000	11.4	6.5	5.2	7.7
$10,000 to $14,999	8.9	7.6	6.1	9.1
$15,000 to $19,999	9.4	8.8	7.4	10.1
$20,000 to $24,999	9.2	9.1	8.6	9.6
$25,000 to $29,999	8.9	9.1	9.4	8.8
$30,000 to $34,999	8.6	9.2	10.1	8.5
$35,000 to $39,999	7.9	8.7	10.0	7.5
$40,000 to $44,999	6.9	7.7	8.7	6.9
$45,000 to $49,999	5.6	6.3	6.9	5.7
$50,000 to $59,999	8.4	9.5	10.4	8.8
$60,000 to $74,999	6.9	8.1	8.5	7.7
$75,000 and over	7.9	9.4	8.8	9.8
Median household income	$31,135	$34,786	$36,206	$32,609

Source: The 1988 Current Population Survey, Bureau of the Census

Note: Numbers may not add to total due to rounding.

Income of All Female Householder Families

INCOME
Appendix

(household income of all female householder families with and without children under 18 at home, numbers for 1988, in thousands, income is for 1987)

	all family households	female householder families total	with children under 18 at home	without children under 18 at home
All households	65,133	10,608	6,273	4,335
Less than $10,000	7,413	3,653	2,846	806
$10,000 to $14,999	5,788	1,536	920	616
$15,000 to $19,999	6,136	1,266	714	552
$20,000 to $24,999	6,013	1,006	562	444
$25,000 to $29,999	5,790	805	389	416
$30,000 to $34,999	5,614	598	249	349
$35,000 to $39,999	5,142	455	198	257
$40,000 to $44,999	4,508	327	114	212
$45,000 to $49,999	3,615	264	82	181
$50,000 to $59,999	5,458	326	94	232
$60,000 to $74,999	4,513	203	55	148
$75,000 and over	5,142	170	49	121

percent distribution	all family households	female householder families total	with children under 18 at home	without children under 18 at home
All households	100.0%	100.0%	100.0%	100.0%
Less than $10,000	11.4	34.4	45.4	18.6
$10,000 to $14,999	8.9	14.5	14.7	14.2
$15,000 to $19,999	9.4	11.9	11.4	12.7
$20,000 to $24,999	9.2	9.5	9.0	10.2
$25,000 to $29,999	8.9	7.6	6.2	9.6
$30,000 to $34,999	8.6	5.6	4.0	8.1
$35,000 to $39,999	7.9	4.3	3.2	5.9
$40,000 to $44,999	6.9	3.1	1.8	4.9
$45,000 to $49,999	5.6	2.5	1.3	4.2
$50,000 to $59,999	8.4	3.1	1.5	5.4
$60,000 to $74,999	6.9	1.9	0.9	3.4
$75,000 and over	7.9	1.6	0.8	2.8
Median household income	$31,135	$15,419	$11,299	$21,939

Source: The 1988 Current Population Survey, Bureau of the Census

Note: Numbers may not add to total due to rounding.

Income of All Male Householder Families

(household income of all male householder families with and without children under 18 at home, numbers for 1988, in thousands, income is for 1987)

	all family households	male householder families total	with children under 18 at home	without children under 18 at home
All households	65,133	2,715	1,047	1,669
Less than $10,000	7,413	397	179	218
$10,000 to $14,999	5,788	289	131	158
$15,000 to $19,999	6,136	307	120	187
$20,000 to $24,999	6,013	286	115	172
$25,000 to $29,999	5,790	290	94	196
$30,000 to $34,999	5,614	235	89	146
$35,000 to $39,999	5,142	180	68	111
$40,000 to $44,999	4,508	184	73	111
$45,000 to $49,999	3,615	105	43	62
$50,000 to $59,999	5,458	191	62	128
$60,000 to $74,999	4,513	133	37	97
$75,000 and over	5,142	120	37	83

percent distribution	all family households	male householder families total	with children under 18 at home	without children under 18 at home
All households	100.0%	100.0%	100.0%	100.0%
Less than $10,000	11.4	14.6	17.1	13.1
$10,000 to $14,999	8.9	10.6	12.5	9.5
$15,000 to $19,999	9.4	11.3	11.5	11.2
$20,000 to $24,999	9.2	10.5	11.0	10.3
$25,000 to $29,999	8.9	10.7	9.0	11.7
$30,000 to $34,999	8.6	8.7	8.5	8.7
$35,000 to $39,999	7.9	6.6	6.5	6.7
$40,000 to $44,999	6.9	6.8	7.0	6.7
$45,000 to $49,999	5.6	3.9	4.1	3.7
$50,000 to $59,999	8.4	7.0	5.9	7.7
$60,000 to $74,999	6.9	4.9	3.5	5.8
$75,000 and over	7.9	4.4	3.5	5.0
Median household income	$31,135	$26,157	$23,638	$27,322

Source: The 1988 Current Population Survey, Bureau of the Census

Note: Numbers may not add to total due to rounding.

Income of All Nonfamily Households

Appendix — INCOME

(household income of all nonfamily households by household type, numbers for 1988 in thousands, income is for 1987)

	total number	living alone total	living alone male householder	living alone female householder	living with others total	living with others male householder	living with others female householder
All nonfamily households:	25,933	21,889	8,788	13,101	4,044	2,521	1,523
Less than $10,000	9,304	8,919	2,646	6,273	385	222	163
$10,000 to $14,999	3,870	3,456	1,345	2,110	414	217	198
$15,000 to $19,999	2,999	2,582	1,035	1,547	417	262	155
$20,000 to $24,999	2,393	2,000	948	1,052	393	260	133
$25,000 to $29,999	1,857	1,485	744	742	371	210	161
$30,000 to $34,999	1,403	1,044	533	511	359	200	159
$35,000 to $39,999	1,056	750	431	319	307	211	95
$40,000 to $44,999	785	514	329	185	271	163	109
$45,000 to $49,999	570	329	195	135	241	157	84
$50,000 to $59,999	683	351	254	98	332	217	115
$60,000 to $74,999	455	207	150	57	248	167	81
$75,000 and over	558	252	180	72	306	235	71

percent distribution	total number	living alone total	living alone male householder	living alone female householder	living with others total	living with others male householder	living with others female householder
All nonfamily households:	100.0%	100.0%	100.0%	100.0%	100.0%	100.0%	100.0%
Less than $10,000	35.9	40.7	30.1	47.9	9.5	8.8	10.7
$10,000 to $14,999	14.9	15.8	15.3	16.1	10.2	8.6	13.0
$15,000 to $19,999	11.6	11.8	11.8	11.8	10.3	10.4	10.2
$20,000 to $24,999	9.2	9.1	10.8	8.0	9.7	10.3	8.7
$25,000 to $29,999	7.2	6.8	8.5	5.7	9.2	8.3	10.6
$30,000 to $34,999	5.4	4.8	6.1	3.9	8.9	7.9	10.4
$35,000 to $39,999	4.1	3.4	4.9	2.4	7.6	8.4	6.2
$40,000 to $44,999	3.0	2.3	3.7	1.4	6.7	6.5	7.2
$45,000 to $49,999	2.2	1.5	2.2	1.0	6.0	6.2	5.5
$50,000 to $59,999	2.6	1.6	2.9	0.7	8.2	8.6	7.6
$60,000 to $74,999	1.8	0.9	1.7	0.4	6.1	6.6	5.3
$75,000 and over	2.2	1.2	2.0	0.5	7.6	9.3	4.7
Median household income	$14,685	$12,544	$16,703	$10,576	$30,573	$32,207	$28,271

Source: The 1988 Current Population Survey, Bureau of the Census

Note: Nonfamilies are either people living alone or living with an individual (or individuals) unrelated to the householder. Numbers may not add to total due to rounding.

Income and Race, All Families

(household income of all family households by race and household type for all ages, numbers for 1988 in thousands, income is for 1987)

		white family households		
	total	*married couple*	*male householder*	*female householder*
All households	56,044	46,644	2,165	7,235
Total	100.0%	100.0%	100.0%	100.0%
Less than $10,000	9.3	6.0	13.7	29.6
$10,000 to $19,999	17.8	16.1	22.7	27.4
$20,000 to $29,999	18.3	18.1	21.2	18.7
$30,000 to $39,999	17.0	17.9	16.8	11.2
$40,000 to $49,999	13.0	14.3	9.8	6.0
$50,000 to $59,999	8.8	9.8	6.8	3.5
$60,000 to $74,999	7.2	8.2	4.8	1.8
$75,000 and over	8.4	9.6	4.0	1.6
Median household income	$32,274	$35,295	$26,230	$17,018

		black family households		
	total	*married couple*	*male householder*	*female householder*
All households	7,177	3,682	421	3,074
Total	100.0%	100.0%	100.0%	100.0%
Less than $10,000	29.9	12.0	31.1	51.3
$10,000 to $19,999	24.2	22.1	28.0	26.2
$20,000 to $29,999	17.0	20.6	18.3	12.3
$30,000 to $39,999	11.9	17.5	8.8	5.7
$40,000 to $49,999	7.5	11.5	5.9	2.8
$50,000 to $59,999	4.0	6.8	4.5	0.7
$60,000 to $74,999	3.0	5.1	1.2	0.6
$75,000 and over	2.5	4.3	1.4	0.5
Median household income	$18,098	$27,182	$17,455	$9,710

Source: Money Income of Households, Families, and Persons in the United States: 1987, *Bureau of the Census, Current Population Reports, Series P-60, No. 162*

Note: Numbers may not add to total due to rounding.

Income and Race, All Nonfamilies

INCOME Appendix

(householder income of all nonfamily householders by race and household type, numbers for 1988 in thousands, income is for 1987)

	white householder			black householder		
	total	male householder	female householder	total	male householder	female householder
All households	22,426	9,592	12,834	3,010	1,429	1,580
Total	100.0%	100.0%	100.0%	100.0%	100.0%	100.0%
Less than $10,000	37.1	26.5	45.0	55.3	48.4	61.6
$10,000 to $19,999	28.5	27.7	29.1	24.2	26.2	22.2
$20,000 to $24,999	9.8	11.5	8.5	8.2	9.1	7.5
$25,000 to $29,999	7.3	9.0	6.1	4.6	5.5	3.8
$30,000 to $34,999	5.3	6.7	4.3	2.9	3.8	2.0
$35,000 to $49,999	7.7	11.3	5.1	3.9	5.4	2.6
$50,000 and over	4.2	7.3	1.9	0.9	1.5	0.4
Median householder income	$13,866	$18,059	$11,313	$8,188	$10,368	$6,654

Source: Money Income of Households, Families, and Persons in the United States: 1987, *Bureau of the Census, Current Population Reports, Series P-60, No. 162*

Note: Numbers may not add to total due to rounding. Householder income is the total money income of the householder only.

Income of All Hispanic Households

INCOME Appendix

(household income of all Hispanic households by household type, numbers for 1988 in thousands, income is for 1987)

family households

	total	married couple	male householder	female householder
All households	4,588	3,204	312	1,072
Total	100.0%	100.0%	100.0%	100.0%
Less than $15,000	36.4	27.7	31.4	63.7
$15,000 to $24,999	21.8	22.1	26.3	19.5
$25,000 and over	41.9	50.2	42.6	16.8
Median household income	$20,628	$24,998	$21,678	$10,591

nonfamily households

	total	male householder living alone	male householder living with others	female householder living alone	female householder living with others
All households	1,109	416	196	429	69
Total	100.0%	100.0%	100.0%	100.0%	100.0%
Less than $15,000	55.6	59.4	22.4	70.4	34.8
$15,000 to $24,999	21.6	22.4	29.1	17.2	21.7
$25,000 and over	22.9	18.3	48.5	12.4	43.5
Median household income	$11,998	$11,712	$24,740	$7,720	–

Source: The 1988 Current Population Survey, Bureau of the Census

Note: Numbers may not add to total due to rounding. Hispanics are of any race. Median income is unreliable and is therefore not given when the category contains fewer than 75,000 households.

Future Expenditures, Detailed for 1990

EXPENDITURES Appendix

(projected aggregate expenditures in 1990 for all households and for households by age of householder, in billions of dollars)

	all households	under 25	25-34	35-44	45-54	55-64	65-74	75+
Number of households (in thousands)	94,227	4,663	21,183	21,245	14,429	12,311	11,672	8,724
Total expenditures (in billions of dollars)	2,203.1	64.2	476.6	628.6	441.2	292.8	197.2	102.5
Food	330.8	9.4	70.3	93.7	64.1	43.9	32.3	17.2
Food at home	225.1	5.9	44.8	64.9	41.8	30.9	23.0	13.7
Food away from home	101.5	3.6	21.2	28.8	22.2	13.0	9.3	3.5
Alcoholic beverages	25.4	1.6	7.5	6.4	4.7	3.0	1.8	0.6
Housing	667.6	19.2	158.3	193.5	121.9	80.8	58.3	35.6
Shelter	385.6	12.4	97.2	115.7	71.7	42.4	28.8	17.5
Owned dwellings	229.7	1.8	50.3	75.8	46.9	28.2	17.9	8.7
Mortgage interest and charges	142.8	1.3	39.3	54.8	29.5	13.0	4.2	0.7
Property taxes	41.4	0.2	4.8	9.7	8.8	7.7	6.5	3.7
Maintenance, repairs, insurance, and other expenses	45.4	0.4	6.3	11.3	8.6	7.4	7.1	4.3
Rented dwellings	115.2	9.5	41.6	27.6	13.1	8.4	7.2	7.6
Other lodging	40.8	1.0	5.2	12.2	11.6	5.8	3.7	1.2
Fuels, utilities, and public services	160.0	3.7	32.0	41.2	29.6	23.2	18.6	11.8
Natural gas	24.3	0.4	4.6	5.9	4.4	3.8	3.1	2.1
Electricity	65.7	1.4	13.0	17.6	12.3	9.4	7.4	4.5
Fuel oil and other fuels	10.5	0.1	1.6	2.2	1.6	1.8	1.8	1.4
Telephone	45.2	1.6	10.3	11.6	8.4	5.9	4.7	2.8
Water and other public services	14.3	0.2	2.5	3.8	2.9	2.2	1.7	1.1
Household operations	34.2	0.7	9.6	10.2	3.8	3.7	2.9	3.3
Domestic services	27.9	0.6	8.5	8.4	2.6	2.7	2.1	2.9
Other household expenses	6.4	0.1	1.2	1.8	1.2	0.9	0.8	0.4
Household furnishings, equipment	87.8	2.4	19.5	26.5	16.8	11.6	8.0	3.0
Household textiles	8.2	0.2	1.4	2.6	1.5	1.2	0.9	0.4
Furniture	29.4	0.9	7.5	9.2	5.1	3.3	2.7	0.7
Floor coverings	5.1	0.1	0.7	1.9	0.9	0.7	0.6	0.2
Major appliances	14.9	0.5	3.2	3.5	3.0	2.4	1.6	0.7
Small appliances, misc. housewares	5.3	0.2	0.9	1.5	1.2	0.8	0.5	0.2
Miscellaneous household equipment	24.9	0.6	5.8	7.7	5.2	3.1	1.7	0.8
Apparel	111.0	4.1	24.6	33.7	22.8	13.8	8.3	3.6
Men and boys	27.5	1.0	6.0	8.9	6.0	3.3	1.7	0.7
Men, 16 and over	21.9	0.9	4.7	6.1	5.1	2.9	1.5	0.6
Boys, 2 to 15	5.6	0.1	1.3	2.7	0.9	0.4	0.2	0.1

(continued next page)

400   Almanac of Consumer Markets

Future Expenditures, Detailed for 1990

EXPENDITURES Appendix

(continued from previous page)

(projected aggregate expenditures in 1990 for all households and for households by age of householder, in billions of dollars)

	\multicolumn{8}{c}{1990 aggregate annual expenditures in billions}
	all households	under 25	25-34	35-44	45-54	55-64	65-74	75+
Women and girls	44.9	1.4	8.6	13.6	9.7	5.9	4.0	1.8
Women, 16 and over	38.2	1.3	7.0	10.1	8.7	5.5	3.8	1.8
Girls, 2 to 15	6.7	0.1	1.6	3.4	1.0	0.4	0.2	0.0
Children under 2	4.1	0.3	1.7	1.0	0.5	0.4	0.1	0.1
Footwear	11.9	0.4	2.5	3.8	2.4	1.5	1.0	0.4
Other apparel products and services	22.5	1.0	5.8	6.5	4.3	2.8	1.5	0.6
Transportation	**464.9**	**15.6**	**107.0**	**130.7**	**98.7**	**61.1**	**37.7**	**14.2**
Cars and trucks, new (net outlay)	137.8	3.5	31.7	39.9	29.7	18.0	11.1	3.9
Cars and trucks, used (net outlay)	85.4	4.0	22.3	23.5	18.9	9.8	5.2	1.7
Other vehicles	2.6	0.3	0.7	0.8	0.5	0.1	0.1	0.1
Vehicle finance charges	26.2	0.8	6.8	8.0	5.7	3.2	1.4	0.3
Gasoline and motor oil	88.2	3.1	19.5	24.3	17.6	12.5	8.0	3.2
Maintenance and repairs	44.2	1.5	9.4	11.8	9.1	6.3	4.4	1.7
Vehicle insurance	40.7	1.2	8.2	11.0	8.7	6.0	3.7	1.9
Public transportation	24.1	0.7	4.8	6.4	5.4	3.1	2.7	1.0
Vehicle rental, licenses, other charges	15.9	0.5	3.6	5.1	3.1	2.0	1.3	0.4
Health care	**103.7**	**1.6**	**14.5**	**21.4**	**16.9**	**16.0**	**17.9**	**15.4**
Health insurance	36.3	0.5	4.9	6.6	5.7	5.5	7.4	5.7
Medical services	49.0	0.8	7.8	11.6	7.9	7.4	6.9	6.7
Medicines and medical supplies	18.4	0.3	1.9	3.1	3.3	3.2	3.6	3.0
Entertainment	**106.0**	**3.1**	**23.3**	**35.2**	**20.6**	**13.0**	**8.0**	**2.6**
Fees and admissions	30.0	1.0	5.8	9.6	6.2	3.8	2.8	0.9
Television, radios, sound equipment	36.1	1.3	8.2	11.2	7.3	4.2	2.6	1.3
Other equipment and services	39.9	0.9	9.3	14.4	7.1	5.1	2.6	0.5
Personal care	**20.1**	**0.6**	**3.7**	**5.2**	**3.8**	**3.1**	**2.3**	**1.3**
Reading	**13.6**	**0.3**	**2.6**	**3.8**	**2.6**	**1.9**	**1.6**	**0.8**
Education	**27.6**	**2.7**	**3.9**	**8.3**	**8.8**	**2.9**	**0.8**	**0.1**
Tobacco and smoking supplies	**22.0**	**0.8**	**4.9**	**5.8**	**4.5**	**3.3**	**2.0**	**0.7**
Miscellaneous	**31.5**	**0.6**	**6.5**	**8.1**	**5.9**	**4.5**	**3.6**	**2.3**
Contributions and support payments	**74.2**	**0.7**	**7.3**	**17.7**	**17.4**	**12.9**	**12.5**	**5.7**
Personal insurance and pensions	**208.9**	**3.9**	**46.4**	**65.2**	**48.5**	**32.6**	**10.0**	**2.3**
Life insurance and other personal insurance	28.9	0.3	4.7	7.8	6.4	5.0	3.7	1.0
Retirement, pensions, Social Security	179.9	3.6	41.7	57.3	42.1	27.7	6.3	1.3

Source: The 1986 Consumer Expenditure Survey, Bureau of Labor Statistics and Projections of the Number of Households and Families:1986 to 2000, Bureau of the Census, Series P-25, No. 986

Note: Aggregate expenditures are the sum of the total expenditures of all households in the nation or of all households in an age group. Projections are based on the average annual expenditures in 1986 and have not been adjusted for inflation. Projections show how total annual expenditures would change as the number of households in the age group changes during the 1990s. All other factors such as price and expenditure pattern are held constant and are not accounted for in these projections.

Future Expenditures, Detailed for 2000

EXPENDITURES Appendix

(projected aggregate expenditures in 2000 for all households and for households by age of householder, in billions of dollars)

	\multicolumn{7}{c}{2000 aggregate annual expenditures in billions}
	all households	under 25	25-34	35-44	45-54	55-64	65-74	75+
Number of households (in thousands)	105,933	4,442	18,004	25,339	21,603	13,903	11,516	11,126
Total expenditures (in billions of dollars)	2,532.4	61.1	405.1	749.7	660.6	330.6	194.6	130.7
Food	379.7	9.0	59.7	111.7	95.9	49.5	31.9	22.0
Food at home	258.9	5.6	38.1	77.4	62.6	34.9	22.7	17.5
Food away from home	117.2	3.4	18.0	34.3	33.2	14.7	9.1	4.5
Alcoholic Beverages	28.3	1.5	6.4	7.6	7.0	3.4	1.7	0.7
Housing	760.3	18.3	134.5	230.8	182.5	91.3	57.5	45.3
Shelter	438.2	11.8	82.6	137.9	107.3	47.9	28.4	22.3
Owned dwellings	265.8	1.7	42.8	90.4	70.3	31.9	17.6	11.1
Mortgage interest and charges	163.9	1.2	33.4	65.4	44.2	14.7	4.1	0.9
Property taxes	48.9	0.2	4.1	11.6	13.2	8.7	6.4	4.7
Maintenance, repairs, insurance, and other expenses	53.0	0.4	5.3	13.5	12.9	8.4	7.0	5.5
Rented dwellings	123.4	9.1	35.4	32.9	19.7	9.5	7.2	9.7
Other lodging	49.1	0.9	4.4	14.6	17.4	6.5	3.7	1.5
Fuels, utilities, and public services	183.6	3.5	27.2	49.1	44.3	26.2	18.3	15.0
Natural gas	27.9	0.4	3.9	7.0	6.6	4.3	3.1	2.7
Electricity	75.6	1.3	11.1	21.0	18.4	10.6	7.3	5.8
Fuel oil and other fuels	12.0	0.1	1.4	2.6	2.4	2.0	1.8	1.7
Telephone	51.4	1.5	8.7	13.8	12.6	6.7	4.6	3.5
Water and other public services	16.7	0.2	2.1	4.6	4.3	2.5	1.7	1.3
Household operations	38.0	0.7	8.2	12.2	5.7	4.1	2.9	4.2
Domestic services	30.6	0.5	7.2	10.1	3.9	3.1	2.1	3.7
Other household expenses	7.3	0.1	1.0	2.1	1.8	1.0	0.8	0.5
Household furnishings, equipment	100.5	2.3	16.6	31.6	25.2	13.1	7.9	3.8
Household textiles	9.5	0.2	1.2	3.1	2.3	1.4	0.9	0.5
Furniture	33.1	0.9	6.4	10.9	7.6	3.8	2.7	0.9
Floor coverings	6.0	0.1	0.6	2.3	1.3	0.8	0.6	0.3
Major appliances	17.0	0.4	2.7	4.2	4.4	2.7	1.6	0.9
Small appliances, misc. housewares	6.2	0.2	0.8	1.8	1.7	1.0	0.5	0.3
Miscellaneous household equipment	28.7	0.6	4.9	9.2	7.8	3.5	1.7	1.0
Apparel	127.6	3.9	20.9	40.2	34.2	15.6	8.2	4.6
Men and boys	31.8	0.9	5.1	10.6	8.9	3.7	1.6	0.9
Men, 16 and over	25.3	0.9	4.0	7.3	7.6	3.3	1.5	0.8
Boys, 2 to 15	6.5	0.1	1.1	3.3	1.4	0.4	0.2	0.1

(continued next page)

Future Expenditures, Detailed for 2000

EXPENDITURES
Appendix

(continued from previous page)

(projected aggregate expenditures in 2000 for all households and for households by age of householder, in billions of dollars)

	\multicolumn{8}{c}{2000 aggregate annual expenditures in billions}
	all households	under 25	25-34	35-44	45-54	55-64	65-74	75+
Women and girls	52.2	1.3	7.3	16.2	14.5	6.6	3.9	2.4
Women, 16 and over	44.6	1.3	6.0	12.1	13.0	6.2	3.7	2.3
Girls, 2 to 15	7.6	0.1	1.3	4.1	1.5	0.4	0.2	0.0
Children under 2	4.4	0.3	1.5	1.2	0.7	0.5	0.1	0.1
Footwear	13.7	0.4	2.1	4.5	3.6	1.6	0.9	0.5
Other apparel products and services	25.5	1.0	4.9	7.8	6.4	3.1	1.5	0.8
Transportation	**533.7**	**14.8**	**90.9**	**155.9**	**147.7**	**69.0**	**37.2**	**18.1**
Cars and trucks, new (net outlay)	158.6	3.3	27.0	47.5	44.5	20.4	10.9	5.0
Cars and trucks, used (net outlay)	97.5	3.8	19.0	28.1	28.3	11.1	5.1	2.1
Other vehicles	2.9	0.3	0.6	0.9	0.8	0.1	0.1	0.1
Vehicle finance charges	29.9	0.8	5.8	9.6	8.5	3.6	1.3	0.4
Gasoline and motor oil	101.0	2.9	16.5	29.0	26.3	14.2	7.9	4.1
Maintenance and repairs	50.7	1.4	8.0	14.1	13.7	7.1	4.4	2.2
Vehicle insurance	47.0	1.2	7.0	13.1	13.0	6.8	3.6	2.4
Public transportation	27.9	0.7	4.1	7.7	8.1	3.5	2.7	1.3
Vehicle rental, licenses, other charges	18.2	0.4	3.0	6.0	4.6	2.2	1.3	0.6
Health care	**120.0**	**1.5**	**12.4**	**25.5**	**25.3**	**18.1**	**17.7**	**19.6**
Health insurance	41.8	0.5	4.2	7.9	8.5	6.2	7.3	7.3
Medical services	56.7	0.8	6.6	13.8	11.8	8.3	6.8	8.5
Medicines and medical supplies	21.6	0.2	1.6	3.7	5.0	3.6	3.6	3.8
Entertainment	**121.7**	**3.0**	**19.8**	**42.0**	**30.9**	**14.7**	**7.9**	**3.3**
Fees and admissions	34.7	0.9	5.0	11.4	9.3	4.2	2.7	1.1
Television, radios, sound equipment	41.5	1.2	6.9	13.4	11.0	4.7	2.6	1.6
Other equipment and services	45.5	0.9	7.9	17.2	10.6	5.8	2.6	0.6
Personal care	23.1	0.5	3.2	6.2	5.7	3.5	2.3	1.7
Reading	15.7	0.3	2.2	4.5	3.9	2.2	1.6	1.0
Education	33.2	2.6	3.3	10.0	13.1	3.3	0.8	0.2
Tobacco and smoking supplies	25.2	0.8	4.2	6.9	6.8	3.7	2.0	0.9
Miscellaneous	36.2	0.6	5.5	9.7	8.9	5.0	3.5	2.9
Contributions and support payments	88.2	0.6	6.2	21.1	26.0	14.5	12.3	7.3
Personal insurance and pensions	**243.2**	**3.7**	**39.4**	**77.7**	**72.7**	**36.8**	**9.9**	**2.9**
Life insurance and other personal insurance	33.8	0.3	4.0	9.4	9.6	5.6	3.7	1.3
Retirement, pensions, Social Security	209.3	3.5	35.4	68.3	63.0	31.2	6.2	1.6

Source: *The 1986 Consumer Expenditure Survey*, Bureau of Labor Statistics and Projections of the Number of Households and Families:1986 to 2000, Bureau of the Census, Series P-25, No. 986

Note: Aggregate expenditures are the sum of the total expenditures of all households in the nation or of all households in an age group. Projections are based on the average annual expenditures in 1986 and have not been adjusted for inflation. Projections show how total annual expenditures would change as the number of households in the age group changes during the 1990s. All other factors such as price and expenditure pattern are held constant and are not accounted for in these projections.

Appendix

Future Expenditures, Detailed for 2000

EXPENDITURES Appendix

(continued from previous page)

(projected aggregate expenditures in 2000 for all households and for households by age of householder, in billions of dollars)

	2000 aggregate annual expenditures in billions

	all households	under 25	25-34	35-44	45-54	55-64	65-74	75+
Women and girls	52.2	1.3	7.3	16.2	14.5	6.6	3.9	2.4
Women, 16 and over	44.6	1.3	6.0	12.1	13.0	6.2	3.7	2.3
Girls, 2 to 15	7.6	0.1	1.3	4.1	1.5	0.4	0.2	0.0
Children under 2	4.4	0.3	1.5	1.2	0.7	0.5	0.1	0.1
Footwear	13.7	0.4	2.1	4.5	3.6	1.6	0.9	0.5
Other apparel products and services	25.5	1.0	4.9	7.8	6.4	3.1	1.5	0.8
Transportation	**533.7**	**14.8**	**90.9**	**155.9**	**147.7**	**69.0**	**37.2**	**18.1**
Cars and trucks, new (net outlay)	158.6	3.3	27.0	47.5	44.5	20.4	10.9	5.0
Cars and trucks, used (net outlay)	97.5	3.8	19.0	28.1	28.3	11.1	5.1	2.1
Other vehicles	2.9	0.3	0.6	0.9	0.8	0.1	0.1	0.1
Vehicle finance charges	29.9	0.8	5.8	9.6	8.5	3.6	1.3	0.4
Gasoline and motor oil	101.0	2.9	16.5	29.0	26.3	14.2	7.9	4.1
Maintenance and repairs	50.7	1.4	8.0	14.1	13.7	7.1	4.4	2.2
Vehicle insurance	47.0	1.2	7.0	13.1	13.0	6.8	3.6	2.4
Public transportation	27.9	0.7	4.1	7.7	8.1	3.5	2.7	1.3
Vehicle rental, licenses, other charges	18.2	0.4	3.0	6.0	4.6	2.2	1.3	0.6
Health care	**120.0**	**1.5**	**12.4**	**25.5**	**25.3**	**18.1**	**17.7**	**19.6**
Health insurance	41.8	0.5	4.2	7.9	8.5	6.2	7.3	7.3
Medical services	56.7	0.8	6.6	13.8	11.8	8.3	6.8	8.5
Medicines and medical supplies	21.6	0.2	1.6	3.7	5.0	3.6	3.6	3.8
Entertainment	**121.7**	**3.0**	**19.8**	**42.0**	**30.9**	**14.7**	**7.9**	**3.3**
Fees and admissions	34.7	0.9	5.0	11.4	9.3	4.2	2.7	1.1
Television, radios, sound equipment	41.5	1.2	6.9	13.4	11.0	4.7	2.6	1.6
Other equipment and services	45.5	0.9	7.9	17.2	10.6	5.8	2.6	0.6
Personal care	23.1	0.5	3.2	6.2	5.7	3.5	2.3	1.7
Reading	15.7	0.3	2.2	4.5	3.9	2.2	1.6	1.0
Education	33.2	2.6	3.3	10.0	13.1	3.3	0.8	0.2
Tobacco and smoking supplies	25.2	0.8	4.2	6.9	6.8	3.7	2.0	0.9
Miscellaneous	36.2	0.6	5.5	9.7	8.9	5.0	3.5	2.9
Contributions and support payments	**88.2**	**0.6**	**6.2**	**21.1**	**26.0**	**14.5**	**12.3**	**7.3**
Personal insurance and pensions	**243.2**	**3.7**	**39.4**	**77.7**	**72.7**	**36.8**	**9.9**	**2.9**
Life insurance and other personal insurance	33.8	0.3	4.0	9.4	9.6	5.6	3.7	1.3
Retirement, pensions, Social Security	209.3	3.5	35.4	68.3	63.0	31.2	6.2	1.6

Source: *The 1986 Consumer Expenditure Survey*, Bureau of Labor Statistics and Projections of the Number of Households and Families:1986 to 2000, Bureau of the Census, Series P-25, No. 986

Note: Aggregate expenditures are the sum of the total expenditures of all households in the nation or of all households in an age group. Projections are based on the average annual expenditures in 1986 and have not been adjusted for inflation. Projections show how total annual expenditures would change as the number of households in the age group changes during the 1990s. All other factors such as price and expenditure pattern are held constant and are not accounted for in these projections.

INDEX

Educational attainment*
  age, by
    18–24 years old, 53
    25–34 years old, 106
    35–44 years old, 160
    45–54 years old, 212
    55–64 years old, 264
    65–74 years old, 316
  higher education, enrollment in
    18–24 years old, 54
  householders
    18–24 years old, 56
    25–34 years old, 108
    35–44 years old, 162
    45–54 years old, 214
    55–64 years old, 266
    65–74 years old, 318
  sex, race, and ethnicity; by
    18–24 years old, 55
    25–34 years old, 107
    35–44 years old, 161
    45–54 years old, 213
    55–64 years old, 265
    65–74 years old, 317
    75 and older, 367
  summary of
    25–34 years old, 105
    35–44 years old, 159
    45–54 years old, 211
    55–64 years old, 263
    65–74 years old, 315
    75 and older, 366

Expenditures
  annual
    18–24 years old, 74–75
    25–34 years old, 126–127
    35–44 years old, 180–181
    45–54 years old, 232–233
    55–64 years old, 284–285
    65–74 years old, 336–337
    75 and older, 376–377
  future
    18–24 years old, 79–80
    25–34 years old, 131–132
    35–44 years old, 185–186
    45–54 years old, 237–238
    55–64 years old, 289–290
    65–74 years old, 341–342
    75 and older, 381–382
    detailed, aggregate 1990, 400–401
    detailed, aggregate 2000, 402–403
  income, by
    18–24 years old, 76–77
    25–34 years old, 128–129
    35–44 years old, 182–183
    45–54 years old, 234–235
    55–64 years old, 286–287

    65–74 years old, 338–339
    75 and older, 378–379
  weekly, detailed
    18–24 years old, 76
    25–34 years old, 130
    35–44 years old, 184
    45–54 years old, 236
    55–64 years old, 288
    65–74 years old, 340
    75 and older, 380

Fertility
  childbearing patterns
    18–24 years old, 51–52
    25–34 years old, 103–104
    35–44 years old, 157–158

Health
  activity restrictions
    under age 5, 14
    5–17 years old, 36
    18-24 years old, 89
    25–34 years old, 143
    35–44 years old, 197
    45–54 years old, 249
    55–64 years old, 301
    65–74 years old, 353
    75 and older, 389
  acute conditions,
    under age 5, 10–11
    5–17 years old, 32–33
    18–24 years old, 85–86
    25–34 years old, 139–140
    35–44 years old, 193–194
    45–54 years old, 245–246
    55–64 years old, 297–298
    65–74 years old, 349–350
    75 and older, 385–386
  cause of death
    under age 5, 15
    5–17 years old, 37
    18–24 years old, 90
    25–34 years old, 144
    35–44 years old, 198
    45–54 years old, 250
    55–64 years old, 302
    65–74 years old, 354
    75 and older, 390
  chronic conditions
    under age 5, 12–13
    5–17 years old, 34–35
    18–24 years old, 87–88
    25–34 years old, 141–142
    35–44 years old, 195–196
    45–54 years old, 247–248
    55–64 years old, 299–300
    65–74 years old, 351–352
    75 and older, 387–388

  height
    18–24 years old, 83
    25–34 years old, 137
    35–44 years old, 191
    45–54 years old, 243
    55–64 years old, 295
    65–74 years old, 347
  status
    under age 5, 9
    5–17 years old, 31
    18–24 years old, 82
    25–34 years old, 136
    35–44 years old, 190
    45–54 years old, 242
    55–64 years old, 294
    65–74 years old, 346
    75 and older, 384
  weight
    18–24 years old, 84
    25–34 years old, 138
    35–44 years old, 192
    45–54 years old, 244
    55–64 years old, 296
    65–74 years old, 348

Households
  number of
    18–24 years old, 46
    25–34 years old, 98
    35–44 years old, 152
    45–54 years old, 206
    55–64 years old, 258
    65–74 years old, 310
    75 and older, 362
  types of
    18–24 years old, 47
    25–34 years old, 99
    35–44 years old, 153
    45–54 years old, 207
    55–64 years old, 259
    65–74 years old, 311
    75 and older, 363
  future types of
    18–24 years old, 48
    25–34 years old, 100
    35–44 years old, 154
    45–54 years old, 208
    55–64 years old, 260
    65–74 years old, 312
    75 and older, 364

Income, household
  age of householder, by
    18–24 years old, 62, 64
    25–34 years old, 114, 116
    35–44 years old, 168, 170
    45–54 years old, 220, 222
    55–64 years old, 272, 274
    65–74 years old, 324, 326
    75 and older, 369

*This index refers to tables by topic. The first topic referenced is educational attainment.

dual–earner married couples
  18–24 years old, *71*
  25–34 years old, *123*
  35–44 years old, *177*
  45–54 years old, *229*
  55–64 years old, *281*
  65–74 years old, *333*
  75 and older, *374*
education, and
  18–24 years old, *72*
  25–34 years old, *124*
  35–44 years old, *178*
  45–54 years old, *230*
  55–64 years old, *282*
  65–74 years old, *334*
  75 and older, *375*
future
  18–24 years old, *73*
  25–34 years old, *125*
  35–44 years old, *179*
  45–54 years old, *231*
  55–64 years old, *283*
  65–74 years old, *335*
family
  18–24 years old, *66*
  25–34 years old, *118*
  35–44 years old, *172*
  45–54 years old, *224*
  55–64 years old, *276*
  65–74 years old, *328*
  75 and older, *371*
  race, by
    all families, 397
    18–24 years old, *68*
    25–34 years old, *120*
    35–44 years old, *174*
    45–54 years old, *226*
    55–64 years old, *278*
    65–74 years old, *330*
  sex, by
    all females, 394
    all males, 395
Hispanic
  all Hispanic, 399
  18–24 years old, *70*
  25–34 years old, *122*
  35–44 years old, *176*
  45–54 years old, *228*
  55–64 years old, *280*
  65–74 years old, *332*
  75 and older, *373*
married couples
  all couples, 393
  18–24 years old, *65*
  25–34 years old, *117*
  35–44 years old, *171*
  45–54 years old, *223*
  55–64 years old, *275*
  65–74 years old, *327*
  75 and older, *370*
nonfamily
  all nonfamily, 396
  18–24 years old, *67*
  25–34 years old, *119*
  35–44 years old, *173*
  45–54 years old, *225*
  55–64 years old, *277*
  65–74 years old, *329*
  75 and older, *372*

race, by
  all nonfamily, 398
  18–24 years old, *69*
  25–34 years old, *121*
  35–44 years old, *175*
  45–54 years old, *227*
  55–64 years old, *279*
  65–74 years old, *331*
Income, individual
  18–24 years old, *63*
  25–34 years old, *115*
  35–44 years old, *169*
  45–54 years old, *221*
  55–64 years old, *273*
  65–74 years old, *325*
Labor force
employment, extent of
  5–17 years old, *27*
  18–24 years old, *58*
  25–34 years old, *110*
  35–44 years old, *164*
  45–54 years old, *216*
  55–64 years old, *268*
  65–74 years old, *320*
occupations, kinds of
  5–17 years old, *28–29*
  18–24 years old, *59–60*
  25–34 years old, *111–112*
  35–44 years old, *165–166*
  45–54 years old, *217–218*
  55–64 years old, *269–270*
  65–74 years old, *321–322*
participation rates
  5–17 years old, *30*
  18–24 years old, *61*
  25–34 years old, *113*
  35–44 years old, *167*
  45–54 years old, *219*
  55–64 years old, *271*
  65–74 years old, *323*
  75 and older, *368*
status
  5–17 years old, *26*
  18–24 years old, *57*
  25–34 years old, *109*
  35–44 years old, *163*
  45–54 years old, *215*
  55–64 years old, *267*
  65–74 years old, *319*
Marital status
marriages and divorces
  18–24 years old, *50*
  25–34 years old, *102*
  35–44 years old, *156*
  45–54 years old, *210*
  55–64 years old, *262*
  65–74 years old, *314*
status
  18–24 years old, *49*
  25–34 years old, *101*
  35–44 years old, *155*
  45–54 years old, *209*
  55–64 years old, *261*
  65–74 years old, *313*
  75 and older, *365*
Population
sex, race, and ethnicity; by
  under age 5, *3*

5–17 years old, *19*
18–24 years old, *41*
25–34 years old, *93*
35–44 years old, *147*
45–54 years old, *201*
55–64 years old, *253*
65–74 years old, *305*
75 and older, *357*
share of total population
  under age 5, *2*
  5–17 years old, *18*
  18–24 years old, *40*
  25–34 years old, *92*
  35–44 years old, *146*
  45–54 years old, *200*
  55–64 years old, *252*
  65–74 years old, *304*
  75 and older, *356*
state populations
  under age 5, *4–6*
  5–17 years old, *20–22*
  18–24 years old, *42–44*
  25–34 years old, *94–96*
  35–44 years old, *148–150*
  45–54 years old, *202–204*
  55–64 years old, *254–256*
  65–74 years old, *306–308*
  75 and older, *358–360*
percent change, 1990–2000
  under age 5, *7*
  5–17 years old, *23*
  18–24 years old, *45*
  25–34 years old, *97*
  35–44 years old, *151*
  45–54 years old, *205*
  55–64 years old, *257*
  65–74 years old, *309*
  75 and older, *361*
School enrollment
5–17 years old, *24*
18–24 years old, *54*
Wealth
composition of
  25–34 years old, *133*
  35–44 years old, *167*
  45–54 years old, *239*
  55–64 years old, *291*
  65–74 years old, *343*
homeownership
  18–24 years old, *81*
  25–34 years old, *135*
  35–44 years old, *189*
  45–54 years old, *241*
  55–64 years old, *293*
  65–74 years old, *345*
  75 and older, *383*
savings
  25–34 years old, *134*
  35–44 years old, *188*
  45–54 years old, *240*
  55–64 years old, *292*
  65–74 years old, *344*
Working mothers,
of children aged
  under age 5, *8*
  5–17 years old, *25*

ABOUT THE AUTHOR

Margaret Ambry is Editor of American Demographics Press. She holds a Ph.D. in demography and consumer economics from Cornell University. A consultant in the areas of demographics, labor force trends, and professional training, Dr. Ambry has also taught with the State University of New York, Cornell University, and Ithaca College. She lives in Ithaca, New York, with her husband and son.